# THE EBIONITES

Their Christology, Soteriology
and Vegetarianism Defended

JOHN VUJICIC

Copyright © 2019 John Vujicic.

All rights reserved. No part of this book may be reproduced, stored, or transmitted by any means—whether auditory, graphic, mechanical, or electronic—without written permission of the author, except in the case of brief excerpts used in critical articles and reviews. Unauthorized reproduction of any part of this work is illegal and is punishable by law.

ISBN: 978-1-6847-1108-6 (sc)
ISBN: 978-1-6847-1107-9 (e)

Because of the dynamic nature of the Internet, any web addresses or links contained in this book may have changed since publication and may no longer be valid. The views expressed in this work are solely those of the author and do not necessarily reflect the views of the publisher, and the publisher hereby disclaims any responsibility for them.

Any people depicted in stock imagery provided by Getty Images are models, and such images are being used for illustrative purposes only.
Certain stock imagery © Getty Images.

Scripture taken from the King James Version of the Bible.

Scripture taken from the World English Version of the Bible.

Lulu Publishing Services rev. date: 09/30/2019

# Contents

Introduction .................................................................................................vii

| Chapter 1 | Ebionite Beliefs and Practices ....................................... 1 |
| Chapter 2 | Who Were the Ebionites? ............................................ 10 |
| Chapter 3 | PAUL The Founder of Christianity............................. 18 |
| Chapter 4 | Was Paul the true Apostle?........................................... 33 |
| Chapter 5 | THE BIBLE Is It Infallible?..........................................46 |
| Chapter 6 | Radical Vegetarianism Of The Original World ..... 113 |
| Chapter 7 | Watchers and their Carnivorous Sons..................... 125 |
| Chapter 8 | Five Conflicting Systems of Worship in the Old Testament.................................................................... 143 |
| Chapter 9 | The Jewish Sacrificial Cult and the Eating of Meat ......... 171 |
| Chapter 10 | Sacrifice in The Desert............................................... 191 |
| Chapter 11 | Quails in the Desert ................................................... 198 |
| Chapter 12 | The Meaning of Sacrifice from the Christian Perspective .................................................................203 |
| Chapter 13 | Paul Had Problems With Vegetarian Believers..... 216 |
| Chapter 14 | Why did Jesus Cleanse the Temple? ........................ 224 |
| Chapter 15 | Did God Allow Noah To Eat Meat? .........................229 |
| Chapter 16 | Did Jesus Eat Fish? .....................................................237 |
| Chapter 17 | Did Jesus Eat the Passover Lamb? ...........................245 |
| Chapter 18 | Anatomy of the Human Body Proves Vegetarianism.........255 |
| Chapter 19 | Cosmic Law of Preservation Proves Vegetarianism............259 |
| Chapter 20 | The Affect Flesh Diet Has on Your Health and the Starving World .......................................................... 264 |
| Chapter 21 | Did Jesus Die For Adam's Sin? ................................. 269 |
| Chapter 22 | Did Jesus Have a Virgin Birth?.................................297 |
| Chapter 23 | Is Jesus God?................................................................325 |

# Introduction

My purpose in writing this book is to demonstrate that Jesus and the Twelve did not establish a new religion and that they were not founders of Christianity. Jesus and the Twelve founded a new branch within Judaism which the Pharisees and the priestly Sadducees identified as the Nazarene sect. This movement which Jesus and his Apostles established was originally known as a Nazarene community and later by the derogatory name Ebionites. To this day Judaists and even Muslims simply call Christians by the name Nazarene. Paul, the self-proclaimed apostle, was the original founder of Christianity and hence he was the first Christian.

The name Christian was first coined in Syrian Antioch where Paul of Tarsus was the chief leader. It is of colossal importance to realize that the followers of the Twelve were not identified as Christians but were still recognized as a deviationist "sect" within Judaism and were known by the name Nazarene even at the time when Paul was arrested in Jerusalem. The Catholic Christianity slowly emerged from the original Paulinist Christian movement which was first established in Syrian Antioch, where the followers of Paul were first named Christians. It is the opinion and conviction of virtually all independent and critical biblical scholars that Paul was the first Christian and that it was he, who in a real sense, actually founded Christianity as an independent religion divorced from Judaism. Overwhelming majority of independent scholars and religious historians recognize the fact that Paul was a self-proclaimed apostle who radically altered the original Gospel Jesus taught. These scholars, many of whom are experts in their fields, actually credit Paul with the founding of Christianity.

Jesus had many disciples and from among them he chose twelve whom he named Apostles and who had special privileges and to whom he revealed secrets that were hidden from others. Paul was not an original disciple of Jesus. He never met Jesus nor did he witness any of his miracles. A true Apostle had to be an eyewitness of Jesus' miracles and he had to be a follower of Jesus who heard his teachings so that he could testify and witness to others who Jesus was and what he taught [Acts 1:21-22].

Paul failed on every point. He could only appeal to his vision of Jesus. But a vision does not prove anything. Muhammad founded Islam on his visions and alleged appearing of Gabriel. Joseph Smith founded Mormonism on his visions and alleged appearance of Moroni. Ellen G. White re-established Adventist Movement on the basis of her visions. It is no wonder then that many questioned Paul's authority and rejected his apostleship. It is evident from Paul's epistles that he had to defend his authority and his apostleship whereas the Twelve did not have to since they were original disciples of Jesus whom Jesus himself appointed and commissioned to preach his Gospel to all nations.

In the Nazarene and the Ebionite circle, the title Apostle exclusively referred to one of the Twelve. Paul however used the title even of himself and Barnabas, as well as others. In Romans 16:7 Paul identified Andronicus and Junia as those who were "outstanding among apostles." Majority of Greek manuscripts give a feminine spelling Junia, and therefore identify this apostle as a woman. A handful of manuscripts give a variant spelling Junias – a masculine name.

The Greek masculine names end with the letter s. Consider the names: Zeus, Dionysus, Achilles, Atlas, Hercules, Oceanus, Andronicus, Hermas, Odysseus... Even the name of Jesus ends with the letter s. His original name in Aramaic was Eshoo and in Hebrew Yeshu. Since the Greeks did not have a letter sh and since in Greek, masculine names end with letter s – hence the transliterated name IESOUS. In Latin it was transliterated as IESUS. Since the 16$^{th}$ century, when the letter i received a j sound in English language, the name is pronounced Jesus. As in Serbian – I was born in Serbia – every feminine name ends with a letter a, so in Greek, masculine names end with the letter s. Therefore, according to the vast majority of Greek manuscripts, Paul referred to a woman apostle named Junia. A handful of Greek manuscripts contain the variant masculine name Junias. This was obviously a corruption by one of the later scribes who objected to female clergy. The Catholic and Eastern Orthodox churches to this day refuse to ordain women to priesthood.

In 1 Corinthians 15, Paul states that after Jesus arose he first appeared to Peter. Then to the Twelve, followed by 500 brethren, then to James and finally to all the apostles. Please note verses 6-7:

"and that he appeared to Cephas, then to the twelve. Then he appeared to over five hundred brothers at once, most of whom remain until now, but some have also fallen asleep. Then he appeared to James, then to all the apostles" [World English Bible].

Who were all these apostles besides the Twelve? There were none. Jesus chose the Twelve from among all his other disciples and them only he called Apostles. Paul referred to others as apostles so that he could adopt the title for himself. The Nazarenes and Ebionites were regarded as a heretical sect by the Jews and later by the emerging Catholic Christianity. In this book I clearly demonstrate that the Ebionites were original believers who were founded by the Twelve. Their principal and fundamental beliefs are defended in this book.

# CHAPTER 1
# Ebionite Beliefs and Practices

In this chapter I will point out some major beliefs and practices of the Ebionites which are known from patristic writings of the early centuries and some surviving documents, apparently stemming from the Ebionites themselves. Later I will argue that they were the original and authentic followers of the Twelve who were not even known as Christians. Christianity was founded by Paul of Tarsus who wasn't even an original disciple of Jesus and who taught doctrines that were repudiated by the Twelve. The first thing I want to point out is the fact that the Ebionites had a very peculiar attitude towards the Jewish Pentateuch and the Bible in general. They argued that the Jewish Pentateuch was falsified and that it contained many pericopes which were of diabolical origin. They likewise believed that the Old Testament, as a whole, was corrupted by the Jewish scribes and was not preserved in its original form.

Of the canonical Gospels they only accepted Matthew in its original Hebrew form. They out rightly rejected all the epistles of Paul. The first Ebionite doctrine therefore holds that the Bible is fallible and that not everything in the Bible is inspired and that many rituals and practices are diabolical in origin which must be rejected. The Church Father Epiphanius, who knew some Ebionites personally, testified that they did not accept the entire Jewish Pentateuch but rather suppressed and rejected certain passages [Panarion XXX, 8]. Epiphanius repeats this statement in Panarion XXX, 18.

The Ebionites believed that original Pentateuch of Moses was corrupted by the lying scribes and contained many falsehoods which, according to them, were contrary to the nature and character of the true God. They claimed that it was the mission of Jesus to purge these falsehoods and restore the true Pentateuch. Rabbi Philip Sigal, in his book Judaism – The Evolution of a Faith, on p. 83, states that the Ebionites believed that it was the mission of Jesus to restore the corrupted Torah of Moses to its original state.

Professor Ferguson, in his book The Backgrounds of Early Christianity, on p. 578, states that the Ebionites removed many passages of the Old Testament because they regarded them as false pericopes. He states that they claimed that the texts supporting Davidic dynasty and especially the sacrificial cult were later interpolations. The *Jewish Encyclopedia*, Art. Jewish Christian Sects, on p. 39, says:

"Similarly discarded were all passages [of the Bible] providing for kingship – an institution which they abhorred – all anthropomorphic expressions of God, and unpraiseworthy stories about the representatives of true prophecy, e.g., Adam's sin, Noah's drunkenness, Abraham and Jacob's polygamy, etc."

Catholic Cardinal Danilou, in his book The Theology of Jewish Christianity, on p. 64, states that the Ebionites saw Jesus as a reformer of the Law and that he brought it back to the true ideas of Moses. The Ebionites claimed that the Torah that the Jews possessed was mixed with elements of diabolical origin. From the preaching of Apostle Peter, preserved in the Clementine Homilies, where many ideas and beliefs of the Jewish "Christians" are preserved, we find that Peter held a very negative opinion of the Jewish Scriptures. In Homily II, Ch. 38, Peter states that to the original true Scriptures many falsehoods were added which are in actual fact contrary to the Law of God. In Homily III, Ch. 9, Peter claims that anyone who teaches against the true nature of God should be rejected, though he may quote some biblical passages since in the Bible both true and false scriptures are found.

In Homily II, Ch. 52, Peter rejects several well known passages of the Jewish Pentateuch which deal with Adam, Noah, Abraham, Jacob, and Moses. Peter states that these passages which he condemns and rejects are "impious imaginations." He does not accept any passage of the Bible which reflects God's character in the bad light or portrays God's true servants in the bad light. He claims that Adam was not a transgressor, neither Noah a drunkard or that Abraham was a polyginist or that Jacob lived with four wives of whom two were sisters. Likewise, Peter states that he does not accept the passages which state that Moses was a murderer or that he learned to judge from his idolatrous father in law.

In Homily II, Ch. 51, Peter categorically states that because there are both true and false sayings in the Bible, Jesus told them to be "good money changers." Peter repeats this assertion in Homily III, Ch. 50, by saying that Jesus told them to be wise money changers because in the Bible there are genuine and spurious words. And, finally, Peter repeats this in Homily XVIII, Ch. 20, in more elaborate form. We are interested only in the final remark which tells us to be judges of the books written because Jesus said that we should be experienced bankers. The need for experienced bankers is because the counterfeit is mixed with the genuine. The statement of Jesus concerning "experienced bankers" was also known to Church Father Origen who quotes it in his Commentary on John 19:7.

As the Pauline Christianity was slowly emerging into Catholic Christianity, its predominantly Gentile adherents began to believe and teach that Jesus was eternal and almighty God – co-equal with his Father. At the same time they taught the virgin birth concept and soon afterwards they added the doctrine of Mary's perpetual virginity. The Ebionites vigorously repudiated and condemned these teachings which, for them, were blasphemous doctrines. Catholic Cardinal Danilou, in his book The Theology of Jewish Christianity, on p. 63, points out that the Ebionites rejected the divinity of Jesus and the virgin birth. He states that they were radically anti-trinitarian. Church historian Eusebius who lived and wrote in the 4th century, testified that Ebionites did not believe in the virgin birth of Jesus and that they denied his deity.

Rabbi Philip Sigal, in his book: Judaism – Evolution of a Faith, on p. 82, says that the Ebionites believed that Jesus was the biological son of Joseph and Mary and that they regarded him as the reformer who restored the Torah of Moses to its original state. The *Encyclopedia of Religion*, Vol. 4, on p. 576, states that the Ebionites regarded Jesus as the greatest Prophet, the One promised in Deuteronomy 18:15, and that they denied the virgin birth. Professor James Dunn, in his book Unity and Diversity in the New Testament, on pp. 241-242, expressly states that one of the most attested feature of Ebionite Christology is their affirmation that Jesus' birth was wholly natural. The Ebionites vigorously opposed the Trinity dogma. They argued that even Jesus, who was the greatest of all the prophets, acknowledged his father as God and prayed to Him and worshipped Him. The Almighty God and father of Jesus never prayed to Jesus or ever bowed down in worship before him.

The Ebionites also rejected the Jewish sacrificial cultus and practiced vegetarianism. They also abstained from wine and other intoxicating beverages. They insisted that Adam was a true prophet and therefore rejected the "original sin" dogma of Paul's Catholic Christianity. They maintained that Jesus' mission was strictly to teach and that it had nothing to do with Christian dogma of atonement.

They believed and dogmatically taught that Jesus was murdered by the Jews simply because they could not accept his views and doctrines and that it had nothing to do with atonement or paying the penalty for a supposed sin of Adam or that of his posterity. When the Ebionites observed the so-called "Lord's Supper" or "Eucharist," commemorating Jesus' death, they did not use wine but actually water – proving that they did not believe in the blood atonement. Cardinal Danilou, in his book The Theology of Jewish Christianity, on pp. 63-64, states that Ebionites saw Jesus as the reformer of the Judaic religion and that he brought the Law back to the true ideas of Moses. He says that they regarded the Law as it existed in Judaism mixed with the elements of diabolical origin. He emphatically states that Ebionites primarily rejected the temple worship, and especially the bloody sacrificial cult.

Great scholar Dr. Larsen, in his book The Essene Heritage, points out that both the Essenes and the Ebionites did not believe that the fall originated with Adam but rather with the fallen Watchers. The Dictionary of Historical Theology, Art. Ebionites, on p. 167, points out that the Ebionites rejected Paul's teaching concerning soteriology and blood atonement and that they emphasized the baptism and parousia of Jesus in contrast to Paul's incarnation and atonement.

The Ebionites maintained that living water and not the blood of the sacrificial victim purified the convert and was administered for the remission of sins. They therefore focused on two major doctrines: baptism and parousia [the return of Jesus in glory]. The Catholic Christianity and the Eastern Orthodox Church, [and later also the Protestant Christianity], focussed on incarnation [God in the flesh theory] and atonement [human sacrifice of Jesus in order to appease the wrath of God and to atone for the sin of Adam]. The *International Standard Bible Encyclopedia*, Vol. 2, Art. Ebionites, on p. 10, says that for the Ebionites Jesus was the great reformer of the Law whereas Paul was its distorter. It says that they believed that the destruction of the temple took place because the Jews resorted to the bloody sacrificial cult.

*Man, Myth and Magic – The Illustrated Encyclopaedia of Mythology, Religion and the Unknown*, Art. St. Paul, on p. 2152, points out that when the original Jewish Christians of Jerusalem realized the nature of Paul's teaching they rejected it and refused to recognize Paul as the true Apostle. It says that they sent their emissaries to Paul's converts in order to present their Gospel as the authentic version of faith. Church Father Epiphanius in his Panarion XXX, 16, points out that the Ebionites did not use wine when they observed the memorial of Jesus' death but rather pure water.

Catholic Cardinal Jean Danilou, in his book The Theology of the Jewish Christianity, on p. 57, comments on the statement of Epiphanius and corroborates the fact that the Ebionites excluded wine when they observed the Eucharist. Church Father Epiphanius also testified that the Ebionites rejected the Jewish sacrificial cultus and that they were in fact vegetarian. He points out that the Ebionites rejected the biblical passages where it was said that any holy patriarch and therefore a true prophet of God ever offered a bloody sacrifice or ate the flesh of an animal. He stated that they did not accept the whole Jewish Pentateuch but that they rejected some portions of it. For example, that Abraham offered meat to the angels or that Noah, Isaac, Jacob or Moses practiced the sacrificial cult [Panarion XXX, 8 and 18].

Rev. Findlay, in his book The Apocryphal Gospels from History of Christianity in the Light of Modern Knowledge, says that the Ebionites were vegetarians and that they despised the flesh diet and condemned the slaughter of animals for sacrifice. In his book Byways in Early Christian Literature, on p. 38, Rev. Findlay says that the Ebionites abhorred the bloody sacrificial cult and the eating of animal flesh. The *International Standard Bible Encyclopedia*, Vol. 1, on p. 184, says that the Ebionites rejected the Old Testament sacrificial laws and that they were in fact vegetarians. The *Catholic Encyclopedia*, Art. Ebionites, on p. 29, says that the Ebionites lived a communal way of life, sharing all goods among themselves, and that they practiced vegetarianism.

From these references it is clear that the Ebionites rejected the sacrificial cultus and that they condemned those who killed animals for either sacrifice or in order to feast on their flesh. It is also apparent that they rejected the Christian view on soteriology and blood atonement and the use of wine as an emblem of Jesus' blood. In their view, the fall did not originate with Adam but rather with the Watchers who corrupted all flesh and introduced men to sacrificial orgies and the eating of animal flesh. There was another major doctrinal difference between the Ebionites and the Pauline or Catholic Christianity. The Church Fathers and later the bishops of the Catholic Christianity discarded God's Law and taught that Jesus abolished and abrogated the Mosaic Law altogether. They maintained that Jesus nailed God's Law to a cross and therefore we are no longer obligated to observe it. In fact, the Catholic Christianity and even its offshoots – Protestant denominations – insist that those who obey God's Law, revealed to Moses on Sinai, are legalists and in bondage. The Ebionites however maintained that every precept God originally revealed to Moses must be observed and that those who reject and nullify the commands revealed to Moses are apostates from the Law and therefore are not and cannot be God's children.

There seems to be a paradox in the Ebionite stance towards the Law of God. On one hand they rejected many commands of the Jewish Pentateuch as uninspired and in fact of diabolical origin, while on the other they maintained that every single precept of God's Law given on Sinai must not be abrogated or discarded. The contradiction altogether disappears once we realize that the Ebionites maintained that the Law which God gave through Moses did not contain all the diabolical commands against which they so vigorously argued. They maintained that the Law which God revealed to Moses was the same and identical spiritual and universal Law which God originally gave through Adam, the true prophet, for all humanity. The Ebionites insisted that God does not change nor His perfect and universal Law. As far as they are concerned, only the corrupted commands and forgeries in the Jewish Pentateuch must be rejected and discarded. All the true and original precepts which originate with God, must be observed, out of love and respect towards God and His will – revealed through His eternal and holy Law. Christian historian Eusebius, of the 4$^{th}$ century, confirmed the fact that the Ebionites of his day emphasized the so-called Mosaic Law – insisting that those who reject and therefore keep on transgressing God's Law are apostates. He said that they did not understand that they could be saved only by faith and corresponding life.

The statement of Eusebius is absurd. He says that salvation should be based on faith and a corresponding life. Indeed, it should. But how can you have a corresponding life if you do not have God's divine Law which tells you how to live a life in accordance with God's will, which is reflected in His Law? Church Father Hippolytus wrote:

"They live, however, in all respects according to the Law of Moses, alleging that they are thus justified" [The Ante-Nicene Fathers, Vol. 5, p. 147].

When Hippolytus says that the Ebionites lived in all respects according to the Law of Moses, he does not mean that they offered sacrifices and killed animals in order to eat their flesh. Nor does he mean that they practiced slavery or did some other Mosaic practices which in fact they abhorred and condemned. He simply means that the Ebionites embraced the Mosaic Law – all the commands – which they believed and argued that originated with God and are therefore binding on all humanity. The *International Standard Bible Encyclopedia,* Art. Ebionites, on pp. 9-10, clearly explains Ebionite position towards the Mosaic Law. It states that although the Ebionites observed the Law they did not however accept the entire Law as it now stands in the Jewish Pentateuch. It points out that they believed that the original and authentic scriptures were adulterated by certain false additions which were post-Mosaic in origin. They rejected these corruptions because they were actually inimical of Moses' teaching.

Apostle Peter in Clementine Homilies, Homily III, Chps. 51-52, explains the Ebionite position of the Law which is based on the teachings of Jesus:

"And also that He [Jesus] said, 'I am not come to destroy the law,' and yet that he appeared to be destroying it, is the part of one intimating that the things which He destroyed did not belong to the law. And His saying, 'The heaven and the earth shall pass away, but one jot or one title shall not pass from the law,' intimated that things which pass away before the heaven and the earth do not belong to the law in reality. Since, then, while the heaven and the earth still stand, sacrifices have passed away, and kingdoms, and prophecies among those who are born of woman, and such like, as not being ordinances of God" [The Ante-Nicene Fathers, Vol. 8].

Peter clearly explains that Jesus believed in and in fact upheld the true Law which Moses originally gave and insisted that his followers must obey every single command of that Law – even those very least [Matthew 5:17-20]. Jesus only condemned and discarded the commands which did not originate with God his father but were rather of diabolical origin, written by the "lying pen of the scribes" [Jeremiah 8:8].

The Ebionites maintained that the true and eternal Law – with universal implications – was originally given through Adam. This Law was generally observed by the first seven generations. In the days of Enoch the fallen Watchers introduced wicked and lewd practices and they have influenced vast majority of humanity to follow in their steps. The true Law was rejected and the whole Earth was filled with violence. All flesh corrupted their original ordinances and began to kill each other and eat one another. Noah eventually restored the true and eternal Law which was later again rejected. At Mt. Sinai this true and universal Law was once again restored through Moses. However, the Law was rejected by the Jews and the Israelites and they walked in the ways of the pagans.

Jesus finally came as the last and the greatest prophet – the Prophet promised in Deuteronomy 18 – who once again restored the true and original spiritual Law. He rejected the corruptions of the lying scribes. The Law that Jesus restored and purified, the Ebionites observed and maintained that all humans are obligated to obey – especially those who claimed to be the followers of Jesus. Paul was the one who rejected this Law and claimed that Jesus abolished this Law. He argued that salvation was now apart from the Law and was possible only and solely through faith in Jesus and his atoning blood.

This was the position of Catholic Christianity, Eastern Orthodox Christianity and virtually all Protestant Christians. Paul did so because he believed that the whole Mosaic Law in the Jewish Pentateuch originated with the true God. Since there were things which he could not accept, he claimed that they were abolished by Jesus. He practically did the same thing the Ebionites did, only in a subtle way. The only difference was that he believed that the Law abrogated was actually the Law of the true God while the Ebionites claimed that all the portions they abrogated never originated with the true God but were rather of a diabolical origin.

# CHAPTER 2
# Who Were the Ebionites?

It is commonly supposed that the original disciples of Jesus were Christians. This however, was not the case. The Twelve and their immediate followers and converts were actually Israelites, who spoke Aramaic and possibly Hebrew. The words *Christ* and *Christian* are not derived from the Hebrew or Aramaic terms, but rather from the Greek words *Christos* and *Christianoi*. Jesus, the Twelve, and all their relatives and associates did not converse in Greek. Nor did they label themselves with any Greek terms. Jesus never used the term Christian. Neither did the Jews of that time identify either Jesus or the Twelve as Christians. The name Christian was coined in the Hellenistic city of Antioch, by the Greek speaking Jews and Gentiles who followed the teachings of Paul. All those who refer to Jesus, the Twelve, and all their immediate associates and converts in Galilee as Christians, are gravely mistaken.

But is it possible that so many Christian theologians and scholars, and even secular historians and intellectuals could be wrong? Is it possible that they are ignorant of the true historical facts? Jesus himself warned his disciples to be on guard lest they be deceived. He maintained that many of his followers will end up being deceived. The worst thing about deception is the fact that those deceived are not aware of it. In order for you to realize that Jesus and the Twelve were not actually Christians, and that many can be led to believe and accept an erroneous view, let me give you an illustration from which this will become very apparent. The natives of America are commonly called Indians. But, strictly speaking, they are not Indians and in fact they never were.

Christopher Columbus ignorantly labelled the natives of America Indians. He believed mistakenly that the land he discovered was part of the islands of Asia, then called Indies. The *Funk and Wagnalls Encyclopedia*, Vol. 2, on p. 20, candidly admits this fact. *Collier's Encyclopedia*, Vol. 12, on p. 642, further corroborates this fact by saying that Columbus mistakenly thought that he reached the islands off the eastern coast of Asia which were then called Indies and hence he identified the natives as Indians.

Here we have it in the plain language. Columbus simply made a mistake. A mistake which was never corrected by later historians. The indigenous peoples of the Americas are not and never were Indians. They were known by their tribal names. The same historians who failed to correct the blunder of Columbus also refer to Jesus [Eshoo or Yeshu] and his earliest followers as Christians. It is an irrefutable fact that Joseph and Mary and all the relatives of Jesus never referred to him by the title Christ. Jesus conversed with his relatives and disciples in either Hebrew or Aramaic and not in Greek or English. Therefore, Jesus never labelled his followers by the name Christian since this name is derived from the Greek term Christianoi – devised in Antioch – by Paul and his followers. The teaching and the life of Jesus, strictly speaking, should not even come under the heading Christianity, since the Galileans and the Judeans never regarded Jesus as a Christian or a founder of a new religion but rather, they viewed Jesus and his earliest followers as another deviationist sect within Judaism. The *Jewish Encyclopedia*, Vol. 5, on p. 506, corroborates this fact:

"Strictly speaking, the career and ministry of Jesus, and his relations with his disciples, do not come under the heading Christianity. They are rather part of the history of Jewish sectarian movements toward the end of the second Temple period."

Before Jesus even began his ministry, there already were various branches of Judaism:

PHARISEES
SADDUCEES
ESSENES/NAZOREANS

HERODIANS
ZEALOTES
GALILEANS
HEMEROBAPTISTS
MASBOTHEANS
SAMARITANS

Church Father Epiphanius who lived and wrote in the 4th century testified that the earliest followers of Jesus did not call themselves by the name Christian but that they were rather identified by the name Nazoreans [Panarion 29:1, 10]. We also know from the Jewish Talmud that the first followers of Jesus were not regarded as followers of a new religion but rather as members of a deviationist sect within Judaism. The Talmud also identifies the first followers of Jesus as Nazoreans. Even the Arabs and the Quran refer to the first followers of Jesus and the community which he led as Nazoreans. Even in this day and age, Christians are simply known as Nazoreans among the Arab Muslims and the Jews. Acts 24:5 irrefutably shows that as far as the Jewish populace of Judea and their leaders were concerned, the followers of Jesus were simply members of a new sect, within Judaism, which they identified by the name Nazorean. The Jewish leaders mistakenly assumed that Paul himself was one of the ring leaders of the Nazorean sect. It was in Antioch that those who accepted Paul's version of the Gospel abandoned the original name Nazorean and instead began to call themselves by the new name Christianoi, that is, Christians. It is imperative for you to realize that the new name Christian was never adopted by the Twelve, of whom James the Just was the chief.

This is evident by the fact that the Jewish populace in general had no knowledge of the name Christian even years after it was adopted by the Gentile followers of Paul. Acts 24:5 uses the term "Nazarene sect" towards the end of Paul's career. Even the Jews in Rome knew nothing of the new religion called Christianity but only of the sect of which the Jews had a bad opinion [Acts 28:22]. The believers in Jerusalem and Galilee retained their original name and were later also known by their derogatory name Ebionites. There were many members in the Nazorean "sect" as is evident from the Book of Acts.

The Nazoreans flourished in Judea and Galilee until 66 c.e., when the Romans besieged Jerusalem. Just prior to the destruction of Jerusalem, Simeon, the relative of Jesus, was instructed in a vision to lead the Nazoreans out of the city. Simeon succeeded James the Just as the leader of the Nazoreans. A Catholic historian Philip Hughes, in his book A History of the Church, on p. 57, points out that the faithful from Judaea and Galilee escaped to Pella, the region across the Jordan river. Church Father Epiphanius wrote that the early believers settled in Pella just before the destruction of Jerusalem. The *Encyclopedia of Early Christianity*, on p. 490, states that as the wars with the Romans began, the Jewish Christians escaped to Pella in Perea. As a matter of fact, Jesus himself warned the disciples to leave Jerusalem when they see the city besieged:

"When you see Jerusalem encircled by armies, then you will know that the time of its desolation has arrived. Then those in Judea must escape to the hills. Let those in Jerusalem flee, and those outside the city should not enter it for the refuge" [Luke 21:20-22 World English Bible].

Jesus specified that the city of Jerusalem and in particular its temple would be destroyed and that this would be the time of punishment – so that everything written concerning it could be fulfilled [Luke 21:22]. The Ebionites believed that the destruction of the temple took place primarily because the Jewish hierarchy and the Sadducee priests refused to discontinue the sacrificial cultus. In the Ebionite Gospel, Jesus is quoted as saying that unless the Jews abolish the sacrificial cult the wrath of God would not depart from them. In the Recognitions of Clement, Apostle Peter points out that the destruction of Jerusalem and its temple was directly brought by God in order that the sacrificial cult could cease.

Peter pointed out that all those who rejected the sacrificial cult and practiced vegetarianism would be preserved and would not perish with the rest in the city. It is significant to note that the believers who were led by Simeon, the successor of James the Just, actually escaped and settled in Pella of Perea – an area which was known as Transjordan. All historians agree that this was the area where the "Jewish Christians" or the "Pristine Christians" did later flourish. The stronghold of the Ebionites was in fact the Transjordan. Rev.

A. F. Findlay in his book Byways in Early Christian Literature, on p. 87, says that the Ebionites were most probably the legitimate descendants of the Palestinian Christians who fled to Pella. The Oxford Dictionary of the Christian Church, on p. 433, locates the Ebionites east of the Jordan River and states that they were Jewish Christians who flourished in the early centuries of the Christian era.

The *Encyclopedia of Religion*, Vol. 4, on pp. 576-577, states that it is possible that the Ebionites go back to the earliest period of Christian history. It says that they were an example of those who were ultimately left behind by the Church who adapted to the needs of the gentile converts. It further states that the Ebionites were eventually rejected as heretics by the emerging great church. Information on the Ebionites is scattered over three centuries, from the middle of the second to the middle of the fifth, suggesting that the sect had a continuous history as a distinct group from the earliest period. The greatest strength of the Ebionites was in Palestine and Syria, areas where Judaism flourished. One community of Ebionites lived in Pella, east of the Jordan River, and claimed to be descended from the original group of Christians, who were thought to have fled Jerusalem at the time of the war with Romans in 70 c.e.

*Encyclopedia Britannica*, Vol. 4, on p. 344, says that the Ebionites were explicitly mentioned by Bishop Irenaeus [185 AD] and that they evidently escaped from Palestine to Transjordan and Syria. It further corroborates the fact that they have later expanded to Asia Minor, Egypt and Rome. *New Age Encyclopedia*, Vol. 9, on p. 309, points out that the word 'ebionim' in Hebrew means 'poor' and that the name was most probably applied to all early believers. It states that the Ebionites although "Christians" remained outside of the emerging Catholic Church. The original followers of Jesus who were known as Nazoreans initially flourished in Transjordan. But soon afterwards, and especially after the rebellion of Bar Cochba, the Jewish Messiah, they were stigmatized by the rabbis of newly emerged Pharisaic Judaism as the "deviationist sect" and were therefore expelled by the rabbis of Normative Judaism.

*Encyclopedia Judaica*, Vol. 5, on p. 511, candidly admits that the Jewish Christians were eventually despised and condemned by the Jewish community. It states that a special formula was created which was to be recited by all present in the synagogue, in order to make the participation of the Jewish Christians impossible. The original believers and followers of Jesus who were established by the Twelve were eventually excommunicated by the rabbis of Pharisaic Judaism. They were despised and rejected as a "heretical sect." *Encyclopedia Judaica*, Vol. 2, on p. 3, says that Samuel ha-Katan composed a benediction which targeted the "Judeo Christians" or more specifically, the Nazoreans.

The Hebrew word "nozerim" is the very word by which the first followers of Jesus were called by the Jewish populace and the rabbis of normative Judaism. It is the very name by which those same believers were identified by the Jews in Acts 24:5. Jesus' followers were henceforth forced to abandon the Jewish synagogues since the new formula required them to pronounce a curse on themselves every time they would assemble with other Jews in a synagogue. Henceforth the Nazoreans/Ebionites were no longer recognized by the Jewish rabbis and they were persecuted and ostracized. While the Jews were looking for a way to get rid of the Nazoreans, the Pauline followers and Christians were transforming his movement into the emerging Catholic Church. Thus, these original true followers of Jesus and the Twelve found themselves in a very peculiar position. They were excluded and rejected by the Jewish community as a whole and at the same time the emerging Catholic Church refused to acknowledge them as true believers but branded them as "heretics" and gave them a new derogatory name Ebionites.

The term in Hebrew simply means "poor ones" but the Catholic bishops and the Church Fathers applied it sarcastically, implying that they had a poor intellect and understanding – since according to them they were poor of intellect, due to their damned doctrines and teaching. Hugh Smith, a Presbyterian writer, in his book History of the Christian Church, on pp. 69,72, states that these Judaic Christians were originally known as Nazarenes and that they were despised and abhorred by the Jews because they attached themselves to Christianity but that at the same time they were despised by the Christians because of their adherence to the Mosaic Law. Finally, he states that they were peculiarly oppressed and unfortunate.

The *Encyclopedia of Early Christianity*, on p. 491, explicitly says that it was not surprising that the Jewish Christians disappeared from the scene since they could not integrate into post-exilic Judaism nor into the emerging Catholic Church. Chadwick, a church historian, in his book The Early Church, on p. 23, points out that from the Church Father Irenaeus onwards the Jewish Christianity was treated as a deviating sect. However, he points out that they had best reasons to claim that they were the offspring of the original community of Jesus in Jerusalem. The most learned of the Church Fathers, Origen, who was at the same time most sympathetic towards the Ebionites, explicitly stated that the Jews who accepted Jesus were called by the name "Ebionites." This fact is pointed out in *Hasting's Encyclopedia of Religion and Ethics*, Vol. 5, on p. 153.

Even though the Ebionites were direct descendants of the Jerusalem and Galilean believers, the emerging Catholic Church and virtually all the Church Fathers vigorously opposed them and regarded them as heretics – condemning them and ostracizing them. The Anglican scholar David L. Edwards, in his book The Real Jesus, on p. 39, candidly admits that Ebionites were direct descendants of Jesus and his earliest followers, and explicitly states that both the Orthodox Jews and the Pauline Christians despised them and condemned them as heretics. He points out that their version of faith and Jesus was based on the account of Jesus' family and the earliest followers of Jesus.

Edwards, although Anglican, candidly admits and frankly states that the original believers who escaped from Jerusalem were regarded as heretics by the mainstream of Christianity – the Pauline Christianity – which was then emerging into the Roman Catholic Church. Edwards is aware of the fact and actually says that "it is certain" that these believers who migrated to Transjordan called themselves Ebionites and that they actually preserved the version of faith which was based on the testimony of the closest relatives of Eshoo/Yeshu and his earliest and closest associates – the twelve Apostles.

The Ebionites suffered persecution by their countrymen – the Jews – just as Jesus said they would.

But they were also ostracized and damned by the "fellow" Christians who allegedly believed in Jesus and followed the Twelve. Jesus did say to his disciples that a time would come that whoever kills them would think that they do God a service. *Man, Myth and Magic: The Illustrated Encyclopaedia of Mythology, Religion and the Unknown*, art. Ebionites, states that what was left of the Jewish Christianity in Palestine, Syria and Egypt in the 5th century is lost to history. It points out that they clung to their faith and that their beliefs are known only through the garbled and prejudiced accounts of the Orthodox Christian writers who rejected them as heretics.

The Church Fathers and the bishops of the emerging Catholic Church condemned the Ebionites and branded them as heretics. Andrew Welburn, who was originally a Fellow at the Warburg Institute at the University of London but is now Fellow of New College, Oxford, argues that the Church Fathers got it all wrong and that the Ebionites were not heretics but rather those who preserved original and true faith. This is evident in his book The Beginnings of Christianity.

Jesus said to his disciples that they can only expect to be treated as he was. Since he was regarded as a heretic by the mainstream Judaism of his day and in fact was killed for his "heretical" views, it was only to be expected that his immediate followers would be also regarded as heretics and that for their views would have to pay with their lives. Jesus never envisaged that his followers would comprise a large and powerful movement, aligned with the secular kingdoms – as was the case with the emerging Catholic Christianity, Eastern Orthodox Church and the mainstream of Protestantism. So, who were the Ebionites? They were the true believers who were directly linked to Jerusalem Apostles and therefore to Jesus himself.

# CHAPTER 3
# PAUL The Founder of Christianity

When we even casually glance at the New Testament it becomes apparent that bulk of the writings come from the pen of Paul. This is not because Paul worked much harder than other Apostles – as is commonly supposed – but rather because the adherents of the Christian Church are based on the teachings of Paul, hence they diligently collected the writings of their founder. When the Church Fathers wrote they used the term "Apostle" exclusively when referring to Paul. Other Apostles had to be named. Many biblical scholars acknowledge that there was a great schism between the Nazarenes who were led by the Twelve and the Christians who followed the teachings of Paul. In fact, many scholars insist that Paul was actually the first Christian, since it was he who caused the believers in Antioch to adopt the name Christian. Church Father Epiphanius stated that the original believers did not apply the title Christ or the name Jesus but rather the name Nazarenes to themselves. He also said that all Christians at that time were simply called Nazarenes but that in Antioch the name Christian was adopted by the Church of God [Panarion 29.1, 10].

The original followers of Jesus were not Christians. They were Nazarenes. Later they were also known by their derogatory name Ebionites. In Antioch for the first time the 'Church of God' became known as the Christian church. Antioch was a Hellenized city where Paul of Tarsus was the leader [Acts 14]. Paul never used the names Nazarenes or Ebionites to refer to any of the assemblies he founded. He always without fail used the term "church of God" as is evident from his own writings. Twelve times the term "church of God" appears in the New Testament – each time used by Paul himself.

James on the other hand never used this term but he rather used the term "synagogue" to identify the place of meeting [James 2:2 – See the Greek text or the Centre Reference of the King James Bible]. Make no mistake about it. After settling at Antioch, Paul drastically altered his views. From this point of history, he no longer used his Hebrew name Shaul [Saul] but adopts a Roman name Paulus [Paul]. St. Jerome informs us why Shaul became known as Paul:

"Paul, formerly called Saul, an apostle outside the number of the twelve apostles…As Sergius Paulus Proconsul of Cyprus was the first to believe on his preaching, he took his name from him because he had subdued him to faith in Christ" [The Nicene and Post Nicene Fathers, Vol. 3, p. 362].

In Acts 13, as soon as the name of Sergius Paulus is mentioned, the name of Shaul [Saul] is also changed to Paulus [Paul]. From this point on Shaul becomes known by his new Roman name. But Paul did not only adopt a Roman name. He also adopted Roman mystic religion into which he injected some of the Judaic flavour and called it Christianity. His views differed drastically from James and other original Apostles. He in fact became the greatest nemesis of the Nazarenes and Ebionites.

The *Encyclopedia of Religion*, Vol. 3, on p. 349 tells us that it was actually Paul who transformed the Jewish sect into a gentile movement by the end of the first century. A Catholic scholar T. Patrick Burke states in his book The Major Religions, on p. 298 that by 70 AD there were practically two Christian movements with very different theology. One was the Jewish movement in Jerusalem and the other the gentile Church completely divorced from anything Jewish and which adhered to Paul's version of the Gospel. Burke admits that there were two very different kinds of Christianity by 70 AD. One became known as Catholic Christianity, the other was known as Nazarene movement.

These Nazarenes were also called Ebionites and are more commonly referred to as Jewish Christians. In a textbook The Holy Land in the Time of Jesus, on page 92, we are explicitly told that it is Paul who should be identified as the first Christian since it was he who split from the original followers and disciples of Jesus. This textbook plainly admits that it was Paul himself who caused the actual break with the original disciples of Jesus who remained faithful to their founder and Messiah. It was he himself who was the first Christian and who was the actual founder of the movement which bears the same name.

The *Encyclopedia of Religion*, Vol. 3. on page 349, states that Paul himself was actually responsible for the transformation of the original Jewish sect to a gentile movement by the end of the first century. It points out that this change is impossible to exaggerate. In a text book Illustrated History of World Religions, on pages 421-422, we are told that the founding or origin of the Christian Church should not be sought in the teachings of Jesus or the Twelve. Here we are explicitly told that the Christian Church did not originate with Jesus and his disciples. Neither is it based on the teaching of Jesus. Religious historian Wilhelm Nestle wrote that the Christian Church is the establishment of Paul and that it replaced Jesus' Gospel with a Gospel about Christ [Krisis des Christentums p. 89].

The original movement of Jesus was simply a variant branch of Judaism. They were permitted to worship in the synagogues and the temple court as were also other Jewish sects. Paul's movement on the other hand made a complete and total break with Judaism and the original movement of Jesus. Paul rejected the authority of the Jerusalem Apostles. He especially disliked James, the brother of Jesus. This fact is also apparent in his epistle to the Galatians. His version of the Gospel was very different from that taught by the original disciples. He insisted that Jesus died as atoning sacrifice in order to redeem the lost mankind. He taught that all were lost because of Adam's rebellion. The original Apostles on the other hand did not believe that Adam rebelled nor did they believe in the sacrificial atonement. Paul did not ask his converts to observe God's true Law.

He in fact rejected the Law and allowed his converts to practice slavery and polygyny. He also allowed them to eat food sacrificed to idols. By persisting in his own ways and by rejecting the original disciples of Jesus, Paul became the major nemesis of the Ebionites. When we carefully read the writings of Paul in the New Testament, it becomes very apparent that he had to deal with those sent by James the Just. He was frequently accused of not having the authority to be a legitimate Apostle. In his epistles he spends much time defending his position. It is very significant that these same "troublemakers" were not following James or other original disciples of Jesus nor did they question their authority.

They never accused them of not having the right to apostleship. Neither do they ever accuse these true Apostles of teaching against the true Law of God. Now if all the Apostles agreed that the true Law is abrogated, and if they preached identical message as Paul of Tarsus – why then all this trouble in which Paul forever found himself? Whenever his authority as an Apostle was questioned, Paul could never state that he walked with Jesus and learned the message from the Master. He could only appeal to his "vision" on the road to Damascus.

But vision in itself proves nothing. Mohammed founded Islam on his visions. Joseph Smith started Mormonism because of his visions. Ellen G. White established the Seventh Day Adventist Church on her visions. Many prophets in the days of Jeremiah spoke of visions and dreams – yet they were deceiving the people. The Ebionites discredited the visions of Paul because they believed that he encountered the demons rather than Jesus in those visions. Please note the frank admission in the *Catholic Encyclopedia*:

"The Ebionites violently opposed the theology of St. Paul because they believed that he had undergone a demoniacal hallucination when he claimed to have had a vision of Christ, and that he had opposed the conversion of the Jews to a perfect observance of the Mosaic Law as intended by St. James in Jerusalem" [Art. Ebionites, p. 29].

The article plainly states that the Ebionites rejected Paul as an apostate. It further admits the fact that James in Jerusalem intended that his associates adhere to a perfect observance of the Law. James insisted on the observance of the Law but not on the corrupted and falsified Law in the Jewish Pentateuch. *Encyclopedia Judaica* states:

"The Jewish Christian opposition to Paul, traditionally ascribed to Peter, was not based only on his use of magic to make impression on the Romans and his denial of the Mosaic laws, but also on the derivation of his apostolic mission from a spurious vision, whereas the true apostles were sent out by Jesus himself" [art. Jewish Christian Sects, p. 39].

Catholic scholar Philip Hughes in regards to the Ebionites states that they regarded Paul as an apostate and the perverter of truth [A History of the Church, p. 57]. Professor James Dunn states that the Ebionites held James, the brother of Jesus, in great esteem and that they denigrated Paul. Church Fathers Irenaeus, Origen, Eusebius and Epiphanius wrote that one of the main Ebionite characteristics was the rejection of Paul. In fact, they considered Paul as the arch enemy who perverted the teachings of Jesus and relaxed his laws so that he could accommodate the gentile converts which were reluctant to get rid of their pagan practices.

*Man, Myth and Magic: The Illustrated Encyclopedia of Mythology, Religion and the Unknown* under Ebionites tells us that Paul's beliefs were rejected by the leaders in the Jerusalem church and that the Jewish Christianity survived into the $5^{th}$ century. It points out that they were known as either Nazarenes or Ebionites and that various peculiar beliefs were ascribed to them. The Christian Church Fathers continually condemned the beliefs of the Ebionites as heresies. But why was this the case? What actually determines a heresy? Heretic is he who simply holds a different view from what is called Orthodox Christianity. If you hold a view that is supported by minority of Christians then you are labelled a heretic.

Please try to understand. The present Christian doctrines regarded as "orthodox," that is, right and correct, were implemented under the penalty of death. Thousands upon thousands were butchered simply because they held different views from those who considered themselves "orthodox Christians." As soon as you come to hold a view that is contrary to the mainstream of Christendom, you become a heretic. But this should not bother you. All God's true prophets were also labelled "heretics" by the mainstream of Judaism. They were not only despised as heretics but many were beaten and ultimately killed. Jesus himself confirmed the fact that those from Jerusalem continued to murder God's prophets who were sent to them – only because the message they preached clashed with the view of mainstream Judaism. You should also realize the fact that Jesus himself was regarded as a heretic.

His view and teachings clashed with that of Pharisees and Sadducees who represented the mainstream opinion of Judaism. For his views – and especially for his attack on the temple cultus – he lost his life. All his original disciples and their Ebionite or Nazarene movement was regarded as a heretical sect. In the third part of the 1st century of the Christian Era, the Nazarene movement was excommunicated from the synagogue. They were banned as heretics. The Jewish daily prayer contained a formula which expressly placed a curse on all "minim" – that is, heretics. This curse was particularly directed against the Nazarene movement.

Knowing these facts, you should never be bothered if Christians regard you as an outcast and a heretic. You should rather be bothered if you belong to "Orthodox Christianity" – since Jesus plainly stated that his followers would comprise a "little flock," which will be despised, rejected and persecuted by the mainstream of Judaism and Christianity. It was Paul of Tarsus who formulated principal Christian doctrines which clashed with those expressed by James and other Apostles. These principal Pauline doctrines were accepted by the Church Fathers, they were elaborated upon and in due time they came to represent "the orthodox Christian doctrines."

They spread so quickly because the padres of the Roman Church, the Eastern Orthodox Church, as well as some of the Protestant churches forced their subjects to adhere to the mainstream Christianity or else face persecution. For the mainstream Christianity Paul was a "god" – for they praised and exalted him far above all other Apostles whom Jesus personally chose. The Christian professor Loraine Boetner in his book The Roman Catholicism states that Paul was the greatest of all Apostles and that he had greater insight concerning the mysteries of life and death than other Apostles. Herbert Lokyer in his book All the Apostles of the Bible, Art. Paul, states that no figure in church history stands as tall as Paul. He writes that Paul is the fountain to which we should turn for the pure water of evangelical faith. He points out that we must assign Paul the foremost place in the glorious company of the Apostles.

On page 206 Lockyer states that Paul was the chief interpreter of Jesus' thoughts and purpose and that he was better suited than the disciples from Galilee to comprehend Jesus' mission and aims. Martin Luther stated that Paul was the preacher of all preachers and that he alone had the right divine to preach Jesus properly. He claimed that Paul alone understood the difference between faith and the Law, grace and works. These comments border on the line of idolatry. They all but bluntly worship Paul – their great hero. They also border on the line of blasphemy.

All these Christian authors degrade and nullify the original Apostles of Jesus. They claim that Paul was the only one who really understood the thoughts and purpose of Jesus. He was the only one who supposedly understood what was Jesus' mission all about. His Hellenistic background gave him advantage over other Apostles. Indeed, it did. That is exactly why he presented Jesus as the pagan Messiah of the Babylon mystery religion. Is it reasonable to assume that all other Apostles were in ignorance of Jesus' true mission? If Jesus could not have enlightened them even though he spent quite some time with them, how then could he have enlightened Paul whom he supposedly met but for a few moments – and that in a vision?

It is obvious that all Christianity follow the steps of the early Church Fathers who accepted Paul and his version of Christianity but nullified and downplayed the role of James and all other original disciples of Jesus who were personally trained by him and sent into the world with his message. Walter I. Meister [a minister of the Apostolic Christian Church] in his booklet God's Master Plan, states:

"To Israel was the Gospel first preached and the first Christians were Jews. From them it spread into all the world as was intended. It is, nonetheless, amazing to observe how slowly Christianity detached itself from the synagogue. The early converts, for years after Pentecost, formed a sect within Judaism and continued the temple and synagogue worship, observing the Mosaic laws. Whether or not to observe The Law, evidently was a weighty problem in the churches for decades. The largest volume of almost all the Epistles of the Bible [Pauline] is dedicated to answering that question... Paul took a clear cut stand against the observation of the Mosaic laws in

Christianity. Yet, even today, this issue is one of major confusion in church circles" [p. 23].

In regards to the original Apostles of Jesus, Meister states:

"They could, and should, immediately have brought the Gospel to the Gentiles. But this they failed to understand. Enormous were their mental obstacles. The concept of Judaism, their nationalism, and the thought that they were the exclusive, chosen, race of God, was so deeply ingrained into the souls of the Jews, Christ's disciples included, that they could not grasp a thought such as making the Gentiles equal to them...It was this stubborn adherence to Judaism that accounts for the early church being integrated with the synagogue. The fact that Moses' Laws actually were from God, and that Israel actually was God's chosen people and His chosen instrument, accounts for God's early tolerance of a natural error. But there can be no justification for a Christian fellowship to be integrated with a pseudo-Christian fellowship. The church is not Israel, nor Zion; neither is grace observation of the Law...Paul explains that the Law was only an appendage added to the covenant with Abraham, and that it was intended to be in effect only until the seed [Jesus Christ] should come. It was only a codicil to the Testament. He also declares that the Law – always meaning the Mosaic – only speaks to those who are under the Law. As a Christian is not under the Law, the same has nothing to tell him" [p. 25].

Meister claims that all original Apostles of Jesus continued in the Jewish error for decades. They could not perceive that the Mosaic Law was abrogated, thus they lingered in Judaism until Paul "the mastermind" enlightened all the original Apostles and made a clear cut with Judaism. Only then the Apostles supposedly came to their senses and followed the course of Pauline Christianity. The Bible tells us that Jesus spent time with his disciples and taught them his true doctrines. They also received the great power on the day of Pentecost. To suppose that the Apostles did not know whether they should have preached the message to the Gentiles is ridiculous. Even more absurd is the idea that the original Apostles of Jesus did not know whether they should observe the Law of God or not. To assume that Paul had to be converted in order to set James, Peter, John and other Apostles straight, borders on the line of blasphemy. Ellen G. White wrote:

"Through the influence of false teachers who had arisen among the believers in Jerusalem, division, heresy, and sensualism were rapidly gaining ground among the believers in Galatia. These false teachers were mingling Jewish traditions with the truths of the gospel" [The Acts of the Apostles, p. 383].

On page 385, she states:

"In the Galatian churches, open, unmasked error was supplanting the gospel message. Christ, the true foundation of the faith, was virtually renounced for the obsolete ceremonies of Judaism."

Ellen White plainly states that the "false teachers" from Jerusalem [the associates of James] taught a heresy to the believers in Galatia. They supposedly taught "the obsolete ceremonies of Judaism." Since James himself was a strict observer of the "Mosaic Law" – that is, the original true Law of God – and since he himself sent his associates to Paul's territory in order to set the believers straight, then he himself must have been the false teacher.

On pages 400-401, White states:

"In the earlier years of the gospel work among the Gentiles some of the leading brethren at Jerusalem, clinging to former prejudices and habits of thought, had not co-operated heartily with Paul and his associates. In their anxiety to preserve a few meaningless forms of ceremonies...there were a few of the leading brethren at Jerusalem who began to cherish anew the former prejudices against the methods of Paul and his associates. These prejudices strengthened with the passing of the years, until some of the leaders determined that the work of preaching the gospel must henceforth be conducted in accordance with their own ideas. If Paul would conform his methods to certain policies which they advocated they would acknowledge and sustain his work; otherwise they could no longer look upon it with favor or grant it their support. These men had lost sight of the fact that God is the teacher of His people; that every worker in His cause is to obtain an individual experience in following the divine Leader, not looking to man for direct guidance; that His workers are to be moulded and fashioned, not after man's ideas, but after the similitude of the divine."

On pages 386 and 387, she states in regards to those who came from James to Galatia the following:

"The apostle urged the Galatians to leave the false guides by whom they had been misled, and to return to the faith that had been accompanied by unmistakable evidence of divine approval. The men who had attempted to lead them from their belief in the gospel were hypocrites, unholy in heart and corrupt in life. Their religion was made up of a round of ceremonies, through the performance of which they expected to gain the favour of God. They had no desire for a gospel that called for obedience to the word, "except a man be born again, he cannot see the kingdom of God" John 3:3. They felt that a religion based on such doctrine, required too great a sacrifice, and they clung to their errors, deceiving themselves and others...In his effort to regain the confidence of his brethren in Galatia, Paul ably vindicated his position as an apostle, "not of men, neither by man, but by Jesus Christ, and God the Father, who raised Him from the dead." Not from men, but from the highest Authority in heaven, had he received his commission."

It absolutely makes me sick when I read remarks like this. How could someone claim that the brothers from Jerusalem – the Ebionites – wanted an easy life when in fact they renounced personal property, alcoholic beverages and meat eating? They lived in great poverty and practiced asceticism. This is much more than Paul or his associates ever did. The adherents of Pauline Christianity lived in urban societies and possessed their own private property. They feasted on wine and meat. They even participated in pagan sacrificial rites and practiced slavery with Paul's consent.

The Ebionites renounced all these and were despised by both Rabbinical Judaism and the Christian Church. Anyone who claims that the Ebionites observed the Law of God because they wanted an easy life must be out of his mind. White charges the leading brothers of Jerusalem with hypocrisy but she did not see herself. In this book she claims that these brothers did not want to offer "too great a sacrifice" – so they resorted to keeping the Mosaic Law. This was supposedly easier than to practice "born-again" Christianity. But in her other books she would tell you how much easier it is to live as a "born-again Christian" than to observe the Mosaic Law which is a yoke and a heavy burden. White denounces the Ebionite movement of Jerusalem but praises and vindicates Paul:

"Relying on the power of God to save, and refusing to recognize the doctrines of the apostate teachers, the apostle [Paul] endeavoured to lead the converts to see that they had been grossly deceived, but that by returning to their former faith in the gospel they might yet defeat the purpose of Satan. He took his position firmly on the side of truth and righteousness; and his supreme faith and confidence in the message he bore, helped many whose faith had failed, to return to their allegiance to the Saviour" [p. 385].

The late Christian professor and lecturer Alexander Whyte boldly speaks on behalf of traditional Christianity and claims that there was no Apostle among the Twelve who was able to understand Jesus' mission and message and that Paul alone understood it. He points out that apart from Jesus, Paul was God's greatest gift to the Church and the world [Saul called Paul, pp. 9-11]. On page 35 of the same book we are told that no prophet of God, no apostle or any other servant of God ever understood the "mystery of God" until the days of Paul. Through him alone, we are told, the "hidden mysteries" from the creation of the world were exclusively revealed. Christians believe that the original disciples of Jesus failed to understand the mission of Jesus.

They believe that if Paul did not come along then the mission of Jesus would have been in vain. But does this seem logical? Is it reasonable to assume that the Twelve established the first believers on the false premises and foundation? Is it possible that the Twelve who were personally taught by Jesus and who were imbued with the Holy Spirit failed to understand their commission? If they were ignorant of the true facts and if they were to be a great obstacle to the true Gospel – why then did Jesus even bother to choose them?

If the Twelve were the "false leaders of Jerusalem" how is it that in the book of Acts we are told that God supported them by giving them power to perform great miracles? Jesus himself stated that he exclusively chose the Twelve to be his witnesses – beginning in Jerusalem and finally extending their witness to the ends of the Earth. The disciple of Jesus had to know Jesus personally. He had to be an eyewitness of his miracles and he had to hear his teachings first hand. Paul fails on every count. He never knew Jesus personally. He never walked with him or heard and saw anything that he did or taught. His name will not be written on the foundations of the heavenly city. He will not sit on one of the twelve thrones reserved for the disciples:

"The city wall had twelve foundations, and the names of the twelve apostles were on them" [Revelation 21:14 World English Bible].

"I tell you the truth, when all things are renewed, when the Son of Man will sit on his glorious throne, you, my followers, will also sit on the twelve thrones, judging the twelve tribes of Israel" [Matthew 19:28 World English Bible].

Paul was not one of the Twelve. He did not follow Jesus. Therefore, he cannot be regarded as an Apostle nor will he actually sit on one of the twelve thrones as a judge. Since the original disciples were to be the judges in the world to come – receiving such a great authority from their Leader and Teacher – how can we even think that they lingered in deception, observing "obsolete rites of Judaism?" How can we even think that Paul is greater than the original Apostles? Is it reasonable to believe that original Apostles were in ignorance until Paul became a convert who supposedly brought them to their senses? If the original Apostles were of great importance, what should we say of James, the brother of Jesus, who was chosen to be the leader among the leaders? But Christians do not hesitate to degrade this Apostle who was holy from his mother's womb. Martin Luther regarded the writings of James as "straw." The writings of Paul, however, he esteemed as "pure gold." Alexander Whyte states that James, the brother of Jesus, was lingering in the decayed past and that the most backward and the reactionaries clung to him and claimed him as their leader and bulwark. He claims that 33 years were not sufficient to convince James of his brother's messiahship [Saul Called Paul, p. 88].

This view is held by majority of Christians. The leader and the greatest pillar of the earliest movement of Jesus is degraded by the adherents of Pauline Christianity. Even in the Gospel of John [as we have it] James is portrayed as unbeliever who refused to identify with Jesus. It is alleged that James converted only after he saw the risen Jesus. This however was flatly denied by the Ebionites. In the original writings of Matthew, James was present at the Last Supper. At that time, he made a vow that he would taste nothing until he sees Jesus arising from the dead.

This proves that James regarded Jesus as the Messiah and that he firmly believed in his brother's claims. Besides, Paul himself says that the risen Jesus appeared to James. Since Jesus appeared only to the believers it must be then that James was a believer prior to Jesus' resurrection. In fact, the Roman Catholic position is that James was the cousin and not the brother of Jesus and that he was actually James the son of Alpheus who was one of the Twelve. The Christian deceivers and admirers of Paul want you to think that James was a Judaizer and steeped in Pharisaic traditions who could not break with Judaism and the sacrificial cult of the temple. But if James was really and truly a Judaizer, how come he was admired by the Ebionites and how come they regarded him as the greatest of all the Apostles? All admit that the Ebionites hated the temple worship and the sacrificial cult, so why would they then regard James as their hero if he endorsed what they abhorred the most?

At least this degrading of James and other original disciples serves some purpose. It should awaken you to the fact that Christian scholars are fully aware that the Twelve most definitely did not believe nor teach the Pauline doctrines Dr. Whyte terms "Great New Testament Doctrines." By carefully studying his statement and the writings of many other Christian authors, you should be aware that the original Apostles were not ignorant and unable to teach such doctrines – as is alleged – but they simply refused to teach them because they regarded such teaching as false.

The Twelve regarded the "hidden mysteries of the Gospel" revealed by Paul as "the modification of the Babylon mystery religion." Dr. Whyte was right in claiming that James was the leader of all those who clung to the past – meaning the Mosaic Law. Albeit he is wrong in saying that they clung to the decayed past. James and the original Apostles dogmatically insisted upon observance of the Law. However, this Law of God was devoid of many diabolical elements present in current Jewish Pentateuch. This Law they called "The Perfect Law," "The Law of Liberty" and "The Royal Law." Paul on the other hand rejected this Law of God and powerfully taught his followers to abandon it.

Paul rejected the teaching of historical Jesus. Instead he propagated the "mythical Christ." He rejected the views of James, Peter and other Apostles. He pursued his own course and ultimately founded a gentile movement which ultimately emerged as the Roman Catholic Christianity. Paul did not preach the message which agreed with James, Jesus and the ancient Nazarites and prophets. Moreover, when we carefully analyse his own writings it becomes evident that he never regarded himself as a convert to the Nazarene movement but rather he believed to be an apostle in his own right who founded his own movement, according to his own principles, which he later named Christianity. He claimed to have been chosen from his mother's womb in order to make manifest the "mysteries of God" which was hidden in past ages. He allowed his converts to practice polygyny and commanded that only the bishops be married to one wife. He permitted his rich converts to practice slavery and commanded the believing slaves to even more vigorously serve their Christian masters instead of commanding the believing masters to free their slaves:

"Let as many as are bondservants under the yoke count their own masters worthy of all honor, that the name of God and the doctrine not be blasphemed. *Those who have believing masters, let them not despise them, because they are brothers, but rather let them serve them, because those who partake of the benefit are believing and beloved.* Teach and exhort these things. If anyone teaches a different doctrine, and doesn't consent to sound words, the words of our Lord, Jesus Christ, and to the doctrine which is according to godliness; he is conceited, knowing nothing, but obsessed with arguments, disputes, and word battles, from which come envy, strife, reviling, evil suspicions" [1 Timothy 6:1-5 World English Bible].

Here Paul states that the practice of slavery was the teaching of Jesus and that whoever rejects it, rejects the sound words of Jesus. But the Gospels show us that Jesus taught that we should do to others what we want them to do to us. He taught that we should love our neighbour as we love ourselves. This teaching nullifies the practice of slavery and in fact commands a believing slave owner to set his slaves free. Contrary to Jesus' teaching, Paul commands the slaves to serve their believing masters even more vigorously instead of commanding the believing masters to set their brothers in Christ free. The Ebionites condemned slavery and in their community it was not possible to have slaves since all believers had everything in common as we are clearly told in Acts 2:44-45. Paul rejected this way of life and in his churches there were many wealthy slave owners. One such man was Philemon who had a runaway slave Onesimus and whom Paul extradited to Philemon as a believing brother, begging Philemon not to punish his runaway slave.

Paul also allowed his converts to eat food sacrificed to idols. He argued that his ministers should be paid for their services. All these doctrines were repudiated by the Twelve and in the community where all had everything in common there could not have been slaves nor paying the ministers for their services. As far as the food offered to idols is concerned, the Twelve prohibited it and even Jesus criticized it in the Book of Revelation and condemned the prophetess Jezebel for teaching the believers to eat food sacrificed to idols. Paul was the false apostle and those who cling to traditional Christianity have a part in a movement that was started by Paul and which drifted from the Twelve and which has nothing to do with Jesus and ultimately the true God.

# CHAPTER 4
# Was Paul the true Apostle?

In the previous chapter I have demonstrated that many scholars believe and maintain that Paul and not Jesus was actually the founder of Christianity and that Paul was a false apostle who twisted and distorted Jesus' original message. In this chapter I will look at this issue from the biblical perspective and see whether their opinion can be substantiated. From Paul's own writings it can be plainly demonstrated that Paul believed that he was a special and unique apostle – unlike the Twelve whom Jesus personally chose.

Paul also insisted on his independence from the Twelve and that he is in no way indebted to them since he never received any instructions from them but rather, he claimed that his gospel was directly and personally revealed to him by the risen Jesus. Paul also claimed that his commission was not as that of the Twelve and that his own gospel was of necessity different from the Gospel the Twelve preached. In Galatians 1:1 Paul testifies concerning himself:

"Paul, an apostle (not from men, neither through man, but through Jesus Christ, and God the Father, who raised him from the dead)" [World English Bible].

In verse 12 Paul goes on to say that the gospel he preached he did not learn from any man but that it was revealed to him directly by Jesus:

"For neither did I receive it from man, nor was I taught it, but it came to me through revelation of Jesus Christ" [World English Bible].

Paul goes on to claim that after he saw "Jesus" in a vision on the way to Damascus, he did not consult any human being concerning the nature of the Gospel nor did he go to Jerusalem to consult the Twelve, but that he immediately went to Arabia and that finally after three years he went to Jerusalem:

"I didn't immediately confer with flesh and blood, nor did I go up to Jerusalem to those who were apostles before me, but I went away into Arabia. Then I returned to Damascus. Then after three years I went up to Jerusalem to visit Peter, and stayed with him fifteen days. But of the other apostles I saw no one, except James, the Lord's brother" [verses 16-17 World English Bible].

Paul assures the Galatians that his testimony is true and that he is not lying. If Paul is indeed saying the truth and not lying, then most certainly Luke is twisting the facts in the book of Acts – as we shall see later. Paul then goes on and tells the Galatians that he was unknown to the believers in Judea until he finally went to Jerusalem the second time – after fourteen years:

"I was still unknown by face to the assemblies of Judea which were in Christ, but they only heard: 'He who once persecuted us now preaches the faith that he once tried to destroy.' They glorified God in me... Then after a period of fourteen years I went up again to Jerusalem with Barnabas, taking Titus also with me. I went up by revelation, and I laid before them the gospel which I preach among the Gentiles, but privately before those who were respected, for fear that I might be running, or had run, in vain." [Galatians 1:22-24; 2:1 World English Bible].

Paul was so sure that he preached the gospel Jesus revealed to him. Why then did he doubt its validity when he went to see the Apostles? Paul goes on and reveals that his gospel was not the same Gospel that Peter and the Twelve actually proclaimed:

"But from those who were reputed to be important (whatever they were, it makes no difference to me; God doesn't show partiality to man) — they, I say, who were respected imparted nothing to me, but to the contrary, when they saw that I had been entrusted with the gospel for the uncircumcision, even as Peter with the gospel for the circumcision (for he who appointed Peter to the apostleship of the circumcision appointed me also to the Gentiles); and when they perceived the grace that was given to me, James and Cephas and John, they who were reputed to be pillars, gave to me and Barnabas the right hand of fellowship, that we should go to the Gentiles, and they to the circumcision" [verses 6-9 World English Bible].

Jesus spoke of all believers being one even as he and his Father are one. He spoke of one flock and the sheep outside the fold which he was going to bring into the fold so that there would be only one united flock. But Paul speaks of two different flocks – the Jews and the Gentiles. He speaks of two different Gospels – one given to Peter which is suitable for the Jews and the other given to him which is suitable for the Gentiles. He speaks of himself and Barnabas as those who were specifically chosen to preach this special gospel exclusively to the Gentiles while Peter and other Apostles were to preach their special Gospel exclusively to the Jews. But if this is true, what Gospel did Peter preach to Cornelius, his household and friends? They were not Jews but rather Gentiles. Did Peter preach to Cornelius Paul's version of the Gospel? What Gospel did he preach to the Samaritans? What Gospel did Peter preach in Pontus, Galatia, Cappadocia, Asia, Bithynia, and later in Rome? And if Peter agreed that he should preach to the Jews while Paul to the Gentiles, why then did he preach his Gospel in all these Gentile regions? Why is his epistle addressed to the Gentiles who lived in these regions?

Let us compare Paul's version of his conversion and apostleship with Luke's version given in the book of Acts. Luke plainly shows that after Paul saw "Jesus" in a vision on the way to Damascus, he did not immediately go to Arabia but rather he went to Damascus. In fact, according to Luke, "Jesus" told Paul to go to Damascus so that he may receive certain instructions from Ananias so that he would know what to do. Please note Acts 9:6:

"But rise up, and enter into the city, and you will be told what you must do" [World English Bible].

Ananias baptized Paul and obviously gave him some instructions – since "Jesus" said that he would be told what to do in the city of Damascus. After spending several days with the believers in Damascus, Paul did not go to

Arabia – as he claims in Galatians – but rather he immediately began to preach in the Damascene synagogues that Jesus is the Son of God [verses 19-20]. The Jews were astonished since they knew that he was the one who came to Damascus in order to imprison Jesus' followers. After spending "many days" preaching in Damascus, the Jews of Damascus conspired to kill him. Instead of going to Arabia, Paul in fact went to Jerusalem and was taken by Barnabas to meet the Apostles. Here is Luke's version of the story – preserved in Acts 9:23-30:

"When many days were fulfilled, the Jews conspired together to kill him, but their plot became known to Saul. They watched the gates both day and night that they might kill him, but his disciples took him by night, and let him down through the wall, lowering him in a basket. When Saul had come to Jerusalem, he tried to join himself to the disciples. They were all afraid of him, not believing that he was a disciple. But Barnabas took him, and brought him to the apostles, and declared to them how he had seen the Lord in the way, and that he had spoken to him, and how at Damascus he had preached boldly in the name of Jesus. He was with them going in and going out at Jerusalem, preaching boldly in the name of the Lord. He spoke and disputed against the Grecian Jews, but they were seeking to kill him. When the brothers knew it, they brought him down to Caesarea, and sent him out to Tarsus" [World English Bible].

Luke flatly contradicts Paul's version given in Galatians. Instead of immediately going to Arabia he in fact ends up going to Jerusalem where he meets the Apostles and where he preaches his gospel not to the Gentiles but rather to the Jews [verse 22]. Paul testifies in Galatians that he was specifically chosen to be an apostle to the Gentiles and was entrusted with the gospel for the Gentiles. He also says that the deal with the Twelve was that he should preach to the Gentiles while they to the Jews. This of course cannot be true if Luke's version and account is accepted as true and inspired. After he left Jerusalem and went to Tarsus, Barnabas found him there and went with him to Antioch where they first named their followers Christians [11:25-26]. Somewhat later, in the days of Claudius Caesar, Barnabas and Paul went to Jerusalem, taking the gift from Antioch [11:28-30. After they delivered the gift to Jerusalem, they took John Mark with them [12:25].

After Barnabas and Paul took John Mark with them, they began what is commonly called "first missionary journey." They went to Seleucia and then to Cyprus [13:1-5].

When they reached Salamis, they began their mission of preaching. But who did they preach to? Gentiles? Luke says that thenceforth they continually preached to the Jews. In Salamis they preached in the Jewish synagogues [13:5]. On the island of Paphos they got involved with a Jewish sorcerer [13:6]. From there they went to Perga in Pamphylia. At this point for some unspecified reason, John Mark deserted them and decided to return to Jerusalem [13:13]. From Perga, Barnabas and Paul went to Antioch in Pisidia. Instead of preaching to the Gentiles they went to the Jewish synagogue and preached to the Jews. When the Jews eventually departed from the synagogue, they preached their gospel to the Gentile proselytes who worshipped with the Jews in their synagogues [Acts 13:14,42]. When two weeks later the Jews rejected Paul's massage, this is what Paul said to them:

"It was necessary that God's word should be spoken to you first. Since indeed you thrust it from you, and judge yourselves unworthy of eternal life, behold, we turn to the Gentiles. For so has the Lord commanded us, saying, I have set you as a light of the Gentiles, that you should be for salvation to the uttermost parts of the earth" [13:46-47 World English Bible].

If Paul was specifically chosen to be an Apostle to the Gentiles and if his gospel was specifically designed for the Gentiles and not the Jews – as Peter's Gospel allegedly was – why did he continually preach to the Jews and try to convert them – thereby breaching the agreement with Peter and the Twelve? And why did he even after leaving Antioch of Pisidia, still continue to preach to the Jews in their synagogues?

Why did he not simply go to the Gentiles as he said he would? That nothing really changed, despite of Paul's promise, is evident from the remaining chapters of Acts. When they arrived in Iconium, Paul did not simply resort to the Gentiles, as he said he would, but he and Barnabas went to the Jewish synagogue in order to preach to the Jews [14:1]. Sometime later Paul and

Barnabas had a bitter argument and so parted company. Never again did they work together. Barnabas took his nephew John Mark and went his way preaching and testifying while Paul chose Silas and with him went his own way – preaching and propagating his own special gospel [15:35-41]. After he parted company with Barnabas, Paul went to Derbe and Lystra.

Did he finally turn to the Gentiles as he promised he would? The fact that he circumcised Timothy because of the Jews, proves that his mission was still very much to the Jews [16:1-3]. In Philippians Paul states that circumcision is "mutilation of the flesh" and calls those who teach circumcision "dogs:"

"Be on guard against those dogs, those evil men, the mutilators of the flesh. For we are the circumcision, we who worship by the spirit f God" [verses 2-3 Author's translation].

By Paul's own definition he was a dog and a mutilator of the flesh, because he circumcised Timothy. After circumcising Timothy, Paul went to Philippi, a major Macedonian city. Paul was again looking for the Jews and the Gentile proselytes, since he went to the river on the Sabbath [16:13]. From there Paul went to Thessalonica, where once again he preached to the Jews and the Gentile proselytes in the Jewish synagogue [17:1-4]. When the Jews in Thessalonica tried to kill Paul and Silas, they went to Berea. Instead of looking for the Gentiles and preaching their gospel to the Gentiles, Paul went to the synagogue of the Jews [16:10]. When the Jews from Thessalonica came to Berea and stirred up trouble, Paul went to Athens where once again he went to preach to the Jews in their synagogues [17:17]. From Athens Paul went to Corinth where again he preaches to the Jews and goes to their synagogues [18:1,4-5]. When the Jews in Corinth opposed him and blasphemed, this is what Paul did:

"When they opposed him and blasphemed, he shook out his clothing and said to them, your blood be on your own heads! I am clean. From now on, I will go to the Gentiles" [18:6 World English Bible].

However, Paul again did not keep his word. Paul stayed next door to a Jewish synagogue for eighteen months with a man who was a Jewish proselyte, preaching to those who were acquainted with Judaism [18:7,8,11]. From there Paul finally went to Ephesus where he did not, as promised, turn to the Gentiles, but rather once again resorted to the Jews and their synagogues [18:19]. At Corinth, Paul met Apollos who was a Jew and got involved with him and some other Jews who were originally baptized by John. Paul decided to re-baptize them since they supposedly never even heard that the Holy Spirit exists [19:1-7]. For three months Paul attended the Jewish synagogue in Ephesus arguing with them about faith [19:8]. When certain Jews of the synagogue opposed, Paul caused a split in the synagogue and took as many members as he could and continued to preach to the Jews in the school of Tyrannus for the next three years [19:9-10].

After being arrested at Jerusalem, Paul later appeared before King Agrippa before whom he plainly confessed that immediately after his vision of "Jesus" on the way to Damascus, where he was supposedly appointed an Apostle to the Gentiles, he actually preached to the Jews in Damascus then those in Jerusalem and throughout Judaea [26:20]. Here, according to Luke's testimony, Paul contradicted his own account in Galatians where he specified that he went to Arabia and not Jerusalem. When Paul finally arrived in Rome, he found himself once again entangled with the Jews and not the Gentiles [28:16-31]. Thus, we see that if Paul was specifically chosen to be an Apostle to the Gentiles and that if he really made a deal with the Twelve to preach among the Gentiles while they among the Jews – he failed to fulfil both his mission and agreement with the Twelve. Another important thing needs to be pointed out. What Gospel did Paul preach to all these Jews that he came in contact with? Was it the Gospel he supposedly received from Jesus on the way to Damascus or was it the Gospel Peter preached among the Jews? Luke, again, gives us the answer. Paul apparently preached to the Jews the same gospel that he preached to the Gentiles. He taught them to abandon the customs of Moses and not to observe the Mosaic commands or to circumcise their children. This is evident from the statement of James to Paul:

"You see, brother, how many thousands there are among the Jews of those who have believed, and they are all zealous for the law. They have been informed about you, that you teach all the Jews who are among the Gentiles to forsake Moses, telling them not to circumcise their children neither to walk after the customs" [Acts 21:20-21 World English Bible].

James the Just knew who Paul was and what he taught. He disagreed with him but despite the fact of believing that he was a false apostle, he tried to save his life in Jerusalem. He advised him to shave his head and along with their four men go and worship in the temple and present a bloodless sacrifice. By this, James said, he would prove to all the Jews that the report they heard was a hearsay and that he himself lives in accordance with the Law [Acts 21:23-24]. Paul, seeing how grave and serious the situation was, agreed to James' proposition. However, later certain Jews from Asia recognized him and confirmed James' allegation that Paul preached everywhere against God's Law and the Mosaic institutions. Please note Acts 21:27-28:

"When the seven days were almost completed, the Jews from Asia, when they saw him in the temple, stirred up all the multitude and laid hands on him, crying out, Men of Israel, help! This is the man who teaches all men everywhere against the people, and the law, and this place" [World English Bible].

Paul of course cowardly denied all these charges claiming that he never said and spoke anything that did not agree with the Mosaic Law or the customs of the Jews. Before Felix he testified:

"But this I confess to you, that after the Way, which they call a sect, so I serve the God of our fathers, believing all things which are according to the law, and which are written in the prophets" [Acts 24:14 World English Bible].

In verse 17 Paul said that he actually came to Jerusalem in order to present sacrifices and that he was ritually clean when presenting them. In verse 18 Paul claimed that the Jews of Asia could not prove their charges against him. During his trial before Festus, Paul falsely testified:

"I sinned neither against the law of the Jews, nor against the temple, or against Caesar" [Acts 25:8 World English Bible].

To the Jews in Rome, Paul lied by saying:

"I, brothers, even though I had done nothing against the people, or the customs of our fathers, still was delivered prisoner from Jerusalem into the hands of the Romans" [Acts 28:17 World English Bible].

Paul distorted the facts and lied to the Jews in order to save his own skin. His epistles clearly show that the Jews of Asia who knew him and his associates were right when they accused him of nullifying the Mosaic Law and teaching against the customs of the Jews. Paul continually negates the Law and claims that those who think that they could be justified through the Law have "fallen from grace." He definitely spoke against the custom of the Jews when he wrote against circumcision and when he called those who practice this rite "dogs" and "mutilators of the flesh." In Galatians he expresses his contempt for the Jewish custom of circumcision by saying that he wished to see the knife slip during the operation or that they would go all the way and emasculate themselves [Galatians 5:4,11-12].

Paul claimed that Jews should live like Gentiles [Galatians 2:14-15]. But if this is so, why then did he say that Peter's Gospel was suited for the circumcised? How then could they live like Gentiles? Throughout his epistles it is evident that Paul adopted an antinomian stance and always spoke and taught against the Law. For this very reason the Ebionites rejected him as an apostate from the Law. Paul also directly violated the decree of the Jerusalem Council [Acts 15] where it was expressly forbidden to the Gentiles to partake of food sacrificed to idols. He permitted his converts to eat of that food since, according to him, idols are nothing. Jesus however held a different view since he condemned those who partook of food sacrificed to idols [Revelation 2:14,20]. Paul taught doctrines contrary to Jesus and the Twelve. He was arrogant and revengeful. Jesus prayed for those who crucified him and said to his God:

"Father, forgive them, for they don't know what they are doing" [Luke 23:34 World English Bible].

Stephen asked Jesus not to take into account the sin of those who were stoning him:

"Lord, don't hold this sin against them!" [Acts 7:60 World English Bible].

This is the character of God and a person who loves and forgives. But Paul was different. He said that Alexander the metal worker did him great harm. Instead of praying to God that he be forgiven, he said:

"the Lord reward him according to his works" [2 Timothy 4:14 King James Bible].

The Corinthian man who had sex with his father's wife [1 Corinthians 5] he delivered to Satan so that Satan may kill him in order that on the last day his spirit may be saved. He also delivered Himenaeus and a different Alexander to Satan [1 Timothy 1:20. Who did Paul think he was? Jesus forgave the woman caught in adultery and did not demand her death. In Revelation we are told that Jesus was willing to forgive those who practiced sexual immorality under the influence of Jezebel the false prophetess. If Jesus did not deliver anyone to Satan and if he taught us to pray that we should be delivered from evil, who was Paul to deliver anyone to Satan and evil and to demand someone's death or payment for doing wrong? Paul was very arrogant and he possessed a judgemental spirit. In Galatians 1 he placed a curse on anyone who would preach a different Gospel than the one he preached to the Galatians.

Since he admits that those who preached a different Gospel and a different Jesus were actually the associates of James, the brother of Jesus, he thus placed a curse on them and their leader. But Paul even dared to place a curse on even an angel if he would dare to preach a different Gospel than he preached. However, even Michael the chief Angel did not dare to condemn Satan [Jude 9], but Paul did not hesitate to condemn and curse anyone who would dare to disagree with him. Jesus told us to bless even our enemies but Paul cursed anyone who did not love the Lord. In 1 Corinthians 16:22 Paul wrote:

"If any man does not love the Lord Jesus Christ, let him be accursed" [World English Bible].

Even Jesus does not curse those who do not believe in him but in fact prays to God not only for the sins of the believers but also for the sins of the world [1 John 2:2]. Paul taught that the children of the believers were holy while those of non-believers were unclean [1 Corinthians 7:14]. Jesus considered all children clean and argued that God's kingdom belongs first and foremost to them [Luke 18:15-17]. Jesus instructed his disciples to be humble and not seek to be the greatest, for those who exalt themselves will be debased. But Paul was extremely arrogant and bragged about his achievements and even claimed that he worked harder than Peter, James and John who were considered to be the pillars among the Apostles. But Paul's ego reached the climax when he said:

"for I would rather die, than that anyone should make my boasting void" [1 Corinthians 9:15 World English Bible].

Paul never knew Jesus nor did he ever walk with him or partake food of his table – as did the Twelve. His vision does not help him since no one was able to verify it. His miracles – if he ever performed them – don't help him either, since he himself testified that even the apostles of Satan perform great miracles. In fact, Jesus predicted that many would cast out demons and perform many miracles in his name – yet would be deceivers and those whom Jesus never knew, because they practiced iniquity – "anomia" – that is, transgressing the Law. The Synoptic Gospels clearly show that Jesus had many disciples who followed him and who were sent to preach his message. But out of all these disciples Jesus especially chose the Twelve to be his closest companions and only to them he gave special power and authority. Luke 6:12-13 says:

"It happened in these days, that he went out into the mountain to pray, and he continued all night in prayer to God. When it was day, he called his disciples, and from them he chose twelve, whom he also named apostles" [World English Bible].

Mark 3:13-15 says:

"He went up into the mountain, and called to himself whom he wanted, and they went to him. He appointed twelve, that they might be with him, and that he might send them out to preach, and to have authority to heal sicknesses and to cast out demons" [World English Bible].

The Twelve were selected so that they would be Jesus' closest companions and associates. To them Jesus gave special powers and abilities to perform miracles. And only to them did Jesus clearly explain all the mysteries of God while to others it was spoken in parables. On the Day of Pentecost, the Twelve were imbued with the power from God and they were now ready to begin their mission. But what was their mission? Was it to preach the Gospel to the Jews only – as commonly supposed? Matthew 28:19-20 clearly shows that after his resurrection Jesus commissioned the Apostles to preach the Gospel "to all nations everywhere" and to make the disciples out of them by baptizing them and teaching them to observe all the commands he taught them. Acts 1:8 shows that Jesus commissioned the Apostles to be his witnesses not only in Jerusalem and Judea but also in Samaria and in fact to the "ends of the earth:"

"But you will receive power when the Holy Spirit has come on you. You will be witnesses to me in Jerusalem, in all Judea and Samaria, and to the uttermost parts of the earth" [World English Bible].

In Mark 16 Jesus also commissioned his Apostles to preach the Gospel to all peoples and nations – throughout the world. The shorter ending of Mark [verse 10] found in some early manuscripts says:

"Following this, Jesus himself sent out through his disciples from the east to the west the holy and ever living message of eternal salvation" [Authors translation].

If you accept the traditional ending of Mark, then please note what Jesus tells his disciples in verse 15:

"Go into all the world, and preach the gospel to the whole creation" [World English Bible].

The Synoptic Gospels and the Book of Acts irrefutably show that Jesus commissioned his Apostles to preach the Gospel not only to the Jews [as Paul later insinuates] but rather he commanded them to preach his message throughout the whole world and to make converts from all nations. The canonical epistle of Peter also shows that Peter preached the Gospel in the provinces of Pontus, Galatia, Cappadocia, Asia, and Bythinia. The author addresses converted Gentiles and not the Jews. Acts 15:7 shows that it was Peter who was specifically chosen to preach the Gospel to the Gentiles:

"Brothers, you know that a good while ago God made choice among you, that by my mouth the Gentiles should hear the word of the gospel, and believe" [World English Bible].

Peter testifies that he was specifically chosen to preach the Gospel to the Gentiles and that in fact he did so. How could Paul then claim that Peter was entrusted with the Gospel for the circumcised – that is, the Jews – while he with the Gospel for the Gentiles? Church tradition shows that Apostle Judas Thomas preached the Gospel among the Indians and Persians, a fact that even the Clementine Homilies confirm. Others went to Europe and other parts of the world. Since Jesus specifically chose the Twelve to be his Apostles and representatives and since they indeed preached his message also among the Gentiles – as he himself commanded them to do – it is plain therefore that there was no need for Paul to be chosen as a special Apostle who would carry the Gospel among the Gentiles.

Jesus would not entrust Paul with a Gospel that was so strikingly different from the Gospel that he taught his most intimate disciples whom he appointed to be witnesses to the "ends of the Earth." The Holy City which will one day descend from heaven has twelve foundations. On them are written the names of the original twelve Apostles of Jesus. Paul's name is nowhere to be found. This in itself proves that he was not a true Apostle who was specifically chosen by God, let alone the most important of all Apostles who allegedly enlightened the Twelve and set them straight. Paul was indeed the champion of Christianity. But not of the Nazarenes who were later known by their derogatory name Ebionites. As far as they were concerned, he was their greatest nemesis.

# CHAPTER 5
# THE BIBLE Is It Infallible?

The Ebionites, as we have seen, claimed that the Bible in the possession of the Jews was by and large a forgery and a corruption of the original scriptures that Moses handed down. In this chapter I will refer to some corruptions and problems detected in the Jewish scriptures. The Bible is replete with problems and discrepancies. This is true of both Old and New Testaments. You only need to know the facts in order to really appreciate this claim. Names do not agree, numbers do not match, genealogies diverge, geography is confused, historical records are inaccurate, and, most importantly, variant ideas and doctrines are propagated by different redactors. It is no wonder that the Ebionites rejected many biblical pericopes as spurious.

**Letter Confusion**

When you carefully compare 1 Chronicles with the book of Genesis it becomes apparent that the Jewish scribes who were responsible to transmit the text to the future generations were often confused and could not tell the Hebrew letters apart. Some Hebrew letters resemble each other very closely. If you compare the genealogies given in 1 Chronicles with those given in Genesis you would discover that no less than 114 names do not agree.

One of the dukes or chiefs of Esau is called Alvah in Genesis 36:40. But the same person is called Aliah in 1 Chronicles 1:51. In this case letters vav [v] and yod [y] were confused. One of the twelve sons of Ishmael is called Hadad in Genesis 25:15 but Hadar in 1 Chronicles 1:30. Likewise, the grandson of Japhet is called Dodanim in Genesis 10:4 while Rodanim in

1 Chronicles 1:7. Here we have the letters daleth [d] and resh [r] confused. In other names for example we have the vowel points confused – hence the following readings: Ebal [Genesis 36:23] for Obal [1 Chronicles 1:40]; Hemam [Genesis 36:22] for Homam [1 Chronicles 1:39; Shepho [Genesis 36:23] for Shephi [1 Chronicles 1:40]; Zepho [Genesis 36:11] for Zephi [1 Chronicles 1:36]. We have already seen that the name of one of the sons of Ishmael was confused. But this is also the case with his royal city. In Genesis it is called Pau [36:39] while in 1 Chronicles 1:50 Pai.

This confusion of letters is not limited to the parallel genealogies of Genesis and 1 Chronicles alone. It is apparent elsewhere in the Bible. One of David's warriors is called Mebbunai [2 Samuel 23:27] but in a parallel passage, that of 1 Chronicles 11:29 he is called Sibbecai. The grandfather of Achan, from the tribe of Judah, is called Zabdi in Joshua 7:1 but Zimri in 1 Chronicles 2:6. The Jewish scribe copying the manuscripts confused these names since in Hebrew they have a close resemblance. The list goes on…

**Transposition of Letters**

Certain names are arranged differently in the Bible – hence they differ. The consonants are the same in each case, but they are transposed in a different manner. For example, King Jehoiachin [2 Kings 24:8] is also called Jeconiah [1 Chronicles 3:16]. The father of Bathshua or Bethsheba – one of the wives of David and the mother of Solomon – is called Amiel in 1 Chronicles 3:5. But in a parallel passage, that of 2 Samuel 11:3 he is called Eliam.

The grandfather of Shallum, the husband of Huldah the prophetess, in 2 Chronicles 34:22 is called Hasrah. But in a parallel passage, that of 2 Kings 22:14 he is called Harhas. This transposition of letters is the same as if I would transpose the letters of the name Daniel and make it read Elidan, Nadiel or Aniled. This "amusement" is also apparent in proper words. The Hebrew word keseb [lamb] is transposed to read kebes. The name of a tree, Almug, is transposed to read Algum. Even the city in Ephraim in which Joshua was buried is called both Timnath-sereh and Timnath-heres. The head of a family of temple slaves who returned from the Babylonian exile is called Shalmai in Ezra 2:46 but Shamlai in Nehemiah 7:48.

## Conflicting Sources in Genesis

In Genesis 1 the name Yahweh [LORD] does not appear. However, Genesis 2, written by another hand uses the name throughout. Genesis 1:20 says that the birds were brought forth out of the water. But another source in Genesis 2:19 says that the birds were formed out of the earth. Genesis 1 shows that heaven and Earth were made on different days and that it took six days for everything to be created. But another source in Genesis 2:4 shows that heaven and Earth were made together and that everything was made "in the day."

Genesis 1:26-28 says that male and female were made together and that Elohim actually blessed them and told them to multiply and increase and be equal rulers of the Earth. But another source in Genesis 2:7 shows that man was made alone and then the Garden of Eden. Then Yahweh paraded all animals before Adam to give them names and to see if he could find a wife from among them. When it became apparent that Adam could not find a suitable female partner, Yahweh put him in deep coma and cloned a woman out of his body. The woman was "bones of his bones and flesh of his flesh" so she was called "Ishah" – female man. The word "woman" means "man with a womb."

Genesis 1:29 says that first created humans were allowed to eat from every tree yielding seed and every herb yielding seed throughout the Earth. No ban was placed on any tree whatsoever. But the Yahwist source says that the first humans were forbidden to eat from one tree and that they were allowed to eat only from the trees planted in the Garden of Eden. Furthermore, the Yahwist source clearly identifies only two beings – Adam and Eve – in the garden. This source further depicts them as strict fruitarians. They were permitted to eat herbs only after they were expelled from the Garden. Eating of herbs was the result of a curse [Genesis 3:18]. Genesis 6:19 says that only two of all animals – male and its female mate – were taken into the ark with Noah [Genesis 6:19]. But the Yahwist source says that two of all the unclean animals were taken but fourteen of all the clean [Genesis 7:2]. Genesis 7:11-13 says that on the day the great deep was broken and the rain began to fall, Noah and those with him entered the Ark. But the Yahwist source says that Noah and his wife with their children and daughters in law and all the animals entered the ark seven days before the flood began [Genesis 7:7,10].

The Yahwist and Elohist sources are clearly detected in the story of Joseph. The two sources use the different names for the servant girl, different names for the sack, and one calls Joseph's father Jacob while the other Israel. The Elohist source in Genesis 37:36 says that the Midianites sold Joseph to Potiphar in Egypt. But the Yahwist source in Genesis 39:1 says that Potiphar actually bought Joseph from the Ishmaelites. The Yahwist source of Genesis 12:8 and Genesis 13:3 shows that the city Bethel was already so named in the days of Abraham. But the Elohist source of Genesis 28:19 and 35:7 shows that the name of Bethel was formerly called Luz and that Jacob was the first who named it Bethel.

**Tablets of Stone and The Ark**

Exodus 25:16 says that Yahweh commanded Moses to place the two stone tablets on which the Ten Commandments were written in the Covenant Box or the Ark of the Covenant which Yahweh also told Moses to make. The Tent of Meeting with all its objects and furniture was completed – including the Ark of the Covenant [Exodus 39:32]. Then on the first day of the first month in the second year the Tent was set up [Exodus 40:16]. Moses then placed the two stone tablets in the Ark and the Ark in the Tent [Exodus 40:20-21]. So, according to the text of Exodus the Ark was not made and the stone tablets were not placed in the Ark until the 1st of Abib in the 2nd year of their wanderings. But Moses contradicts this in the book of Deuteronomy. In chapter 10 verses 1-5 Moses says:

"At that time Yahweh said to me, Hew you two tables of stone like the first, and come up to me onto the mountain, and make an ark of wood. I will write on the tables the words that were on the first tables which you broke, and you shall put them in the ark. So I made an ark of acacia wood, and hewed two tables of stone like the first, and went up onto the mountain, having the two tables in my hand. He wrote on the tables, according to the first writing, the ten commandments, which Yahweh spoke to you on the mountain out of the midst of the fire in the day of the assembly: and Yahweh gave them to me. I turned and came down from the mountain, and put the tables in the ark which I had made; and there they are as Yahweh commanded me" [World English Bible].

According to the words of Moses recorded in this text, he made the Ark of the Covenant at the same time he made the two new tablets of stone. He placed the tablets of stone in the Ark as soon as he came down from the mountain and the tablets were there "ever since" – almost forty years. This text proves that this Ark was a permanent resting place of the tablets of stone. Moses did not destroy this Ark and transferred the tablets of stone in the Ark which was supposedly made nine months later – along with the Tent and all its utensils. There is therefore a clear contradiction between the texts of Exodus and Deuteronomy.

**Who Wrote the Ten Commandments?**

In Deuteronomy 5:22 it is said that Yahweh wrote the Ten Commandments on the tablets of stone. But this is contradicted in Exodus 34:27-98 where we are told that Yahweh actually asked Moses to write them and that Moses actually wrote the Ten Commandments on the tablets of stone and carried them both with him as he went back to the people. Some Bible translations conceal this fact but the Hebrew, as well as the King James Bible and most other English versions make this fact very clear.

**The Passover**

The Exodus account related in chapter 12 shows that only lambs and goats were permitted for this kind of sacrifice [verse 3]. The lamb or goat had to be roasted – raw meat or boiled meat was prohibited [verse 9]. The Festival was to be observed for full seven days – with the first and seventh days being the special sabbaths [verses 15-16]. Leviticus 23:5-8 agrees with the text of Exodus. But the text of Deuteronomy 16 disagrees. Here the cattle could also be slaughtered for the Passover meal and the meat is to be boiled – a thing the text of Exodus 12 forbids. Some translators – including those of the King James Bible – incorrectly use the word "roast" in 16:7. The Hebrew word is "bashal." It means "to boil, cook." The word is number #1310 in Strong's Hebrew Dictionary and you can verify this fact. It does not really matter to argue what exactly the word "bashal" means. What is important is this: it was the very word "bashal" used in Exodus 12 in order to prohibit "boiling" the victim. So then in the text of Exodus to "bashal" the victim was prohibited but in the text of Deuteronomy it was actually commanded. In the text of Exodus, the first of the seven days and the seventh of the seven days were special days – holy convocation was commanded on those days. But the text of Deuteronomy 16 does not agree. This text prescribes holy convocation only on the seventh day of the Festival which lasted for seven days. This text commands to slaughter the Passover victim on the evening of the first day and to return home [the tents] the next morning. The Festival was to be observed for the next six days and the holy convocation was to take place only on the seventh day. Likewise, the Deuteronomy text commands that the Passover be observed only in the chosen place of worship. Whereas the Exodus and Leviticus texts know nothing of this. There is therefore a clear discrepancy between these texts which actually deal with the observance of the Passover.

**Benjamin An Old Man or A Little Child?**

One account of Genesis makes it very plain that Joseph was Jacob's favourite son because he was born in his old age [Genesis 37:3]. At the age of 17 Joseph was sold [Genesis 37:2]. When Joseph was 30 years old, he interpreted the dream of Pharaoh and was consequently appointed ruler of Egypt [Genesis 41:46]. Seven years of plenty followed [Genesis 41:47-49]. In the $2^{nd}$ year of famine the brothers of Joseph went to Egypt to buy some food [Genesis 45:6]. Therefore, it follows that Joseph was 39 years old when his brothers went to Egypt and when Jacob and his whole family relocated to Egypt. Jacob was 130 years old when he migrated to Egypt and appeared before Pharaoh [Genesis 47:9]. Since Joseph was 39 when Jacob was 130 it follows that Jacob was 91 when Joseph was born. Thus, it could be truly said that Joseph was born to Jacob in his old age.

Benjamin was born to Jacob after Joseph was sold. When Joseph was 39, he addressed Benjamin by the term "my son" [Genesis 43:29] proving that he was significantly older than Benjamin. Likewise, at the time Benjamin accompanied his brothers on their second journey to Egypt, Judah plainly said to Joseph that Benjamin was at that time a little child [Genesis 44:20]. Therefore, Benjamin must have been born after Joseph was sold into slavery. Had Benjamin been born shortly after Joseph, then he and not Joseph would have been the favourite, since then he and not Joseph would have been the youngest and the son of Jacob's old age. Joseph's sons – Manasseh and Ephraim – were born to Joseph before the famine began and therefore no later than Joseph's 37th year [Genesis 41:50]. When Jacob met them, they were young lads [Genesis 48:8].

Joseph lived to see Ephraim's grandchildren. He finally died at the age of 110 [Genesis 50:23]. Another biblical source portrays Benjamin not as a little child but rather as a grandfather when he joined his brothers on their trip to Egypt. Genesis 46 states that Jacob and his whole family – 66 in all – migrated to Egypt. With Jacob himself, plus Joseph and his two sons – Ephraim and Manasseh – the number of Jacob's whole family is set at 70. In verse 21 we are explicitly told that the ten sons of Benjamin accompanied their father and Jacob on this trip to Egypt. The names of Benjamin's ten sons are given as follows: Bela, Bechir, Ashbel, Gera, Naaman, Ehi, Rosh, Muppim, Huppim, and Ard. The Hebrew word bene can mean both son and grandson. Indeed, Numbers 26:40 clarifies that Ard and Naaman were not actually Benjamin's sons but rather grandsons. They were sons of Bela, Benjamin's son. The lying pen of the scribes therefore clearly depicts Benjamin as both father and a grandfather at the time when the true Genesis account says that he was merely a little child.

A thirty-nine year old Joseph could hardly address Benjamin as my son if Benjamin was old enough to be his own father. The lying scribe has built his case quite well and the lying hand has interwoven its narrative so well that only those who read with a watchful eye can discover a real conflict in the two stories. We are told that Esau was 40 years old when he married two foreign wives [Genesis 26:34]. At this time Jacob was also 40 years old, since he was Esau's twin [Genesis 25:24]. Shortly afterwards, Jacob allegedly stole Esau's blessing and was forced to flee to his uncle Laban who lived in Paddan Aram.

## THE EBIONITES

After Jacob left, Esau married another wife – this time of the Semitic stock [Genesis 28:6-9]. Jacob stayed in Mesopotamia with his uncle for twenty years [Genesis 31:38,41]. After his arrival, Jacob worked for Rachel seven years. At the end of this time Laban allegedly tricked him and gave him Leah instead. Seven days later he was also given Rachel but continued to work another seven years for Leah [Genesis 29:15-30]. By the end of his 20 year stay in Mesopotamia – all his eleven sons were born [Genesis 32:22]. After his 20 year stay with his uncle Laban, Jacob finally took all he had and returned to Canaan. As he was approaching his brother Esau, he divided his children and allocated them with their mothers. He put his concubines first with their children. Leah was next with her children. Finally, Rachel approached with Joseph [Genesis 33:2,7]. His eleven sons at that time were young and tender [Genesis 33:13].

As Jacob met Esau, they were both about 60 years old. Since Jacob was 130 years old when he migrated to Egypt and since his eleven sons were born to him in Paddan Aram – it follows then that according to the lying pen of the scribes, Jacob's sons were aged between 71 and 82. Since it is said that Rachel was pregnant with Benjamin as Jacob was returning to Canaan from Mesopotamia and since she gave birth to Benjamin while on this trip, Benjamin then would have been 71 years old when he went to Egypt with his brothers – at the time when the true Genesis account says that his brother Joseph was actually 39 years old. It is said that Rachel died while giving birth to Benjamin – at the time when Jacob was 60 years old [Genesis 35:16-20 and 48:7]. Neither Joseph nor Benjamin then could be said to have been born to Jacob in "his old age."

Thus, this source furnishes enough evidence that Benjamin was 71 years old when he met Joseph and directly contradicts another Genesis account which says that Joseph was 39 at this time. How could Benjamin be 71 and Joseph 39 when Joseph was actually older than Benjamin and in fact called him my son? For many Christians all these contradictions are trifling. But that's so only because they do not really realize the significance and the colossal implications involved here.

Just think for a moment. If Benjamin was really a mere child when he met Joseph in Egypt and if Joseph was truly 39 years old when Jacob was 130, then so many stories told in Genesis are actually forgeries and insertions by the lying pen of the scribes. For example, the story that Jacob stole Esau's blessing is simply not true. That he went to Paddan Aram and that he married two sisters is not true. That his two wives gave Jacob their maidens as concubines is also a lie. That Rachel was pregnant and that she died while giving birth to Benjamin is also a farce.

Rachel supposedly died on their return trip from Paddan Aram – after they spent 20 years there. But if Joseph was 39 when his father was 130 that means that Jacob was 91 when Joseph was born. Jacob would have been 108 when Joseph was sold – since Joseph was 17 when sold. Benjamin was born sometime after Jacob was 108 years old. If Rachel was the mother of Benjamin and if she died while giving birth to Benjamin – as the lying pen of the scribes says – then Rachel would have been past child bearing age since she married Jacob when he was about 47 years old. Rachel therefore could not have died while giving birth to Benjamin on their return trip from Paddan Aram – when Jacob was about 60 years old. Nor could have all the eleven sons been born to Jacob in Paddan Aram by the age of 60. If Rachel died on the return trip from Paddan Aram while giving birth to Benjamin, how could Joseph later dream that the "sun" [his father] and the "moon" [his mother] along with the "eleven stars" [his eleven brothers] bowed before him in obeisance? Jacob clearly identified himself with the "sun" and Rachel with the "moon," while his eleven sons with the "stars." Jacob's comment proves that Rachel was alive at the time Joseph dreamt this dream:

"What is this dream that you have dreamed? Will I and your mother and your brothers indeed come to bow ourselves down to you to the earth?" [Genesis 37:10 World English Bible].

Jacob could hardly speak of Rachel bowing down before Joseph if she died some years earlier. There is a clear discrepancy between the two Genesis accounts concerning Benjamin. No wonder Apostle Peter made a remark that he just did not believe that Jacob cohabited with four wives – of which two were sisters. This remark is preserved in the Clementine Homilies – written no later than the 2nd century. The lying pen of the scribes assumed that the readers of their forged material are ignorant fools. They expected their readers to believe that Isaac was fooled by Jacob so cheaply [Genesis 27]. They expected you to believe Jacob could not recognize Leah all the night through – although he was intimately involved with her [Genesis 29:21-25]. They also expect you to believe a score of other incredible and absurd stories. And, finally, how could have Rachel been pregnant and given birth to Benjamin on the return trip from Paddan Aram, when she actually told her father that then she had her menstruation? [Genesis 31:35].

**Isaac and Jacob's Stolen Blessing**

Isaac was forty years old when he married his relative Rebecca [Genesis 25:20]. He was sixty years old when his twins Esau and Jacob were born [verse 26]. In Genesis 27:1 we are told that Isaac got very old and became blind of his old age. But how old was he? Since he was sixty years old when Esau was born and since Esau was forty at that time, it would make Isaac hundred years of age. When I dealt with Benjamin, I pointed out this fact and also the fact that the lying scribe made Jacob 91 years old when Joseph was born to Jacob and Benjamin when he was even older. When Abraham was 99 years old, he was circumcised. Some years later he was able to travel three days journey with Isaac in order to sacrifice him on the mount he was told to go. At that time Abraham was over 100 years of age and was still strong and well since he died at the age of 175. How then could Isaac at 100 years of age be so feeble and blind from his old age when we are told that he died at the age of 180? [Genesis 35:28]. In the chapter where we read how Jacob deceived Isaac so naively, we obviously deal with the invented event and with the pen of the lying scribe.

**Hagar and Her Son Ishmael**

Abraham was 99 years old when he was circumcised and Ishmael 13 years old [Genesis 17:24]. Sometime after their circumcision Sarah got pregnant and then Isaac was born. By then Ishmael was at least 14 years old. When Isaac was weaned Abraham made a great feast [Genesis 21:8]. The child in those days was usually weaned when 3 years of age. By then Ishmael would have been between 16-17 years old. Sometime after that Sarah saw Ishmael playing with Isaac and she told Abraham to send Ishmael and his mother Hagar away. Abraham was reluctant but we are told that God instructed him to do as Sarah asked him [Genesis 21:9-13]. Then the next morning Abraham obeyed his God and his wife and put some bread, water and the boy on Hagar's back and sent them away. In the wilderness the water ran out and Hagar placed the boy under a shrub and went a distance away not to see the boy die of thirst. An angel appeared to her and showed her a well of water. She filled the leather bag with water and took the boy in her arms [Genesis 21:14-20]. The author of this portion of Genesis portrays Ishmael as a little child who could be placed under a shrub and who could be carried in the arms of his mother or on her back. But we have seen that Ishmael at this time would have been at least 16 years old and most probably closer to 18. Thus, there is a clear discrepancy here.

**Inheritance or No Inheritance for The Levites?**

The book of Deuteronomy and some other texts simply prohibit the Levites to own any land or to receive any inheritance whatsoever. They were to live off the sacrifices and the tithes of the people. Deuteronomy 10:9 says that the Levites received no land as other tribes did. In Deuteronomy 18:1-2 we read:

"The priests the Levites, [even] all the tribe of Levi, shall have no portion nor inheritance with Israel: they shall eat the offerings of Yahweh made by fire, and his inheritance. They shall have no inheritance among their brothers: Yahweh is their inheritance, as he has spoken to them" [World English Bible].

In Numbers 18:20-24 we read:

"Yahweh said to Aaron, you shall have no inheritance in their land, neither shall you have any portion among them: I am your portion and your inheritance among the children of Israel. To the children of Levi, behold, I have given all the tithe in Israel for an inheritance, in return for their service which they serve, even the service of the tent of meeting. Henceforth the children of Israel shall not come near the tent of meeting, lest they bear sin, and die. But the Levites shall do the service of the tent of meeting, and they shall bear their iniquity: it shall be a statute forever throughout your generations; and among the children of Israel they shall have no inheritance. For the tithe of the children of Israel, which they offer as a heave-offering to Yahweh, I have given to the Levites for an inheritance: therefore, I have said to them, Among the children of Israel they shall have no inheritance" [World English Bible].

According to these texts, the Levites were not to receive any inheritance in the land of Canaan. They were to live off the sacrifices and offerings and the tithes the Israelites paid. But this is contradicted elsewhere in the Jewish Pentateuch. In Numbers 35:1-8 we read:

"Yahweh spoke to Moses in the plains of Moab by the Jordan at Jericho, saying, Command the children of Israel that they give to the Levites of the inheritance of their possession cities to dwell in; and suburbs for the cities round about them shall you give to the Levites. "The cities shall they have to dwell in; and their suburbs shall be for their cattle, and for their substance, and for all their animals. The suburbs of the cities, which you shall give to the Levites, shall be from the wall of the city and outward one thousand cubits round about. You shall measure outside of the city for the east side two thousand cubits, and for the south side two thousand cubits, and for the west side two thousand cubits, and for the north side two thousand cubits, the city being in the midst. This shall be to them the suburbs of the cities" [World English Bible].

"The cities which you shall give to the Levites, they shall be the six cities of refuge, which you shall give for the manslayer to flee to: and besides them you shall give forty-two cities. All the cities which you shall give to the Levites shall be forty-eight cities; them [shall you give] with their suburbs. Concerning the cities which you shall give of the possession of the children of Israel, from the many you shall take many; and from the few you shall take few: everyone according to his inheritance which he inherits shall give of his cities to the Levites" [World English Bible].

There were 23,000 Levites. The Levites who were of Aaronic lineage received thirteen cities while others the rest. If we were to settle 23,000 in

48 cities which they received, we would realize that each city would have been inhabited by only 479 persons. Joshua 21 says that the Levites came to Joshua and reminded him of Yahweh's instructions concerning their property. They asked for the cities and the pasture land for their cattle. Joshua assigned the thirteen cities to the Aaronic priests and the rest to other Levites. Some of these cities were of quite a good size. Thus, the Levites had their own cities, the pasture land, the flocks and herds, and the tithe on which to live. The Aaronic priests had all that plus a thigh and a shoulder of every sacrificial victim. Not a bad deal for those who supposedly were to have no property at all in the land of Canaan. Now please note the text of Numbers 18:23-24 once again:

"But the Levites shall do the service of the Tent of Meeting, and they shall bear their iniquity. It shall be a statute forever throughout your generations. Among the children of Israel, they shall have no inheritance. For the tithe of the children of Israel, which they offer as a wave offering to Yahweh, I have given to the Levites for an inheritance. Therefore, I have said to them, 'Among the children of Israel they shall have no inheritance" [World English Bible].

Now please compare this text with that of Leviticus 25:32-34 very carefully:

"Nevertheless, the cities of the Levites, the houses in the cities of their possession, the Levites may redeem at any time. The Levites may redeem the house that was sold, and the city of his possession, and it shall be released in the Jubilee; for the houses of the cities of the Levites are their possession among the children of Israel. But the field of the pasture lands of their cities may not be sold; for it is their perpetual possession" [World English Bible].

**Did Joshua Conquer the Promised Land or Not?**

The adherents of Pharisaic Judaism and those of traditional Christianity believe that Yahweh swore to Abraham that he would greatly multiply his descendants and that he would give the land of Canaan to them:

"To your descendants I will give this land" [Genesis 12:7 World English Bible].

"I will give to you, and to your seed after you, the land where you are travelling, all the land of Canaan, for an everlasting possession" [Genesis 17:8 World English Bible].

"In that day Yahweh made a covenant with Abram, saying, To your seed have I given this land, from the river of Egypt to the great river, the river Euphrates: the Kenites, the Kenizzites, the Kadmonites, the Hittites, the Perizzites, the Rephaim, the Amorites, the Canaanites, the Girgashites, and the Jebusites" [Genesis 15:18-21 World English Bible].

In Genesis 26:3-5 we are told that Yahweh also appeared to Isaac and confirmed his unconditional promise, telling him that his descendants will inherit the whole land of Canaan:

"Sojourn in this land, and I will be with you, and will bless you. For to you, and to your seed, I will give all these lands, and I will establish the oath which I swore to Abraham your father. I will multiply your seed as the stars of the sky, and will give to your seed all these lands. In your seed will all the nations of the earth be blessed, because Abraham obeyed my voice, and kept my charge, my commandments, my statutes, and my laws" [World English Bible].

Yahweh swore to Abraham an unconditional oath that he would give the whole land of Canaan to his descendants. The oath was sworn after Abraham was allegedly prepared to sacrifice his own son Isaac to Yahweh. Because of Abraham's unrestrained devotion and obedience, it is said that Yahweh swore the unconditional oath [Genesis 22:18-19]. In Genesis 28:13-14 this unconditional promise was also repeated to Jacob:

"Behold, Yahweh stood above it, and said, I am Yahweh, the God of Abraham your father, and the God of Isaac. The land whereon you lie, to you will I give it, and to your seed. Your seed will be as the dust of the earth, and you will spread abroad to the west, and to the east, and to the north, and to the south. In you and in your seed will all the families of the earth be blessed" [World English Bible].

That Yahweh swore an unconditional oath to Abraham, Isaac and Jacob is repeated in Deuteronomy 7:6-8:

"For you are a holy people to Yahweh your God: Yahweh your God has chosen you to be a people for his own possession, above all peoples who are on the face of the earth. Yahweh didn't set his love on you, nor choose you, because you were more in number than any people; for you were the fewest of all peoples: but because Yahweh loves you, and because he would keep the oath which he swore to your fathers, has Yahweh brought you out with a mighty hand, and redeemed you out of the house of bondage, from the hand of Pharaoh king of Egypt" [World English Bible].

Clearly the alleged oath to the Patriarchs had nothing to do with the obedience of the Israelites. It was unconditional and Yahweh was going to give them the whole land of Canaan even though they did not deserve it because of their repeated rebellion. This fact is expressly stated by Moses in Deuteronomy 9:1-6:

"Hear, Israel: you are to pass over the Jordan this day, to go in to dispossess nations greater and mightier than yourself, cities great and fortified up to the sky, a people great and tall, the sons of the Anakim, whom you know, and of whom you have heard say, Who can stand before the sons of Anak? Know therefore this day, that Yahweh your God is he who goes over before you as a devouring fire; he will destroy them, and he will bring them down before you: so shall you drive them out, and make them to perish quickly, as Yahweh has spoken to you. Don't speak in your heart, after that Yahweh your God has thrust them out from before you, saying, for my righteousness Yahweh has brought me in to possess this land; whereas for the wickedness of these nations Yahweh does drive them out from before you. Not for your righteousness, or for the uprightness of your heart, do you go in to possess their land; but for the wickedness of these nations Yahweh your God does drive them out from before you, and that he may establish the word which Yahweh swore to your fathers, to Abraham, to Isaac, and to Jacob. Know therefore, that Yahweh your God doesn't give you this good land to possess it for your righteousness; for you are a stiff-necked people" [World English Bible].

Moses goes on to remind the Israelites of their repeated rebellion and disobedience in the desert. The text therefore explicitly and irrefutably says that the oath given to Abraham, Isaac, and Jacob was unconditional and that Yahweh was going to conquer the whole land of Canaan so that his oath and promise to the Patriarchs could be fulfilled. In Deuteronomy 4:37-38 these words are ascribed to the lips of Moses:

"Because he loved your fathers, therefore he chose their seed after them, and brought you out with his presence, with his great power, out of Egypt; to drive out nations from before you greater and mightier than you, to bring you in, to give you their land for an inheritance, as at this day" [World English Bible].

Yahweh pledged to give the whole land of Canaan to the descendants of Abraham, Isaac, and Jacob even though they were rebellious and wicked. Even after the worship of the golden calf, Yahweh still pledged to lead the people to the land of Canaan, because of his oath to the Patriarchs. In Exodus 32:34 and 33:1-2 Yahweh commanded Moses:

"Now go, lead the people to the place of which I have spoken to you. Behold, my angel shall go before you.Yahweh spoke to Moses, Depart, go up from here, you and the people that you have brought up out of the land of Egypt, to the land of which I swore to Abraham, to Isaac, and to Jacob, saying, 'I will give it to your seed.' I will send an angel before you; and I will drive out the Canaanite, the Amorite, and the Hittite, and the Perizzite, the Hivite, and the Jebusite" [World English Bible].

When Moses grew old and was 120 years of age, he appointed Joshua as the leader of Israel and charged him to go and lead the people to the land of Canaan. Moses solemnly promised that Yahweh would conquer the land for his people because of the oath he gave to the Patriarchs. Deuteronomy 31:1-8 explicitly says:

"Moses went and spoke these words to all Israel. He said to them, I am one hundred twenty years old this day; I can no more go out and come in: and Yahweh has said to me, you shall not go over this Jordan. Yahweh your God, he will go over before you; he will destroy these nations from before you, and you shall dispossess them: [and] Joshua, he shall go over before you, as Yahweh has spoken. Yahweh will do to them as he did to Sihon and to Og, the kings of the Amorites, and to their land; whom he destroyed. Yahweh will deliver them up before you, and you shall do to them according to all the commandment which I have commanded you. Be strong and of good courage, don't be afraid, nor be scared of them: for Yahweh your God, he it is who does go with you; he will not fail you, nor forsake you. Moses called to Joshua, and said to him in the sight of all Israel, Be strong and of good courage: for you shall go with this people into the land which Yahweh has sworn to their fathers to give them; and you shall cause them to inherit it. Yahweh, he it is who does go before you; he will be with you, he will not fail you, neither forsake you: don't be afraid, neither be dismayed" [World English Bible].

In Deuteronomy 31:16, 19-21 we are told that Yahweh knew that the Israelites were going to forsake him and serve the hinder gods, once they inherit the land of Canaan. Nevertheless, Yahweh still promised to lead them to that land because of the oath he gave to the Patriarchs:

"Yahweh said to Moses, Behold, you shall sleep with your fathers; and this people will rise up, and play the prostitute after the strange gods of the land, where they go to be among them, and will forsake me, and break my covenant which I have made with them. Then my anger shall be kindled against them in that day, and I will forsake them, and I will hide my face from them, and they shall be devoured, and many evils and troubles shall come on them; so that they will say in that day, Haven't these evils come on us because our God is not among us? I will surely hide my face in that day for all the evil which they shall have worked, in that they are turned to other gods. Now therefore write you this song for you, and teach you it the children of Israel: put it in their mouths, that this song may be a witness for me against the children of Israel. For when I shall have brought them into the land which I swore to their fathers, flowing with milk and honey, and they shall have eaten and filled themselves, and grown fat; then will they turn to other gods, and serve them, and despise me, and break my covenant. It shall happen, when many evils and troubles are come on them, that this song shall testify before them as a witness; for it shall not be forgotten out of the mouths of their seed: for I know their imagination which they frame this day, before I have brought them into the land which I swore" [World English Bible].

Even though Yahweh was aware that the Israelites were going to desert him and serve the hinder gods, the very gods of Canaan, he still purposed to deliver them to the land of Canaan and give them the whole land just as he swore both to them and their fathers. After the death of Moses, Yahweh told Joshua to go ahead and lead the people to the land of Canaan. He told him to take possession of the whole land and not to be afraid since no man would be able to withstand him:

"Now it happened after the death of Moses the servant of Yahweh, that Yahweh spoke to Joshua the son of Nun, Moses' minister, saying, Moses my servant is dead; now therefore arise, go over this Jordan, you, and all this people, to the land which I do give to them, even to the children of Israel. Every place that the sole of your foot shall tread on, to you have I given it, as I spoke to Moses. From the wilderness, and this Lebanon, even to the great river, the river Euphrates, all the land of the Hittites, and to the great sea toward the going down of the sun, shall be your border. There shall not any man be able to stand before you all the days of your life. As I was with Moses, so I will be with you; I will not fail you, nor forsake you. Be strong and of good courage; for you shall cause this people to inherit the land which I swore to their fathers to give them" [Joshua 1:1-6 World English Bible].

Please note the boundaries of the land they were to possess. Their empire was to stretch as far as the river Euphrates and in fact any land on which they stepped with their feet was to be theirs. Joshua 10:40-43 expressly says that Joshua did everything Yahweh told him to do and that in one campaign Joshua conquered the whole land:

"So Joshua struck all the land, the hill-country, and the South, and the lowland, and the slopes, and all their kings: he left none remaining, but he utterly destroyed all that breathed, as Yahweh, the God of Israel, commanded. Joshua struck them from Kadesh-barnea even to Gaza, and all the country of Goshen, even to Gibeon. All these kings and their land did Joshua take at one time, because Yahweh, the God of Israel, fought for Israel. Joshua returned, and all Israel with him, to the camp to Gilgal" [World English Bible].

This claim is repeatedly stated in the book of Joshua. Please carefully note Joshua 11:6-15:

"Yahweh said to Joshua, Don't be afraid because of them; for tomorrow at this time will I deliver them up all slain before Israel: you shall hamstring their horses, and burn their chariots with fire. So Joshua came, and all the people of war with him, against them by the waters of Merom suddenly, and fell on them. Yahweh delivered them into the hand of Israel, and they struck them, and chased them to great Sidon, and to Misrephoth-maim, and to the valley of Mizpeh eastward; and they struck them, until they left them none remaining. Joshua did to them as Yahweh bade him: he hamstrung their horses, and burnt their chariots with fire. Joshua turned back at that time, and took Hazor, and struck the king of it with the sword: for Hazor before was the head of all those kingdoms. They struck all the souls who were therein with the edge of the sword, utterly destroying them; there was none left who breathed: and he burnt Hazor with fire. All the cities of those kings, and all the kings of them, did Joshua take, and he struck them with the edge of the sword, and utterly destroyed them; as Moses the servant of Yahweh commanded. But as for the cities that stood on their mounds, Israel burned none of them, save Hazor only; that did Joshua burn. All the spoil of these cities, and the cattle, the children of Israel took for a prey to themselves; but every man they struck with the edge of the sword, until they had destroyed them, neither left they any who breathed. As Yahweh commanded Moses his servant, so did Moses command Joshua: and so did Joshua; he left nothing undone of all that Yahweh commanded Moses" [World English Bible].

Now please note Joshua 11:23:

"So Joshua took the whole land, according to all that Yahweh spoke to Moses; and Joshua gave it for an inheritance to Israel according to their divisions by their tribes. The land had rest from war" [World English Bible].

Joshua 21:43-45 says:

"So Yahweh gave to Israel all the land which he swore to give to their fathers; and they possessed it, and lived therein. Yahweh gave them rest round about, according to all that he swore to their fathers: and there stood not a man of all their enemies before them; Yahweh delivered all their enemies into their hand. There failed not anything of any good thing which Yahweh had spoken to the house of Israel; all came to pass" [World English Bible].

If this is not clear and plain then I guess nothing in the Bible is clear. The texts plainly say that Yahweh through Joshua conquered the entire region and the whole land, the land which he swore to give them. Joshua left nothing undone. The Israelites settled in the land and the entire population was wiped out. After conquering the entire region, the Israelites finally lived in safety and rested from war. Time and time again, the conquered peoples were named in the land prophecies: the Amorites, the Canaanites, the Girgashites, the Hittites, the Hivites, the Jebusites, and the Perizzites. But as always, the authors of the Bible disagree among themselves and the redactors played a role in the final revision of the Bible. This author [s] present a completely different scenario, claiming that in fact most of the land Yahweh swore to give the Israelites was in fact unconquered as long as Joshua was alive and in fact remained unconquered. These alternative passages clearly and unblushingly state that the Israelites in fact were unable to conquer the Canaanites because they had iron chariots. This author either was unaware that Yahweh was going to fight the battles himself or else he did not think Yahweh was able to conquer these mighty nations. This author/redactor unreservedly says that Joshua in fact did not conquer the land nor did he accomplish everything just as Moses said he would. Please note the text of Joshua 13:1-6:

"Now Joshua was old and well stricken in years; and Yahweh said to him, You are old and well stricken in years, and there remains yet very much land to be possessed. This is the land that yet remains: all the regions of the Philistines, and all the Geshurites; from the Shihor, which is before Egypt, even to the border of Ekron northward, [which] is reckoned to the Canaanites; the five lords of the Philistines; the Gazites, and the Ashdodites, the Ashkelonites, the Gittites, and the Ekronites; "also the Avvim, on the south; all the land of the Canaanites, and Mearah that belongs to the Sidonians, to Aphek, to the border of the Amorites; and the land of the Gebalites, and all Lebanon, toward the sunrise, from Baal-gad under Mount Hermon to the entrance of Hamath; all the inhabitants of the hill-country from Lebanon to Misrephoth-maim, even all the Sidonians; them will I drive out from before the children of Israel: only allot you it to Israel for an inheritance, as I have commanded you" [World English Bible].

This passage directly contradicts the claim in Joshua 11:23 that Joshua "took the whole land, according to all that Yahweh spake unto Moses so that the land had rest from war. All of the territorial regions specified in this text as land that remained unconquered in fact lay within the boundaries that were laid out in Joshua 1:1-6. So if Joshua had indeed taken "the whole land, according to all that Yahweh spake unto Moses," as stated in Joshua 11:23, how could it be said later that "very much land" remained to be possessed?

We have seen previously that both Moses and Yahweh promised the Israelites that they would easily conquer the whole land since Yahweh would go ahead of them as a "consuming fire." The promise was repeated to Joshua and the previous passages clearly show that Joshua and the Israelites conquered the whole land and then rested from war. But another hand in Joshua 15:63 plainly says that the Israelites could not drive out the Jebusites nor could they actually take Jerusalem, a city which was supposedly to be their one and only place of worship:

"As for the Jebusites, the inhabitants of Jerusalem, the children of Judah couldn't drive them out: but the Jebusites dwell with the children of Judah at Jerusalem to this day" [World English Bible].

Why could not the tribe of Judah defeat the Jebusites when they were one of the nations "greater and mightier than you" of which both Moses and Yahweh said that they would be destroyed on behalf of the Israelites? Joshua 16:10 says:

"They didn't drive out the Canaanites who lived in Gezer: but the Canaanites dwell in the midst of Ephraim to this day, and are become servants to do forced labor" [World English Bible].

The Canaanites however were specifically listed as one of the seven nations that would be completely destroyed and they were to be completely destroyed and in fact were according to other source of Joshua. In Joshua 17:12-13 we are explicitly told that Manasseh could not defeat the Canaanites because the Canaanites were determined to live in their homeland. How could this be when elsewhere we are told that Joshua conquered the whole land and that nothing was left undone?

There are other places where it is said that the Israelites could not drive out the inhabitants of the Promised Land. Yet both Moses and Yahweh promised that they will defeat all those nations and drive them out "without fail." IF Yahweh gave to Israel ALL the land which he swore to give to their fathers [Joshua 21:43-45], and IF they possessed it and dwelt therein [same verses], and IF Yahweh gave them rest round about, according to ALL that he swore to their fathers [same verses], and IF there stood not a man of ALL their enemies before them [same verses], and IF Yahweh delivered all their enemies into their hand [same verses], and IF there failed nothing of any good thing which Yahweh had spoken to the house of Israel [same verses], and IF all came to pass [same verses], how then could another source say that when Joshua grew old there was still very much land to be conquered?

Those who believe that the Bible is infallible and inerrant have much to explain. If the alternative passages in Joshua present problems and serious discrepancies, the texts in the book of Judges cause even more serious problems. In Judges 1:1-4 we are told that Judah was to start his campaign against the Canaanites and Perizzites only after the death of Joshua. In fact, the same text also says that Simeon had not as yet received his inheritance and Judah promised to help him in his campaign if he would help Judah defeat the Canaanites and Perizzites. In the same chapter, verses 10-15 a great blunder is made. Here we are told that Judah conquered Hebron formerly called Kirjath Arba actually after the death of Joshua and that the three sons of Anak were then killed. But Joshua 14:6-15 says that it was in fact Joshua himself who gave Caleb the city Hebron and in 15:14-15 we read:

"To Caleb the son of Jephunneh he gave a portion among the children of Judah, according to the commandment of Yahweh to Joshua, even Kiriath-arba, [which Arba was] the father of Anak (the same is Hebron). Caleb drove out there the three sons of Anak: Sheshai, and Ahiman, and Talmai, the children of Anak. He went up there against the inhabitants of Debir: now the name of Debir before was Kiriath-sepher" [World English Bible].

After Caleb took possession of Hebron it is said [verse 15] that the land had rest from war, since the whole land was conquered by then. The two texts are therefore in variance. But there is even a greater blunder yet to be discovered when we deal with Caleb and his inheritance. In Joshua 15:15-19 we read how Caleb also conquered the city of Kirjath Sepher, that is, Debir. This of course took place while Joshua was still alive. The same account, almost word for word, is recorded in Judges 1:11-15 only here is claimed that this conquest did not take place while Joshua was alive but in fact after his death. Please note the two texts:

"He went up there against the inhabitants of Debir: now the name of Debir before was Kiriath-sepher. Caleb said, He who strikes Kiriath-sepher, and takes it, to him will I give Achsah my daughter as wife. Othniel the son of Kenaz, the brother of Caleb, took it: and he gave him Achsah his daughter as wife. It happened, when she came [to him], that she moved him to ask of her father a field: and she alighted from off her donkey; and Caleb said, What would you? She said, Give me a blessing; for that you have set me in the land of the South, give me also springs of water. He gave her the upper springs and the lower springs" [Joshua 15:15-19 World English Bible].

"From there he went against the inhabitants of Debir. (Now the name of Debir before was Kiriath-sepher.) Caleb said, He who strikes Kiriath-sepher, and takes it, to him will I give Achsah my daughter as wife. Othniel the son of Kenaz, Caleb's younger brother, took it: and he gave him Achsah his daughter as wife. It happened, when she came [to him], that she moved him to ask of her father a field: and she alighted from off her donkey; and Caleb said to her, What would you? She said to him, Give me a blessing; for that you have set me in the land of the South, give me also springs of water. Caleb gave her the upper springs and the lower springs" [Judges 1:11-15 World English Bible].

Identical event and the same account but with two major contradictions. The Joshua's account makes it plain that the incident took place before the death of Joshua and that after this conquest the Israelites rested from war since the whole land of Canaan was conquered by then. The Judges account however, makes it very clear that the incident took place after the death of Joshua and that this was the very beginning of conquest and that the Promised Land was not as yet conquered. An amazing thing is stated in Judges 1:19. It is said that Yahweh was with the warriors of Judah and that they were able to conquer much land but that although Yahweh was with them they could not defeat the Canaanites in the valley because they possessed the chariots of iron and were therefore too strong for the warriors of Judah:

"Yahweh was with Judah; and drove out [the inhabitants of] the hill-country; for he could not drive out the inhabitants of the valley, because they had chariots of iron" [World English Bible].

There are numerous texts where both Moses and Yahweh encouraged the people not to fear the nations of Canaan because they would defeat them all without fail. The spies were condemned because they said that the Israelites could not defeat the fortified cities and because there were even Anakim warriors who were of gigantic statue and who were the descendants of ancient Nephilim. How then could it be said that Judah could not drive out the Canaanites from the valleys because of their iron chariots even though Yahweh was with him? Moreover, why was there a need for Judah to fight for his territory when, as we have already seen, the whole land was conquered and Judah in fact already inherited the whole allotment while Joshua was still alive? Joshua 14:1-5 explicitly says that the conquered land was divided among the tribes of Israel in accordance with the instructions of Moses. Chapter 15 describes in detail the land Judah inherited while Joshua was still alive. Judges 1:27-28 also shows that Manasseh could not drive out the Canaanites from the valleys, as was the case with Judah.

The Canaanites were determined to preserve their land. What about the promise that they would take possession of the whole land without fail? The same chapter goes on to say that also Ephraim, Zebulun, Asher, and Naphtali also failed to drive out the natives out of their territories. Verse 34 says that the Amorites were too powerful for the tribe of Dan and that they forced them to the mountains, since they were determined to hold onto their homeland. In Judges 3:1-5 the redactor inserted a gloss in order to explain the failure of the tribes to drive out and defeat the enemies in the land of Canaan. The redactor claimed that it was Yahweh himself who left all these nations in the land so that the Israelites who were untrained warriors could learn to fight and that Yahweh could also test the Israelites through these nations:

"Now these are the nations which Yahweh left, to prove Israel by them, even as many [of Israel] as had not known all the wars of Canaan; only that the generations of the children of Israel might know, to teach them war, at the least such as before knew nothing of it: [namely], the five lords of the Philistines, and all the Canaanites, and the Sidonians, and the Hivites who lived on Mount Lebanon, from Mount Baal-hermon to the entrance of Hamath. They were [left], to prove Israel by them, to know whether they would listen to the commandments of Yahweh, which he commanded their fathers by Moses. The children of Israel lived among the Canaanites, the Hittites, and the Amorites, and the Perizzites, and the Hivites, and the Jebusites" [World English Bible].

Here we find the Canaanites, Hittites, Amorites, Perizzites, Hivites, and the Jebusites very much alive and in fact very powerful, possessing iron chariots and great strength, so much so that in Judges 1 we are told that their survival had nothing to do with later warfare training but rather that the Israelites simply could not defeat them. But both texts are forgeries. Neither Judges 1 nor Judges 3:1-5 could be true if the previous texts of Joshua are true. In Joshua 11:3 we read of the Canaanites, Amorites, Hittites, Preizzites, Jebusites, and the Hivites, exactly the same six nations named in Judges 3:5, mustering their armies against Joshua and the Israelites. Yahweh told Joshua not to be afraid but to go and fight these nations since they would all be delivered into their hands. Verses 6-12 describe in detail how the

Israelites defeated these six nations and how they destroyed their cities and killed everything that breathed in those cities. Verse 15 says that Joshua did to these six nations everything that Moses commanded him to do. He left nothing undone. The whole land was destroyed and all these nations were completely annihilated and the Israelites and the whole land had rest from war. Judges and the books of Samuel clearly show that the Israelites never had rest from war but that until the days of King David they were continually mistreated by the very nations which Joshua allegedly completely destroyed and wiped out.

The Israelites were weak and continually served the native peoples of the Promised Land. Judges 18:1 shows that the tribe of Dan was basically without territory and that even at that time they still did not inherit bulk of the territories which belonged to them, despite of the fact that in Joshua it was said that all the tribes received their inheritance in the days of Joshua and rested from war. It follows then that the burden of explaining rests on those who believe in the inerrancy of the Bible and not those who believe that the Bible is fallible and that many passages were corrupted and written by the "lying pen of the scribes" [Jeremiah 8:8]. The Ebionites were right to reject the bulk of the Jewish Scriptures as forgeries and of diabolical origin.

**A Sample of Other Discrepancies in The Bible**

In 2 Chronicles 36:9 we are told that King Johoiachin was 8 years old when he became king. But 2 Kings 24:8 contradicts this and says that he was 18. In 2 Kings 8:26 we are told that King Ahaziah was 22 years of age when he ascended the throne. But 2 Chronicles 22:2 contradicts this and says that he was 42. If this was true then he would have been two years older than his own father who died at the age of 40. But, then, "all things are possible" for those who "have faith." In 1 Kings 4:26 we are told that Solomon had 40,000 stalls whereas 2 Chronicles 9:25 places the number at 4000. In 1 Kings 9:23 we are told that Solomon had 550 overseers but in 2 Chronicles 8:10 the number is 250.

In 1 Kings 5:13 we are told that Solomon conscripted men from Israel for his forced labour projects. Adoniram was in charge of this force [verse 14].

In 1 Kings 12:4 it is confirmed that Solomon placed a heavy burden on the shoulders of the Israelites and that he actually flogged the Israelites [verse 11]. When Rehoboam, Solomon's son refused to deal with this issue, the Israelites rebelled and killed Adoniram who was in charge of the forced labour [verse 18].

But all this is flatly contradicted in 2 Chronicles 8:9 where it is said that Solomon did not use any of the Israelites for his forced labour projects. 1 Chronicles 19 describes the battle in which David defeated Syrians and Ammonites. In verse 18 we are told that David killed 7000 charioteers and 40,000 foot-soldiers. But this is contradicted in 2 Samuel 10, describing the same battle. Verse 18 says that David actually killed 700 and not 7000 charioteers and 40,000 horsemen and not foot men.

In 2 Samuel 24 and 1 Chronicles 21 we find a detailed account of how David numbered all his fighting men and how thousands of innocent Israelites were butchered for his sin. There are a number of problems in these two accounts. But I will point out only four significant and blunt contradictions. In Samuel's account it was Yahweh who stirred up David to number the people [verse 1] but in the account of Chronicles it was actually Satan [verse 1].

In Samuel's account the number of the fighting men is given as: 800,000 fighters in Israel and 500,000 fighters in Judah [verse 9]. But in the account of Chronicles the number is 1,100,000 fighters in Israel and 470,000 fighters in Judah [verse 5]. In Samuel's account the prophet Gad went to David with three options from Yahweh [verse 13]:

> SEVEN YEARS OF FAMINE
> THREE MONTHS OF DEFEAT
> THREE DAYS OF PESTILENCE IN ISRAEL

But in the version of Chronicles [verse 11] the three options were:

> THREE YEARS OF FAMINE
> THREE MONTHS OF DEFEAT
> THREE DAYS OF PESTILENCE IN ISRAEL

In one account the option was seven years of famine while in the other three. [Some new English Bible versions read three in both texts in order to reconcile the discrepancy. In the footnote however it is pointed out that the Hebrew text of Samuel reads seven – as does also the King James Bible]. The fourth blunt contradiction between the two accounts has to do with the site or the thrashing floor of Arunah the Jebusite from whom David bought it. In Samuel's account the site was purchased by David for fifty shekels of silver [verse 24] but according to the version given in Chronicles the amount was six hundred shekels of gold [verse 25].

In 2 Chronicles 16:1 we are told that Basha, king of Israel came against Ramah and fortified it in order to prevent anyone entering the city or escaping to the territory of Judah. According to this text this occurred in the 36$^{th}$ year of Asa, king of Judah. But 1 Kings 16:6 says that Basha died in the 26$^{th}$ year of Asa, king of Judah. How could Basha fortify the city of Ramah 10 years after he was dead? In 2 Chronicles 36:10 we are told that after King Jehoiachin was arrested and taken as prisoner to Babylon, his brother Zedekiah was appointed in his place. But 2 Kings 24:17 contradicts this by saying that Zedekiah was not Jehoiachin's brother but rather uncle, the brother of his father. In 2 Samuel 6:23 we read that Michal, the daughter of King Saul, had no children until the day she died. But 2 Samuel 21:8 contradicts this by saying that she had five sons whom David handed to be killed. The father of the children is actually the husband of her sister Merab. The children were most likely Merab's and not Michal's. Either the scribe made a mistake or someone wrote it who was ignorant of the facts. In either case it is obvious that they were not inspired and that therefore the Bible is not infallible.

For the Bible to be fully inspired and inerrant, the original authors, the copyists, and even the translators would have to be fully inspired so that every word could be preserved as it actually was in the autograph. Anything less than this results in the fallible Bible. One source of Joshua says that Yahweh commanded Joshua to send twelve men – one from each tribe of Israel – to take twelve stones out of the midst of Jordan where the priests were standing, as the people were crossing Jordan and to take them with them and erect them at the place where they were to camp that night [Joshua

4:2-3]. Verse 8 says that the men did as commanded and that they carried the stones to the place where they camped and laid them there. But another source contradicts this by saying that the twelve stones were actually erected in the midst of Jordan – where the priests stood – and that they were still there [sticking out of the water?] at the time the book of Joshua was written [verse 9]. Thus, this source says that the stones were erected in exactly the same place whereas another source says they were actually taken from it and carried away.

In Joshua 15:15-19 we find a text that is rewritten in Judges 1:11-15. The text says that Caleb went to fight against Debir. He promised to give his daughter in marriage to the man who conquers the city. Othniel, the son of his younger brother Kenaz conquered it and thus he married Caleb's daughter. The two texts are identical. But there is one major contradiction. According to Joshua's text this conquering of Debir took place while Joshua was still alive. But the text of Judges shows that the conquest took place after Joshua actually died [verse 1]. Also, Joshua 15:14 says that Caleb had only expelled out of Hebron the three sons of the giant Anak. Their names were: Sheshai, Ahiman, and Talmai. But the text in Judges 1:10 says that Caleb actually killed them. [See King James Bible and the Hebrew text].

In 2 Chronicles 11:20-21 we are told that Maacah, the daughter of Absalom was the mother of King Abijah. She was Rehoboam's favorite wife and Abijah his favorite son [verses 21-22]. But 2 Chronicles 13:2 denies that Maacah the daughter of Absalom was the mother of Abijah by saying that Abijah's mother was actually Micaiah, the daughter of Uriel from Gibeah. In 1 Samuel 22:9,11-12 we learn that Ahimelech was the son of Ahitub and the father of Abiathar. He and all his relatives were killed by King Saul. Verse 20 says that only Abiathar the son of Ahimelech escaped. But in 1 Chronicles 24:6 and 2 Samuel 8:17 the relationship is reversed. Here Abiathar is not the son of Ahimelech but actually his father.

We cannot reconcile these passages by assuming that there were two persons called Ahimelech. The grandfather Ahimelech and the grandson Ahimelech – with Abiathar in between. According to 2 Samuel 8:17 the Ahimelech served as priest during the reign of David. Therefore, he had to precede Abiathar and could not have been his son. Besides, Abiathar was later deposed by Solomon and expelled to the town of Anathoth and none of his descendants were allowed to serve in the temple [1 Kings 2:26-27]. These texts therefore contradict each other. Jesus also contradicted the account given in the Hebrew Scriptures by saying that David went to the House of Yahweh [in Nob] in the days when Abiathar was the High Priest [Mark 2:26]. The Hebrew Scriptures show that in fact Ahimelech was the High Priest at that time and not Abiathar. In Daniel 1:5,18 we are told that Daniel and his three friends were trained for three years and that only after that training time they actually appeared before Nebuchadrezzar.

At the end of three years Nebuchadrezzar found them to be ten times wiser than all others in any field of knowledge and Daniel remained in the palace until the first year of King Cyrus [verses 18-21]. But Daniel 2:1 contradicts this by saying that in the second year of Nebuchadrezzar's reign Daniel appeared before Nebuchadrezzar and interpreted the king's famous dream that no one else could. Thus Daniel 2:1 does not allow Daniel to complete his three-year training course and has him the Governor of Babylon in the second year of his training. The same is true of his three friends.

Daniel spoke to Nebuchadrezzar and they were given important jobs in the kingdom [2:49]. There is a clear contradiction between the two accounts. Daniel 1:21 says that Daniel continued until the first year of King Cyrus. But Daniel 10:1 has the prophet see a vision at the river Tigris in the third year of King Cyrus. According to Daniel 10:1 the prophet was still in exile in the third year of Cyrus – two years after he was supposedly dead. But if he was truly alive in the third year of Cyrus how is it that he was still in exile when already in the first year of Cyrus, Ezra and all other Jews were free to return to Jerusalem? [Ezra 1:1-4]. There is clearly a problem and a discrepancy here.

In Daniel 1:1-2 we are told that in the 3rd year of King Jehoiakim's reign, King Nebuchadrezzar of Babylon besieged Jerusalem. Verse 2 says that Jehoiakim was captured and the temple was spoiled and all the vessels were taken to Babylon and were used in the services of the Babylonian gods. There is a problem here. The 3rd year of King Jehoiakim's reign was 606 B.C.E., but Nebuchadrezzar at that time was not yet king. It wasn't until 597 B.C.E.

that Nebuchadrezzar actually took Jerusalem and the first exiles were taken to Babylon. By then King Jehoiakim was already dead. In 1 Kings 7:14 we are told that King Hiram's mother was of the tribe of Nephtalim while 2 Chronicles 2:14 contradicts this by saying that his mother was of the tribe of Dan.

In 2 Kings 9:1-3 we are told that one of the prophets in accordance with Elisha's instructions anointed Jehu as king of Israel. This took place after Elijah was taken away. But in 1 Kings 19:15-16 we are told that Elijah was commissioned to do that at the same time he was to anoint Elisha as his successor. In Exodus 20:8-11 the Sabbath is said to be given as a memorial of six day creation, but in Deuteronomy 5:15 it was given to be a memory of exodus from Egypt.

Shortly after Moses placed the tablets of stone in the Ark he made, they left and departed for Moserah. Aaron died there – sometimes in the second year and his son Eleazar succeeded him as High Priest [Deuteronomy 10:6]. But this is contradicted elsewhere. In Numbers 33:38 it said that Aaron died on the first day of the fifth month in the fortieth year on Mount Hor. In 1 Kings 8:5 we are told that when the temple was completed and the Ark of the Covenant was placed in the Holy of Holies, Solomon sacrificed "so many sheep and cattle that they could not be recorded or counted."

But apparently the author of 2 Chronicles 7:5,8 was both able to count them and record them. He says that Solomon sacrificed 22,000 cattle and 120,000 sheep and goats – during the space of seven days. In verse 7 we are told that the altar itself was insufficient for this occasion so Solomon dedicated the middle part of the front court for the purpose of burning the holocausts. The animals had to be killed, their blood poured at the altar, their carcases skinned, the flesh washed, and then the bodies burned on the altar. Twelve sheep and goats and two bulls would have to be killed and prepared and also completely consumed by fire every minute for 24 hours a day and for seven days straight. An impossible task indeed.

In 2 Kings 16:2 we are told that King Ahaz was 20 years old when he became king and that he reigned 16 years. Verse 20 shows that when Ahaz died at the age of 36 his son Hezekiah became king in his place. Then in 18:1-2 we are told that Hezekiah was 25 years old when his father died. This data would make King Ahaz 11 years old when his son Hezekiah was born. Since gestation period is about nine months it would mean that Ahaz fathered his son Hezekiah when he was ten years old – something which he could not have done under normal biological circumstances. Did Hezekiah have a miraculous birth? The Bible does not say so and I do not know of any Christian denomination which claims so. In Genesis 48:7 we are told that Rachel's tomb was near Bethlehem in Judah. But in 1 Samuel 10:2 Rachel's tomb was near Ramah in the territory of Benjamin.

**Corruption of the Synoptic Gospels**

Church of all branches maintains that the Synoptic Gospels are fully inspired and that they were independently written by Matthew, Mark and Luke. But I will demonstrate that the three Gospels are actually corrupted and forged by an unknown hand and that they are written in such a way that Matthew and Luke would disagree virtually on any and every point. We may begin with parents of Jesus and find out whether they lived in Nazareth of Galilee before Mary conceived Jesus in her womb or after they had returned from Egypt. I will demonstrate that this is the very first fundamental disagreement between Matthew's and Luke's Gospels. Matthew states that Jesus was born in Bethlehem and that King Herod the Great issued an order to kill all the infants in Bethlehem in hope to kill the newborn Jesus. In order to save Jesus alive, Joseph escaped with Mary and his son to Egypt where he remained until the death of Herod. After his death they returned from Egypt but would not settle in Judea since Herod's son Archelaus ruled in his father's place. Receiving instructions in a dream they settled in Nazareth of Galilee [Matthew 2:19-23].

Therefore, according to the version of Matthean Gospel, the parents of Jesus settled in Nazareth only after their return from Egypt. But the version of Luke's Gospel clearly shows that Joseph and Mary lived in Nazareth before Gabriel even announced Mary's pregnancy. In fact, in this Gospel we are told that Gabriel appeared to Mary in Nazareth and told her that she will conceive Jesus [Luke 1:26-31]. Joseph himself lived in Nazareth since he went to Bethlehem from Nazareth [Luke 2:4]. Six weeks after Jesus' birth they went to Jerusalem and then returned back home to Nazareth:

"When they had accomplished all things that were according to the law of the Lord, they returned into Galilee, to their own city, Nazareth" [Luke 2:39 World English Bible].

Even the genealogies of Jesus differ. Matthew traces Jesus to David through Solomon whereas Luke through Solomon's brother Nathan. Now I will demonstrate just how Matthew and Luke disagree on virtually any topic. Mark is a stable source and if Luke agrees with Mark then Matthew's version deviates from Mark in order to disagree with Luke and when Matthew agrees with Mark then Luke's version deviates from Mark in order to disagree with Matthew. Later I will show that even when Matthew and Luke say something that is not written in Mark's Gospel, they disagree and give conflicting versions – whatever the subject.

**Matthean Deviation from Mark**

Mark says that when Jesus and his disciples crossed the Sea of Galilee, they arrived at the region called Gadarenes. As soon as they arrived, a demoniac met them whom Jesus eventually healed [Mark 5:1-8]. Luke agrees with Mark in his version of this story. He likewise says that the region was called Gadarenes and that only one demoniac was involved [Luke 8:26-29]. But the Gospel of Matthew must not agree with that of Luke, so the Matthean account now deviates from that of Mark. Matthew calls the region not Gadarenes – as Mark and Luke do – but actually Gergesenes. He also states that there was not one but two demoniacs [Matthew 8:28-29]. The Matthean account even changes the singular pronouns of Mark and Luke to plural.

Mark writes that Jesus sent two of his disciples to bring him a colt and that he eventually entered Jerusalem riding on this colt [Mark 11:1-2,7]. Luke agrees with Mark. He also states that only a colt was involved and that Jesus was riding only a colt [Luke 19:29-30,35]. But Matthew again deviates from Mark in order not to agree with Luke. Matthew emphasizes that the disciples brought an ass and her colt and that Jesus actually rode them both as he entered Jerusalem [Matthew 21:1-2,6].

It is hard to imagine Jesus riding the two animals at the same time. But Matthean account maintains this in order to disagree with Luke – even if in doing so means to be stupid and tell a lie. Several days after entering Jerusalem, Jesus sent two of his disciples to prepare a room where Jesus and the Twelve could eat the last meal. Mark places these words on the lips of the two disciples when they approached the owner of the house:

"Where is the guest room, where I may eat the Passover with my disciples?" [Mark 14:14 World English Bible].

Luke agrees with Mark:

"Where is the guest room, where I may eat the Passover with my disciples?" [Luke 22:11 World English Bible].

But Matthew deviates from Mark and so accomplishes his purpose – to disagree with Luke:

"My time is at hand. I will keep the Passover at your house with my disciples" [Matthew 26:18 World English Bible].

Here again we have two against one and Matthew disagreeing with Luke. One particular Sabbath Jesus went to Simon's house and found that his mother in law was sick. He healed her of her fever. Now when Mark referred to Peter he uses the name Simon [Mark 1:29-31]. Luke agrees with him. Referring to the same incident, Luke also uses the name Simon [Luke 4:38-39]. But Matthew now must deviate from Mark in order to disagree with Luke. So what does he do? He uses the name Peter instead [Matthew 8:14-15]. John the Baptist spoke of Jesus. He said something about the shoes of Jesus:

"the thong of whose sandals I am not worthy to stoop down and loosen" [Mark 1:7 World English Bible].

Luke agrees with Mark. His text reads:

"the latchet of whose sandals I am not worthy to loosen" Luke 3:16 World English Bible].

Matthew must disagree with Luke. So, he alters Mark's version, and makes his own text say:

"whose shoes I am not worthy to carry" [Matthew 3:11 World English Bible].

The Synoptic Gospels portray Judas Iscariot as traitor. He went to the chief priests and offered to deliver Jesus into their hands. Mark says that they promised Judas money [Mark 14:11]. Luke agrees with him. He also uses the word money [Luke 22:5]. But Matthew cannot use the same word since by doing so he would agree with Luke so he changes his text to read thirty pieces of silver [Matthew 26:15]. Mark says that one day Jesus led his disciples through cornfields [Mark 2:23]. Luke agrees with him. He also uses the word cornfields [Luke 6:1]. Matthew of course must deviate from Mark so that he can disagree with Luke. He chooses the word corn instead [Matthew 12:1]. Would the Holy Spirit opt to play word games? Would She inspire the original authors to distort the truth in order to uphold the Synoptic principle? Jesus spoke concerning the important subject of divorce. Mark places this statement on the lips of Jesus:

"Whoever divorces his wife, and marries another, commits adultery against her" [Mark 10:11 World English Bible].

Luke agrees with him:

"Everyone who divorces his wife, and marries another, commits adultery" [Luke 16:18 World English Bible].

Mark and Luke agree: marriage is unconditional. No divorce – full stop. But Matthew cannot agree. Even though we are faced with an important and very significant doctrine, Matthew must resort to his word play in order to disagree with Luke. So, he adds a clause in the mouth of Jesus:

"I tell you that whoever will put away his wife, except for sexual immorality, and will marry another, commits adultery" [Matthew 19:9 World English Bible].

Shortly before his death Jesus made a remark concerning the temple after some of his disciples pointed out its massive stones and beauty. As they were sitting on the Mount of Olives his disciples asked him to clarify his remark. Mark places these words in the mouth of the disciples:

"...when will these things be? What is the sign that these things are all about to be accomplished?" [Mark 13:4 World English Bible].

Luke agrees with Mark. His text reads:

"when therefore will these things be? What is the sign that these things are about to happen?" [Luke 21:7 World English Bible].

Mark and Luke agree that the question had to do only and exclusively with the destruction of the temple – when there was not going to be one stone left upon another – as Jesus pointed out. But Matthew must deviate from Mark so that he may disagree with Luke. So, he places the following words in the mouth of the disciples:

"Tell us, when will these things be? What is the sign of your coming, and of the end of the world?" [Matthew 24:3 World English Bible].

Jesus began explaining that there would first of all come deceivers in his name saying I am Christ [Mark 13:6]. Luke agrees with Mark. He also uses the expression I am Christ [Luke 21:8]. You will note that in the King James Bible the word Christ is in italics. This means that it was supplied by the translators and that it does not appear in the Greek text. The Greek text simply uses "Ego eimi" [I am].

Virtually all new English versions omit the italicized word Christ. So, Mark and Luke simply use the phrase "I am." But Matthew deviates from Mark and uses the phrase "Ego eimi o christos" – that is, "I am the Christ." You will note that the word "Christ" in Matthew is not in italics in the King James Bible. So, again we have two against one and Matthew disagreeing with Luke. When Jesus was crucified, Pilate wrote an inscription as to why he was crucified. Mark says that this inscription read:

"THE KING OF THE JEWS" [Mark 15:26 World English Bible].

Luke agrees with Mark:

"THIS IS THE KING OF THE JEWS" [Luke 23:38 World English Bible].

But Matthew deviates from Mark and makes the inscription read:

"THIS IS JESUS, THE KING OF THE JEWS" [Matthew 27:37 World English Bible].

Now I will present the Synoptic passages in which Luke deviates from Mark and therefore causes his Gospel to disagree with Matthew.

**Lukan Deviation from Mark**

Mark reports that Peter and his brother Andrew were chosen by Jesus at the Sea of Galilee while they were throwing their fishing nets into the sea [Mark 1:16-18]. Then shortly afterwards, but independently of this incident, Jesus chose James and John at the same sea while they were mending the fishing nets with their father. He called them and they became his disciples [Mark 1:19-20]. Matthew agrees with Mark. He says the same thing [Matthew 4:18-20 and 4:21-22]. But Luke deviates from Mark in order to disagree with Matthew.

He reports that Peter, Andrew, James, and John were chosen all together and at the same time at a different place, at a different chronological date and under different circumstances than reported by Mark and Matthew [Luke 5:1-11]. Mark identifies the twelve disciples of Jesus by the following names: Simon Peter, Andrew, James, John, Philip, Bartholomew, Thomas, Matthew, James, Thaddaeus, Simon the Canaanite, and Judas Iscariot [Mark 3:16-19].

Matthew agrees with Mark but he slightly rearranges the order of the names [Matthew 10:2-4]. Luke however deviates from Mark so that his list of names would not agree with that of Matthew. Simon the Canaanite becomes Simon Zelotes, and Thaddaeus is replaced with Judas. Luke ends up with two disciples named Judas [Luke 6:14-16]. Thus, again we have two against one and Matthew and Luke not agreeing. Jesus promised that some of his disciples would live to see his glory.

It was six days after this promise that Jesus fulfilled it. Matthew agrees with him. He also says six days. But Luke disagrees and says eight days. Mark and Matthew say that he took Peter, James, and John to a high mountain and was transfigured. But Luke disagrees by reversing the names, deleting "high" and using the word "altered" rather than "transfigured." Compare Mark 9:1-2, Matthew 16:28; 17:1-2 with Luke 9:27-28].

When Jesus spoke of the destruction of the temple, he used the term "the abomination of desolation" [Mark 13:14]. Matthew agrees with him. He uses the identical term [24:15-16]. But Luke disagrees and alters Mark's account to "Jerusalem compassed with armies" – so that he may disagree with Matthew [Luke 21:20-21]. Jesus told the disciples that they should learn the lesson from the "fig tree" according to Mark 13:28 and Matthew 24:32. But Luke changes this to "fig tree and all the trees" [Luke 21:29].

Jesus said that when all was about to be fulfilled, they should know that the destruction is at "the doors" [Mark 13:29 and Matthew 24:33]. But Luke again disagrees and changes his version to "at hand" [Luke 21:30]. The Synoptic principle or pattern continues unabated and we always have two against one and Matthew and Luke disagreeing. During the night of his arrest – while serving the supper – Jesus pointed out that the betrayer's hand "dippeth in the dish" [Mark 14:20 and Matthew 26:23]. But according to Luke it was "on the table" [Luke 22:21]. Jesus took bread and broke it and then gave it to his disciples and said to them:

"Take, eat. This is my body" [Mark 14:22 World English Bible].

Matthew agrees with Mark:

"Take, eat; this is my body" [Matthew 26:26 World English Bible].

But Luke distorts the text of Mark so that he may disagree with Matthew and makes his text read:

"This is my body which is given for you. Do this in memory of me" [Luke 22:19 World English Bible].

According to Mark 14:23-24 and Matthew 26:27-28 the wine represented the blood of Jesus "which was shed for many." But Luke has it "for you" [Luke 22:20]. A little later Jesus told his disciples that the Son of Man will be indeed killed "as it was written" [Mark 14:21 and Matthew 26:24]. But Luke changes this to "determined" [Luke 22:22]. When Jesus was arrested, he told the chief priests and the mob that they are arresting him in order to "fulfil the scripture" [Mark 14:49 and Matthew 26:56]. But Luke disagrees and points out that the arrest took place because it was "their hour and power of darkness" [Luke 22:53]. Mark reports that Jesus died with a loud cry and that his last words were Eloi, Eloi, lama sabachtani [Mark 15:34]. Matthew agrees with Mark. He says the same thing [Matthew 27:46]. But Luke deviates from Mark in order to make his text read differently from that of Matthew. He reports that the last words spoken were "Father, into your hands I commit my spirit!" [Luke 23:46]. After Jesus died, the centurion was amazed at the events he saw. Mark and Matthew have him say the following words:

"Truly this man was the Son of God!" [Mark 15:39 World English Bible].

"Truly this was the Son of God" [Matthew 27:54 World English Bible].

But Luke disagrees. He makes the centurion say the following words:

"Certainly, this was a righteous man" [Luke 23:47 World English Bible].

Mark and Matthew agree that Jesus was crucified and died on Golgotha [Mark 15:22; Matthew 27:33]. But Luke deviates from Mark and does not use the name Golgotha but rather Calvary [Luke 23:33]. Mark and Matthew agree that there was only one angel at the tomb of Jesus:

"Entering into the tomb, they saw a young man sitting on the right side, dressed in a white robe, and they were amazed. He said to them, Don't be amazed. You seek Jesus, the Nazarene, who has been crucified. He has risen. He is not here. Behold, the place where they laid him! But go, tell his disciples and Peter, He goes before you into Galilee. There you will see him, as he said to you" [Mark 16:5-7 World English Bible].

"Behold, there was a great earthquake, for an angel of the Lord descended from the sky, and came and rolled away the stone from the door, and sat on it. His appearance was like lightning, and his clothing white as snow. For fear of him, the guards shook, and became like dead men. The angel answered the women, Don't be afraid, for I know that you seek Jesus, who has been crucified. He is not here, for he has risen, just like he said. Come, see the place where the Lord was lying. Go quickly and tell his disciples, He has risen from the dead, and behold, he goes before you into Galilee; there you will see him. Behold, I have told you" [Matthew 28:2-7 World English Bible].

Mark and Matthew agree that there was only one angel who was sitting – dressed in white. He spoke with the women and told them to go and tell the disciples that Jesus is alive and that he was on his way to Galilee. That is where the disciples were told to go in order to see him. But Luke deviates from Mark in order to disagree with Matthew. He says that there were two angels and that they did not instruct the disciples to go to Galilee since, according to him, the appearance actually occurred in Judaea – Jerusalem – and not Galilee. Please note how Luke changes Mark's account and the words spoken to the women:

"They found the stone rolled away from the tomb. They entered in, and didn't find the Lord Jesus' body. It happened, while they were greatly perplexed about this, behold, two men stood by them in dazzling clothing. Becoming terrified, they bowed their faces down to the earth. They said to them, Why do you seek the living among the dead? He isn't here, but is risen. Remember what he told you when he was still in Galilee, saying that the Son of Man must be delivered up into the hands of sinful men, and be crucified, and the third day rise again? They remembered his words" [Luke 24:2-8 World English Bible].

Mark's account was changed so that Luke's version would not agree with Matthew. He has two angels, in shining rather than white garment, poses a question to the women rather than a statement. And most significantly, Luke completely changes the context of the words concerning Galilee. He does so in order to be able to also disagree with Matthew as to where the actual first appearance of Jesus to his disciples took place. In Luke 24:9 Luke says that the women went and reported the matter to the eleven apostles and the rest but they did not believe their story. Verses 13-32 state how Jesus met two of the disciples [not of the Twelve] on the way to a village called Emmaus. One of them was named Clopas. He was invited to their place late that afternoon. When he broke bread before meal the two disciples realized that it was Jesus. As soon as they realized this, they immediately returned to Jerusalem which was about 10 kilometres from Emmaus. Please note:

"They rose up that very hour, and returned to Jerusalem, and found the eleven gathered together, and those who were with them, saying, The Lord is risen indeed, and has appeared to Simon! They related the things that happened along the way, and how he was recognized by them in the breaking of the bread. As they said these things, Jesus himself stood in the midst of them, and said to them, Peace be to you. But they were terrified and filled with fear, and supposed that they saw a spirit. He said to them, Why are you troubled? Why do doubts arise in your hearts? See my hands and my feet, that it is truly me. Touch me and see, for a spirit doesn't have flesh and bones, as you see that I have. When he had said this, he shown them his hands and his feet. While they still didn't believe for joy, and wondered, he said to them, Do you have anything here to eat? They gave him a piece of a broiled fish and some honeycomb. He took it, and ate in front of them" [Luke 24:33-43 World English Bible].

There is no doubt at all that this text most plainly reveals that Jesus ate fish and honey on that evening in the presence of his eleven Apostles and some others. Luke clearly portrays Jesus in Jerusalem that very night and that is where his first appearance to the disciples takes place. In his claim he deviates from Mark in order to disagree with Matthew – as we shall now see. On the night of his arrest Jesus is quoted by Mark as saying:

"However, after I am raised up, I will go before you into Galilee" [Mark 14:28 World English Bible].

The angel said to the women at the tomb on Sunday morning:

"But go, tell his disciples and Peter, He goes before you into Galilee. There you will see him, as he said to you" [Mark 16:7 World English Bible].

According to the testimony of Mark, Jesus clearly told his disciples that after he is risen from the dead he would go to Galilee and that is where the disciples were going to see him. Matthew 26:32 also quotes Jesus as telling his disciples that after he is risen from the dead, he would go ahead of them to Galilee:

"But after I am raised up, I will go before you into Galilee" [World English Bible].

Matthew quotes the angel as saying to the women:

"Go quickly and tell his disciples, He has risen from the dead, and behold, he goes before you into Galilee; there you will see him. Behold, I have told you" [Matthew 28:7 World English Bible].

Jesus himself appeared to the women and said:

"Don't be afraid. Go tell my brothers that they may go into Galilee, and there they will see me" [Matthew 28:10 World English Bible].

Then in Matthew 28:16 we read the following:

"But the eleven disciples went into Galilee, to the mountain where Jesus had sent them. When they saw him, they bowed down to him, but some doubted" [World English Bible].

According to Matthew the eleven Apostles went to Galilee to a mountain Jesus specified. There, in Galilee, the disciples saw Jesus for the first time after his resurrection. The account of Luke therefore cannot be reconciled with the text of Mark and especially that of Matthew. Again, we have two against one. Digressing here just for a moment, I would like to point out that in Luke 24:41-43 it is explicitly stated that Jesus actually ate meat. But now you know that this text is simply not true if you believe Mark and Matthew.

Jesus was not in Jerusalem that evening but was on his way to Galilee. Jesus' first appearance did not take place in Jerusalem but rather in Galilee – as Mark and Matthew clearly point out. Therefore, the text of Luke so often cited as proof that Jesus was a meat eater and therefore not a vegetarian – as many sources prove – is a forgery. By now it has been demonstrated that the Synoptic principle dictates that Luke and Matthew would not agree. Not only is this true of the material all three evangelists have in common but even of the material that Matthew and Luke only have in common. This fact will now be demonstrated.

**Matthean And Lukan Discrepancies**

Matthew maintains that Joseph and Mary lived in Judaea when Mary fell pregnant and that Mary gave birth in Bethlehem. From Judaea they escaped to Egypt. After Herod died, they returned to the "land of Israel" – meaning Judea. After they learnt that Herod's son reigned over Judaea in his father's place, they were afraid and decided to go to Galilee instead. Matthew has them settle in Nazareth only after they returned from Egypt:

"But when Herod was dead, behold, an angel of the Lord appeared in a dream to Joseph in Egypt, saying, Arise and take the young child and his mother, and go into the land of Israel, for those who sought the young child's life are dead. He arose and took the young child and his mother, and came into the land of Israel. But when he heard that Archelaus was reigning over Judea in the place of his father, Herod, he was afraid to go there. Being warned in a dream, he withdrew into the region of Galilee, and came and lived in a city called Nazareth; that it might be fulfilled which was spoken through the prophets: He will be called a Nazarene" [Matthew 2:19-23 World English Bible].

Matthew has Joseph and Mary living in Bethlehem of Judaea. That is why he says nothing about taxing and their journey to Bethlehem. They did not have to journey to Bethlehem since they lived there. They wanted to return to Bethlehem from Egypt but were afraid and so they settled in Nazareth instead. But Luke has both Joseph and Mary living in Nazareth of Galilee while they were still unmarried and before Mary even fell pregnant.

In fact, Luke says that Gabriel was sent to the city of Nazareth in order to tell Mary that she was going to become pregnant with the Messiah. Luke 1:26 says that Gabriel went to see Mary in Nazareth. Luke 2:4-5 says that Joseph and Mary went from Nazareth to Bethlehem. Matthew says that Joseph, Mary and Jesus escaped to Egypt, while Luke says that they went to Jerusalem's temple in order to perform the rites of purification. Luke knows nothing about Herod's wish to kill Jesus and the children of Bethlehem.

For Luke there was no need to run to Egypt but rather it was perfectly safe to travel to Jerusalem and even to the very temple. After Joseph and Mary finished their rites in the temple they returned to Nazareth – their own town [Luke 2:39]. Matthew has the Magi come from Persia and visit the child. Luke knows nothing of this. He has the shepherds visiting Bethlehem and the angelic hosts singing. Matthew has God saying at Jesus' baptism the following words:

"This is my beloved Son, in whom I am well pleased" [Matthew 3:17 World English Bible].

Luke changes this to read:

"You are my beloved Son. In you I am well pleased" [Luke 3:22 World English Bible].

After his baptism, Jesus went to the desert where he was tempted by the devil. Matthew says that the order of temptation was in the following manner:

1. TO TURN STONES INTO BREAD [Matthew 4:3].
2. TO JUMP FROM THE PINACLE OF THE TEMPLE [Matthew 4:5].
3. TO BOW DOWN AND WORSHIP SATAN [Matthew 4:9].

Now Luke of course can't agree with Matthew. So, what does he do? He reverses the order of temptation:

1. TO TURN STONES INTO BREAD [Luke 4:3].
2. TO BOW DOWN AND WORSHIP SATAN [Luke 4:7].
3. TO JUMP FROM THE PINACLE OF THE TEMPLE [Luke 4:9].

One of Jesus' disciples was originally a tax collector. In Matthew's Gospel he is called Matthew:

"As Jesus passed by from there, he saw a man called Matthew, sitting at the tax collection office. He said to him, Follow me. He got up and followed him" [Matthew 9:9 World English Bible].

Luke can't agree with Matthew so he names this disciple Levi:

"After these things he went out, and saw a tax collector, named Levi, sitting at the tax office, and said to him, Follow me. He left everything, and rose up and followed him" [Luke 5:27-28 World English Bible].

Matthew has Jesus saying to the Pharisees that he casts out demons "by the Spirit of God:"

"But if I by the Spirit of God cast out demons, then the kingdom of God has come on you" [Matthew 12:28 World English Bible].

Luke must deviate from Matthew so he uses the phrase "finger of God:"

"But if I by the finger of God cast out demons, then the kingdom of God has come to you" [Luke 11:20 World English Bible].

Now let us compare the "beatitudes" and the rest of this important speech of Jesus. Matthew says that Jesus ascended the mountain and then delivered his speech in a sitting position [Matt. 5:1]. Luke says that Jesus descended from the mountain to a plain and delivered his speech in a standing position [Luke 6:12,17].

In Matthew, Jesus uses the pronouns "they, theirs," [verses 3-10] while in Luke "you, yours" [verses 20-21]. In Luke, Jesus also pronounces "woes" while Matthew knows nothing of these. In Matthew, Jesus uses the term "Kingdom of Heaven" while in Luke "Kingdom of God." In Luke 6:20 the poor are blessed while in Matthew 5:3 the poor in spirit. In Matthew 5:4 "mourners shall be comforted" while in Luke 6:21 "mourners shall laugh."

In Matthew, Jesus says "revile you, persecute you" [verse 11] while in Luke "hate you, ex-communicate you" [verse 22]. All this was to be done "for my sake" [Matthew 5:11] but "for the Son of Man's sake" in Luke 6:22. In Matthew 5:15 people do not put a candle "under a bushel" while in Luke 8:16 "under a bed."

When hated and persecuted the disciples should "rejoice and be exceedingly glad" [Matthew 5:12] but according to Luke 6:23 Jesus said "Rejoice ye in that day, and leap for joy." When Jesus spoke of doing good, he said to do good even to "publicans" [Matthew 5:46] but according to Luke 6:33 "sinners." In Matthew 5:48 the audience was to strive to be "perfect as the Father is perfect" while in Luke 6:36 they were to strive to be "merciful as the Father is merciful."

In Matthew 5:45 the righteous are "Children of the Father" while in Luke 6:35 "Children of the Highest." In Matthew 5:45 God is kind to "just and unjust" while in Luke 6:35 to "unfaithful and evil." In Matthew 7:16 Jesus said that people do not collect "grapes from thorns" and "figs from thistles" while in Luke 6:44 he says "grapes from bramble bush" and "figs from thorns." In Matthew 7:26 the foolish man builds his house "upon the sand" while in Luke 6:49 "upon the earth."

During this speech Jesus also taught his disciples and the general public how to pray. He taught them the prayer commonly called "The Lord's Prayer" [Matthew 6:9-13]. But according to Luke, Jesus did not teach his disciples this prayer then but rather later – when the disciples asked him to do so – since John the Baptist also taught his disciples how to pray [Luke 11:1-4]. Matthew and Mark do not only disagree on their chronology but they also disagree on the content of the prayer. But then so they should. The Synoptic principle dictates that they should disagree just about on any subject. Here is the comparison of the "Lord's Prayer" according to the two versions – that of Matthew and Luke: Matthew 6:9-13

"Our Father, who is in heaven, may your name be kept holy. May your kingdom come. May your will be done, as in heaven, so on earth. Give us this day our daily bread. Forgive us our debts, as we also forgive our debtors. Bring us not into temptation, but deliver us from evil. For yours is the kingdom, the power and the glory forever. Amen" [World English Bible].

Luke 11:2-4

"Our Father in heaven, May your name be kept holy. May your kingdom come. May your desire be done on Earth, as it is in heaven. Give us day by day our daily bread. Forgive us our sins, For we ourselves also forgive everyone who is indebted to us. Bring us not into temptation, But deliver us from the evil one" [World English Bible].

A close comparison reveals that either Matthew or Luke deliberately rearranged and changed the content of the prayer so that they would not agree. Now let us continue and see that there are further deliberate alterations by either Matthew or Luke so that their Gospels would simply not agree. In Matthew 8:5-10 a centurion's servant was "sick of the palsy, grievously tormented" while in Luke 7:1-9 he was "sick and ready to die." In Matthew the centurion personally goes to Jesus for his help while in Luke he sends "elders of the Jews." In Matthew 12:39-40 Jesus says this concerning the sign of Jonah:

"An evil and adulterous generation seeks after a sign, and there will no sign be given it but the sign of Jonah, the prophet. For as Jonah was three days and three nights in the belly of the whale, so will the Son of Man be three days and three nights in the heart of the earth" [World English Bible].

But in Luke 11:29-30 Jesus has this to say instead:

"This is an evil generation. It seeks after a sign. No sign will be given to it but the sign of Jonah, the prophet. For even as Jonah became a sign to the

Ninevites, so will also the Son of Man be to this generation" [World English Bible].

According to Matthew 23:23 the scribes and Pharisees pay tithe "of mint and anise and cummin" while according to Luke 11:42 "mint and rue and all manner of herbs." In Matthew 23:27 the scribes and Pharisees are like "whited sepulchres, which indeed appear beautiful outward, but are within full of dead man's bones, and of all uncleanness." But according to Luke 11:44 they are as "graves which appear not, and the men that walk over them are not aware of them." In Matthew 23:4 the scribes and Pharisees "bind heavy burdens" which they would not lift with even one finger."

In Luke 11:46 it is not the scribes and Pharisees who do this but actually lawyers. In Matthew 23:29 the scribes and Pharisees "build the tombs of the prophets, and garnish the sepulchres of the righteous" while in Luke 11:47 the lawyers actually do that. In Matthew 23:13 it is the scribes and Pharisees who neither entered the kingdom themselves nor allowed other to do so. But in Luke 11:52 it is not the scribes and Pharisees who did so but rather lawyers. In Luke 12:24 "ravens" are fed by "God" while in Matthew 6:26 "fowls" by "Heavenly Father."

According to Luke 18:35-43 a blind man met Jesus in Jericho as he was on his way to Jerusalem. Jesus gave him sight. But according to Matthew 20:29-34 there was not one man but two. I can go on and on – citing other examples. But this is not necessary. The quotations provided indisputably prove that the Gospels of Matthew and Luke were written in such a way so that they would simply not agree. It is not surprising then that Jesus told his disciples to be wise bankers so that as bankers identify the forged money, so they could identify the forgeries in the Bible.

### *Forgeries in the New Testament*

The Christian New Testament is comprised of 27 books. They have been translated from koine Greek. This New Testament is sanctioned by Roman Catholics, Eastern Orthodox Church and all Protestants. It is however, rejected by Eastern Christians of the Near East and India, the Church of the East, the Roman Catholic Church in the East, the Monophysites, and Indian

Christians. The Assyrian Church, or as it is known, the ancient Apostolic and Catholic Church of the East, was one of the major Christian churches in the world. Not until the 14$^{th}$ century was the church rivalled by any other church. It was the most powerful branch of Christendom in the Near East, Palestine, Arabia, Lebanon, Iran, India and elsewhere. The churches of the East rejected the Greek New Testament which is comprised of 27 books. The Eastern Church recognizes only the Peshitta – Aramaic text of the New Testament. The Peshitta New Testament is comprised of only 22 books. Excluded are 2 Peter, 2 and 3 John, Jude and Revelation.

Even in the Western churches these books were rejected for several centuries until they were finally incorporated in the canon. Peshitta manuscripts are very ancient indeed. Some scholars insist that the Greek New Testament was actually translated from Aramaic Peshitta. Most scholars however, believe that at least Luke, Acts and the epistles of Paul were originally written in Greek. There are only a handful of Peshitta manuscripts available today. On the other hand, there are thousands of Greek manuscripts. But these manuscripts differ significantly one from another. There is virtually no sentence in the New Testament that does not have at least several variant readings.

The *Lion Encyclopedia of the Bible* on p. 66, subtitle: How the New Testament came Down to Us tells us that the New Testament scholars are faced with thousands of different and conflicting manuscripts in Greek and some other ancient languages. The encyclopedia states that scholars must decide which of these manuscripts most accurately preserve the original. When you are fully aware of these facts it is quite natural and logical to ask the question: just which one of all these manuscripts actually comprise the so-called infallible Word of God? *Collier's Encyclopedia* Vol. 17 on p. 466 tells us that original manuscripts have disappeared. It tells us that today we have over 5,000 Greek manuscripts which were copies of earlier ones, as well as 10,000 of ancient versions and about 80,000 New Testament quotations by the Church Fathers. Practically nobody knows how many variant and different readings there are. More than 30,000 variant readings were discovered in one examination of 150 manuscripts of the Gospel of Luke. It concludes by saying that there is probably not one sentence in the New Testament which does not have several variants.

For the sake of those who are not very well informed on the subject, certain things need to be clarified. The first thing we must realize is the fact that we do not possess the original manuscripts called autographa – whether they were written in Greek or Hebrew. The next thing we need to realize is the fact that the Greek manuscripts in the hands of Bible scholars are uncial [written in capital letters] and miniscule [written in small letters]. We also need to be aware of the fact that the Greek manuscripts were written with no marks, punctuation, or separation of words. The modern scholars have edited and compiled these texts and have also separated the words according to their understanding and whim. They have also inserted punctuation – often in a manner to uphold certain traditional doctrines of the Christian Church.

The oldest Greek form does not have a space between words or punctuation of any type. This is a crucial fact to realize, because certain words have not been correctly separated by certain scholars. This is one of the reasons why we have so many different Bible versions. The most important thing to realize is the fact that not even one of the bibles available has been actually translated directly from one single Greek manuscript. All English bibles have been translated from one of the Greek texts compiled by an editor. The editor would examine different Greek manuscripts and then choose and decide what material to take from what manuscript. The editor must decide for himself which texts are closest to the original writings.

The first compiled Greek-Latin text was printed between 1514 and 1517 c.e. This text was known as Complutension Diaglot. Then in 1516 c.e. Dutch scholar Desidorius Erasmus published his first edition of the compiled Greek text. This text was prepared in haste and contained many errors. This initial text was somewhat corrected through the following four editions between 1519 and 1535 c.e. The third edition of Stephanus' Greek text [issued in 1550] became in principal, the Received Text [Textus Receptus], upon which the King James translators were based in 1611. After Erasmus, a great number of scholars have applied themselves to the task of constructing a reliable Greek text of the mass of variant readings. This fact is plainly admitted by virtually all Bible scholars and can be read in almost all Bible prefaces.

In the introduction of the Interlinear Greek-English New Testament by Alfred Marshall on p. 5, we are told that not even one scholar has taken one particular manuscript from which to make his translation. We are told that they rather adopted the principle of "pick and choose" and also the principal of "textual criticism" and even of "higher criticism." From the mass of variant readings, they have compiled their own Greek texts from which others have made translations into other languages. Wescott and Hort have probably come closest to one single manuscript – that of Codex Vaticanus. In the introduction of the New English Bible on p. 7, we are told that the translators had no choice but consider the variant readings and weigh the evidence for themselves and choose the reading which to the best of their ability to discern represented the original meaning.

Do you realize the tremendous significance of this admission? The translators of the New English Bible admit that they sifted through the mass of contradicting Greek texts and manuscripts – selecting each passage from whatever source they thought most accurately preserved the original. Different translators choose different texts and therefore their translations will naturally differ. Which of them all is actually fully inspired? In the preface of the New International Version on p. 7, we are told that the text used for the translation is an electric one. We are told that no other ancient literature had such an abundance of witnesses as the New Testament. When faced with conflicting texts and variant readings, the translators adopted the accepted principle known as textual criticism.

Just what is textual criticism? The word *criticism* denotes, primarily, a judgement, or an act of judging; its derivation from Greek verb "krino" meaning: to discern, or to try, or pass judgement upon, or to determine. The textual criticism is a method which the Bible scholars apply to determine which manuscripts or part thereof are fraud and which genuine. These textual critics sift through thousands of Greek manuscripts and countless variant readings, in order to compile the text which, they think is the best and most reliable.

Different scholars choose different material. Thus, even the Greek texts they themselves compile are at odds with each other. For example, the Greek text compiled by Stephanus on which the King James Bible is based differs in some 6000 places from the text compiled by two Anglican scholars Westcott and Hort. Most modern bibles are based in principal on the text of Wescott and Hort. When you become aware of all these facts then you realize how complex the issue really is. Then you realize that if you yourself were to make a translation from Greek manuscripts, the task would be enormous and difficult. You yourself would be faced with a dilemma as to which passages to accept and which to discard. Knowing all this, can you still claim that the New Testament as we have it is really infallible?

There are myriads of conflicting readings but in here we are primarily interested how the orthodox Christian scribes forged many original readings in order to bolster the anti adoptionist view of the Ebionites and to substantiate the orthodox view of Jesus' pre-existence and his divinity. We can begin with the fact how these lying scribes tried to hide the fact that Joseph was actually the biological father of Jesus. There were manuscripts which emphatically show that Joseph was Jesus' biological father. The Syriac or Aramaic manuscript discovered in St. Catherine's Monastery on Mount Sinai gives the following version of Matthew 1:16:

"Jacob begot Joseph; Joseph, to whom was betrothed the virgin Mary, begot Jesus, who is called the Christ."

Then in verse 25 we are told the following:

"and he [Joseph] had no relations with her [Mary] until she bore to him a son."

Compare this with the King James Bible, based on the Textus Receptus:

"And knew her not till she had brought forth her firstborn son."

Various manuscripts show how the Orthodox scribes have corrupted the original renderings whenever we are told that Joseph was the father of Jesus or where the phrase "the parents" of Jesus occur in the earlier manuscripts. In Luke 2:33, some manuscripts read:

"father and mother began to marvel."

But majority of the manuscripts read:

"Joseph and his mother."

In Luke 2:48 one important but fragmentary Greek manuscript $C^{vid}$ and two Old Latin manuscripts β and e read:

"Your relatives and I have been grieved."

Other manuscripts [a b ff² g¹ I r¹ and syr^c read:

"We have been grieved."

The earlier reading was:

"Your father and I have been grieved."

This is the reading even in the Textus Receptus and the King James Bible. Why such variations if not because someone wanted to remove the idea of the Ebionite adoptionist teaching concerning Jesus? When Jesus stayed behind in the temple, his parents did not know it. They assumed that he went to Galilee with their relatives and friends. The original reading was:

"his parents knew it not"

but this was changed in other manuscripts to

"Joseph and his mother knew it not."

The Textus Receptus and the King James Bible are based on this version of Luke.

In the speech of Peter [Acts 2] he stated that Jesus was to come "from the loins of David – clearly implying that through Joseph [the royal line] he would be David's biological descendant. But this was changed to "from the heart of David" in Codex Bezae it[d]. In John 1:13 we read:

"But as many as received him, to them he gave the right to become God's children, to those who believe in his name: who were born not of blood, nor of the will of the flesh, nor of the will of man, but of God" [World English Bible].

Please note the plural "who were born," implying that all those who are born of God are God's children. But this was later changed in Old Latin manuscript to singular "who was born." This change had to take place before the end of the second century for the Church Father Irenaeus was aware of this and argued that the text referred to Jesus. Tertulian later also argued in favour of the singular rendering in order to counter the Ebionite adoptionist view. In John 1:14 the earlier reading was:

"the word became flesh," but this was later changed to "God became flesh." In John 1:18 the earlier reading was "the only begotten son," but this was later changed to read variously as "the unique God," "the only begotten God" and "God the only son."

In John 19:40 we are told that Nicodemus and Joseph wrapped the "body of Jesus." This was later changed to the "body of God" [Codex Alexandrinus]. In Luke 2:26 we are told that the Holy Spirit told Simeon that he will not die until he sees the "Lord's Christ." Old Latin MS ff[2] changes this to "Christ, namely God." In Luke 9:20 Peter acknowledged Jesus as "Christ of God," but this was later changed to "Christ, God" in the Coptic manuscripts. In Mark 3:11 the demon referred to Jesus as "Son of God," but this was later changed to "God, the Son of God" [MS 69].

In Luke 7 we are told how a Roman centurion went to Jesus in order to ask him to heal his sick servant. In verse 9 we read: "when Jesus heard." This was changed to "When God heard" [miniscule MS 124]. In Luke 8:28 the demon referred to Jesus as "Jesus, Son of God Most High." This was changed to "Jesus, the Highest God" [MS 2766].

In Luke 20:42 Jesus quotes the words of David: "The LORD said to my Lord." This was changed to "God said to my God" [Persian Diatesseron]. In Jude verse 5 we are told that "the Lord" saved the people from Egypt. This was changed to "Jesus" in MSS A B 3381 1241 1739 and 1881. In the following MSS C² 623 and VG$^{ms}$ the reading is "God." In one manuscript P$^{72}$ the reading is "the God Christ."

In Galatians 2:20 the earliest reading is:

"...I live by the faith of the Son of God, who loved me, and gave himself for me" [King James Bible].

This was changed in MSS P$^{46}$ B D F and G to read:

"by the faith of God even Christ."

Miniscule MSS 330 reads:

"by the faith of God."

MS 1985 reads:

"by the faith of God the Son."

In Titus the original reading "through Jesus Christ our Savior" was changed to "through Jesus Christ our God." In Hebrews 13:20 "our Lord Jesus" was changed to "our God Jesus" [MS d]. In Ephesians 3:9 the words "by Jesus Christ" are added later in some manuscripts. Majority of English bibles omit these words as do also Greek manuscripts coded A B C D F G, Syriac, Arabic of Erpen, Coptic, Ethiopic, Vulgate, and Itala. These words were added so that the reader would think that Jesus was present with God when the creation took place and that everything was made by Jesus.

The most significant and evil text added to the New Testament is found in 1 John 5:7 – a text bolstering the Trinity dogma. This verse was not in any of the Greek manuscripts prior to the fifteenth century. The Benjamin Wilson in his *Emphatic Diaglott*, p. 803, omitted this text and explains why:

"The received text reads, For there are three that bear witness in heaven, the Father, the Word, and the Holy Ghost, and these three are one. And there are three that bear witness in earth. This text concerning the heavenly witnesses is not contained in any Greek manuscript which was written earlier than the 15th century. It is not cited by any of the Greek ecclesiastical writers; nor by any of the early Latin fathers, even when the subjects upon which they treat would naturally have led them to appeal to its authority. It is therefore evidently spurious."

Adam Clarke, himself a trinitarian states in his Clarke's Commentary, Vol. 6, p. 923, in regards to 1 John 5:7 that no ancient manuscript contains this passage. He states that prior to the 15th century it is missing from the Syriac, Arabic, Ethiopic, the Coptic, Sahidic, Armenian and Slavonic. He points out that only the later Vulgate Latin manuscript contains it but that the earlier and more ancient Vulgate manuscripts have it not. Do you realize what this means? People who lived prior to the fifteenth century simply knew nothing about 1 John 5:7. They never referred to it because they could not refer to something that was not in existence. St. Gregory urged the Roman hierarchy to delete this text since "God does not need our lies" – he said. However, his church most certainly does and consequently on January 13, 1897 Pope Leo XIII forbade anyone to question the authenticity of this text.

Despite the fact that this text is a wicked forgery, many Christians still use it in order to prove their erroneous teaching on Trinity. Moreover, they sternly condemn those who reject this text as scribal interpolation. Even some Bible scholars retain this verse in their translations even though they frankly admit it to be a forgery. J.P. Green retains this verse in his Interlinear Bible, yet in the preface he plainly states that he does not regard this text as true Scripture.

There is another trinitarian text added in the New Testament. On the basis of this text many Christians baptize their converts in the name of the Father, Son and the Holy Spirit. The text in question is found in Matthew 28:19. Reinach says that this text and that of 1 John 5:7 are not authentic. The *Encyclopedia Britannica*, 1911 edition, under Baptismal Formula, p. 365 states that the Trinitarian formula and trine immersion was not used from the beginning. The *International Standard Bible Encyclopedia*, Vol. 4, p. 2637, under Baptism points out that the Matthean formula in 28:19 was canonized later and that this trinitarian formula was foreign to the mouth of Jesus.

Schaff-Herzog *Encyclopedia of Religious Knowledge*, on p. 435, states that Jesus did not give this Trinitarian formula for baptism. The *Catholic Encyclopedia*, Vol. II, on page 263, says:

"The baptismal formula *was changed* from the name of Jesus Christ to the words Father, Son, and Holy Spirit by the Catholic Church in the second century."

And, finally, the verses 18-20 in the Hebrew Gospel of Matthew omit the Trinity formula. The formula is missing even in the quote of the fourth century Church historian Eusebius. How are the disciples made and admitted into the fold of Jesus? By baptism, of course. And in whose name did Jesus say to make the disciples? In his name, of course. Therefore, it is no wonder that apostles baptized in the name of Jesus only as is evident from the following passages:

Acts 2:38:

"Then Peter said unto them, Repent, and be baptized every one of you in the name of Jesus Christ for the remission of sins" [King James Bible].

Acts 8:16:

"...they were baptized in the name of the Lord Jesus" [King James Bible].

Acts 10:47-48:

"And he commanded them to be baptized in the name of the Lord [King James Bible].

It is necessary to point out that practically only the King James Bible states "in the name of the Lord" while basically every other English translation states "in the name of Jesus Christ."

Acts 19:5:

"When they heard this, they were baptized in the name of the Lord Jesus" [King James Bible].

Galatians 3:27:

"For as many of you as have been baptized into Christ have put on Christ" [King James Bible].

Water in baptism represents the grave and the plunging in the water, the death of old self. As Jesus died, so do we in baptism. As Jesus rose from the dead to a new life, so do we.

Please note Romans 6:3-4:

"Know ye not, that so many of us as were baptized into Jesus Christ were baptized into his death? Therefore, we are buried with him by baptism into death: that like as Christ was raised up from the dead by the glory of the Father, even so we also should walk in newness of life" [King James Bible].

Furthermore, whenever the apostles performed any miracle they did so in the name of Jesus and not the trine name – Father, Son and the Holy Spirit.

In Colossians 3:17 we read:

"And whatsoever ye do in word or deed, do all in the name of the Lord Jesus, giving thanks to God and the Father by him" [King James Bible].

If whatever we do, we should do in the name of Jesus, then this most surely applies to baptism as well. Those who baptize in the name of the Father, Son and the Holy Spirit must believe that the Father and the Holy Spirit also died and were raised from the dead. Paul said that those who were baptized into Jesus, were baptized into his death. The Father and the Holy Spirit did not die and therefore baptism which symbolizes death and resurrection cannot be performed in their names but rather only in the name of Jesus who died and was raised and with whom we die and shall be made alive. The baptism or submersion pictures burial while the ascension out of the water symbolizes the resurrection. Paul himself was aware of this fact. In Colossians 2:12 he wrote:

"Buried with him in baptism, wherein also you are risen with him through the faith of the operation of God, who hath raised him from the dead" [King James Bible].

Neither sprinkling nor pouring could possibly represent the burial and resurrection – therefore christening is the false mode of baptism. Only when one is plunged into the water, he or she is literally in a watery grave. A person submerged under water would not live unless brought up out of the watery grave – unless risen from the water. Therefore, when one is immersed into water, he or she is symbolically buried. The Father and the Holy Spirit did not die and therefore we cannot be baptized in their names since we cannot die with them.

The baptism pictures the death, burial and the resurrection of Jesus and it also pictures the same of all of us who are baptized in his name. Through repentance we crucify our old selves and the old man of sin. After mortifying the old self of sin, we are then buried in the waters of baptism. When we reappear from the watery grave, we are newborn babies – dead to the world and its principles. The Holy Spirit is then given to take hold of the newborn children of God, to teach, guide, spiritually nourish and protect the children until they reach maturity and are ready to be united with the Infinite One through all eternity. The trine baptismal formula is therefore blasphemous since it symbolically represents the death and burial of the Father and the Holy Spirit. This formula has neither Jesus' nor the apostolic approval.

Paul stated in 1 Corinthians 10:2 that the Israelites were baptized in the sea and cloud. They were not baptized in the name of the Father and the Holy Spirit but rather "into Moses." In 1 Corinthians 12:2 Paul said that we are all baptized by one spirit into one body. But the one who baptizes with the spirit is Jesus. John the Baptist said that it was Jesus who will baptize with the Holy Spirit. With Jesus we have died and through him we shall live. In John 6:40 he said that it is he who will raise the believer from the dead on the last day. Jesus said that the dead will hear his voice and will come out of their graves. He said that even the judgement the Father has entrusted to him. He will judge the world on the last day and not the Father or the Holy Spirit [John 5:21-29].

Jesus said in Matthew 25:31-33 the following:

"But when the Son of Man comes in his glory, and all the holy angels with him, then will he sit on the throne of his glory. Before him all the nations will be gathered, and he will separate them one from another, as the shepherd separates the sheep from the goats. He will set the sheep on his right hand, but the goats on the left" [World English Bible].

Jesus alone was crucified and died. Jesus alone was baptized and not God the Father or the Holy Spirit. Jesus was resurrected. With Jesus we have died and with him we are raised and therefore baptism should be in his name, as Apostles have given us an example.

### Gospel of John and Jesus' Divinity

John's Gospel is most loved by Christians and it is regarded as the most beautiful and inspiring. This may be so but how reliable is this Gospel? How much historical truth does it really contain? The Gospel of John is strikingly different from the Synoptic Gospels. Only about eight percent of its content is actually paralleled in the Synoptics. In the Synoptics the disciples are referred to as Apostles. This word never appears in John's Gospel. The Synoptics [especially Matthew and Luke] contain many parables which Jesus actually taught the public. In fact, it is expressly said that Jesus never spoke to the public in any other way but the parables. There is not even one single parable in John. On the contrary, Jesus engages in many long doctrinal and theological discourses with the Jews.

In the Synoptics, Jesus never claimed to be the "Son of God" or "Messiah." In fact, when someone tried to identify him as the "Messiah" or the "Son of God," Jesus sternly forbade them to ever mention that again or to say so to anyone. According to John's version, Jesus does not only tolerate such statements but actually personally states and makes it public on many occasions that he is the "Messiah" and the "Son of God." He does not only say so but actually expects others to identify him as such, as was the case with the man born blind [John 9].

In this Gospel he tells the Jews that he is one with God. He tells them that he came down from heaven. He tells them that Abraham saw his day and was glad. All these statements clearly imply his pre-existence. In the introduction of the Gospel we are told that Jesus as the Word was with God in the beginning and that everything was created through him. This Gospel places Jesus in Jerusalem and Judea virtually throughout his ministry. In fact, according to this Gospel Jesus spends most of his time in Jerusalem and among the Jews in Judea.

In the Synoptics, Jesus never visits Jerusalem. Throughout his ministry he restricts himself to Galilee and the region of Sidon. He never visits Jerusalem – even when the annual festivals were observed there. But John depicts Jesus observing at least two Passovers in Jerusalem, one Feast of Dedication, and the Feast of Tabernacles. On several occasions the Jews attempted to stone him but he miraculously escapes. The Synoptics are full of stories how Jesus cast out many demons. Not even a single word is said of this in John's Gospel. Many miracles are recorded in the Synoptics. John records only seven miracles. In the Synoptics, Jesus offers only the sign of Jonah as proof who he is. In John's Gospel he offers seven signs. Here they are in their chronological order:

TURNING WATER INTO WINE IN CANA OF GALILEE
HEALING THE SON OF A CERTAIN ROYAL PERSON IN CAPERNAUM

HEALING OF AN INVALID AT BETHESDA'S POOL
FEEDING THE FIVE THOUSAND
WALKING ON WATER
OPENING THE EYES OF THE MAN BORN BLIND
RAISING LAZARUS BACK TO LIFE

Miracles three, six, and seven, could not be historical events if the Synoptic Gospels are correct. For there we discover that Jesus never stepped on the soil of Jerusalem until he actually went there several days before he was killed. In fact, when he finally entered Jerusalem, the Jerusalemites did not know who he was. They had to be told that it was Jesus a prophet from Galilee [Matthew 21:10-11]. Even the temple guards could not identify Jesus although he supposedly spent most of his time in the temple. Judas allegedly identified him with a kiss.

If the Synoptics are correct, that is, if Jesus restricted his ministry to Galilee and the Gentile regions, then these Jerusalem and Bethany miracles are fictions. The Synoptics show that Jesus did not begin his public ministry until John was actually imprisoned [Mark 1:14]. But the Gospel of John has Jesus and John both working and preaching at the same time. John says that Jesus, through his disciples, baptized and made more converts than John did. The Gospel has Jesus baptizing in the Judean countryside while John in Aenon – near Salim [John 3:23]. Verse 24 explicitly states that all this took place "before John was put in prison," and therefore directly contradicts the account of the Synoptic Gospels – especially that of Mark 1:14.

John contradicts both Mark and Matthew as well as the account of Luke as to how the first disciples were chosen. Mark and Matthew show that Peter and Andrew were chosen first – at the Sea of Galilee. They were chosen together and at the same time. Shortly afterwards, James and John were chosen at the same sea. But John's Gospel maintains that Andrew was originally a disciple of John the Baptist and with him also another person, presumably John. John's Gospel says that it was not really Jesus who chose and selected Andrew but rather Andrew offered himself – after hearing John the Baptist's remark concerning Jesus. According to John, Andrew became the disciple of Jesus the day after John baptized Jesus.

The first thing Andrew did after being accepted as a disciple of Jesus, says John, he looked for Peter and when he had found him, he told him that he had found the Messiah. Then Andrew brought Peter to Jesus and he became a disciple of Jesus [John 1:35-42]. The day after, Jesus found Philip and he became his disciple. Philip found Nathanael who also became one of the twelve. All this took place in the next few days after his baptism.

But according to the Synoptic Gospels, immediately after his baptism Jesus went to the wilderness in order to be tested by Satan. Only after his 40-day trial did he return to Galilee in power and only then did he choose Peter and Andrew and then James and John. John's account therefore cannot be reconciled with the Synoptic story. In John 2 we are told how Jesus went to Jerusalem in the very beginning of his ministry and from the temple drove all those who were buying and selling.

He set free all the animals and birds which were intended for sacrificial ritual. This account directly contradicts the Synoptic record. According to the first three Gospels this event is placed at the very end of Jesus' ministry and this event triggered his sudden death. According to the Synoptic record, this event could not have taken place for two reasons. First, Jesus never went to Jerusalem during his entire ministry. And, secondly, because they say that he cleansed the temple only several days before he was actually killed.

The Synoptic Gospels report that on the night of his arrest, Jesus prayed to his Father to bypass death if at all possible. This prayer can nowhere be squeezed in the narrative of John. In John's Gospel Jesus could not pray to bypass the cup since he was divine and God in the flesh. The Synoptic Gospels say that Jesus was crucified at "the third hour" – that is, nine in the morning. But John's Gospel says that it was "the sixth hour" when Jesus was still before Pilate [John 19:14].

This account cannot be reconciled with that of the Synoptic Gospels. Oh, there are some enthusiastic Christians who try to reconcile the problem by insisting that John used Roman computation of time while the Synoptists the Jewish. By Judean computation the "third hour" would be nine in the morning – being the third hour from daybreak. John's sixth hour, they argue, would be six in the morning – being the sixth hour from midnight. But this argument cannot hold water. Elsewhere in the Gospel of John we find irrefutable evidence that John did not use the Roman computation of time but rather the Judean. In John 4:6 we are told that Jesus stopped at Jacob's well in order to have a drink – since he was tired from his journey. His disciples have gone to town to buy some food. The Samaritan woman met Jesus "about the sixth hour" – that is, about noon. Jesus could not have been before Pilate at six in the morning since Luke says that it wasn't until daybreak that the Jewish Council arranged the trial of Jesus.

Only after the Jewish trial ended Jesus was led to Pilate. John's Gospel clearly states that Jesus was before Pilate at noon and most modern versions so render the text. It therefore flatly contradicts the Synoptic accounts – especially that of Mark. The Synoptic Gospels show that Jesus refused to drink wine that he was offered by the Roman soldiers. But Luke goes further than this. He points out that Jesus made a vow on the night of his arrest that he would never again taste of the wine until he drinks it anew in the Kingdom [Luke 22:18]. But John clearly states that while hanging on the stake Jesus actually drank wine [John 19:28-29].

The Synoptic Gospels say that the women took spices with them to the tomb on Sunday morning in order to anoint the body of Jesus. They did so since they did not have time to do so on the day of the crucifixion – since it was too late. But John flatly contradicts the Synoptic testimony. John's Gospel plainly says that Nicodemus brought one hundred pounds of spices and that they have anointed the body of Jesus – according to the Jewish burial custom [John 19:39-40]. For this reason, in John's Gospel there are no women going to the tomb with spices in order to anoint his body since it was already done on the day of his burial. Everything else reported about the resurrection contradicts the Synoptic accounts. Luke's Gospel points out that all eleven disciples were present on Sunday night when Jesus allegedly appeared to them in Jerusalem.

The Markan added text also confirms this. But John maintains that Thomas was absent and that he later refused to believe that Jesus was alive. When finally, he saw him a week later he said "my Lord and my God." Whether he addressed Jesus with those titles or simply in the moment of shock referred to God as we do sometimes when we say: Oh my God! Oh my Lord! is neither here nor there, since this appearance was not historical if we accept the versions of Mark and Matthew. The Gospel of John also maintains that Jesus first appeared to Mary Magdalene and therefore gives her the pre-eminence above all other Apostles. For this reason, the same author in 2 John refers to the leader of the congregation as lady. The Markan version has Jesus first appearing to Peter. The Jewish Christian Gospel has Jesus appearing first to James, his brother. Now the Tridentine Council has stated that every word in the Bible was dictated by the Holy Spirit. Did the Holy Spirit dictate the Synoptic Gospels in such a way that generally two Gospels would agree against one and the Gospels of Matthew and Luke to disagree? Historically we can deduce that the current Gospel of Matthew is not the same Gospel that Matthew actually wrote. Church Father Jerome – who lived and wrote in the 4$^{th}$ century – was aware of the Hebrew version of the Gospel of Matthew.

This Gospel was used in the early centuries by the believers commonly called Jewish Christians or Pristine Christians. St. Jerome wrote that this Hebrew Matthew was preserved in the library of Caesarea even in his own time. Please note what Church Father Jerome actually said concerning this Gospel:

"Matthew, also called Levi, apostle and aforetimes publican, composed a gospel of Christ at first published in Judea in Hebrew for the sake of those of the circumcision who believed, but this was afterwards translated into Greek though by what author is uncertain. The Hebrew itself has been preserved until the present day in the library of Caesarea which Pamphilus so diligently gathered. I have also had the opportunity of having the volume described to me by the Nazarenes of Beroea, a city of Syria, who use it" [The Nicene and Post Nicene Fathers, Vol. 3, p. 362 WM. B. Eerdmans Publishing Company, Grand Rapids, Michigan].

Papias was the first to refer to the Hebrew Gospel of Mathew. Hegesepius also spoke of its existence. Church Father Epiphanius and Church historian Eusebius – both of the 4$^{th}$ century – also testified of the existence of the

Hebrew Matthew. This Hebrew Matthew has since disappeared. We now have only some fragments of it preserved in the quotations of the Church Fathers. But enough has been preserved to demonstrate that this Hebrew Matthew was strikingly different from the present Greek Matthew – incorporated in the Christian New Testament.

The earliest followers of Jesus who were known as Nazoreans and later by their derogatory name Ebionites, rejected the four canonical Gospels and they used the Gospel of Matthew which was strikingly different from the canonical Matthew. From what we have seen, it is no wonder that they could not accept all these conflicting versions. Finally, I want to state why the Gospel of John was written and also that it was not and could not have been written by Apostle John.

### Would Apostle John write against the Ebionites?

We know from the writings of the Church Fathers that allegedly the bishops of Asia compelled Apostle John to write a Gospel in which he would repudiate the doctrine of the Ebionites concerning Jesus' origin and his divinity. Church Father Jerome wrote:

"John, the apostle whom Jesus most loved, the son of Zebedee and brother of James the apostle, whom Herod, after the Lord's passion, beheaded, was the last one to write a Gospel, at the request of the bishops of Asia, against Cerinthus and other heretics and *especially against the growing doctrine of the Ebionites*, who asserted that Christ did not exist before Mary. For this reason, he was compelled also to announce his divine nativity" [Jerome, Vir. ill. 9].

Eusebius of the 4th century also quotes St. Clement of Alexandria and states that he also wrote of this fact [Ecclesiastical History, 6.14.7]. Church Father Epiphanius also confirmed that John wrote his Gospel in order to repudiate the Ebionite Christology [Panarion 51:2; 69:23].

At least this proves that the Ebionites were already in existence and flourished before the end of the first century and during the lives of the original Apostles of Jesus. I have argued in this book that the Ebionites were the true believers who were ostracised by both the rabbis of Judaism and by the Pauline Christianity. Why would Apostle John write against the Ebionites and the true doctrine that the Twelve taught? In order to accept this testimony concerning the Gospel of John and Apostle John, we would have to nullify and reject all the arguments I have presented this far concerning Jesus and his nature.

It is generally agreed that John's Gospel was not written before 95 A.D. Many scholars prefer even a later date. It is also generally held in the traditional Christian circles that Apostle John was also the author of the three epistles and the book of Revelation. But many scholars reject the idea that the Gospel of John, the epistles of John, and the Book of Revelation were written by the same author.

The Book of Revelation was written in a poorer Greek and the style and vocabulary differs. Even the name of Jerusalem is spelled differently in Revelation than in the Gospel of John. Many independent and critical scholars believe that the Gospel and the epistles were written by John the Elder. As a matter of fact, the author of the second and third epistles identifies himself as an Elder.

The Elders were not Apostles. This is clear from Acts 15:6 since Apostles and Elders got together at the council. James also stated that if a believer was sick he should call an Elder to anoint him and pray for his recovery. Elders were not Apostles. Therefore, on this basis alone John the Apostle could not have written second and third epistles of John.

# CHAPTER 6
# Radical Vegetarianism Of The Original World

Not many Christians would argue that angels in heaven run modern and sophisticated slaughterhouses where billions of animals are butchered so that God and all those in His realm could dine and feast on animal flesh. There is neither suffering nor death in God's realm. If angels do not eat animal flesh nor are fond of veal, steak, a lamb chop or a chicken schnitzel, what is then their daily food? The Bible says that the Israelites were fed manna which was actually the food of angels:

"Yet he commanded the skies above, And opened the doors of heaven. He rained down manna on them to eat, And gave them food from the sky. Man ate the bread of angels" [Psalm 78:23-25 World English Bible].

The text strongly implies that manna which God rained in the desert was the type of food consumed by the heavenly beings. In this text the manna is said to be bread made from grain. In the Jewish Pentateuch it is said that manna was used to make bread and that it resembled the coriander seed. Both coriander and grain are plants and therefore it follows that all the celestial beings in God's realm are radical vegetarians. Even those who would be accounted worthy of the eternal life and immortality are not promised dainty foods and barbecued meat but rather a "hidden manna" and the "fruit" of the Tree of Life. Isaiah 11 clearly shows that in God's kingdom which is to come, there will be no killing of animals for food. Rather, even the present carnivorous animals will become tame and the lion will eat grass like an ox. In that restored paradise the wolf and the lamb will dwell together and there will be neither harm nor destruction on all God's Holy Mountain – because then the whole world will be full of the knowledge of God. In other words, the present ignorance and deception will be lifted and humanity and animals will come to know God and the principles He stands for. Genesis 1:29-30 explicitly states that at creation God prescribed a radical vegetarianism to both humans and all animal species. At that long- forgotten beginning, no living soul was permitted to consume the flesh of another living soul. All living creatures were created to be herbivorous:

"God said, "Behold, I have given you every herb yielding seed, which is on the surface of all the earth, and every tree, which bears fruit yielding seed. It will be your food. To every animal of the earth, and to every bird of the sky, and to everything that creeps on the earth, in which there is life, I have given every green herb for food." And it was so" [World English Bible].

"And so it was" tells us that this was not only an ideal of God but rather a fact of life. Both humans and animals implemented this radical vegetarian diet. It thus follows that all the celestial beings are vegetarian and that the first humans and animals were created to be radical vegetarians. It is therefore fair to say that the idea and concept of vegetarianism did not originate with some heretical man but rather with God Himself. Many Christians however, assume that vegetarianism was only short lived and that Adam became a carnivorous being immediately after his alleged fall and partaking of the forbidden fruit. In fact, most Christians ascribe the first killing, rather murder, [since an innocent lamb was slaughtered] to God Himself, in order to make the garments for Adam and his wife. But was this really the case?

Did Adam really kill animals in order to eat their flesh? Did the righteous Abel really butcher an innocent lamb in order to present it as a burnt-offering to God? Could it be that the "lying pen of the scribes" did reverse the role of Abel and Cain? Genesis 3:17-19 irrefutably shows that Adam remained vegetarian all his life and that his sustenance came from the plants of the earth which he was to plant and cultivate with the sweat on his brow:

"Cursed is the ground for your sake. In toil you will eat of it all the days of your life. Thorns also and thistles will it bring forth to you; and you will eat the herb of the field. By the sweat of your face will you eat bread until you return to the ground" [World English Bible].

Even if you do believe in Adam's fall and the curse, you still must concede that Adam was to remain radical vegetarian *all his life* – since he was to cultivate his food *from the earth* and the *plants* were to be his food *until the day he died*. There was no promise of meat. Even all those who are obedient to God and who obey His true and perfect Law, are not promised animal flesh but rather fruits and vegetables – the produce of the land [Isaiah 1:18-19].

Many object and argue that Adam must have been permitted to kill animals since he allegedly taught his sons how to present burnt-offerings to God. Genesis 4 in the Jewish canonical form clearly shows that Abel must have killed a fattened lamb which he burnt on the altar as a pleasing and a sweet-smelling aroma to God. Cain in contrast presented an oblation – that is, a bloodless sacrifice. God spurned Cain and his sacrifice but loved and accepted the sacrificial lamb which Abel allegedly presented. But some other ancient literature which is not incorporated in the Jewish and Christian bibles has preserved an alternative version and the record which actually reverses the roles of Cain and Abel. In the *Essene Humane Gospel* these words are ascribed to the lips of Jesus:

"But ye believe that Moses commanded such creatures to be slain and offered as a sacrifice unto God and eaten. Ye believe wrongly; ye do not know of temple oblations; for at no time did the True God delight in or demand flesh and blood offerings, but only the *pure oblation the unbloody sacrifice*…For Abel offered up the *grains and the fruits of the earth*…But I tell ye: Satan, the evil one, maketh the truth a lie, and giveth to the sons of man, flesh and blood, the burnt offering, the unholy law of evil doers, things that my Holy Father hateth and abhoreth. Know ye not, before ye standeth one greater than even Moses! Yea, even the holy one, who Moses spake of is here and restoreth the truth of the law, that all may for a certainty know that God is true and every man whosoever keepeth not the Holy Law is a liar. For I tell ye, the Holy Law of Moses and Adam are one; even as my Prophets spake unto Israel, I speak. The Holy Law changeth not, but evil men speak according to their desires of the flesh and lust after things unlawful. For of that, which ye offer unto God in purity, ye may eat of freely, for it is lawful, but of that kind which ye offer not in purity, shall ye not eat. The hour cometh when all sacrifices and blood feasts shall cease, and ye shall again worship God according to holy law and a *pure oblation."*

Here we are told that Abel actually offered a *pure oblation* and in fact the *bloodless sacrifice – fruits and grains*. This ancient gospel [if genuine] therefore reverses the roles of Cain and Abel. But there is another ancient manuscript which likewise reverses the roles of Cain and Abel. The *World Bible Publishers* have put a book together which is compiled of ancient manuscripts which did not find their way into the canonical Bible. This book is entitled *The Lost Books of the Bible and the Forgotten Books of Eden*. Various translators were used to translate the manuscripts from their original tongues. The manuscript we are interested in is entitled A*dam and Eve*. For the translation of this manuscript we are indebted to two great Bible scholars: Dr. S.C. Malan, Vicar of Broadwindsor and Dr. E. Trumpp – Professor at the University of Munich. Ethiopic and Arabic originals were used for the current English translation.

In the 77$^{th}$ chapter we find a story of Cain's and Abel's offerings. At that time Cain was fifteen and his brother Abel twelve. Adam instructed both of his sons to take something "of their sowing" and to offer it to God. Abel did exactly what his father told him, but Cain offered a lamb instead. It is said that God accepted the offering of Abel but rejected the offering of Cain and condemned his "murderous thoughts." It is also pointed out that Abel actually did as was the custom of his father – implying that Adam himself *was always presenting a pure oblation and not a bloody sacrifice*. The Book of Jubilees – written in Hebrew – which was discovered among the Dead Sea Scrolls and which was held in great esteem at Qumran, corroborates the fact that Adam actually offered an *oblation* and therefore a *bloodless* sacrifice [Jubilees 3:27].

This is quite interesting since we also know for certain that the Jews who lived in Egypt, in an area known as the Elephantine, although they built a temple there – an exact replica of the Jerusalem one – did not kill the lamb during their Passover observance nor did they ever offer blood sacrifices.

They only authorized and sanctioned the practice of a "pure oblation." The *International Standard Bible Encyclopaedia*, Vol. 2, on p. 60, says that only oblations were prescribed as formerly and that an Aramaic text states that sheep, oxen and goats were not offered.

This ancient papyrus which is dated to the 5$^{th}$ century B.C.E., clearly shows that in Elephantine the Jews did not follow Hezekiah's and Josiah's reforms nor did they, like other Jews, sacrifice only in Jerusalem or present bloody sacrifices. The document clearly shows that these Jews appealed to the former practice of *pure oblation only*. It is also of great significance to point out that in the *Essene Humane Gospel*, [if genuine], Jesus clearly points out that Abel in fact offered a *pure oblation* while Cain offered the *bloody sacrifice* and that for this very reason his offering was not accepted:

"And did not Abel know the *pure oblation* and was put to death on account – for Satan entered into Cain and bloodshed was manifested in the earth, and man and beast crieth unto God and God heareth their cries. 'But I did not recognize Cain's *blood offering*' nor did God the evil of Satan but grieved over the evil of mankind that spread over the land even as waters cover the sea basin. For truly, I say to you, for this end have I come into the world that I may put away *all blood offering and eating of flesh*."

Christians generally believe and argue that the reason why Cain's sacrifice was rejected is because it was not a *blood sacrifice*. But Jesus, according to this Essene gospel argues that exactly opposite is true. Jesus says that Abel was killed because of his *pure sacrifice* and that bloodshed was manifested in the Earth against both animals and humans through Satan's influence on Cain. Jesus further pointed out that his explicit mission on this Earth was to put an end to both animal sacrifice and meat eating. Remarkably, Hebrews 11:4 strongly implies that the text of *Essene Humane Gospel* is and must be true and correct. Please note the text as it stands in the King James Bible:

"By faith Abel offered unto God a *more excellent sacrifice* than Cain, *by* which he obtained witness that he was righteous, God testifying of his gifts: and by *it* he being dead yet speaketh."

God rejected Cain's *gift* and approved of Abel's *gifts* [plural], because this kind of sacrifice was *righteous*. The Greek word *dikaios* implies "justice" and that what is "morally right" – as can be ascertained from virtually all Greek-English lexicons and dictionaries. Because Abel's gifts represented what is "just" and "ethical," God accepted it and declared Abel to be right and just. On the other hand, God rejected Cain's gift because it was representing bloodshed, death and ultimately what is morally wrong and unjust. Abel's gifts were indeed nobler and by far more excellent than Cain's gift which demanded bloodshed and great suffering to one of God's innocent creatures. That the story of Genesis 4 is reversed by the "lying pen of the scribes" is evident from the fact that Abel offered *gifts*.

The plural Greek word is used in Hebrews 11:4 and refers to *various fruits of the ground* which Abel offered. In contrast, Cain offered one kind of a gift – the fat portions of the firstborn. If Abel killed the animal and presented it as sacrifice – as the "lying pen of the scribes" insinuates, how then could the author of Hebrews argue that his sacrifice is morally and ethically better than his brother's bloodless sacrifice? Is it morally right and just to slash the throat of an animal? Is it just and humane to subject an animal to terror, pain and great suffering? How would you like if someone subjected you to pain and suffering? How would you feel if you were locked up awaiting the butcher's knife? In the *Clementine Homilies* – an early document which contains the preaching of Apostle Peter – points out that Adam and his son Abel could not have possibly sacrificed animals to God, since Peter plainly states that Adam, as the true Prophet, hated bloody sacrifices, bloodshed and wine libations [Homily III, Chps: 21 nad 26].

Since Peter says that Adam hated bloody sacrifices and libations, that is, wine offerings, it is obvious then that he, being a true Prophet, would not offer the same. It logically follows that Abel would not do so either since it is testified that he was righteous and in fact followed the example of his father Adam. In chapter two a further proof will be supplied which irrefutably proves that Abel did not and could not have offered a bloody sacrifice, since men in general at that time did not kill animals either for food or sacrifice. Christians and all those who crave and lust after animal flesh try to justify the killing of animals on the grounds that they do not possess a soul. They claim that only humans possess a soul. But is this claim true? The account of Genesis proves beyond refute that animals, just like humans, are actually *living souls*. They are composed of the same material humans are. They breathe the same oxygen that humans do. They also have *the same and identical spirit*. This is somewhat obscured in the King James Bible and some other versions but is crystal clear in the Hebrew Bible. The King James translators often differentiate between animals and humans by referring to animals as "living creatures" but to Adam as "living soul."

In Genesis 1:20-21 the King James Bible uses the term "living creature" in reference to all marine life. Then in verse 24 it uses the same term "living creature" to describe all animals on the dry ground and the birds of the air. But in Genesis 2:7 the King James translators used the term "living soul" in reference to Adam. The Hebrew Bible however uses the term "nephesh hayah" which always means "living soul" or "air breathing creature." The term is equally applied to animals as it is to Adam. In Genesis 1:20 it is explicitly said that *animals actually have a soul*:

"And God said, let the waters bring forth abundantly the moving creature that *hath life*" [King James Bible].

The moving creatures in the sea *had life*. In the Centre Reference of the King James Bible it is admitted that the word should have been translated *soul*. The text therefore plainly says that all animals in fact have a *soul*. In Genesis 2:7 we are told that God made man out of the ground. Genesis 1:24 tells us that animals were likewise made out of the ground. Thus, they were all made of the same substance.

All living creatures received the *breath of life* by which they maintained their existence. Likewise, all living creatures die once they run out of *breath of life*. In the Hebrew text the expression "chay ruwach" is used which means "living spirit." Man maintains his existence in exactly the same way that animals do. They also die in exactly the say manner. In Job 34:14-15 we read:

"If He [God] set His heart upon man: if He gather unto Himself *his spirit* [ruwach] and *his breath* [neshamah]: all flesh shall perish together" [King James Bible].

In Ecclesiastes 3:18-20 we read:

"I said in my heart concerning the estate of the sons of men, that God might manifest them, and that they might see that *they themselves are beasts*. For that which befalleth the sons of men befalleth beasts; even one thing befalleth them: as the one dieth, so dieth the other; yea, *they have all one breath*; so that a man hath no preeminence above a beast: for all is vanity. All go unto one place; all are of the dust, and all turn to dust again. Who knoweth the spirit of man that goeth upward, and the *spirit of the beast* that goeth downward to the earth?" [Ecclesiastes 3:18-21 King James Bible].

In this text we are told in the plainest language that animals and humans are of the same composition and both have the same breath. The word *breath* has been translated from the Hebrew word *ruwach* which means "spirit." Thus, the author tells us that beasts and the sons of men have *the same and identical spirit*. Even in the New Testament animals are likewise called *souls*. In Revelation 16:3 we read:

"And the second angel poured out his vial upon the sea; it became as the blood of a dead man: and every *living soul* died in the sea" [King James Bible].

The Bible plainly states that all marine creatures are in reality *living souls*. Thus, it becomes apparent that the Christian argument for killing animals cannot be justified on the grounds that animals are beasts that do not possess a soul. The next argument Christians, Jews and Muslims use in order to justify their butchering of animals is based on a claim that animals are *irrational beings* – unable to perceive right from wrong. But if this is the criteria we should use in order to distinguish between men and animals, then by the same reasoning we should regard all little children as animals – since they, too, cannot tell right from wrong.

Likewise, those who were born with a retarded mind should be regarded as animals since they are not rational beings. What about the human embryos? They are not rational beings yet Jews, Muslims and Christians alike strongly condemn abortion as murder while at the same time clear consciously condone the butchery of billions of animals. When God originally created animals He created them *rational* – with ability to speak, think and reason. In Genesis 3:1 we read:

"Now the serpent was more subtle than any beast of the field which the LORD God had made" [King James Bible].

The serpent was the most cunning. In verses 2-3 we are told that the serpent led a conversation with Eve. It was able to speak, think and reason. All other animals had the same ability, only the serpent was most cunning. Jesus advised his disciples to be *wise* like serpents. This implies that serpents are intelligent. In the book of Jubilees 3:28 we read that all animals originally spoke one language. In Job 12:7-10 we read:

"But ask now the beasts, and they shall teach thee; and the fowls of the air, and they shall tell thee: and the fishes of the sea shall declare unto thee. Who knoweth not in all these that the hand of the LORD hath wrought this? In whose hand *is* the soul of every living thing, and the breath of all mankind" [King James Bible].

Job states that all animals are aware of who was their creator. It is also plainly stated that all animals also have souls and that their souls are in God's care. In Revelation 5:13 we are plainly told that all creatures of the universe actually are capable of praising God with a rational mind.

Please note:

"Then I heard every animate creature that is in heaven and on the earth and beneath the earth and in the sea offer praise. Collectively, all of them were saying, praise, honour, glory, and might forever and ever to the One who sits on the throne and to the Lamb" [Author's translation].

The four living creatures [animals] around the throne of God also speak and are rational beings. One of them is a lion, one a bull and one an eagle [Revelation 4:7]. In Isaiah 43:20 we read:

"Even the wild animals will honour Me" [Author's translation].

When we realize all these significant facts – how, then, can we insist that it's all right to kill and eat all the living souls who are identical to us in almost every respect? Genesis 9:5 also alludes to the fact that animals will also be held responsible for their evil deeds:

"I will surely require your blood of your lives. At the hand of every animal I will require it. At the hand of man, even at the hand of every man's brother, I will require the life of man" [World English Bible].

In the *Secrets of Enoch* 58:7 we read that not only the souls of men are according to number but that even the animals will not perish. We are told that even their souls God created and that they will accuse man for ill treatment. All this then explains just why God was fond of and favoured Abel's gifts and rejected and despised Cain's sacrifice. God hated Cain's sacrifice because it necessitated pain and bloodshed. He accepted Abel's sacrifice because it was a *pure oblation* and did not cause any pain, suffering or death to God's innocent creatures. If Abel killed an animal for sacrifice – as the lying pen of the scribes insinuates – then God could not testify that his sacrifice was much more excellent than Cain's nor could He declare Abel morally and ethically right and just.

If Abel slashed the throat of an innocent lamb, and if God sanctioned and praised this deed, then this innocent lamb could rightly and justly accuse God of cruelty and murder and extreme injustice. Just think rationally and with an open mind. Is it right and ethically just to kill innocent animals in sacrifice? Is it right to shed their blood in order to atone for the sins of others? And if their blood does not and cannot really wash the sins away – as Christians themselves admit – would God resort to murder and violence just to prove some symbolic and metaphoric gesture? The true followers of Jesus and those who really love God and adhere to His precepts are instructed by Jesus thus to pray:

"Thy will be done on earth as it is in heaven" [King James Bible].

It should be the sincere desire and honest prayer of every individual believer who loves God and adheres to His noble precepts, that God's will be implemented on this Earth as it is being carried out in heaven. Do you realize what this means? If God's will would be administered on this Earth as it is administered in heaven, then there would be no wars, no lying and cheating, no adultery and blasphemy – and, yes, no slaughterhouses. Just think for a moment. According to Australian Bureau of Statistics, [1987] Australia slaughters 152,379 cattle, 620,209 sheep, 90,859 pigs, and 5,213,498 chickens *each week*. In addition to this, more than 300 tonnes of fish are killed *each week*. United States of America on the other hand slaughters over ten billion animals annually.

This figure of course does not include the marine creatures. If all the slain bodies of these poor innocent souls were laid next to each other, the line would stretch about one million kilometres. In addition to this cruel carnage, animals are often subjected to cruel and inhumane conditions and are crammed in the trucks and rail cars for days without any food or water. Animals are often forced fed and chemicals and hormones of other animals are used to speed up their growth and increase their size and weight. In America farm animals are fed ground up carcasses of dogs and cats that have been euthanized. They are fed recycled chicken manure and given liquid wastes from manure pits to drink. Young calves are treated cruelly and inhumanely so that gluttons could eat "veal" and other cattle are fed *only corn* so that man may eat "corned beef."

The world's largest slaughterhouse is located in Wallula, Washington, and is owned by IBP, the world's largest slaughterhouse conglomerate. A documentary video was shown in early 2001 on NBC News/Dateline. Among other things it was shown how poor and innocent cows were skinned alive. Seventeen IBP employees put their jobs on the line when they signed an affidavit reporting the inhumane practices at the plant. It was reported that 30% of cattle are dismembered without being rendered unconscious. There were cases when some of these poor souls were screaming in agony after all their hide was stripped off. Often their stomachs were cut open while they were still alive and cruelly suffering at the hands of those whose feelings are as hard as stones. Workers are pushed and warned not to care or stop the assembly line since it costs too much.

While in Europe laws are being enacted to somewhat protect animals in the slaughterhouses and adopt more "humane" technique of killing them, in the U.S., Congress is repealing the "humane" slaughter. Lobbying by slaughterhouses has caused many states to repeal even the weak laws now in existence. The Bush Administration has cut way back on USDA personnel and instructed them to forget about humane slaughter. This "born again" Christian monster and mass murderer who reads his Bible daily and who prays daily was trying to set Iraq straight while his hands were stained with innocent blood both at home and abroad.

American people are proud that their country is a Christian nation and on their money a motto is found: "In God We Trust" but it is against the law to pray in school. Americans are so greedy and their appetite for beef is slowly but surely destroying the world environment and exploiting the Third World countries. American slaughterhouses and even those where more "humane" techniques are adopted are living hell for the innocent creatures which God Himself created both for His and man's pleasure.

Animals are living creatures just as we are. They are identical to us in almost every respect. Just as you enjoy a refreshing drink when thirsty, so do they. As you eat food to sustain your body, so do they. As you sleep when tired, so do they. As you express joy and pleasure, so do they. As you procreate and enjoy sex, so do they. As you show affection towards your wife and children, so do they. As you grieve for your loved ones when they die, so do they. As you cry when subjected to pain and sorrow, so do they. As the blood flows in your veins and as your heart pumps the blood to all parts of your body, so does theirs. And, yes, as you fear pain and butcher's knife, so do they. Why then terrorize and mistreat your distant relatives that God created both for His and your pleasure? Long before this world was created, God was vegetarian and all those in His realm practiced radical vegetarianism. All the living creatures were created to be herbivorous and God expressly forbade any living soul to consume the flesh of another living soul. Why then disobey God and why rely on the lying pen of the scribes?

# CHAPTER 7
# Watchers and their Carnivorous Sons

Genesis 1:29-30 clearly reveals that both man and animals were vegetarian and that no living soul was permitted to kill another living soul for food. All those in the celestial realm are vegetarian and in the end, all will be vegetarian and wolf and the lamb will live together in peace [Isaiah 11]. We have seen that Abel pleased God because his *pure oblation* was much more excellent sacrifice than the bloody sacrifice of his brother Cain. In this chapter I will endeavour to demonstrate just how and when both humanity and the animal kingdom ceased to be vegetarian and who was responsible for the carnivorous diet and the fall from vegetarianism.

Essenes and the Ebionites did not believe in the fall of Adam as Christians do today. They believed that the world was relatively calm and with few exceptions both humans and animals lived in accordance with the original ordinances they were given. From their point of view all this has changed after certain heavenly Watchers married the human daughters and with them procreated giants who were responsible for all evil and violence in this world. Through them, all living souls corrupted their way of life and through them for the first time, humanity resorted to sexual immorality and the eating of strange flesh.

The Essenes were strict vegetarians and they condemned the bloody sacrificial cult of the Jews. They regarded the Jewish temple in Jerusalem as a slaughterhouse and would not participate in their bloody sacrifices. Professor Charles Pfeiffer in his book The Dead Sea Scrolls and the Bible on p. 43 states that the Essenes took no part in the temple worship and that they condemned the sacrificial cult.

The *Jewish Encyclopedia,* art. Essenes, on p. 90, candidly admits that the Essenes recognized only the *pure oblation* and would not take any part in the *bloody sacrifice*:

"While the Pharisees took an active part in the daily Jewish life of the masses, even when the Temple worship was controlled by the Sadducees, the Essenes formed a separate sect. The reason seems evident: they deemed themselves the only true Israel and they regarded the religious observances in the cities and the Temple as corrupt. They refused, therefore, to participate in them and went to the wilderness of Judea, to seek God there. Nevertheless, this refusal was confined to animal sacrifices only and they did make offerings of flour and oil, as well as incense."

The Essenes, just like the Jews of Elephantine, offered only a *pure oblation* and vigorously repudiated and condemned any form of animal sacrifice. The same is true of the Ebionites. Early manuscripts and the writings of the Church Fathers plainly show that the Ebionites repudiated bloody sacrifices and they maintained that one of the main reasons why Jesus was born was in fact to do away with bloody sacrifices and the eating of strange flesh. But there was another Jewish sect which existed in old times and was located by the Church Father Epiphanius in ancient Gilead and Bashan. Epiphanius identifies them by the name *Nasaraeans*. These ancient Nazarenes rejected the Jewish Pentateuch claiming that many passages were corrupted and forged by the lying Jewish scribes. The Bishop of Salamis, Epiphanius, testified that they claimed to possess the true Law.

In *Panarion* 1:18 he supplies further information saying that these Jews from the Transjordan acknowledged that Moses received the Law from God but not the one the Pharisaic Judaism used. Epiphanius most emphatically stated that these ancient Nazarenes did not offer bloody sacrifices nor did they eat animal flesh. Matthew Black in his book: The Scrolls and Christian Origins, on p. 66, comments on Epiphanius' statement saying that these ancient Nazarenes declared that the Jewish Pentateuch of their day was not the one Moses received from God but a later fabrication. He also points out that they out rightly rejected all animal sacrifice and that they did not eat animal flesh.

Dr. M.D. Magee in his article entitled *Pre-Christian Nazarenes* states that these Nazarenes, just like the Samaritans, were opposed to the traditions of the Jews. He points out that they were vegetarian who also opposed animal sacrifices. In *Panarion* 1:19 Epiphanius further states that the Ebionites and the Nazoreans produced a great prophet named Elxai who was also accepted by Essenes and the pre-Christian Nasaraeans who vigorously taught against animal sacrifices claiming that the true Law banned such a practice and that the true believers must not eat meat. He was esteemed by all these true believers who rejected the bloody sacrificial cult of the Jews and who condemned those who killed animals in order to eat strange flesh. They held that the original vegetarian world was deceived and corrupted by the fallen angels identified as Watchers in the book of Enoch. In the Book of Enoch, we are told that as the population on Earth increased, Semyaz and some of his companions, being the children of heaven, married human daughters and with them procreated giants who became perverts on Earth. The Book of Jubilees, discovered among the Dead Sea Scrolls also describes how these fallen angels procreated giants who have perverted everything and who have taught humanity to do all sort of evils.

Both the book of Enoch and the book of Jubilees clearly reveal that all injustice and violence, especially the sexual perversion and the eating of strange flesh, was introduced to humanity by the fallen angels identified as Watchers. Daniel 4:13 confirms that there are angels called by this name. Through the corrupt teaching of the Watchers and through brutality of their bastard sons who are identified as *giants* [nephilim], the Earth was full of injustice and *violence. All flesh corrupted and altered their way of life* and *began to shed blood and eat the strange flesh.* These giants were beings of great and enormous stature. The people of the earth could not produce enough food in their fields to feed these ever-hungry bastards and *so they began to eat animals and humans in order to satisfy their enormous appetite.* The Bible itself shows that these giants could have indeed been very tall and of enormous strength. In Amos we read that the Amorites were of enormous stature and strength.

They were tall as cedars and strong as oaks [2:9]. Cedars are trees which grow to 40 metres in height. Some species even higher. An oak tree is indeed a strong and powerful and an enormous tree. The sons of Anak were also of gigantic stature and the spies who spied the land of Canaan confirmed this:

"The land, through which we have gone to spy it out, is a land that eats up the inhabitants of it; and all the people who we saw in it are men of great stature. There we saw the Nephilim, the sons of Anak, who come of the Nephilim: and we were in our own sight as grasshoppers, and so we were in their sight" [World English Bible].

Revelation 10:1-2 shows that one powerful angel stood with his right foot on the sea and with his left on the land. Only a being of gigantic stature could do this. Soviet cosmonauts aboard space station Salyut 7 reported seeing seven angels hovering outside the portholes of their craft. These angels were of gigantic stature. The report is recorded in *The Reader's Digest Almanac of the Uncanny* on p. 432. The Soviet cosmonauts reported that the angels were as big as an airliner. An international airliner is over 60 metres long. The Book of Enoch therefore is not wrong when it says that the bastard giants were about 300 cubits tall. Before I go into the Bible in order to show that the story in the Book of Enoch is genuine and true and that the Watchers who fell procreated the gigantic offspring who caused humanity to fall from vegetarianism, it is essential to present some excerpts from the *Clementine Homilies* where Apostle Peter clearly shows that Adam was not responsible for the sin in this world but rather the fallen angels and their bastard sons:

"But thus the matter stands. The only good God having made all things well, and having handed them over to man, who was made after His image, he who had been made breathing of the divinity of Him who made him, being a true prophet and knowing all things, for the honour of the Father who had given all things to him, and for the salvation of the sons born of him, as a genuine father preserving his affection towards the children born of him, and wishing them, for their advantage, to love God and be loved of Him, showed them the way which leads to his friendship, teaching them by what deeds of men the one God and Lord of all is pleased; and having exhibited to them the things that are pleasing to Him, appointed a perpetual law to all, which neither can be abrogated by enemies, nor is vitiated by any impious one, nor is concealed in any place, but which can be read by all. To them, therefore, by obedience to the law, all things were in abundance, – the fairest of fruits, fullness of years, freedom from grief and from disease, bestowed upon them without fear, with all salubrity of the air" [The Ante-Nicene Fathers].

The Fall was instigated by the Watchers and their offspring. Peter explains in *Clementine Homilies*:

"For of the spirits who inhabit the heaven, the angels who dwell in the lowest region...having become in all respects men, they also partook of human lust, and being brought under its subjection they fell into cohabitation with women; and being involved with them, and sunk in defilement and altogether emptied of their first power, were unable to turn back to the first purity of their proper nature...but from their unhallowed intercourse spurious men sprang, much greater in stature than ordinary men, whom they afterwards called giants...wild in manners, and greater than men in size, inasmuch as they were sprung of angels; yet less than angels, as they were born of women. Therefore God, knowing that they were barbarized to brutality, and that the world was not sufficient to satisfy them [for it was created according to the proportion of men and human use], that they might not through want of food turn, contrary to nature, to the eating of animals, and yet seem to be blameless, as having ventured upon this through necessity, the Almighty God rained manna upon them, suited to their various tastes; and they enjoyed all that they would. But they, on account of their bastard nature, not being pleased with purity of food, longed only after the taste of blood. Wherefore they first tasted flesh. And the men who were with them there for the first time were eager to do the like. Thus, although we are born neither good nor bad, we become one or the other; and having formed habits, we are with difficulty drawn from them. But when irrational animals fell short, these bastard men tasted also human flesh. For it was not a long step to the consumption of flesh like their own, having first tasted it in other forms" [The Ante- Nicene Fathers, Vol 8].

Peter goes on to show how the pure Earth was violated and the long lives shortened on account of poisonous juices of the flesh. He also states that the spirits of the giants survived their bodily destruction and were later known as the evil spirits or demons that are responsible for sacrificial cults, the butchering of animals, sex orgies and other evils which are rampant in this world. Peter points out that these demons have the power only over those who permit them to enter their bodies. In the *Recognitions of Clement* Peter goes on to say how the demons enter the human bodies because they are disembodied spirits and by a vicarious way, try to satisfy their cravings and lusts for sex and strange flesh:

"But the reason why the demons delight in entering into men's bodies is that, being disembodied spirits and having perverted desires after meat and sex, but not being able to partake of these due to being spirits, and wanting organs fitted for their enjoyment, they enter the bodies of men in order to gain organs with which to satisfy their lusts, both meat and sex" [The Ante-Nicene Fathers, Vol. 8].

Apostle Peter explained that the best way to prevent demon possession is to live a pure and simple life. Especially clean sex life and the abstention from animal flesh keeps the demons at bay. Jesus himself pointed out that worst kinds of demons come forth only through prayer and *fasting*. When demons are deprived of *food and pleasure,* they are looking for, they leave in haste in search of other bodies where they could fulfil their depraved and degenerate nature. Apostle Jude clearly refers to the writings of Enoch and the fallen angels who indulged in perverted sex and partook of strange flesh:

"And the angels which kept not their first estate, but left their own habitation, he hath reserved in everlasting chains under darkness unto the judgement of the great day" [King James Bible].

This fact is clearly related in the Book of Enoch to which Jude in fact refers. From 2 Peter 2:4 we learn that these angels were actually locked in Tartarus. Tartarus, in the light of Greek mythology, was a place where the rebellious Titans were locked. These angels had nothing to do with the so-called rebellion of Lucifer. Nor were these angels identical with demons or evil spirits. The demons and their chief evil spirit – Satan – are free to roam on this Earth and are not in chains nor are they locked in Tartarus or the Abyss.

Only the angels who did not retain their first state of existence but did voluntarily exchange their first estate for human bodies in order to marry the human daughters are locked away in the Abyss or Tartarus. Jude clearly states that the angels who are imprisoned in chains *left their own original dwelling* place. Rebelling angels in Christian tradition and teaching did not *leave* heaven but were rather expelled and thrown out. On one occasion the demons begged Jesus not to send them to Abyss [Luke 8:31]. These demons were the disembodied spirits of the giants whose fathers [Watchers] were locked away in Tartarus or Abyss. That is why they begged Jesus not to send them to the same place of terror. In Christian theology, Lucifer Satan and all his angels were never imprisoned in Tartarus or Abyss but were simply hurled down to this Earth where they are free to roam it and deceive the people.

But Jude knows nothing of this theology but rather he refers to the Book of Enoch and the Watchers who were imprisoned in the Abyss [rendered bottomless pit, or deep in the King James Bible]. During the thousand years reign all the demons and their chief leader, Satan, will finally be locked away with their fathers in the Abyss [Revelation 20:3]. This also proves that Satan and his demons are now free to deceive and take possessions of the bodies of those who permit them – just as Peter says in the *Clementine Homilies* and the *Recognitions of Clement*.

But Jude also points out something else. He refers to Sodom, Gomorrah, and their surrounding towns and points out that they have practiced the same evil rites as the imprisoned angels did. They, just like those angels, were guilty of fornication and the eating of strange flesh [verse 7]. The word "strange" means "foreign, alien." Dr. Spiros Zodhiates points out in his Complete Word Study Dictionary Of The New Testament on p. 665, that the Greek word "heteros" in Jude 7 means "foreign, strange." He goes on to say that the same Greek word is used in Exodus 30:9 of the Greek Septuagint Bible where the offering of a strange incense is prohibited.

The word "strange" in this text implies "foreign" or "forbidden" incense. The Hebrew word in the Masoretic text is "zuwr" which means "strange" and "profane." Jude thus says that the Sodomites were guilty of sexual perversion and of eating strange, forbidden and profane flesh of animals. Jesus also had something to say concerning the ante Deluvian world. According to him they were guilty of perverted sex, eating of flesh and drinking of wine. Jesus' statement is recorded in the *Essene Humane Gospel:*

"for as in the days that were before the flood they were eating flesh and drinking sour wine, [fermented wine] and marrying for unnatural reasons, until the day that Noah entered into the ark and knew not until the flood came, and took them all away, so shall also the coming of the Son of Man be."

The canonical Mathean version mentions only "eating and drinking" and "marrying" which of course occurs at all times of human history and does not constitute any special sign at all which would help us identify the times we live in. But the saying recorded in the *Essene Humane Gospel* makes all the difference. Jesus here points out that the final age would experience the same degradation and perversion as did the age just before the Deluge. As in those days the Earth was filled with violence due to the slaughter of animals for food so shall it be in the final age. And as people married and indulged in sexual activities for "unnatural" reasons, so shall it be in the final age.

Just look around you today. Billions of animals are butchered in our modern and sophisticated slaughterhouses so that carnivorous beings could gratify their barbarous habit and craving for animal flesh. Just take a look at all the available intoxicating beverages and the amount of alcohol consumed today and you will immediately realize just how accurate Jesus was. In addition, take a look at all the sexual activities in this world and all the pornography available which has nothing to do with the marriage for "natural" purposes, and again you will see just how accurate Jesus was. In fact, Jesus was much more specific when he spoke of the final age and the killing of animals for their flesh. He spoke of things that could not be applied to any previous age. Please note some excerpts of his predictions, recorded in the *Essene Humane Gospel*:

"For many things shall take place upon earth that hath not taken place before, nay, nor seen by any generation, except those of that generation… Those that have power, shall gather to themselves in greed, the lands and the riches of the earth, for their own lusts, and thus shall oppress the greater number who have not. For in those days, the many shall be held in bondage, but yet not in prison, and they shall be used to increase the riches of the greedy. Yea, even the innocent beasts of the field shall be greatly oppressed, for every cruelty and lust shall be worked against my innocent brothers and sisters of the great household of God; for many shall lust after the taste of flesh, and blood shall flow freely as high as the bridle of a horse!…For I say unto ye this day, that a strange saviour shall rule the minds of many, and that generation shall believe not in the evil of the world, but shall judge all evil, good, and all good, evil…Yea, I tell ye, in that age to come, the Father's Name shall be blasphemed in a manner like never before in the history of the world, greater than even the star count of heaven itself! For hands dripping with the innocent blood of my creatures will take up my name in vain and mislead many, and they will follow the ways of the Pharisees and not the true path of the pure oblation. Yea, many lies will be spoken of me in that age, things I spoke not unto ye, nor taught not, for they will lust after much flesh and sin, and their evil will mount higher than a new moon of thy season and many will believe, and be lost…For verily I say unto ye, that age shall not pass till all those things be fulfilled…Yea, in that age to come, there shall be great lawlessness in the land, for every man shall seek his own advantage, and there shall be no natural love between brothers and sisters and mothers and fathers, for great shall the division of faith and belief be in that age of the end.

In that age to come all things the prophets spoke shall come to pass yea, every sacred word to the letter, for in that time, troubles and tribulations shall engross the nations, and men shall not know a way to escape, for by their evil shall they be caught as a bird in a snare, and none shall escape just rewards. For in that age, many shall fall into Satan's traps and be misled, striving after riches and material goods; many shall leave off from my laws and the love of riches shall blind them to truth. I tell ye, truly, never in the history of the world shall slavery be manifest as in that age, for Satan shall enslave the masses in manners unknown to thy generation, and the masses shall put their faith and hope in the vain promises of ever-speaking man.

For all done in that age, will be accredited to man alone, for few shall know the tricks and deceptions of the evil one, who worketh every strange miracle and fooleth the people and leadeth them to destruction. For many shall not profess God, but believe in their own might and strength and entire nations shall war in my name and deceive many."

Jesus also pointed out that the true believers and disciples are not gathered around "dead things" like vultures, but only round the table where "living" food is:

"For remember, wheresoever the carcass is, there will the vultures be gathered together. For these birds eat of the dead and do gather round for the feast and know not the living. Know ye also, therefore, that the true disciples of Christ are among the living only and are not found gathered round dead things."

So many of those who claim the name of Jesus and who maintain that they are true followers of Jesus, feast like vultures on carrion and enjoy the flesh of the innocent creatures cruelly slaughtered and decapitated in the slaughterhouses. I have demonstrated from several extra-canonical sources that humanity did not eat animal flesh before the Watchers fell and their bastard sons caused havoc on this Earth. But most Christians would dismiss them since they are not quoted from the Bible – the only scriptures they recognize as canonical. But they could not prove that all these canonical books are genuine and inspired and that they were originally written by God's true prophets and apostles. Nevertheless, I will now refer to Genesis 6 and plainly demonstrate that this chapter of the Bible in reality agrees and teaches exactly the same truth this extra-canonical literature does. The first thing we are told in this chapter is the fact that when humanity increased on this Earth and many beautiful girls were born, the "Sons of God" fell in love with them and desired them. After marrying them they procreated "nephilim" that is, *giants* who became mighty warriors and heroes. Please note the text as is translated in the King James Bible:

"And it came to pass, when men began to multiply on the face of the earth, and daughters were born unto them, that the sons of God saw that the daughters of men that they were fair; and they took them wives of all which they chose…There were giants in the earth in those days; and also after that, when the sons of God came in unto the daughters of men, and they bare children to them, the same became mighty men which were of old, men of renown."

Who were these sons of God? Those who blindly accept the traditional Christian view will tell you that they were holy men from the lineage of Seth. The beautiful daughters of men, they say, were girls from the lineage of Cain. The problem, therefore, is intermarriage between supposedly the righteous lineage of Seth and the sinful lineage of Cain. These conservative scholars argue that the Sons of God could not be angels since, in their view, angels are sexless and therefore could not marry. To support their view, they always refer to the words of Jesus:

"For when they shall rise from the dead, they neither marry, nor are given in marriage; but are as the angels which are in heaven." [Mark 12:25 King James Bible].

Since Jesus said that angels in heaven neither marry nor are given in marriage, they conclude that they therefore must be sexless. But we shall see a little later that nothing can be further from the truth and that this text, along some other evidence, in fact proves that there are both male and female angels and that they could engage in sexual activities if they so choose. But before I demonstrate this fact, let us first of all see some other versions of the Bible and see how these translators understood the text and who they thought were these Sons of God. *The Tanakh* [released by the Jewish Publication Society uses the phrase "divine beings." The Bible for Today "supernatural beings." The Good News Bible the same phrase. The Living Bible "beings from the spirit world." The Book of Yahweh "sons of the gods." The New American Bible for Catholics: "sons of heaven." In a footnote, the translators say that these "sons of heaven" were celestial beings of mythology. And, finally, Dr. James Moffat in The Moffat Bible renders the phrase "bene elohim" as "angels."

All these Bible translators [and many others], clearly understood that "bene elohim" are in fact the *supernatural beings* and not men from the lineage of Seth. Those who believe that Genesis 6 speaks of offspring crossed between holy and unholy lineages fail to satisfactorily explain just why the offspring was of *gigantic stature* and why were they the legendary heroes of the dim past. If the *giants* were born because their fathers were of the holy lineage then Isaac should have been even a greater *giant* since both his father and mother were holy. And John the Baptist then should have been the *super-giant* since both Zechariah and Elizabeth were blameless before God and kept all his commandments [Luke 1:6].

Let us closely examine some passages of the Hebrew Bible and see how the term "Sons of God" was used and to whom did it always refer. This term appears several times in the Book of Job and virtually all commentators agree that it refers to the *supernatural beings*. In Job 1:6 and 2:1 the term "bene elohim" or "bene elim" is translated variously by Bible translators. Some use the term "sons of God" while others "divine beings," "supernatural beings," and "angels." No Christian commentator even insinuates that "sons of God" here are of the lineage of Seth. They all unanimously agree that the term refers to angels or some other higher divine beings, the members of the Divine Council. Job 38:1, 7 clearly shows that the "Sons of God" were in existence long before there was any human being. The term therefore does not and cannot be applied to any earthly people or lineage, since the Old Testament invariably uses the term in reference to the *divine beings*.

In Psalm 29:1 the term "bene elohim" occurs. But in this passage the King James translators did not use the term "sons of God" but rather they translated the term "mighty." The Psalmist actually calls on the "Sons of God" to praise God. In Psalm 89:6 [King James Bible 7] the Psalmist says that none among the "bene elim" [Sons of God] could be compared with God. Clearly the reference is to the higher Divine Beings and not men from the lineage of Seth.

Another crucial text is found in Deuteronomy 32:8 where the term "sons of God" appears. The King James Bible uses the term "sons of Israel" because it is based on the Hebrew Masoretic Text, composed in the 6th century of the

Christian era. The early manuscripts and the versions of the Bible, including the Hebrew version discovered with the Dead Sea Scrolls uses the term "bene elohim" rather than "bene Yisrael." The notion in this text is that the Most High assigned the nations to His sons to govern them. Deuteronomy 32:7-9 ascribes these words to the lips of Moses:

"Remember the days of old, consider the years of many generation: ask thy father, and he will shew thee, thy elders, and they will tell thee. When the Most- High divided to the nations their inheritance, when he separated the sons of Adam, he set the bounds of the people according to the number of the children of Israel. For the LORD'S portion is his people; Jacob is the lot of his inheritance" [King James Bible].

Here we have a song of antiquity, ascribed to Moses. This division of the nations took place many generations prior to the days of Moses. The text says that Elyon [Most High] divided the nations "according to the number of the Children of Israel." The King James Bible follows the reading of the Masoretic Text. Some other English versions follow a different Hebrew text which reads "according to the number of the *Sons of God*." This reading is also supported by some LXX manuscripts, by the version of Symmachus, Old Latin and the scroll from Qumran. The *International Standard Bible Encyclopedia*, on p. 584, states that the Jewish Masoretic Text erroneously uses the phrase "sons of Israel" and that the reading "Sons of God" is supported by the Septuagint, the translation of Symmachus, the Old Latin and the Dead Sea Scroll from Qumran.

The translators understood the text of Deuteronomy 32:7-9 differently. Those who were influenced by modern monotheism identified Elyon [the Most-High] and Yahweh as one and the same God. James Moffat understood that a "guardian angel" [Moffat Bible] was appointed over every nation except the nation of Israel which was ruled by the Most-High personally. The translators of the Good News Bible understood that "a god" was appointed over each nation by the Most-High but that He ruled over Israel personally.

The translators of the Living Bible – Life Application Bible – understood that "a supervising angel" ruled over each nation while the Most-High ruled over Israel directly. The compilers of *The International Standard Bible Encyclopedia* understood that the Most-High and Yahweh are two distinct beings and that Yahweh, like all other Sons [gods] was merely an heir who inherited Israel from his father Elyon [Vol. 5, art. Sons of God, p. 584].

Now it becomes clear why Jephtah recognized Chemosh as the national and authentic God of the Ammonites. It also becomes clear why so many passages in the Hebrew Bible clearly state that Israel is the actual *inheritance* of Yahweh. If Yahweh was the Most-High God then he could not inherit anything – since everything would be his. But this fact proves that Yahweh was just one of the 72 sons who were appointed over the 72 nations of the ancient world. There are numerous texts in the Hebrew Bible which say that Israel is Yahweh's *inheritance* [See: Deuteronomy 4:20; 9:26; 1 Samuel 10:1; 2 Samuel 14:6; 1 Kings 8:53; 2 Kings 21:14 and Psalm 33:12]. Psalm 82:1 correctly translated reads:

The Gods stand in the assembly of El, who judges in the midst of the Gods.

Now the picture is somewhat clearer. The Gods were the 72 Sons of Elyon [Most High] who ruled over the nations. These Gods were accused by the Most- High of misrule and injustice and tells them that they will die like mortals even though they were Gods, as the Sons of the Most-High [verses 2-7]. This psalm depicts the Heavenly Council in session. All the gods, rulers of the 72 nations, are assembled before the Most-High. He accuses them of misconduct and tells them that even though they are all his sons and therefore divine, they will die just like mere men. For full details regarding this subject read my book Yahweh Conspiracy, available from Lulu.com and Amazon.com. In the New Testament all new born believers are "sons of God" because they are begotten of His Spirit and therefore partake of His divine nature. But none of new born believing humans ever beget *nephilim* that is, *great giants,* no matter how holy the person may be, thus proving that the fathers of the nephilim spoken of in Genesis 6 were indeed *angels*, just as the Book of Enoch clearly states.

All the evidence therefore points to the fact that the fallen Watchers and their bastard sons were the first to taste *flesh* and *kill for food*. They were those who influenced humanity to pervert their original way of life and ordinances of God. Prior to this time all the living souls were vegetarian and they followed the way of life God prescribed for them in the beginning and they observed His ordinances. Only after the Watchers fell and the giants were born to them did all flesh corrupt their way and the Earth was filled with *violence*. This fact is actually clearly recorded even in the King James Bible. Please note the text of Genesis 6:11-12:

"The earth became corrupt in God's sight, and the earth was filled with violence. And God looked upon the earth, and, behold, it was corrupt; for all animate creatures had corrupted their way upon the earth" [Author's translation].

The first thing I want to point out is the fact that the word "was" in the King James Bible should actually be "became." The Hebrew word "hayyah" was so correctly translated in Genesis 2:10 where it is said that the river *became* four branches. The word "hayyah" is defined by James Strong in his Strong's Exhaustive Concordance Hebrew Dictionary as "to become; to come to pass." The Earth was not always full of violence. The creatures on Earth were not always corrupt. The Earth *became* full of violence and all flesh *corrupted* their way of life only *after* the Sons of God cohabited with the beautiful daughters of men and through this unnatural and forbidden union procreated monstrous Nephilim giants. The word "corrupt" means: made inferior to the original version; immoral, debased or depraved; a disintegration of something once good and pure.

All flesh on Earth altered their original way of life and they became corrupt, just as the Book of Enoch explains. This fact alone proves that prior to that time the Earth was not corrupt nor was it full of violence. Only after the fall of the Watchers and after their bastard sons were born and they resorted to carnivorous diet and caused others to do the same did Earth become full of violence and thus all flesh corrupted their original way of life and good ordinances they received from Adam. The Fall therefore did not originate with Adam but rather with the Watchers and the giants they procreated. You will recall that in the Book of Enoch we were told that the giants had monstrous appetite and that the people resented feeding them. You will also recall that the descendants of these Nephilim giants were living in the land of Canaan. The spies reported that the land of Canaan was very fertile and that its fruits were the best on Earth. A bunch of grapes was carried by two persons. Yet the land *starved its inhabitants* and was not able to satisfy the enormous appetite of the Anakim who were legitimate descendants of the Nephilim giants spoken of in Genesis 6. Thus Numbers 13: 32 speaks of the Nephilim giants in the same manner that the Book of Enoch does and therefore gives weight to the story of Enoch. Therefore, those who kill animals in order to eat their flesh walk on the path of the monstrous Nephilim giants who were the first to kill for food and who thus filled the Earth with violence.

Today billions of animals are cruelly slaughtered by merciless people so that they could gratify their lusts just like those bastard sons of the fallen Watchers. Some are sure to argue that Watchers could not have married women since they are sexless! The Bible however, nowhere says that angels are sexless. Nor does the Bible anywhere say that angels cannot resort to metamorphosis. On the contrary, the Bible shows that angels did resort to metamorphosis when they appeared to people and at times were even able to partake of the earthly food. If angels are sexless, why then do they wear garments? What do they have to hide? Even God is portrayed as wearing a garment. In Revelation all the saints are portrayed as wearing garments. If they will all be sexless, as generally supposed, why then wear garments?

There are at least two passages in the Bible which strongly imply that angels do have genitals. In Isaiah 6:2 we are told that Seraphim have six wings. With two they fly, with two they cover their face, and with the remaining two they cover their *feet*. It is impossible to cover the feet with wings. The two wings which cover the face cover the body from waist upward. The two wings which cover the *feet* cover the body from waist down. The word "feet" is often used metaphorically in the Bible. They euphemistically represent the *genitals*. In Isaiah 7:20 "pubic hair" is referred to as "hair of the feet." In Deuteronomy 28:57 it is said that good and tender mother would resort to cannibalism and would consume the afterbirth which comes from "between her feet," a clear reference to genitalia. In 2 Kings 18:27, King James Bible uses the word "piss" [urine]. The Hebrew however says "foot water." The same text is also recorded in Isaiah 36:12. In Ezekiel 16:25 God condemns Judah for offering her "feet" to her lovers. All these expressions are used euphemistically to describe the male and female genitalia.

Therefore Isaiah 6:2 strongly implies that angels are both male and female. This then also explains why Jesus said that the saved ones will neither marry nor be given in marriage but will be like the "angels" in heaven. If angels were sexless then Jesus would not have used them as an example, since sexless beings naturally do not marry. Only if the angels are indeed male and female, but do not resort to marriage, does the illustration make perfect sense. The other text which strongly implies that angels are indeed either male or female also comes from Isaiah. In Isaiah 34:14 the name *Lilith* appears in connection with the Satyrs, male goat demons. The translators of the King James Bible have rendered the name Lilith as "screech owl." In the Center Reference this is corrected to "night monster." Lilith is number #3917 *in Strong's*, where it is rendered "night specter." The word "specter" means: "spirit of the dead person; ghost; something that haunts or disturbs the mind." *The Brown-Driver-Briggs Hebrew and English Lexicon*, on p. 359, says that Lilith is a "name of a female night-demon haunting desolate Edom."

*The Zondrvan Pictorial Encyclopedia of the Bible*, on p. 96, says that Isaiah referred to the familiar Akkadian female demon Lilitu by the Hebrew name of Lilith. Good News Bible renders "Lilith" in Isaiah 34:14 as "night monster." In a footnote however, it says that she is a female demon who lived in desolate places. Jesus himself confirmed that demons lived in desolate places [Matthew 12:43]. *Man, Myth and Magic, Illustrated Encyclopedia of Mythology, Religion and the Unknown*, on p. 163, art. "Lilith," says that she was chief of the demonesses. Lilith is also known as Succubus. Succubus is a female demoness, seeking sexual intercourse with men in their sleep. Succubus is a female counterpart of male demon called "Incubus." Incubus is a male demon who seeks sexual pleasure with women in their sleep. *The Jewish Encyclopedia*, on p. 1226, says of "Lilith:"

"according to a popular etymology the "demon of the night." She is mentioned in Isaiah 34:14. In the Talmud, Lilith is described as having human face, long hair, and wings, but the term Lilith also occurs as a noun denoting female demons generally. In mystical literature [Cabala], she became the queen of demons and the consort of Satan-Samael."

Therefore, those who reject the story told in the Book of Enoch and Jubilees and who deny that the Sons of God in Genesis 6 are actually angels, on the grounds that angels are sexless and therefore unable to copulate, cannot substantiate their belief.

# CHAPTER 8
# Five Conflicting Systems of Worship in the Old Testament

For a long time now the adherents of Pharisaic Judaism, Christendom and Islam have acknowledged the bloody sacrificial system as part of Mosaic Code – originally sanctioned and implemented by God Himself. Very few realize the fact that Jesus, his Apostles and the earliest believers called Nazarenes who were later known by their derogatory name Ebionites, commonly referred to as Jewish Christians, rejected the sacrificial commands as false pericopes and uninspired interpolations. Ebionites were not the first to regard the sacrificial system as interpolations. The Nazarenes and Essenes of the pre-Christian times displayed the same tendencies. They themselves rejected the sacrificial cult as not authentic and also abstained from eating any kind of animal flesh. The true prophets of Israel also entertained this view.

Jeremiah in particular regarded the sacrificial rites as interpolation by the lying pen of the scribes. When we carefully study the Bible, we come to a realization that it actually contains five systems of religious worship – each one supposedly sanctioned by the true God. These texts were originally written by independent writers representing the view of different Jewish sects which were later fused by Ezra – the priest and scribe of Judah. These texts are not preserved in their original form but have actually undergone certain corrections, deletions and interpolations. By careful and thorough study, it is possible to trace each independent system throughout the writings of the Bible. One system prescribes Jerusalem and its temple as the only centralized shrine where all the tribes of Israel were required to present their bloody sacrifices and burnt offerings. In the same place they were to celebrate three annual festivals: The Feast of Unleavened Bread, the Pentecost, and the Feast of Tabernacles. This religious system was embraced and propagated by the Aaronid priests – descended from Aaron through Eleazar and Phinehas. The rabbis of Judaism likewise embraced this system during the Second Temple period. The Christian Church also recognizes the temple Solomon built as the only authentic House of the LORD – where all sacrificial rites occurred, foreshadowing the supreme and divine sacrifice of Jesus. The second system prescribes Mount Ebal [Mount Gerizim in the Samaritan version of the Pentateuch] as the only authentic shrine where all the sacrificial rites and annual festivals were to occur.

The next system prescribed the Tabernacle, which was supposedly constructed by Moses in the desert, as the only authentic place where all types of sacrificial rites were to take place. Even the animals which were to be consumed by people had to be slaughtered on the altar at the entrance of the Tent of Meeting. The blood was to be poured upon the altar. This system condemned anyone who killed an animal anywhere else but the place where the altar for sacrifices stood in front of the Tabernacle.

The fourth system rejects the centralized shrine and instead prescribes the local worship on the high places – called bamoth in Hebrew. This system recognized many places where the sacrificial altar was to be erected. At all these places where altars were erected it was lawful to perform sacrificial rites and the slaughtering of animals for human consumption. The fifth system rejects all other systems of worship. It rejects the sacrificial rites as not authentic. It claims that the bloody sacrifices and burnt offerings were interpolations by the lying pen of the scribes. It rejects the claim that sacrifices were offered to the true God during forty years the Israelites wandered through the desert. It rejects the idea that the true God implemented the sacrificial system after He led the Israelites out of Egypt. It plainly reveals that the Most-High God actually abhorred the sacrificial rites.

In order for you to realize this fact it is essential to closely examine the biblical texts related to these sacrificial systems. For only then will you be able to see that they fundamentally contradict each other. By the time you finish reading this book you will become aware that the Bible as we have it is not infallible as the Christian Church claims. You will also realize that the original true religion implemented by the Most High was radically different from the Pharisaic Judaism, Islam and traditional Christianity.

## *The Centralized Worship*

The adherents of Normative Judaism claim that the book of Deuteronomy sanctions Jerusalem and its temple built by Solomon as the only recognized and authentic centralized shrine for worship and sacrificial rites:

"Destroy completely all the places on the high mountains and on the hills and under every green tree where the nations you are dispossessing worship their gods. Break down their altars, smash their sacred stones and burn their wooden poles in the fire; cut down the idols of their gods and wipe out their names from those places. You must not worship Yahweh your God in their way. But you are to seek the place Yahweh your God will choose from among all your tribes to put His Name there for a dwelling. To that place you must go; there bring your burnt offerings and sacrifices, your tithes and special gifts, what you have vowed to give and your freewill offerings, and the firstborn of your herds and flocks. There in the presence of Yahweh your God, you and your families shall eat and shall rejoice in everything you have put your hand to, because Yahweh your God has blessed you...But you will cross the Jordan and settle in the land Yahweh your God is giving you as an inheritance, and He will give you rest from all your enemies around you so that you will live in safety. Then to the place Yahweh your God will choose as a dwelling for His Name – there you are to bring everything I command you: your burnt offerings and sacrifices, your tithes and special gifts, and all the choice possessions you have vowed to Yahweh. And there rejoice before Yahweh your God, you, your sons and daughters, your menservants and maidservants, and the Levites from your towns, who have no allotment or inheritance of their own. Be careful not to sacrifice your burnt offerings anywhere you please. Offer them only at the place Yahweh will choose in one of your tribes; there you shall offer your burnt offerings" [Deuteronomy 12:2-14 World English Bible].

Here we find the contrast between the system of Canaan and that of Judaism. The Canaanites erected stone pillars and wooden poles beside the altars on the high places where they worshipped their gods with bloody sacrifices. The Israelites in contrast were to have one centralized shrine – according to the Deuteronomic texts.

"You must not sacrifice the Passover in any town Yahweh your God gives you except in the place He will choose as a dwelling for His Name. There you must sacrifice the Passover" [Deuteronomy 16:5-6 World English Bible].

"Be sure to set aside a tenth of all that your fields produce each year. Eat the tithe of your grain, new wine and oil, and the firstborn of your herds and flocks in the presence of Yahweh your God at the place He will choose as a dwelling for His Name, so that you may learn to revere Yahweh your God always. But if that place is too distant and you have been blessed by Yahweh your God and cannot carry your tithe [because the place where Yahweh will choose to put His Name is so far away], then exchange your tithe for silver, and take the silver with you and go to the place Yahweh your God will choose. Use the silver to buy whatever you like: cattle, sheep, wine or fermented drink, or anything you lust for. Then you and your household shall eat there in the presence of Yahweh your God and rejoice" [Deuteronomy 14:22-26 World English Bible].

"Three times a year all your men must appear before Yahweh your God at the place He will choose: at the Feast of Unleavened Bread, the Feast of Weeks and the Feast of Tabernacles" [Deuteronomy 16:16 World English Bible].

Undoubtedly these texts of Deuteronomy insist on a centralized shrine. Later we find Solomon and other writers claim that these texts applied to the choosing of Jerusalem and the temple he built. We shall see that Solomon claimed that no city or tribe was chosen until the tribe of Judah was chosen in the days of David. Others used these texts to sanction their shrines at Shiloh, Beth El, Mizpah, Gilgal, Nod...They did this despite the fact that the Deuteronomic source plainly names the chosen place as Mount Ebal and its adjacent Mount Gerizim. The Deuteronomic source demands that all tribes go to the place Yahweh will choose. This is to be done even if the place is too distant. The Israelites were to convert their property into silver and then go to the chosen place. These texts expressly forbid them to present sacrifices and burnt offerings in any place they choose. They were also expressly forbidden to sacrifice the Passover lamb anywhere but in the place Yahweh was to sanctify. The following texts plainly reveal that the tribe of Judah understood these Deuteronomic texts to sanction Jerusalem and its temple as the only authorized central shrine:

"When Solomon had finished the Temple of Yahweh and the royal palace, and had succeeded in carrying out all that he had in mind to do in the Temple of Yahweh and in his own palace, Yahweh appeared to him at night and said: I have heard your prayer and have chosen this place for Myself as a temple for sacrifices. When I shut up the heavens so that there is no rain, or command locusts to devour the land or send a plague among My people, if My people, who are called by My Name, will humble themselves and pray and seek My face and turn from their wicked ways, then will I hear from heaven and will forgive their sin and will heal their land. Now My eyes will be open and My ears attentive to the prayers offered in this place. I have chosen and consecrated this temple so that my name may be there forever. My eyes and My heart will always be there" [2 Chronicles 7:11-16 World English Bible].

This text plainly states that Yahweh exclusively chose and consecrated the temple Solomon built on Mount Moriah in Jerusalem as the temple for sacrifices. It further claims that Yahweh would dwell and place his name in this temple forever. Obviously, the author was unaware that the temple was going to be desecrated twice and finally destroyed. Otherwise he would not have claimed that Yahweh would forever be present within its walls. Rehoboam the son of Solomon was forty-one years old when he was crowned king. He ruled seventeen years in Jerusalem,

"the city Yahweh had chosen out of all the tribes of Israel in which to put His Name" [1 Kings 14:21 World English Bible].

Whoever wrote this text he regarded Judah as the only authentic tribe in which Yahweh chose to establish his name. In this tribe alone – in Jerusalem, more particularly, the temple Solomon constructed – all the tribes of Israel were required to take their burnt offerings and sacrifices along with all their other gifts and presents. In this place alone the males of all the tribes were required to present themselves three times a year. The temple in Jerusalem was to be the exclusive shrine for worship. When the prophet Ahijah from Shiloh announced to Jeroboam that he was to become the king of the Ten Tribes of Israel, he also told him that Yahweh would make sure Rehoboam the son of Solomon would retain the rule over the tribe of Judah. This was so that David would always have a lamp in the place where Yahweh supposedly chose to establish his name:

"But he shall have one tribe, for my servant David's sake and for Jerusalem's sake, the city which I have chosen out of all the tribes of Israel; To his son will I give one tribe, that David my servant may have a lamp always before me in Jerusalem, the city which I have chosen me to put my name there" [1 Kings 11:32,36 World English Bible].

Again, the author had no idea that Jerusalem was going to be destroyed. Neither was he aware that David's dynasty was going to come to an end. He assumed that David would always have a descendant to rule in Jerusalem. But this was not to be. This author insisted that Jerusalem was to remain a chosen place of worship even if David's descendants turn against Yahweh and worship hinder gods. When Solomon deserted Yahweh and became guilty of gross idolatry, he did not lose his throne because of supposed unconditional oath to David.

Rehoboam his son was also guilty of gross sins but did not lose his throne because Jerusalem was supposedly eternal, invincible city where all the tribes were required to worship. The redactor explicitly states that even though the descendants of David would practice idolatry – Yahweh would not end their reign no reject the temple and Jerusalem he chose to place his name:

"He walked in the ways of the kings of Israel, as the house of Ahab had done, for he married a daughter of Ahab. He did evil in the eyes of Yahweh.

Nevertheless, for the sake of His servant David, Yahweh was not willing to destroy Judah. He had promised to maintain a lamp for David and his descendants forever" [2 Kings 8:18-19 World English Bible].

"He committed all the sins his father had done before him...Nevertheless, for David's sake Yahweh his God gave him a lamp in Jerusalem by raising up a son to succeed him and by making Jerusalem strong" [1 Kings 15:3-4 World English Bible].

Yahweh supposedly ignored gross idolatry and horrible abominations of David's descendants in order to preserve Jerusalem and its temple forever. If these texts are genuine and if Yahweh indeed swore to David that he will always have a son to rule in Jerusalem – the chosen city – how is it then that Jerusalem was destroyed and the Davidic dynasty became extinct? It is obvious to me that these claims are either spurious and interpolations by the lying pen of the scribes – or else they were written by the original author who was led to believe and practice the false religious system. Yahweh supposedly rejected Eli and his descendants for some technical sin, while at the same time fully ignored the wicked abominations of David's descendants. He rejected King Saul for minor mistakes, but ignored the wicked abominations of the kings of Judah and even David himself.

Now please pay a special attention to the following text recording the very words of Solomon:

"But I have built you a house of habitation, and a place for you to dwell in forever. The king turned his face, and blessed all the assembly of Israel: and all the assembly of Israel stood. He said, Blessed be Yahweh, the God of Israel, who spoke with his mouth to David my father, and has with his hands fulfilled it, saying, Since the day that I brought forth my people out of the land of Egypt, I chose no city out of all the tribes of Israel to build a house in, that my name might be there; neither chose I any man to be prince over my people Israel: but I have chosen Jerusalem, that my name might be there; and have chosen David to be over my people Israel" [2 Chronicles 6:2-6 World English Bible].

If Solomon really made such a statement and if other claims in the Bible are true, then Solomon credited Yahweh with a false statement. He emphatically stated that since Yahweh brought the Israelites out of Egypt, he never chose a city where he would establish his name. But this is simply not true providing the text in Jeremiah 7:12 is correct:

"But go you now to my place which was in Shiloh, where I caused my name to dwell at the first, and see what I did to it for the wickedness of my people Israel" [World English Bible].

Here we are plainly told that Shiloh, a city in the tribe of Ephraim, was first chosen where Yahweh established his name. We know from other scriptures that it was at the very temple of Shiloh that the boy Samuel served and was raised. We know that there was a temple there for we are told that Eli sat "beside the doorpost of Yahweh's temple" [1 Samuel 1:3,9]. Some would want you to believe that this was not actually a built temple but rather the Tabernacle Moses supposedly constructed in the desert. But this could not have been the case. The Tabernacle was not destroyed at that time. It was in existence even in the days of David and Solomon.

The temple of Shiloh however was destroyed because of people's wickedness. Yahweh threatened to destroy the temple in Jerusalem just as he destroyed the temple in Shiloh. He threatened to reject the tribe of Judah just as he rejected the whole tribe of Ephraim [Jeremiah 7:14-15]. The Tabernacle in Shiloh was apparently erected in the days of Joshua [Joshua 18:1]. In the book of Judges, we are told that Jonathan and his sons served as priests in Dan "all the time that the House of God was in Shiloh" [Judges 19:31]. If these texts are authentic then the text preserving the speech of Solomon must be spurious. If the text faithfully preserved the speech of Solomon then he must have either lied or was ignorant of the true facts.

In Psalm 78 Asaph states:

"So that he forsook the tent of Shiloh, The tent which he placed among men; Moreover, he rejected the tent of Joseph, And didn't choose the tribe of Ephraim, But chose the tribe of Judah, Mount Zion which he loved. He built his sanctuary like the heights, Like the earth which he has established forever" [verses 60,67-69 World English Bible].

According to this text, Yahweh never chose the tribe of Ephraim but rather the tribe of Judah. He deserted the temple of Shiloh and instead supposedly built the Sanctuary [Solomon's temple] in Judah to endure forever.

The Samaritans claim that the temple of Shiloh was established by Eli the High Priest who deserted the original temple built at Shechem. The Bible itself reveals that indeed there was a Sanctuary at Shechem even in the days of Joshua:

"Joshua gathered all the tribes of Israel to Shechem, and called for the elders of Israel, and for their heads, and for their judges, and for their officers; and they presented themselves before God. Joshua wrote these words in the book of the law of God; and he took a great stone, and set it up there under the oak that was by the sanctuary of Yahweh" [Joshua 24:1,25 World English Bible].

This text plainly states that there was a Sanctuary at Shechem. It also reveals that a stone pillar and the oak were beside the Sanctuary. We shall see later that the redactors sanctioning the tribe of Judah and the temple of Jerusalem sternly condemned the practice of erecting stone pillars and wooden poles beside the altar or Sanctuary. From Joshua 22 it is evident that the Israelites in his days regarded Shiloh as the sole centralized shrine at which alone it was lawful to offer burnt offerings and perform other sacrificial rites. There we are told that the tribes of Reuben, Gad and half the tribe of Manasseh built an altar in Geliloth near Jordan. When the other tribes learned of this, they assembled all their armies at the central shrine at Shiloh intending to make war with Reubenites, Gadites and Manasseh. Before attacking however, the Israelites sent Phinehas, the son of Eliazar, along with ten chieftains:

"So the Israelites sent Phinehas son of Eliazar, the priest, to the land of Gilead – to Reuben, Gad and the half tribe of Manasseh. With him they sent ten chief men, one for the each tribe of Israel, each the head of the family division among the Israelite clans. When they went to Gilead – to Reuben, Gad and the half tribe of Manasseh – they said to them: The whole assembly of Yahweh says: How could you break faith with the God of Israel like this? How could you turn away from Yahweh and build yourselves an altar in rebellion against Him now?...If you rebel against Yahweh today, tomorrow He will be angry with the whole community of Israel. If the land you possess is defiled, come over to Yahweh's land, where Yahweh's Tabernacle stands, and share the land with us. But do not rebel against Yahweh or against us by building an altar for yourselves, other than the altar of Yahweh your God...

Then Reuben, Gad and the half tribe of Manasseh replied to the heads of the clans of Israel: God, God Yahweh...He knows! And let Israel know! If this has been in rebellion or disobedience to Yahweh, do not spare us this day. If we have built our own altar to turn away from Yahweh and to offer burnt offerings and grain offerings, or to sacrifice fellowship offerings on it, may Yahweh Himself call us to account. No! We did it for fear that someday your descendants might say to ours, What do you have to do with Yahweh, the God of Israel? Yahweh has made the Jordan a boundary between us and you – you Reubenites and Gadites! You have no share in Yahweh. This is why we said, Let us get ready and build an altar – but not for burnt offerings or sacrifices.

On the contrary, it is to be a witness between us and you and the generations that follow, that we will worship Yahweh at His Sanctuary with our burnt offerings, sacrifices and fellowship offerings. Then in the future your descendants will not be able to say to ours, You have no share in Yahweh. And we said, If they ever say this to us, or to our descendants, we will answer: Look at the replica of Yahweh's altar, which our fathers built, not for burnt offerings and sacrifices, but as a witness between us and you. Far be it from us to rebel against Yahweh and turn away from Him today by building an altar for burnt offerings, grain offerings and sacrifices, other than the altar of Yahweh our God that stands before His Tabernacle" [Joshua 22:13-29 World English Bible].

When Phinehas and the other chiefs heard their reply, they no longer spoke about going to war with their brothers [verse 33]. It is not possible to know for certain whether this text represents an actual historical event or whether it is a later gloss. What is clear however, is the fact that the tribes at this point of history were fully convinced that no altar was to be erected anywhere in Israel apart from the one Moses supposedly constructed in the desert. Only at this altar which was placed at the entry of the Shiloh Sanctuary all the tribes were to present their bloody sacrifices. At this place alone they were also to kill their fellowship sacrifices. The fellowship sacrifices consisted of partaking of animal flesh and holding community festivities.

Whoever wrote Joshua 22 most certainly believed the texts of Deuteronomy 12, 14 and 16, as well as the text of Leviticus 17 – where worship in the central shrine was enforced. He however, was either ignorant or rejected the text of Exodus 20:24-25 which allowed building an altar in all the places Yahweh was to choose. According to this text of Exodus the tribes of Reuben, Gad and Manasseh were at liberty to build an altar in Geliloth and present their bloody sacrifices there. This will become apparent later.

In 2 Chronicles 6, Solomon did not only claim that Yahweh never chose a tribe and a city prior to choosing Judah and Jerusalem – a claim that cannot be justified on the evidence presented. He also stated that Yahweh never chose anyone to be the leader of Israel until he chose David his father. This claim is at odds with other scriptures. According to certain texts of the Bible, Yahweh chose Saul the son of Kish to be the king of Israel before David. It is claimed that Samuel in fact anointed Saul as king over the whole Israel [1 Samuel 10:1]. In order to accept the text of 2 Chronicles 6, we must discard all other texts in the Bible which contradict Solomon's claim. It is just not possible to accept all the conflicting views propagated by various authors and redactors in the Bible. We must make a choice and decide which texts are reliable and credible – in harmony with the perfect character of the true God – and which are later gloss and lying interpolations. By the time you finish reading this book the decision will not be all that difficult to make.

### *The Centralized Shrine of Mount Ebal*

We have already seen that the descendants of Judah believed that Yahweh chose the tribe of Judah and the temple of Jerusalem where to place his name in fulfilment of Deuteronomy 12, 14 and 16. We have also seen that others claimed Shiloh to be the centralized shrine in fulfilment of the same texts.

The Samaritans however claimed that neither of these places were chosen by Yahweh. They insisted that Mount Gerizim [adjoining Mount Ebal] was the only legitimate central shrine where all sacrificial rites were to take place. To this day they kill their Passover lambs in Shechem [modern Nablus] – at the foot of Mount Gerizim. Their original temple which once stood on Mount Gerizim was destroyed by Jewish king John Hyrcanus. Who were the Samaritans and on what grounds do they claim that Mount Gerizim and not Jerusalem was the chosen place?

Jews insist that the Samaritans were Gentiles who settled in the land of Israel when the Ten Tribes were enslaved by the Assyrians. Samaritans on the other hand claim that they are legitimate descendants of Ephraim and Manasseh. In the New Testament itself it is evident that Jews and Samaritans did not associate. The Samaritan woman told Jesus that the Jews claimed the place of worship was in Jerusalem while the Samaritans claimed it was on the Mount Gerizim. She stated that Jacob whom she identified as their father worshipped on Mount Gerizim. Jesus however rejected both Jerusalem and Mount Gerizim. He claimed that neither Jewish view nor the Samaritan view was pleased to God. The true worshippers, said Jesus, worship everywhere in spirit and in truth [John chapter 4]. Believe it or not, the Samaritans likewise appealed to the book of Deuteronomy in order to prove that their shrine was the only legitimate centralized place of worship. They appealed to the following texts:

"Behold, I set before you this day a blessing and a curse: the blessing, if you shall listen to the commandments of Yahweh your God, which I command you this day; and the curse, if you shall not listen to the commandments of Yahweh your God, but turn aside out of the way which I command you this day, to go after other gods, which you have not known. It shall happen, when Yahweh your God shall bring you into the land where you go to possess it, that you shall set the blessing on Mount Gerizim, and the curse on Mount Ebal "Deuteronomy 11:26-30 World English Bible].

Please note that chapter 12 follows this text. The Samaritans claim that it is actually continuation of the thought expressed in chapter 11. However, there is an explicit text in Deuteronomy which plainly singles out Mount

Ebal and Mount Gerizim as the only authentic places to worship and present sacrifices:

"It shall be on the day when you shall pass over the Jordan to the land which Yahweh your God gives you, that you shall set yourself up great stones, and plaster them with plaster: and you shall write on them all the words of this law, when you are passed over; that you may go in to the land which Yahweh your God gives you, a land flowing with milk and honey, as Yahweh, the God of your fathers, has promised you. It shall be, when you are passed over the Jordan, that you shall set up these stones, which I command you this day, in Mount Ebal, and you shall plaster them with plaster. There shall you build an altar to Yahweh your God, an altar of stones: you shall lift up no iron [tool] on them. You shall build the altar of Yahweh your God of uncut stones; and you shall offer burnt offerings thereon to Yahweh your God: and you shall sacrifice peace-offerings, and shall eat there; and you shall rejoice before Yahweh your God. You shall write on the stones all the words of this law very plainly" [Deuteronomy 27:2-8 World English Bible].

In verses 12 and 13 of the same chapter we are told that six of the tribes should stand on Mount Gerizim while they pronounce the blessings and other six should stand on Mount Ebal while they pronounce the curses. When the Israelites entered the land, Joshua, so it is claimed, actually built the altar according to the instructions of Moses:

"Then Joshua built an altar to Yahweh, the God of Israel, in Mount Ebal, as Moses the servant of Yahweh commanded the children of Israel, as it is written in the book of the law of Moses, an altar of uncut stones, on which no man had lifted up any iron: and they offered thereon burnt offerings to Yahweh, and sacrificed peace-offerings. He wrote there on the stones a copy of the law of Moses, which he wrote, in the presence of the children of Israel. All Israel, and their elders and officers, and their judges, stood on this side of the ark and on that side before the priests the Levites, who bore the ark of the covenant of Yahweh, as well the sojourner as the native; half of them in front of Mount Gerizim, and half of them in front of Mount Ebal; as Moses the servant of Yahweh had commanded at the first, that they should bless the people of Israel. Afterward he read all the words of the law, the blessing and the curse, according to all that is written in the book of the law. There was not a word of all that Moses commanded, which Joshua didn't read before all the assembly of Israel, and the women, and the little ones, and the sojourners who were among them" [Joshua 8:30-35 World English Bible].

If we were to accept the Deuteronomic texts which prescribe the centralized national worship, we would have to admit that Mount Ebal and Mount Gerizim with its altar was the only authentic place where the sacrificial rites were to be performed. How and why the Shiloh was chosen is an enigma. Why the tribe of Judah rejected the altar of Mount Ebal is also an enigma. Joshua supposedly erected the shrine at Shiloh – forbidding anyone to erect another anywhere else. Yet the same Joshua supposedly erected the altar on Mount Ebal according to the instructions of Moses.

Later, prophet Samuel ignores the Deuteronomic texts and supposedly sacrifices on high places of Beth El, Giboah, Mizpah and other towns. Prophet Elijah rejects the temple of Jerusalem and supposedly sacrifices on Mount Carmel – recognizing many altars of Yahweh in the land of Israel and not Judah. Amos, Isaiah, Jeremiah, Hosea and Micah altogether rejected the shrine worship of any kind. All the texts which prescribe the sacrificial cult of any sort they regard as interpolations – claiming that the true God never implemented it. This will be fully documented when we deal with the fifth system of worship – the system which flatly rejects the sacrificial cult.

### *The Altar at the Tent of Meeting*

According to the text of Exodus – Moses was shown a pattern of the Sanctuary of Yahweh. He was instructed to erect the Tent of Meeting [Tabernacle] which was to consist of two apartments: The Holy Place and the Most Holy Place. He was also told to make an altar of acacia wood and overlay it with bronze. On this altar all the sacrificial rites were to be performed. On the golden altar which he was also instructed to make, the incense was to be burned perpetually.

He was also to make a golden lampstand [The Menorah], as well as all sort of utensils required for the sacrificial cult. The most holy object that was supposedly constructed in the desert was the Ark of the Covenant which was overlaid with gold and whose lead was made of pure solid gold. This Ark was to rest between two cherubim which Moses was to make of pure gold. This Ark was called the throne of Yahweh and the mercy seat. In it, Yahweh lived. The cherubim creatures were animals resembling bulls. They had human faces and long wings. On the Day of Atonement – 10$^{th}$ of the Jewish seventh month – the High Priest was to enter the Most Holy Place and sprinkle blood on the mercy seat in order to atone for the sin of his nation. Each day – morning and evening – the priests were to present a lamb as a perpetual sacrifice. This rite became known as the daily sacrifice.

The Tabernacle was erected on the first day of the first month in the second year after exodus from Egypt [Exodus 40:17]. The altar for burnt offerings and sacrifices was placed near the entrance to the Tent of Meeting. There the priests kept performing the sacrificial rites [40:20]. In Leviticus 17 we find the following clear instructions regarding the Tent of Meeting and its sacrificial altar:

"Yahweh spoke to Moses, saying, Speak to Aaron, and to his sons, and to all the children of Israel, and tell them: This is the thing which Yahweh has commanded, saying, Whatever man there be of the house of Israel, who kills an ox, or lamb, or goat, in the camp, or who kills it outside of the camp, and hasn't brought it to the door of the tent of meeting, to offer it as an offering to Yahweh before the tent of Yahweh: blood shall be imputed to that man; he has shed blood; and that man shall be cut off from among his people: To the end that the children of Israel may bring their sacrifices, which they sacrifice in the open field, even that they may bring them to Yahweh, to the door of the tent of meeting, to the priest, and sacrifice them for sacrifices of peace-offerings to Yahweh. The priest shall sprinkle the blood on the altar of Yahweh at the door of the tent of meeting, and burn the fat for a sweet savor to Yahweh. They shall no more sacrifice their sacrifices to the male goats, after which they play the prostitute. This shall be a statute forever to them throughout their generations" [17:1-7 World English Bible].

This priestly source commands all the tribes of Israel to bring their sacrifices and burnt offerings and present them on the altar in front of the Tabernacle. The text also forbade any Israelite or an alien to slaughter his animals anywhere else but the altar of the Tabernacle. They were to bring it there as fellowship offerings – and eat them in the 'presence of Yahweh.' This law was not to be in force only while they were in the desert but "everlasting, through all their generations."

The first book of Samuel plainly reveals that the Israelites prior to the days of David and Solomon at least partially adhered to this command. They never slaughtered their animals for human consumption at their homes. They brought them to the place of worship. They accepted the fact that they could not kill their animals apart from the altar, but they did not always bother to bring it to the Tent of Meeting. They took their animals to Shiloh, Beth El and other sacrificial centres – or simply erected their own altars. Elkanah, the father of Samuel, took his animals to Shiloh every year. There he and his family ate of the flesh. Since he loved his wife Hannah more than his other wife or children, he gave her double portion of meat [1 Samuel 1:3-4].

When King Saul conquered the Philistines, the army seized the animals and killed them on the ground rather than the altar. Then they ate the meat. Some soldiers came to Saul and told him that the people are sinning against Yahweh because they ate meat by bloodshed. Saul was very disturbed and ordered the soldiers to bring the animals to him. He took a large stone and commanded the people to kill their animals on this stone so that they would not be guilty of bloodshed – that is, murder.

When Christians, Muslims and the adherents of Judaism read the text of 1 Samuel 14:31-34, they fail to realize the real meaning of it. Most assume that their sin was eating flesh together with the blood. But this was not the case. The text first of all states that they slaughtered the animals. Since they were slaughtered that means that they were bled. The Hebrew word "shachat" means "to kill or slaughter animal for food, sacrifice or human being in sacrifice." They cut the throat of their animals and so they were bled. But they slaughtered the animals on the ground and not an altar. Saul commanded that large stone be brought to him upon which they should slaughter their animals. This act plainly reveals that Saul believed [at least it is so claimed] that it was lawful to kill the animals for human consumption only upon the altar. On this occasion he built his first altar to Yahweh. The correct translation of this text from Hebrew is as follows:

"That day, after the Israelites had defeated the Philistines from Mikmash to Ayalon, they were exhausted. They pounced on the plunder and, taking sheep, cattle and calves, they slaughtered them on the ground and ate them through bloodshed [murder]. Then someone said to Saul, Look, the men are sinning against Yahweh by eating flesh through bloodshed. You have broken faith, he said. Roll a large stone over here at once. Then he said, go out among the men and tell them, each of you bring me your cattle and sheep, and slaughter them here [on the stone] and eat them. Do not sin against Yahweh by eating meat through bloodshed. So, everyone brought his ox that night and slaughtered it there. Thus, Saul built an altar to Yahweh; it was the first time he had done this" [Author's translation].

Please recall that the text of Leviticus 17 regarded the slaughter of an animal as murder unless it was done so on the altar near the entrance of the Tabernacle. Saul did not build the altar near the Tent of Meeting but he nevertheless obeyed the rest of the Levitical text. Also, there was Ahijah the priest with him there [verses 18-19]. The rabbis of Judaism teach that it is forbidden to sacrifice animals to Yahweh when there is no temple in Jerusalem. That is why the Jews do not present sacrifices and burnt offerings since the temple was destroyed in 70 c.e. But the rabbis allow eating of flesh regardless where the animal was killed. By forbidding animal sacrifice but allowing the slaughtering of animals in order to gratify their lusts they are most definitely guilty of bloodshed.

According to the Levitical text they should be cut off from among their people. The rabbis teach that the Pentateuch was written by Moses and claim the inspiration of every letter. Why then do they reject the text of Leviticus which orders the Israelites and the aliens to slaughter their animals on the altar of Yahweh alone? This rule was to be an everlasting ordinance – throughout the Hebrew generations.

## *Worship on the High Places*

The phrase *high place* occurs more than hundred times in the Bible. It comes from the Hebrew word *bamah* and primarily refers to a cultic site of some sort. St. Jerome rendered the Hebrew word *bamah* as *excelsus* in his Latin Vulgate Bible and hence the high place in the King James Bible. The Hebrew word *bamah* means more than just a high place. New English Bible renders 'bamah' 'high shrine' while Revised Standard Version and New Jewish Publication Society render it 'shrine.' The Jerusalem redactors sternly condemn 'bamot' [plural of bamah] of any sort. The Deuteronomic and Levitical sources prescribed the sacrificial worship in one place alone. Yet we find the Israelites continuously associated with many altars on the high places. When Saul first met Samuel he went with him to bamah – because Samuel had to officiate at the shrine since there was a festival to be observed and sacrifices to be presented [1 Samuel 9:11-25].

After having a sacrificial meal with Saul, Samuel sent him to Bethel, to the hill, where the company of prophets met him. [Beth El was the important shrine to the Patriarchs and the Israelites. Later it became one of the two main shrines of the Ten Tribes. Its name means: House of El]. How is it that the Israelites had many sacred shrines in the high places when the original Tabernacle Moses supposedly made in the desert was available to them and was actually situated at the high place of Gibeon? [1 Chronicles 21:29]. How is it that even the men of Yahweh, such as Samuel, actually worshipped on high hills and in different locations and offered sacrifices at the shrines of Beth El, Mizpah, Shiloh, Gibeah, Galgal, Ramah...?

Why did he not worship only at the Tent of Meeting which was located at Gibeon? Why was there also a Sanctuary at Shechem as well as Shiloh and Nod – when all along the Israelites had the mobile Sanctuary which Moses allegedly constructed? By building all other shrines and sanctuaries on the high places they most definitely sinned if the Deuteronomic texts which enforce the centralized worship are authentic.

They were guilty of murder by shedding blood of animals on altars other than the one Moses supposedly constructed in the desert for all times. Why did even Elijah recognize various altars on the high places as the altars of Yahweh – when the temple Solomon built in Jerusalem still stood erect? All these questions have haunted the rabbis of Judaism, as well as Christian theologians, for thousands of years. To date they have been unable to solve the enigma. This however, did not prevent them from claiming that every letter in the five books of Moses is inspired and infallible. The rabbis of Normative Judaism pronounce a curse on anyone who even questions Mosaic authorship of the entire Pentateuch. The Christian Church went as far as claiming that every word in the entire Bible is inspired and infallible. If the true God was indeed the Author of the entire Bible, why then is it full of errors and contradictions? Why did the Ebionites reject many portions of it? Why did Jeremiah himself charge the Jewish scribes of falsifying the Pentateuch? Why are so many books missing from the original Bible? Why these conflicting accounts concerning the chosen place and where the sacrificial cult should be practiced?

Let us now return to the subject of the shrines on the high places. Where did King David worship Yahweh and offer sacrifices and burnt offerings? Most definitely not in Gibeon where the Tent of Meeting was located. He most definitely offered sacrifices in different places – if the Bible as we have it is to be trusted. He pitched a tent in Jerusalem in which he placed the Ark of the Covenant. In the same place he offered bloody sacrifices [2 Samuel 6:17-18]. Yahweh supposedly told him to do so despite the fact that the Tent of Meeting and its sacrificial altar was located in Gibeon. By commanding David to build an altar in Jerusalem and to present sacrifices thereupon did not Yahweh violate His own command given to Moses and the Israelites in the desert [Lev.17], commanding the Israelites to present their sacrifices on the altar of the Tabernacle throughout their generations? David presented sacrifices on the altar he built in Jerusalem where he placed the Ark of the Covenant. He built an altar on the threshing floor of Araunah and there he performed sacrificial rites [2 Samuel 24:18-25]. Please pay attention to the following text:

"So David gave to Ornan for the place six hundred shekels of gold by weight. David built there an altar to Yahweh, and offered burnt offerings and peace-offerings, and called on Yahweh; and he answered him from the sky by fire on the altar of burnt offering. Yahweh commanded the angel; and he put up his sword again into the sheath of it. At that time, when David saw that Yahweh had answered him in the threshing floor of Ornan the Jebusite, then he sacrificed there. For the tent of Yahweh, which Moses made in the wilderness, and the altar of burnt offering, were at that time in the high place at Gibeon" [1 Chronicles 21:25-29. See also 1 Chronicles 6:31-32 World English Bible].

But now please note the following text which reveals an amazing act of David:

"It happened, as the ark of the covenant of Yahweh came to the city of David, that Michal the daughter of Saul looked out at the window, and saw king David dancing and playing; and she despised him in her heart They brought in the ark of God, and set it in the midst of the tent that David had pitched for it: and they offered burnt offerings and peace-offerings before God. When David had made an end of offering the burnt offering and the peace-offerings, he blessed the people in the name of Yahweh. He dealt to everyone of Israel, both man and woman, to everyone a loaf of bread, and a portion [of flesh], and a cake of raisins. He appointed certain of the Levites to minister before the ark of Yahweh, and to celebrate and to thank and praise Yahweh, the God of Israel and Zadok the priest, and his brothers the priests, before the tent of Yahweh in the high place that was at Gibeon, to offer burnt offerings to Yahweh on the altar of burnt offering continually morning and evening, even according to all that is written in the law of Yahweh, which he commanded to Israel; " [1 Chronicles 15:29 - 16:3-4,40 World English Bible].

Here most plainly we are told that David established two places of worship. In both places sacrificial rites took place. We are also plainly told that the Ark of the Covenant was placed in the tent David pitched in Jerusalem and not the Tabernacle Moses allegedly built which was situated at Gibeon. Yet on the sacrificial altar at Gibeon he charged Zadok to offer daily sacrifice in accordance with the supposed command of Yahweh written in the so-called Mosaic Law. Of what value was the Tabernacle in Gibeon since its most sacred object was not there? This Tabernacle was deserted since

Yahweh supposedly resided in the Ark – which was placed in Jerusalem. By establishing two places of worship, did David fulfil the commands of Deuteronomy 12, 14 and 16 – prescribing only one centralized shrine? Did he fulfil Leviticus 17 by slaughtering animals for either sacrifices or human consumption on the altar at the entry of the Tent of Meeting? The answer is resounding no!

Just what are we supposed to make of all these absurd and contradicting texts? Which ones are authentic and inspired – revealing the perfect will of the true God? As far as God's true prophets, Jesus, his apostles and the Ebionites were concerned – none of them. They altogether rejected the sacrificial rites of any kind – whether in Jerusalem, Tent of Meeting or any other high shrine. This fact will become crystal clear in this book. In 1 Kings 3, the Deuteronomic redactor attempts to justify people who continued to sacrifice in the high places saying:

"Only, the people sacrificed in the high places, because there was no house built for the name of Yahweh until those days" [verse 2 World English Bible].

But what difference does this make? They had the most sacred Sanctuary at Gibeon. And why on a high place if it was something Yahweh hated as I have already pointed out in the quoted text previously? How could he justify the sacrificial rites on the high places if the text of Leviticus 17 is authentic? In 1 Kings 3:3 Solomon himself is criticized for worshipping Yahweh on the high places:

"Solomon loved Yahweh, walking in the statutes of David his father: only he sacrificed and burnt incense in the high places" [World English Bible].

Whoever wrote this text obviously believed that it was wrong to sacrifice on shrines of the high places. Yet in the same chapter we are told that Solomon presented 1000 cattle on the most sacred high place in Gibeon. There, at that very high shrine Yahweh supposedly appeared to Solomon and told him to ask of Yahweh whatever he will. He did not ask for riches but rather for wisdom so that he would be able to lead the Israelites wisely [1 Kings 3:4-5].

How is it that Yahweh never told Solomon that to present sacrifices on the high place of Gibeon was wrong? It is obvious to me that not all the texts in the Bible were inspired by the true God. Many texts were written by various redactors in the name of someone else in order to bolster their religious views and convictions. The redactor of the book of Kings attempted to justify the people for sacrificing on the high places because the temple in Jerusalem was not as yet built. But on what grounds would he justify the action of Elijah who lived many years after Solomon built the temple in Jerusalem? The Prophet Elijah did not recognize that temple as the only authentic place for worship. As a matter of fact, he did not even worship in the temple at Jerusalem. He was preaching in the Kingdom of Israel – during the days of Ahab and Jezebel. Please note the following text:

"Now therefore send, and gather to me all Israel to Mount Carmel, and the prophets of Baal four hundred fifty, and the prophets of the Asherah four hundred, who eat at Jezebel's table. So Ahab sent to all the children of Israel, and gathered the prophets together to Mount Carmel…Elijah said to all the people, Come near to me; and all the people came near to him. He repaired the altar of Yahweh that was thrown down. Elijah took twelve stones, according to the number of the tribes of the sons of Jacob, to whom the word of Yahweh came, saying, Israel shall be your name. With the stones he built an altar in the name of Yahweh; and he made a trench about the altar" [1 Kings 18:19-20,30-32 World English Bible].

This text claims that there was an altar of Yahweh on Mount Carmel. Baal's prophets demolished it and left it in ruins. Elijah supposedly repaired it and offered a sacrifice on it. Yahweh supposedly responded with fire. How could there be an altar on Mount Carmel after the temple in Jerusalem was supposedly exclusively consecrated for sacrifices and burnt offerings? How could Elijah repair this altar and present a sacrifice to Yahweh in a place other than the one Yahweh supposedly chose to place his name? By sacrificing a bull on Mount Carmel, Elijah was guilty of murder. He should have taken it to the entrance of the Tent of Meeting as the Levitical text commanded to be done forever – through all generations. Or if this is a forged text, then to the temple Solomon built. Why offer a sacrifice on a high place [bamah]? How could he even offer sacrifices when he was not a priest? How could even Samuel, David and others in the Bible offer sacrifices when they were not priests? Samuel was a descendant of Korah and was not a descendant of Aaron. In 1 Kings 19:14 Elijah supposedly said to Yahweh:

"I have been very jealous for Yahweh, the God of hosts; for the children of Israel have forsaken your covenant, thrown down your altars, and slain your prophets with the sword; and I, even I only, am left; and they seek my life, to take it away" [World English Bible].

How could Elijah state that there were alters of Yahweh in the kingdom of Samaria when we are told elsewhere that the only authentic altar for sacrifices was the one Moses supposedly constructed in the desert? What about the altar Solomon built and which stood at the entrance of the temple? That altar was supposedly exclusively chosen by Yahweh for sacrifices and burnt offerings. Why then all the altars in the kingdom of Israel? These are baffling questions which you must answer if you want to serve the true God in spirit and truth. By the time you read this book it will become apparent that all these texts sanctioning various shrines are not authentic. You will realize that they are interpolations by the lying pen of the scribes. That is why they fundamentally contradict each other.

In the books of Kings and Chronicles – Hezekiah, King of Judah implemented a great religious reform. The Jewish redactor of the book of Kings who strongly supported the Jewish claim regarding Jerusalem and the temple of Solomon – identifies King Hezekiah as most righteous of all kings:

"He did that which was right in the eyes of Yahweh, according to all that David his father had done. He removed the high places, and broke the pillars, and cut down the Asherah: and he broke in pieces the brazen serpent that Moses had made; for to those days the children of Israel did burn incense to it; and he called it Nehushtan. He trusted in Yahweh, the God of Israel; so that after him was none like him among all the kings of Judah, nor [among them] that were before him" [2 Kings 18:3-5 World English Bible].

It is claimed that no king as righteous as Hezekiah arose after him. Yet we are told the same about King Josiah who himself also implemented a great religious reform not many years after Hezekiah's reform. It is claimed that no king before or after Josiah was as righteous as he who served Yahweh with all his heart and soul. More about Josiah's reform later. When people read the last text quoted from the book of Kings – they usually suppose that the high places Hezekiah destroyed were the places where Israelites worshipped Baal. It is true that Hezekiah destroyed the altars of Baal but he also destroyed the altars of Yahweh built by the worshippers in the Ten Tribes. The Ten Tribes erected sacred stone pillars and wooden poles [asherim] beside the altars they built for Yahweh. The tribe of Judah hated this system of worship. That is why Hezekiah smashed all the altars and the stone pillars and wooden poles – commanding all the tribes to worship in Jerusalem alone – at the temple Solomon built. In the Torah itself we find texts sanctioning and forbidding the stone pillars and wooden poles. We find the people both erecting and demolishing them. Moses himself is depicted as erecting twelve stone pillars beside the altar he supposedly built [Exodus 24:4]. Jacob erected a stone pillar at Beth El beside the altar he supposedly built [Genesis 28:18,22; 35:6-7]. Joshua himself erected the large stone pillar beneath the same oak tree Jacob did [acting as a wooden pole] beside the Sanctuary at Shechem [Joshua 24:25-25]. Even in the days of Gedeon this stone pillar was in existence. For we are told that Abimelech was crowned King of Israel beside this pillar [Judges 9:6].

The Israelite altars in honour of Baal or Yahweh were always associated with sacred stone pillars [masaboth] and wooden poles or oaks – rendered *groves* in the King James Bible. The tribe of Judah sternly condemned this practice. That is why we find a redactor's insertion which prohibits this practice:

"You shall not plant you an Asherah of any kind of tree beside the altar of Yahweh your God, which you shall make you. Neither shall you set yourself up a pillar; which Yahweh your God hates" [Deuteronomy 16:21 World English Bible].

If Yahweh hates this practice, why then did Jacob erect the pillars near the altar? Why did Moses do it and even Joshua? Hezekiah destroyed all these shrines built by the Israelites. He even dared to destroy the bronze serpent [Nehushtan] which Moses made in the desert. But he did not touch the altars Solomon erected in honour of the pagan gods. Solomon built altars to the gods of his pagan wives. Hezekiah did not touch these altars but he destroyed all altars which were erected to Yahweh in the territory of the Ten Tribes – especially those in Ephraim and Manasseh. It was Josiah who smashed the altars Solomon erected to the pagan gods [2 Kings 23:13]. Solomon was Hezekiah's 'hero' and the 'founder' of the religion he reformed. That Hezekiah also destroyed the altars the Israelites regarded to be those of Yahweh – is also evident from the following text:

"The king of Assyria sent Tartan and Rab-saris and Rabshakeh from Lachish to king Hezekiah with a great army to Jerusalem. They went up and came to Jerusalem. When they were come up, they came and stood by the conduit of the upper pool, which is in the highway of the fuller's field. When they had called to the king, there came out to them Eliakim the son of Hilkiah, who was over the household, and Shebnah the scribe, and Joah the son of Asaph the recorder. Rabshakeh said to them, Say you now to Hezekiah, Thus says the great king, the king of Assyria, What confidence is this in which you trust? You say (but they are but vain words), [There is] counsel and strength for the war. Now on whom do you trust, that you have rebelled against me? Now, behold, you trust on the staff of this bruised reed, even on Egypt; whereon if a man lean, it will go into his hand, and pierce it: so is Pharaoh king of Egypt to all who trust on him. But if you tell me, We trust in Yahweh our God; isn't that he whose high places and whose altars Hezekiah has taken away, and has said to Judah and to Jerusalem, You shall worship before this altar in Jerusalem? Now therefore, Please give pledges to my master the king of Assyria, and I will give you two thousand horses, if you are able on your part to set riders on them. How then can you turn away the face of one captain of the least of my master's servants, and put your trust on Egypt for chariots and for horsemen? Am I now come up without Yahweh against this place to destroy it? Yahweh said to me, Go up against this land, and destroy it" [2 Kings 18:17-25 World English Bible].

Hezekiah was forced to pay the tribute to the king of Assyria. He took all the gold he could find but was also forced to strip the gold from the doors and posts of the temple in order to pay his tribute [1 Kings 18:16]. What an irony! The most "righteous" king of Judah was forced to desecrate the temple in order to pay his tribute to the Gentile king. Please note how this text resembles the text in connection with Josiah:

"After all this, when Josiah had prepared the temple, Neco king of Egypt went up to fight against Carchemish by the Euphrates: and Josiah went out against him. But he sent ambassadors to him, saying, What have I to do with you, you king of Judah? [I come] not against you this day, but against the house with which I have war; and God has commanded me to make haste: forbear you from [meddling with] God, who is with me, that he not destroy you. Nevertheless Josiah would not turn his face from him, but disguised himself, that he might fight with him, and didn't listen to the words of Neco from the mouth of God, and came to fight in the valley of Megiddo" [2 Chronicles 35 20-22 World English Bible].

Hezekiah became subject to the king of Assyria. Josiah was killed in a battle against Neco, the king of Egypt. Yet both kings instituted great religious reforms and each is said to be more righteous than any other king that ruled in Judah. Why then were they defeated by the pagan kings? There is obviously something drastically wrong with these stories. When we carefully compare the story of Hezekiah given in 2 Kings 18-20 with that given in 2 Chronicles 29-32 – we discover some significant differences. The same can be said about the two stories in regards to Josiah and his reform. So far, we have examined the four systems of worship which are sanctioned in one way or another in the Bible. We have seen that there are many conflicting texts – each one written by someone in order to uphold a certain religious system concerning the sacrificial cult. Those who built altars in various places and offered sacrifices there, appealed to the example of the Patriarchs and especially the text of Exodus 20:24-25:

"An altar of earth thou shall make me, and shalt sacrifice thereon thy burnt offerings, and thy peace offerings, thy sheep, and thine oxen: in all places where I record my name I will come unto thee, and will bless thee" [King James Bible].

This text of Exodus commands the Israelites to make an altar of the earth. This was preferred. If made of stones they must not cut them in any way. But

Moses built an altar of stones. So did Joshua. So did Elijah repair the altar of stones. This text allows the erection of altars to Yahweh in more than one place – in all the places Yahweh will establish his name. In all these places they were allowed to perform sacrificial cult. The text of Deuteronomy allowed them to build an altar only in one place – the very place Yahweh was to choose from all the tribes of Israel. Another Deuteronomic source sanctioned only the altar on Mount Ebal. The text of Leviticus 17 altogether forbade the Israelites to build any altar whatsoever. It regarded the altar Moses supposedly built in the desert as the only authentic altar for all times. Only at this altar which was located at the entrance of the Tabernacle they were to slaughter their sacrifices of all types. When Solomon built the temple, he altogether ignored this text. He did not even use the altar Moses supposedly built in the desert of acacia wood overlaid with bronze – whose size was 3 cubits high, five cubits long and five cubits wide [Exodus 27:1]. Please note the following text:

"Moreover he made an altar of brass, twenty cubits the length of it, and twenty cubits the breadth of it, and ten cubits the height of it. Also he made the molten sea of ten cubits from brim to brim, round in compass; and the height of it was five cubits; and a line of thirty cubits compassed it round about. Under it was the likeness of oxen, which did compass it round about, for ten cubits, compassing the sea round about. The oxen were in two rows, cast when it was cast. It stood on twelve oxen, three looking toward the north, and three looking toward the west, and three looking toward the south, and three looking toward the east: and the sea was set on them above, and all their hinder parts were inward. It was a handbreadth thick; and the brim of it was worked like the brim of a cup, like the flower of a lily: it received and held three thousand baths " 2 Chronicles 4:1-5 World English Bible].

The altar of Exodus text was 3 cubits [1 meter] high. It could not have been any higher since the text forbade the erection of any steps in connection with the sacrificial altar [Exodus 20:26]. Since Solomon's altar was more than 3 meters high – it had to have steps in order for the priests to be able to lay the timber and sacrifice on top of the altar. This would have contradicted the Exodus text. But then Solomon would have ignored it anyway since this text of Exodus sanctions more than one place of worship. He could have paid attention to the latter Jewish tradition which allowed the altars with steps but commanded the priests to wear underpants in order not to expose their nakedness [Exodus 28:40-42, Ezekiel 43:13-17]. We are now ready to carefully examine the texts which endorse the fifth system – the system which claims that the sacrificial cult did not originate with the true God. Those who accepted and practiced this religious system discarded all texts supporting the sacrificial rites. I urge you to read it very carefully and with an open mind. Then draw your own conclusions.

# CHAPTER 9
# The Jewish Sacrificial Cult and the Eating of Meat

Animal sacrifice and the eating of animal flesh were closely intertwined in the Old Testament. One without the other was not possible. The Most-High God was always against the idea of sacrifice and very much against the eating of animal flesh because both practices necessitated butchery and the murdering of animals. There are many passages in the Bible where God categorically rejects the idea that He ever commanded such barbaric rituals. Jeremiah 7:21-26 is just one such passage. But regrettably, this passage has come down to us in its three variant versions. All three however convey basically the same message, although in different words.

"Add your burnt offerings to your sacrifices, and eat you flesh. For I didn't speak to your fathers, nor command them in the day that I brought them out of the land of Egypt, concerning burnt offerings or sacrifices: but this thing I commanded them, saying, Listen to my voice, and I will be your God, and you shall be my people; and walk you in all the way that I command you, that it may be well with you. But they didn't listen nor turn their ear, but walked in [their own] counsels [and] in the stubbornness of their evil heart, and went backward, and not forward. Since the day that your fathers came forth out of the land of Egypt to this day, I have sent to you all my servants the prophets, daily rising up early and sending them: yet they didn't listen to me, nor inclined their ear, but made their neck stiff: they did worse than their fathers" [World English Bible].

According to the priestly injunctions, there was a distinction between a "burnt offering" and a "fellowship offering." A burnt offering was wholly burnt and consumed by fire on the altar. It was Yahweh's "meal" or "food" and was offered in order to please him with a "pleasant aroma" of the barbecued meat. The fellowship sacrifice was presented in order that worshippers could feast on barbecued meat.

Only a part of it was offered to Yahweh and the rest was consumed by participants. God however, plainly says through Jeremiah that He never gave any commands concerning either a burnt offering or a sacrifice. That's why he tells them that they may as well eat the whole lot themselves since He most certainly does not need the meal they offered Him. God says that He did not speak to their forefathers concerning these barbaric and sick rituals but He rather told them to walk "in all my ways." His "all ways" most certainly excluded "burnt offerings and sacrifices" and God clearly made a contrast here. The lying pen of the scribes however inserted a passage in Leviticus 7:37-38 where God is directly contradicted and where we are told that God actually gave commands and regulations concerning burnt offerings and all other sacrificial rituals. God allegedly gave these commands on Mount Sinai with all other laws and commands. But God categorically denies this in Jeremiah 7.

But the lying scribes did not only resort to lies in the days of Jeremiah, but they are also very much at work today. Gradually the NIV Bible, that is, the New International Version, has become the most popular and most widely used Bible among liberal Christians today. We can also clearly detect the lying pen of the scribes in the text of Jeremiah in this version. The scribes have opted to pull out of a hat only one little word which completely changes the context of the text. This "little lie" hides the truth and contributes to the deception of many people. The word is "just" so that the reading implies that God did not only speak concerning sacrifices and burnt offering but also about other things as well.

Here we find this little word which deceives the reader and prevents him to detect the problem or detect a contradiction between this passage and that of Leviticus 7:37-38. This word does not exist in the Hebrew text. It is lacking in virtually all English bibles. Chances are that you are usually reading the NIV Bible and therefore I urge you to discard this "lying word" which was inserted by the lying scribes who comprised the International Committee in order to bolster their belief and conviction that it was actually God Himself who prescribed and commanded the sacrificial cult.

We have seen the version of the World English Bible which is generally the same rendering of virtually all English bibles since they, like World English Bible, are based on the Hebrew Masoretic text which was compiled by the Jewish scribes called Masoretes in the 6th century of the Christian era. But there is another version which is to be found in the Eastern text or the Bible commonly called Peshitta. This version has preserved a different reading in the Aramaic and it is necessary to refer only to first two sentences since the rest of the passage is the same as that of the Masoretic Text. The text states that God told them to eat meat which He did not command their fathers to eat and that He did not give them commands concerning burnt offerings and sacrifices.

The Eastern text or the Peshitta Bible is believed by all adherents of the Eastern Christianity. The Patriarch of the East actually claims and maintains that their Peshitta Bible was directly handed to their ancestors by the very Apostles. You may not be aware but those who accept only this Peshitta version number into many, many millions. All Eastern Christians of the Near East, the Church of the East, the Roman Catholic Church in the East, the Monophysites, and the Indian Christians accept and acknowledge the canonicity and authenticity only of the Aramaic Peshitta Bible.

The Assyrian Church, or as it is known, the ancient Apostolic and Catholic Church of the East, was one of the major Christian churches in the world. Not until the 14th century was the church rivalled by any other church. It was the most powerful branch of Christendom in the Near East, Palestine, Arabia, Lebanon, Iran, India, and elsewhere. All these Christians use the Peshitta Bible and therefore their version of Jeremiah 7:21-26 clearly shows that God neither authorized the killing of animals for burnt offerings nor for eating of their flesh.

But this text of Jeremiah is also preserved in another form and version. The words are quoted by no lesser authority than Jesus himself. The words are ascribed to Jesus in the *Gospel of the Holy Twelve* which has been translated by Rev. Jasper Gideon Eusely in the late 1800's, and which may or may not be authentic. Here Jesus talks with the Pharisees about sacrifice and in order to condemn sacrifice and support his view he quotes the text of Jeremiah saying:

"Is it not written in the prophets, put your bloody sacrifice to your burnt offerings, and away with them, and cease ye from the eating of flesh, for I spake not to your fathers nor commanded them, when I brought them out of Egypt, concerning these things. But this thing I commanded saying: Obey my voice and walk in the ways that I have commanded you, and ye shall be my people, and it shall be well with you. But they harkened not nor inclined their ear."

Both Peshitta and this version speak dually – concerning sacrifice and meat eating. Neither of these two practices God actually commanded or endorsed when He led them out of Egypt. In the early centuries of the Christian era the epistle of Barnabas was accepted by virtually all Church Fathers and Christians of their time as genuine and authentic. It was only later that its authenticity was questioned and finally rejected and is now classified with other apocryphal books. In chapter 2 verses 4-10 Barnabas writes:

"For He hath revealed to us by all the prophets that He needs neither sacrifices, nor burnt-offerings, nor oblations, saying thus, What is the multitude of your sacrifices unto Me, saith the Lord? I am full of burnt-offerings, and desire not the fat of lambs, and the blood of bulls and goats, not when ye come to appear before Me: for who hath required these things at your hands?...And again He says to them, Did I command your fathers, when they went out of Egypt, to offer unto Me burnt-offerings and sacrifices? But this rather I commended them, Let no one of you cherish any evil in his heart against his neighbour, and love not an oath of falsehood" [The Epistle of Barnabas, The Ante-Nicene Fathers, Vol. I, WM. B. Eerdmans Publishing Company, Grand Rapids, Michigan].

Barnabas quotes this from the Old Testament of his day. Whoever wrote the epistle of Barnabas could not have invented this passage any more than I could invent a passage now that is not in our canonical bibles. The author would have been challenged by his opponents. It is therefore certain that latter part of this text was dropped later by the Masoretes in the 6th century and that's why it is now not found in the Masoretic Text or the bibles based on that text.

The passage of Barnabas supports the passage of Jeremiah and also shows that God did not speak about sacrifice nor did He give them permission or injunctions concerning the fellowship sacrifices from which they could eat meat. The text of Leviticus 7 therefore must be a forgery and insertion by the lying scribes and priests.

There is also another passage in the canonical Bible which clearly shows that God did not and could not have given any commands concerning the sacrificial cult. In Isaiah 43:22-24 God says according to the Greek Septuagint Bible the following:

"I did not now call you, O Jacob; neither have I wearied you O Israel. You did not bring me sheep for the burnt-offering; neither did you glorify Me with your sacrifices. I did not cause you to serve with sacrifices, nor did I weary you with frankincense. You did not purchase victims for Me with your silver, neither did I desire the fat of your sacrifices" [Author's translation].

These passages clearly contradict the passages inserted by the lying scribes and they plainly show that God never asked for nor did He ever give any commands concerning sacrifices and burnt offerings. We have seen from the passage of Isaiah 1:11-12 which Barnabas quoted from the Greek Septuagint Bible that God asked the Jews concerning sacrifices and burnt-offerings: "who has required these from your hands?" If God prescribed all the commands in the Jewish Pentateuch, then He could not have asked them this question since they could have answered: You did require them and commanded them. So many Christian commentators try to downplay this passage arguing that God did not reject sacrifices per se but rather He objected to sacrifices presented without respect and those which are not accompanied by faith and the corresponding holy life. But this is not true. If that is the case then God could not ask: "who has required these things [sacrifices and burnt-offerings] from your hands?" It certainly was not God. That God did not prescribe the sacrificial cult and that He never gave any commands concerning sin offerings and trespass offerings is clearly stated in Psalm 40:6-7:

"Sacrifice and offering you didn't desire. My ears have you opened: Burnt offering and sin offering have you not required" [World English Bible].

But the lying pen of the scribes has written many passages where God allegedly demands and prescribes sacrificial victims and their blood in order to atone for sins of the Israelites. In Psalm 51:16-19 the psalmist says to God in prayer:

"For you don't delight in sacrifice, or else I would give it. You have no pleasure in burnt offering. The sacrifices of God are a broken spirit. A broken and contrite heart, O God, you will not despise. Do well in your good pleasure to Zion. Build the walls of Jerusalem. Then will you delight in the sacrifices of righteousness, In burnt offerings and in whole burnt offerings. Then they will offer bulls on your altar" [World English Bible].

David did not write this psalm, despite of the statement in the introduction. This is evident from the fact that the author lived at the time when Jerusalem was destroyed by the Babylonians. He prayed for the walls of Jerusalem to be rebuilt. The author did not believe in the sacrificial cult. He, like the Essenes, only believed that incense should be offered as a symbol of prayer and a righteous life. The last verse seems to contradict the rest of the passage since we are told that if the walls of Jerusalem are rebuilt, then bulls will be offered on the altar. But offering bulls in sacrifice is not and cannot be "a sacrifice of righteousness" but rather of "iniquity."

Most English versions of the Bible incorrectly translate the Hebrew word "qatar" as "bulls." This word is number #6999 in Strong's Hebrew Dictionary and actually means "incense." Gesenius' Hebrew-Chaldee Lexicon to the Old Testament on p. 730, likewise states that the primary meaning of the word "qatar" is "incense." The Brown-Driver-Briggs Hebrew and English

Lexicon on p. 883, also defines the word "qatar" as "incense." The NAS Old Testament Hebrew Lexicon also defines the word "qatar" primarily as "incense." The word "qatar" was never translated "bulls" in any other passage but in this one. The Hebrew words "par, egel, baqar and showr" refer to bulls but not the word baqar.

Therefore, the author of this psalm plainly stated that the true God does not delight in sacrifice or burnt offerings of animals. If He did, then he would offer them. He believed that the true sacrifice was the contrite heart and a broken or meek spirit. He believed that if the walls of Jerusalem were rebuilt then they could offer the righteous sacrifice on the altar, namely "baqar," that is, "incense." Incense represented a righteous prayer of the saints [Revelation 8:4]. God does not need incense either but the opponents of blood sacrifice used incense, a sweet-smelling aroma, as a symbol of thanksgiving and righteousness. Just as water in baptism replaced blood in sacrifice for the remission of sin, so did the aroma of incense replace the aroma of a burnt offering.

Jesus himself pointed out on several occasions that God desires *mercy* and *not sacrifice*. The psalmist points out that God would not despise *prayer* as He despised *sacrifice*. In Isaiah 1 God clearly stated that He hates and despises burnt offerings and sacrifices and that He was disgusted with the fat and blood of slaughtered animals. It is very clear that the psalmist did not believe in a sacrificial system since he said that he would have offered sacrifices if God asked him to do it. But since God never asked for sacrifices, he therefore would not offer the same. In the Epistle of Barnabas 2:12 we read:

"A sacrifice pleasing to God is a broken spirit; a smell of pleasing aroma to God is a heart that glorifies Him that made it" [The Ante-Nicene Fathers, Vol. I].

Again, Barnabas quotes a passage from the Old Testament which was not preserved in the Hebrew Masoretic text and therefore most of the English bibles. In Psalm 50 God points out that He does not want burnt offerings which the Jews presented daily as His food. God categorically says that He does not eat flesh and that He does not drink blood but that He wants only spiritual sacrifices – praise and thanksgiving. The text is controversial even though the context clearly shows that most translators render it wrong. I guess they do so because they are influenced by the traditional concept that God was pleased with whole-burnt-offerings since it was presented to Him as a "pleasant aroma." I will quote the text as it stands in the King James Bible:

"Hear, O my people, and I will speak; O Israel, and I will testify against thee: I *am* God, *even* thy God. I will not reprove thee for thy sacrifices or thy burnt offerings, *to have been* continually before me. I will take no bullock out of thy house, *nor* he goats out of thy folds. For every beast of the forest *is* mine, *and* the cattle upon a thousand hills. I know all the fowls of the mountains: and the wild beasts of the field *are* mine. If I were hungry, I would not tell thee: for the world *is* mine, and the fullness thereof. Will I eat the flesh of bulls, or drink the blood of goats? Offer unto God thanksgiving; and pay thy vows unto the most High…Whoso offereth praise glorifieth me" [verses 7-14, 23].

The Hebrew text could be also rendered "Will I not reprove you?" If we apply the words "I will not reprove you" and if we should understand that God was pleased with all their burnt-offerings which they continually presented to Him, why then did He refuse to take them and why does He say that He does not eat flesh or drink blood? If God had no problem with their sacrificial cult, why then did He introduce the text by saying that He will speak to His people and *testify against them*? The context of the text necessitates the interrogative statement: "Will I not reprove you?" If this is however denied, then the only other possible way to understand the text is in a manner that some translators do, adding a clause "for the lack."

Either way the text shows that God condemned the sacrificial cult and that the only sacrifice He wants is actually the sacrifice of "thanksgiving" and "praise." God does not only say that He will not accept their slaughtered animals, but He also directly contradicts several lying insertions of the lying scribes where it is directly and plainly stated that God actually eats the flesh and drinks the blood of the victims offered as whole-burnt-offerings. In Leviticus 1:9, 13 and 17 we are told that the burnt offerings and the fat thereof are "sweet savour" [King James Bible] to God. The phrase "sweet savour" comes from the word number #5207 in Strong's Hebrew Dictionary and is defined: "pleasant," "delight." According to this text the *fat and blood were to be a delightful fragrance* to God.

In Exodus 29 we are told how often the *meal* for God was to be presented. Please note the following text:

"Now this is that which you shall offer upon the altar; two lambs of the first year day by day continually. The one lamb thou shalt offer in the morning; and the other lamb thou shalt offer at even: And with the one lamb a tenth deal of flour mingled with the fourth part of an hin of beaten oil; and the fourth part of an hin of wine for a drink offering. And the other lamb thou shalt offer at even, and shalt do thereto according to the meat [meal: see Center Reference] offering of the morning and according to the drink offering thereof, for a sweet savour, an offering made by fire unto the LORD. This shall be a continual burnt offering throughout your generations at the door of the tabernacle" [King James Bible, verses 38-42].

This morning and evening offering had nothing to do with expiation for sin. They were completely consumed on the altar. They were daily food or meal for God. The wine was to be His drink. In this meal God supposedly delighted. It was a sweet odour to His nostrils. In Leviticus 3 we find the following statement:

"...and he shall offer of the sacrifice of the peace offering an offering made by fire unto the LORD; the fat that covereth the inwards, and all the fat that is upon the inwards, and the two kidneys, and the fat that is on them, which is by the flanks...and Aaron's sons shall burn it on the altar upon the burnt sacrifice, which is upon the wood that is on the fire: it is an offering made by fire, of a sweet savour unto the LORD...and the priest shall burn it upon the altar: it is the food of the offering made by fire unto the LORD...all the fat is the LORD's. It shall be a perpetual statute for your generations throughout your dwellings, that ye eat neither fat nor blood" [King James Bible].

This text tells us that all the fat belonged to God. It was to be presented to Him as a *meal* which was to *"delight"* His appetite. The Israelites were forbidden to eat blood. This is because the blood of animals was offered as a *drink* to God along with wine libations. In Ezekiel 44:7 it is explicitly stated that God's *bread* [food] was *fat and blood*. The following verse is from the King James Bible:

"In that ye have brought into my sanctuary strangers, uncircumcised in heart, and uncircumcised in flesh, to be in my sanctuary, to pollute it, even my house, when ye offer MY BREAD, the FAT AND THE BLOOD."

Thus, it is evident from all these texts that burnt offerings were presented to God so that He may partake of a meal and nourish Himself. Its smell was to *delight* Him. The true Prophets who protested against the sacrificial cult most definitely did not recognize Leviticus 1-7. They most definitely did not believe that fat and blood were to be presented to God as His food, bread, or meal. Neither did they recognize the priests who believed they offered daily bread [food, meal] to God. That priests offered bread to God can be verified from the following text:

"They [priests] shall be holy unto their God, and not profane the name of their God: for the offerings of the LORD made by fire, and the *bread of their God*, they do offer: therefore they shall be holy…No man that hath a blemish of the seed of Aaron the priest shall come nigh to offer the offerings of the LORD made by fire: he hath a blemish; he shall not come nigh to offer the *bread of his God*. He shall eat the *bread of his God*, both of the most holy and, the holy" [Leviticus 21:6, 21-22 King James Bible].

No priest with any blemish was allowed to present a meal offering to God. He however, was allowed to join God in His meal and eat the "bread of his God." In Isaiah 1:11 God explicitly states that fat of the sacrifice does not please Him. He claims that He *does not delight* in it. But the deceived Jews believed that the fat and blood was the *sweet odour* to His nostrils. In Isaiah 43:23 [Greek Septuagint] God says that He did not desire the fat of their sacrifices. God does not depend on food and drink. He is transcendent, self-sufficient. Can't you realize that the self-sufficient and immortal being cannot possibly depend on food for nourishment? If God was dependent on fat and blood of the animals then He would have starved to death when they were not presented to Him. How can God who is *immortal* depend on *mortal* food? For whatever is sustained by causes and things external to itself, must be mortal and on the way to decay, when anything on which it lives begins to be wanting.

How can God who is far transcendent from us and who lives in unapproachable light, whose face no mortal can see, who has no physical body that can be touched, whose very angels are "flame of fire," be possibly nourished on things pertaining to the body, that that which is mortal should support that which is immortal? The deceived Jews completely failed to understand God's character. They refused to worship Him on His terms but rather chose to worship Him in the exact manner the pagans worshipped their gods and goddesses.

You may agree that God did not actually consume the fat, blood, grain, oil and whatever else was offered to Him. You may believe that He only enjoyed the pleasing aroma of the sacrifice. You may think that burnt offerings and incense were presented to Him in order to give Him some pleasure and delight. Whoever wrote the text of Genesis 8:20-22 must have believed that the aroma from the sacrificed victims Noah supposedly sacrificed delighted the nostrils of God so much that He actually regretted the act of destroying the Earth with its life. Can you really think that God who knows the end from the beginning, who is absolutely perfect Being can be actually a subject to temporal pleasure and sensual enjoyment?

Can He really be soothed and made gentle by a scent which is soon passing away? For if God can be overcome by pleasure and delight then He also must be subject to its opposite, sorrow, pain and grief. God however should be free from passions and weakness of the mortals if we believe that He is everlasting and immortal. Moreover, every kind of pleasure is in a way a flattery to the mortal body and is related to the well-known five senses. But if God above feels the five senses, He then also must have a physical body which relates to them. If God can appreciate the sweet fragrance arising in smoke towards heaven, then He should also be annoyed by the stench arising from the Earth. Just what pleasure and delight could God possibly get from burnt offerings?

Does He delight to see an innocent creature slaughtered and bled to death? Does His ear take pleasure in continually hearing their cries and moans? Does He delight in seeing the rivers of blood? Does He delight in seeing stomachs cut open, blood and excrement gushing out? Does He delight to see the heart of a dead animal still pounding with the life left in it and the trembling, palpitating veins in the viscera? Even we humans are moved with sympathy and grief when we witness the slaughter of innocent animals. The children cry and resist their slaughter.

Try to spend a day in the modern slaughterhouse where thousands of innocent animals are slaughtered, butchered and cut to pieces. I wonder if the smell of all the bloody mess would really delight your appetite. Since we who are evil do not delight in the butchery of animals but kill them and eat their flesh only because we are slaves to our savage lusts, how then can we even think that God Who is the source of love, kindness, tenderness and compassion could possibly delight and take pleasure in burnt offerings or other kinds of sacrifice? Since God Himself insisted that sacrifices and burnt offerings did not please and delight Him, why then continue to believe that He actually instituted these pagan, barbaric rites?

But someone will say that the burnt offerings were presented to God in order to calm His wrath and to appease Him. But why should God change His mind and angry state just because someone kills a bull, lamb, goat or pair of doves? What "magic" is there in their fat, blood or smell to cause Him to forget the wrong and evil one has done against Him? Was this sacrifice to be some kind of a bribe? Does God need "toys" like a little child in order to cool His fits of rage? Those who believed so and actually presented burnt offerings in order to *appease* God were grossly deceived and totally failed to understand the perfect nature, justice and ethics of God.

In Numbers 28:2 God allegedly said:

"Command the children of Israel, and tell them, My offering, my food for my offerings made by fire, of a sweet savor to me, shall you observe to offer to me in their due season" [World English Bible].

In verse 6 it is alleged that this system was commanded by God on Mount Sinai:

"*It is* a continual burnt offering, which was ordained in mount Sinai for a sweet savour, a sacrifice made by fire unto the LORD"[King James Bible].

In these two chapters [28 and 29] we find a detailed description of sacrifices and drink offerings which were to be presented on Sabbaths and annual Sabbaths – New Moons, Passover, Unleavened Bread Festival, Pentecost, Feast of Trumpets, Day of Atonement and Feast of Tabernacles. After listing all these additional sacrificial victims God allegedly stated:

"These you shall offer to Yahweh in your set feasts, besides your vows, and your freewill-offerings, for your burnt offerings, and for your meal-offerings, and for your drink-offerings, and for your peace-offerings" [Numbers 29:39 World English Bible].

The lying pen of the scribes has introduced and sanctioned a system that was identical to that of the pagan nations. God however, clearly stated that He never spoke to them on Mount Sinai after He led them out of Egypt concerning burnt-offerings and sacrifices and He categorically states that He never caused them to worship Him with burnt-offerings and sacrifices. Prophet Micah was a good and a righteous man. If God really and truly commanded that His "bread" be offered to Him as a "pleasing aroma" then most certainly he would have done so. However, Micah clearly says that He would not offer any burnt-offering to God since that is not what God wants and that is not what He asked His people to do. In Micah 6:6-8 the righteous prophet says:

"Wherewith shall I come before the LORD, *and* bow myself before the high God? shall I come before him with burnt offerings, with calves of a year old? Will the LORD be pleased with thousands of rams, *or* with ten thousands of rivers of oil? shall I give my firstborn *for* my transgression, the fruit of my body *for* the sin of my soul? He hath shewed thee, O man, what *is* good; and what doth the LORD require of thee, but to do justly, and to love mercy, and to walk humbly with thy God?" [King James Bible].

Micah asked a good and valid question. He asked how and with what should he appear before God in order that his worship would be pleasing and acceptable to Him. If God really and truly commanded the Israelites to honor Him with whole-burnt-offerings and various sacrificial gifts and to please and delight Him with all the "fat and blood" of calves and rams, then Micah would have done so. If Micah came before God with calves and rams and the pleasant aroma of their fat, at least then the Christian commentators could not say that the burnt-offerings were presented by a sinful person without respect and a corresponding holy life. But Micah knew better.

He, just like all holy and righteous prophets, knew that the sick and disgusting sacrificial cult was never instituted by God and that is why he says that he would never kill and burn neither humans in sacrifice nor an animal victim. Micah clearly points out that God had plainly shown to humanity what He wants and in what He delights. What God wants us to do is diametrically opposed to the pagan and barbaric sacrificial rituals where innocent creatures of God are cruelly immolated. But there was another hand that wrote a psalm and obviously the person whose hand wrote this psalm did not agree with Micah. This person delighted in and was very proud to worship God with burnt-offerings and to delight Him with "fat animals" and the "incense of rams." Please note Psalm 66:13-15:

"I will come into your temple with burnt offerings. I will pay my vows to you, which my lips promised, And my mouth spoke, when I was in distress. I will offer to you burnt offerings of fat animals, With the offering of rams, I will offer bulls with goats" [World English Bible].

This person relied on the lying passages of the Jewish Pentateuch and this person believed that the temple in Jerusalem was God's House where He actually lived in the darkest room called "Holy of Holies." But Micah did not believe in this and he would not offer any burnt-offerings to God. He knew that those who slaughtered animals and presented "fat animals" did so "unlawfully" and in fact transgressed God's Law by murdering innocent and beautiful creatures of God. In Proverbs 21:27 we find this statement:

"The sacrifice of the wicked *is* an abomination to the LORD: but the prayer of the upright *is* his delight" [King James Bible].

The Greek Septuagint Bible states that the sacrifice was an abomination to God because it was unlawful to present them. How could they have been unlawful if God commanded them in the Pentateuch? The author clearly understood that those who offer sacrifices are stained with blood and guilt and through that act become sinful and ungodly. God very much hated the violence and the immolation of His creatures and that is why He abhors the burnt-offering. In Proverbs 15:8 we are told that to God "sacrifice" is an abomination while the prayer is His delight. We are told that those who offer sacrifices are "wicked" while those who offer their prayers in sacrifice are "just:"

In Ecclesiastes 5:1 we read:

"Keep thy foot when thou goest to the house of God, and be more ready to hear, than to give the sacrifice of fools: for they consider not that they do evil" [King James Bible].

Fools offered sacrifices because they did not know that in doing so they were doing evil. Many Bible translators render the text in this way. A righteous and a wise man knows that he goes to the temple to learn and give God a sacrifice of praise and thanksgiving. Micah was such a wise man and therefore he would not offer any sacrificial victim. The fools however, go to the temple to present burnt-offerings – fat and blood – and in doing so they do not realize that they are doing a wicked and an abominable thing. The author of Psalm 66 was one of such fools who was proud to present "fat animals" and the "sweet aroma of rams."

In Isaiah 66:2-3 God categorically states that any Israelite who resorts to the worship of sacrifice with the so-called "clean" animals is no better in His sight than the pagans who resorted to human sacrifice and the sacrifice of animals that the Jews regarded as unclean and abominable. To God, a Jew or an Israelite who sacrificed a "bull" was as guilty as a pagan who sacrificed a "human." Please read very carefully and prayerfully this very powerful passage:

"...but to this man wil I looke, euen to him that is poore and of a contrite spirit, and trembleth at my word. He that killeth an oxe is as if he slew a man: he that sacrificeth a lambe, as if he cut off a dogs necke...yea, they haue chosen their owne wayes, and their soule delighteth in their abominations" [King James Bible as was written in archaic English of 1611].

Paraphrased in modern English it should read:

But I respect the man who is of poor and humble spirit and who honours My word. But he who sacrifices an ox is as he who sacrifices a human being. He who sacrifices a lamb, as he who cuts the head of a dog... yes, they have chosen their own ways and their souls delight in their abominations.

God esteems or is pleased with those who are humble and of a contrite spirit but He is appalled with those who sacrifice bulls or lambs. To him they are as guilty as those who sacrifice humans and dogs. God clearly shows that the sacrificial cult was of their "own way" and therefore most certainly an abomination to Him. God was most definitely displeased and in fact appalled with the sacrificial cult of the Israelites and all other pagans for that matter. God emphatically states that Israel's statutes which they have devised are "strange" that is, something "forbidden" and He says that those who sacrifice animals and eat of its flesh He will just not accept. Please note Hosea 8:11-13:

"The multiplied altars of Ephraim are his beloved, but they have made him sinful. I will write many commands for him since his statutes are forbidden, even his beloved altars. For if they will offer a sacrifice and eat flesh, the Lord will not accept them" [Author's translation based on Greek Septuagint].

How much clearer and emphatic does God need to be before you could actually believe Him? Just one more thing I wish to say in this chapter concerning sacrifices. It will show that the lying pen of the scribes was indeed at work. In 1 Kings 8:5 we are told that when the temple was completed and the Ark of the Covenant was placed in the Holy of Holies, Solomon sacrificed "so many sheep and cattle that they could not be recorded or counted."

But apparently the author of 2 Chronicles 7:5, 8 was both able to count them and record them. He says that Solomon sacrificed 22,000 cattle and 120,000 sheep and goats – during the space of seven days. In verse 7 we are told that the altar itself was insufficient for this occasion so Solomon dedicated the middle part of the front court for the purpose of burning the holocausts. The animals had to be killed, their blood poured at the altar, their carcases skinned, the flesh washed, and then the bodies burned on the altar. Twelve sheep and goats and two bulls would have to be killed and prepared and also completely consumed by fire every minute for 24 hours a day and for seven days straight. An impossible task indeed. Considering that today it takes 2-3 hours to cremate a human body in extremely high temperatures, how much longer it would have taken to fully burn and consume all those thousands of animals?

I have stated earlier that animal sacrifice and the eating of meat are intertwined and that one without the other was not possible. Therefore, it is now necessary to refer to certain passages of the true prophets and those who knew the truth. These passages clearly show that all the true prophets were vegetarian and that they strongly condemned those who killed animals in order to eat their flesh. In Amos 6:4-7 we find evidence that God did not approve of those who killed animals in order to eat their flesh nor did He approve of those who drank wine and those who slept on beds of ivory. God said that they would be the first to be exiled to Babylonia.

God condemned those who sleep on beds of ivory. In order to enjoy this luxury, one must slaughter many elephants. There were many wicked people in the days of Amos. But God especially despised those who killed animals in order to gratify their craving for flesh. They were more guilty than even the harlots. Jesus himself stated that tax collectors and harlots would enter the Kingdom of God before the religious leaders of his day [Matthew 21:31]. The harlots and the tax collectors did not kill, but the priests and the Pharisees daily immolated God's innocent animals and in doing so have turned the

House of Prayer into a graveyard of murderers. The slaughterhouse is more abhorrent than a brothel.

God could not stand the "winebibers" and the "gluttonous eaters of flesh." The author of Proverbs 23:20 was aware of this fact. That is why he gave this advice to those who would read his sayings:

"Be not among winebibbers; among riotous eaters of flesh" [King James Bible].

'Don't make wine your habitual drink, neither feast long at feasts, or purchase of flesh' [Author's translation based on Greek Septuagint].

A "wine-bibber" means "a habitual drinker of alcohol." The ancient Nasaraeans of Gilead and Bashan, the Essenes and the Ebionites regarded any feast where wine and flesh were served as revelry. For them anyone who ate animal flesh was a glutton. Jesus himself warned his disciples against meat eating and wine. Only this is not easy to detect in the canonical Gospel of Luke. The oldest version of this text known as Evangelion Da-Mepharreshe, written in old Syriac or Aramaic gives a different version:

"Be on guard lest your hearts become heavy from eating meat and from drinking intoxicating wine" 21:34 Author's translation].

In Ezekiel 34 we find a parable which God spoke. From this parable we can clearly see that God cares for the sheep and is displeased when they are mistreated. Although the sheep represent the Israelites and the shepherds their leaders, the literal application must also be valid. Otherwise, no logical comparison could be made. God says to the shepherds:

"Son of man, prophesy against the shepherds of Israel, prophesy, and say unto them, Thus saith the Lord GOD unto the shepherds; Woe be to the shepherds of Israel that do feed themselves! should not the shepherds feed the flocks? Ye eat the fat, and ye clothe you with the wool, ye kill them that are fed: but ye feed not the flock. Behold, I am against the shepherds; and I will require my flock at their hand, and cause them to cease from feeding the flock; neither shall the shepherds feed themselves any more; for I will deliver my flock from their mouth, that they may not be meat for them" [King James Bible].

And please also note Zechariah 11:4-6:

"The Lord Almighty says: feed the sheep which are destined for slaughter; whom their possessors have slaughtered AND HAVE NOT REPENTED: they sold them saying, blessed be the Lord; for we have become wealthy. Their shepherds did not feel sorry for them" [Author's translation].

The Good News Bible says that although they slaughtered the sheep, they "go unpunished."

God condemns both sellers and buyers who think they could slaughter His innocent creatures and get away with it. God in the beginning forbade anyone to kill for food. All creatures were created to be strictly herbivorous beings. At the end of time, when God's eternal kingdom will be established, all creatures will again be forced to revert to herbivorous diet. No living soul will be permitted to consume another living soul. Therefore, you better learn to live on a vegetarian diet while still in the flesh, for to do so later might be too late. Isaiah 11:6-9 gives us a vivid picture of the wonderful vegetarian world of the future:

"The wolf also shall dwell with the lamb, and the leopard shall lie down with the kid; and the calf and the young lion and the fatling together; and a little child shall lead them. And the cow and the bear shall feed; their young ones shall lie down together: and the lion shall eat straw like the ox. And the sucking child shall play on the hole of the asp, and the weaned child shall put his hand on the cockatrice' den. They shall not hurt nor destroy in all my holy mountain: for the earth shall be full of the knowledge of the LORD, as the waters cover the sea" [King James Bible].

The only reason why no one will harm and kill any living soul at that time is because everyone then will realize just what kind of God is the true God and the father of Jesus. Then all will know the good and compassionate nature of God. The reason why many kill today and consume the flesh of innocent animals is because they don't know God, nor His true Holy Law, due to the fact that they have put their trust in the "lying pen of the scribes."

Another major reason why so many Christians believe that it's perfectly all right to butcher innocent animals for food is due to the fact that they rely on the teachings of Paul and his writings – not realizing that the earliest and true believers did not accept Paul as the legitimate Apostle. Remember that Jesus did not promise us barbecued meat and Mc Donalds in the Kingdom of God, but rather manna and the fruit from the Tree of Life. No carnivorous diet in the celestial realm.

# CHAPTER 10
# Sacrifice in The Desert

The Mosaic Law is replete with injunctions, ordinances and commands which were to regulate the sacrificial system. These commands and laws concerning the bloody sacrificial cult were supposedly given by God to Moses on Mount Sinai. I am a vegan and I maintain that God never gave these commands and that these laws were later interpolated and written by the lying scribes. The Church on the other hand maintains that every word in the Mosaic Law is inspired and was actually commanded by God and written down by His servant Moses. Therefore, in this chapter I intend to give irrefutable evidence and absolute proof that these passages in the Mosaic Law were not originally spoken by God nor were they a part of the original writings of Moses. They are later forgeries and false pericopes by the lying scribes.

In order to prove my point and demonstrate beyond refute that the sacrificial cult was no part of the Book of the Law Moses wrote, it is necessary to demonstrate to the reader certain facts which will prove that the priests did not and could not have dealt with all those injunctions and ordinances which were to regulate the sacrificial cult in the desert. Let us begin with the text of Leviticus 17. Here we are told that every sacrifice which the Israelites offered to God had to be brought to the altar which was situated at the entrance of the Tabernacle. The priests alone were allowed to officiate at the altar. They were to slaughter the victim and sprinkle the blood against the altar. Then they were to burn the fat for a "pleasing aroma to the LORD."

In Leviticus 4:11-12 we are told that whenever a sin offering was made by the priest, which was a daily and constant service "the skin of the bullock, and all his flesh,...even the whole bullock shall he [the priest] carry forth without the camp unto a clean place, where the ashes are poured out, and burn him on the wood of fire" [Leviticus 4:11-12]. The Tabernacle or the Tent of Meeting was situated in the midst of the camp.

The bullock was to be slaughtered on the altar which was situated at the entrance of the Tabernacle and then it was to be carried by a priest to a place outside of the camp. In order to visualize this incredible scenario and the impossibility of this, it is necessary to demonstrate to the reader just how large the camping ground was and how far the bullock had to be carried. Please carefully read all evidence presented, since this will prove beyond refute that the commands in the Mosaic Law concerning sacrifices and offerings were not and could not have been given by God, nor were they performed in the desert.

### How Large Was the Community?

The Jewish Pentateuch says that at the time of exodus from Egypt there were 603,550 men alone. Please note Exodus 12:37:

"The children of Israel journeyed from Rameses to Succoth, about six hundred thousand on foot who were men, besides children" [World English Bible].

This number is also confirmed in Numbers 11:21. The census taken in the wilderness, in the $2^{nd}$ year from the date of exodus, confirms that there were actually 603,550 male soldiers who were 20 years and over. Numbers 1:45-47 says:

"So all those who were numbered of the children of Israel by their fathers' houses, from twenty years old and upward, all who were able to go out to war in Israel; even all those who were numbered were six hundred three thousand five hundred fifty. But the Levites after the tribe of their fathers were not numbered among them" [World English Bible].

That this figure is correct can be verified by the text of Exodus 38:25-26:

"The silver of those who were numbered of the congregation was one hundred talents, and one thousand seven hundred seventy-five shekels, after the shekel of the sanctuary: a beka a head, that is, half a shekel, after the shekel of the sanctuary, for everyone who passed over to those who were numbered, from twenty years old and upward, for six hundred three thousand five hundred fifty men" [World English Bible].

There were 3000 shekels to a talent. Therefore 100 talents and 1,775 shekels comes to exactly 603,550 half shekels:

3,000 x 100 = 600,000 half shekels

1,775 shekels = 3,550 half shekels

600,000 + 3,550 = 603,550.

When 22,000 Levites who were later counted, and all the women and children are included, as well as all those males who were outside of conscription age – the Israelites must have numbered about three million in all. This is quite a conservative figure and is readily confirmed by most Bible commentators as well as the *Jewish Encyclopedia*. In addition to this figure, Exodus 12:38 says that there was also a multitude of strangers who went out with the Israelites and a large number of herds and flocks:

"A mixed multitude went up also with them, with flocks, herds, and even very much cattle" [World English Bible].

It would be a waste of time to speculate just how many strangers there were with them. All we can say with certainty is that there were many or a multitude – as the Hebrew word implies. But we can get a fairly good idea of how many sheep and goats there were with them. Exodus 12 says that the Israelites observed the Passover in the land of Goshen. For their meal they were commanded to use either a lamb or goat [the same Hebrew word is used for both kinds of animals].

The lamb was to be of the 1st year. Allowing liberally ten persons in a family per lamb, the Israelites would have required 300,000 lambs of the 1st year in order to observe their first Passover in Egypt. They would have also required this number of lambs each succeeding year in the wilderness – since the Jewish Pentateuch says that they kept on observing the Passover in the desert.

In addition, they would have needed myriads of other animals for all their multiple sacrifices prescribed in the book of Leviticus. For there to be some 300,000 lambs of the 1st year, a flock of about 3,000,000 to 4,000,000 sheep and goats were required. In addition to this the Exodus text says that many bovine animals went out with them. We have no way of determining the size of this herd except that it was very large.

**The Camping Ground**

Did it ever occur to you just how big a space did the Israelites need every time they wanted to set up their camp? The Jewish Pentateuch clearly shows that the Israelites lived in tents and that they erected and dismantled them every time they stopped to lodge. In order to accommodate only for the Israelites, you would need some 300,000 tents. Each tent would have to be 5x5 metres, and would occupy an area of 25m$^2$ – packing ten persons in each tent.

Thus, 300,000 tents would cover an area of 7,500,000m$^2$. But I have not allowed a single square metre for walking tracks – the area covered takes into account only 300,000 tents pitched one next to another. Some space was also required to accommodate the Tabernacle or the Tent of Meeting with an area for the congregation to gather in front of the Tabernacle. In order to accommodate all the Israelites and the Tabernacle with some walking tracks an area of some 10,000km$^2$ would be required. But you also must provide an area for the multitude of strangers who were with the Israelites. You also must provide an area for some 3,000,000 to 4,000,000 flocks. If you were to pack two sheep in a square metre, you would need 1,500,000m$^2$ to accommodate 3,000,000 sheep.

That is an area of 1500km$^2$. Add to this the multitude of cattle and you will see just how large the camp was. Remember, the altar was situated at the entrance of the Tent of Meeting and the Sanctuary was situated in the midst of the camp. The three tribes were commanded to camp on each side of the Tabernacle [Numbers 2]. The priest therefore would have had to drag the bullock kilometres away from the altar in order to burn it outside the camp. There were myriads of other sacrifices the priests had to perform as described in Exodus 29 and the first 7 chapters of Leviticus. Likewise, every woman who gave birth was required to present a lamb for a burnt offering and a pigeon for a sin offering at the end of her purification period. The Jewish Pentateuch says that all those who were 20 and over died in the wilderness except Joshua and Caleb.

But since the census in the 40$^{th}$ year shows that the number was basically the same as in the 2$^{nd}$ year – you can imagine how many births there must have been and how many sacrifices the priests would have offered for each woman at the end of her purification period. It is estimated that at least two million died in the desert and therefore there must have been additional two million births to compensate for the loss. These births distributed over the period of 40 years would have resulted in some 300 births per day. The priests would have therefore been required to offer some 300 sacrifices each day for the women who needed their purification rites performed.

This was in addition to all other sin offerings, free will offerings, fellowship offerings, and the daily sacrifices presented each morning and evening. In addition, the priests had to burn incense and clean the Holy Place, eat the flesh of the holy offerings in the Holy Place, prepare shewbread and replace it every seventh day. They also had to make special perfumes and myriads of oblations – bread and cakes which accompanied many sacrifices. Just think for a moment. If it took one priest to kill, clean, wash, burn, and sprinkle the blood against the altar just 15 minutes, he could only perform 48 such sacrifices in the space of 12 hours. To accomplish this task in this space of time he could not take even a moment off. But imagine if the priest had to stop his job in order to go to the toilet. He would have to walk kilometres to relieve himself, for it was commanded that no toilet could be situated within the borders of the camp.

The Israelites had to relieve themselves outside of the camp [Deuteronomy 23:12]. Therefore, it follows that even if there were many priests, they could never manage to present all the myriads of sacrifices already described. But the crux of the matter is this: the Jewish Pentateuch clearly says that there were only 5 priests in the desert – Aaron and his four sons, Nadab, Abihu, Eleazar, and Ithamar. Shortly after their ordination, Nadab and Abihu were killed. The whole Israelite community was thus left with only two capable priests and their aged father Aaron who was over 80 years old. Many misinformed people assume that all Levites were priests and that they all had a legitimate right to serve at the altar and present burnt offerings and other Jewish ritual sacrifices. This however was not the case. Most Bible scholars are aware of this fact and they are also aware that no Levite was allowed to serve at the altar or ever enter the Holy Place unless he belonged to the lineage of Aaron, the brother of Moses. The priestly duties were entrusted to Aaron and his four sons: Nadab, Abihu, Eleazar and Ithamar. Initially only these five were allowed to burn incense in the Holy Place and to offer sacrifices and burnt offerings at the sacrificial altar which was situated at the entrance of the Tabernacle.

After the death of Abihu and Nadab – only Aaron and his two sons Eleazar and Ithamar were allowed access to the altar and the Holy Place. All other Levites were banned from the Holy Place and were forbidden to approach the altar. In fact, all Levites who were not of the lineage of Aaron were forbidden to even look at any holy object which was situated in the Tabernacle. All the descendants of Levi – whether through Gershon, Kohath, or Merari were banned from the Tabernacle and could carry the sacred objects of the Tabernacle only after they were covered by the sons of Aaron who alone acted as priests. Furthermore, all the other Levites could carry out their duties only under a supervision of the sons of Aaron. It is therefore evident that there were only two active priests and their aged father officiating in the desert. Where would these three Aaronic priests – the only ones permitted to officiate at the altar and the Holy Place – find the time to take care of all the myriads of sacrifices described in the Jewish Pentateuch? Where would they find the time to carry the skins of the bullocks outside the camp and to relieve themselves on daily basis – since the camp was so large? Where would they find the time to eat all the "holy offerings" in the "Holy Place" and how could the three men eat so much flesh?

On a certain occasion Aaron and his sons did not eat the holy flesh of a goat – and Moses was supposedly furious with them. Anyone with an unbiased mind would immediately realize that no such sacrifices could have taken place in the desert and in the camp of that enormous size and under the circumstances and conditions described in the Jewish Pentateuch. It is no wonder that God denies in Jeremiah 7:22 that He ever instituted or commanded such sacrifices after the Israelites left Egypt. No wonder Stephen stated that the Israelites did not offer sacrifices to the true God in the desert. [Acts 7:42-43].

# CHAPTER 11
# Quails in the Desert

Exactly one month after their departure from Egypt, the Israelites came to the wilderness of Sin. There they murmured and complained to Moses that they were starving to death:

"We wish that we had died by the hand of Yahweh in the land of Egypt, when we sat by the flesh-pots, when we ate our fill of bread, for you have brought us out into this wilderness, to kill this whole assembly with hunger" [Exodus 16:3 World English Bible].

Miracle of miracles! The whole community was starving to death even though elsewhere we are told that at that time they had with them millions of sheep and cattle. The Bible unequivocally states that when the Israelites lived in Egypt, they possessed livestock. When all the livestock of the Egyptians perished not even a single animal perished that belonged to the Israelites [Exodus 9:4-6]. When Pharaoh asked Moses, who was to go to the desert he replied:

"We will go with our young and our old; with our sons and our daughters, with our flocks and our herds, we will go, for we must hold a feast to Yahweh" [Exodus 10:9 World English Bible].

Pharaoh rejected Moses' proposition. He told Moses to take only adult males. Later however Pharaoh agreed to let all the people go but not the flocks and herds:

"Then Pharaoh called to Moses and said, Go, serve Yahweh; only let your flocks and your herds be kept back. Let your little ones also go with you. But Moses said…our livestock also shall go with us; not a hoof shall be left behind" [Exodus 10:24-26 World English Bible].

When Pharaoh finally agreed to let them go, he said:

"Up, depart from among my people, you and the Israelites with you! Go, worship Yahweh as you said! Take also your flocks and your herds, as you said, and begone!" [Exodus 12:31 World English Bible].

Verse 38 states:

"Moreover, a mixed multitude went up with them, and very much livestock, both flocks and herds" [World English Bible].

But how much is "very much?" In the previous chapter I have demonstrated that they would have had some three to four million sheep and goats. In addition, they had a large herd of bovine animals. The Israelites left Egypt on the 15$^{th}$ of the first month which was called Abib [Numbers 33:3]. Exactly a month later they arrived at the Wilderness of Sin. At this point of time they were starving to death. What about all the milk and cheese they could have had? Be it as it may, Yahweh promised to give them quails in the evenings and manna in the mornings [Exodus 16:8]. Verse 35 states that they ate manna throughout the forty years they were wandering through the desert until they reached the land of Canaan. About a year after this scenario the Israelites arrived at the wilderness of Paran [Numbers 10:11-12]. In chapter 11 we are told how the Israelites again complained to Moses saying:

"Who will give us flesh to eat? We remember the fish which we ate freely in Egypt, the cucumbers, the melons, the leeks, the onions, and the garlic; but now our whole being is dried up; there is nothing at all except this manna before our eyes!" [Numbers 11:4-6 World English Bible].

One wonders why on earth would the Israelites wail and crave flesh when only about a month earlier they ate the Passover lambs. The Israelites had large number of flocks and herds. They slaughtered the Passover lambs each year while they wandered through the desert. They were given quails in the evenings. In Deuteronomy 32:13-18 we are told how the Israelites were so well fed that they grew fat and rebelled:

"He made him ride on the high places of the earth, He ate the increase of the field; He made him to suck honey out of the rock, Oil out of the flinty rock; Butter of the herd, and milk of the flock, With fat of lambs, Rams of the breed of Bashan, and goats, With the finest of the wheat; Of the blood of the grape you drank wine. But Jeshurun grew fat, and kicked: You have grown fat, you are grown thick, you are become sleek; Then he forsook God who made him, Lightly esteemed the Rock of his salvation. They moved him to jealousy with strange [gods]; With abominations provoked they him to anger. They sacrificed to demons, [which were] no God, To gods that they didn't know, To new [gods] that came up of late, Which your fathers didn't dread. Of the Rock that became your father, you are unmindful, Have forgotten God who gave you birth" [World English Bible].

A vivid picture of plenty and abundance. The Israelites gorged themselves on flesh and also sacrificed animals to demons. In Leviticus 17:1-9 we find this pertinent information:

"Yahweh spoke to Moses, saying, Speak to Aaron, and to his sons, and to all the children of Israel, and tell them: This is the thing which Yahweh has commanded, saying, Whatever man here be of the house of Israel, who kills an ox, or lamb, or goat, in the camp, or who kills it outside of the camp, and hasn't brought it to the door of the tent of meeting, to offer it as an offering to Yahweh before the tent of Yahweh: blood shall be imputed to that man; he has shed blood; and that man shall be cut off from among his people: To the end that the children of Israel may bring their sacrifices, which they sacrifice in the open field, even that they may bring them to Yahweh, to the door of the tent of meeting, to the priest, and sacrifice them for sacrifices of peace-offerings to Yahweh. The priest shall sprinkle the blood on the altar of Yahweh at the door of the tent of meeting, and burn the fat for a sweet savor to Yahweh. They shall no more sacrifice their sacrifices to the male goats, after which they play the prostitute. This shall be a statute forever to them throughout their generations. You shall tell them, Whatever man there be of the house of Israel, or of the strangers who sojourn among them, who offers a burnt offering or sacrifice, and doesn't bring it to the door of the tent of meeting, to sacrifice it to Yahweh; that man shall be cut off from his people" [World English Bible].

The two texts agree. The Israelites had plenty of flesh to eat. They made their sacrifices in the open to the demons. They were commanded to present their sacrifices to Yahweh at the altar which was situated at the entrance of the Tabernacle. They were also to give choice portions of their flesh offerings to the priests who officiated on their behalf. Only a month or so before the Israelites wailed and craved flesh, they observed the Passover in the Wilderness of Sinai [Numbers 9]. They craved for flesh in Kibroth Hattavah – which was 12$^{th}$ camping site [Numbers 33:16]. The episode described in Numbers 11 occurred before the spies were sent to spy the land of Canaan [Numbers 13:3; Deuteronomy 9:22-23; Numbers 33:16-18; Numbers 10:11-12]. Thirty-nine years later Moses died.

Various Pentateuch sources reveal that Moses offered sacrifices when he came down from Mount Sinai and made the covenant between Yahweh and the Israelites. They also offered sacrifices on various occasions. On the first day of the first month in the second year from exodus – that is, just a little less than a year from the departure from Egypt, the Tabernacle was erected and the regular sacrificial cult began [Exodus 40:17; Leviticus 1-6]. There are different sources in the Jewish Pentateuch. Obviously, the scribe who wrote the story of quails in Numbers 11 was unaware of the source which clearly states that Yahweh provided the Israelites with manna every morning and quails every evening. Neither was this scribe aware that according to the other source the Israelites had millions of herds and flocks with them. If this scribe was aware of this, he could not have said that the Israelites murmured against Moses because they had no flesh but only manna. But this scribe was also unaware of his lies and just how incredible his lies were.

We are told that the quails lay around the camp on all four sides a day's journey and were two cubits high. In Numbers 1 and 2 we are given the figures of the warriors of each tribe and the layout of the camp. The Tabernacle was situated in the midst of the camp. To these numbers you need to add approximately two and a half million Israelites plus the multitudes of strangers that were with them. In addition, they needed space for millions of flocks and herds. Then you can imagine how large the camping site was and how many quails there were scattered around the camp. In 11:31-32 we read:

"And there went forth a wind from the LORD, and brought quails from the sea, and let them fall by the camp, as it were a day's journey on this side, and as it were a day's journey on the other side, round about the camp, and as it were two cubits high upon the face of the earth. And the people stood up all that day, and all that night, and all the next day, and they gathered the quails: he that gathered least gathered ten homers: and they spread them all abroad for themselves round about the camp" [King James Bible].

In the footnote of the New International Version we are told that "ten homers" equates to 1.75 tons. The Good News Bible says that the one who gathered least actually gathered "fifty bushels." Bushel is an American measure which equals 35 litres. Fifty bushels thus give 1750 litres or kilograms or 1.75 tons. Since we are told that there were about three million Israelites in all, plus many strangers with them, plus millions of flocks and herds, the camping ground for that multitude had to be of enormous size. To accommodate three million people, they needed 300,000 tents. Each tent had to be 5x5 metres and ten persons had to be accommodated in each tent. This would have required 7,500,000m². There is no provision for walking passages or the Tent of Meeting with its quarters for the congregation gatherings, nor any space whatsoever for the strangers and flocks and herds. It is almost impossible to envision the scenario of millions of people and flocks in a camp, let alone at least 300,000 tons of quails. If one person collected a ton of quails per tent that gives 300,000 tons. Just where did they spread them to dry in the camp in already such a crowded space? Where and how did they dispose of all the feathers and internals?

# CHAPTER 12
# The Meaning of Sacrifice from the Christian Perspective

Virtually all Christians believe and maintain that the sin offerings of the Jewish Pentateuch were typical of the sacrifice of Jesus. Thus, we are to believe that the sin offerings of the falsified Jewish Pentateuch typified or symbolized the sacrifice of Jesus. If you carefully study the sacrificial system of the Old Testament and all the references to the same in the New – especially in the Book of Hebrews – you will realize that there are enormous problems and difficulties once we accept the principal of typology between the so called Mosaic sin offerings and the offering of Jesus.

The Hebrew word used in the Jewish Pentateuch and elsewhere for the purification or sin offering is "hattat." The first most fundamental principle of the Book of Hebrews is that there can be no forgiveness of sin without the shedding of blood [Hebrews 9:22]. According to this principle, atonement or remission or forgiveness of sin can be obtained only through a bloody sacrifice or a bloody sin offering. This principle and argument of the author of Hebrews [and virtually all Christians] does not agree with the principal and instructions allegedly given by God in the Jewish Torah. Leviticus 4 gives us a detailed account which deals explicitly with a sin offering. The offering had to be presented according to the rank or status of the individual in the community. If the priest sinned, he had to present a young bull [verse 3]. If the whole Israelite community sinned the same victim was prescribed [verse 14]. If a leader sinned, he had to present a male goat [verse 23]. The first three laws or principles were non-negotiable.

Neither the priest nor the community or the prominent leader could make a substitute and present a victim of a lesser ranking. This is due to the fact that the legislator of this law regarded the priest, the whole community and the prominent leader wealthy enough to present the prescribed victims. If however, an average Israelite person sinned, he was obligated to present a female goat [signifying a lesser rank of both the offerer and the offering]. The offerer had to lay his own hand on the animal and slaughter it personally. The offerer was also allowed to bring a female lamb as a substitute for the female goat. The procedure was the same. He had to lay his hand on the animal and slaughter it personally [verses 27-31].

If an ordinary person could not afford to offer a female goat or a lamb then he was required to offer two doves or young pigeons [Leviticus 5:7]. If a person could not even afford these victims then he was to bring an oblation or bloodless sacrifice. Please note the text of Leviticus 5:11-13:

"But if he can't afford two turtledoves, or two young pigeons, then he shall bring his offering for that in which he has sinned, the tenth part of an ephah of fine flour for a sin offering. He shall put no oil on it, neither shall he put any frankincense on it, for it is a sin offering. He shall bring it to the priest, and the priest shall take his handful of it as the memorial portion, and burn it on the altar, on the offerings of Yahweh made by fire. It is a sin offering. The priest shall make atonement for him concerning his sin that he has sinned in any of these things, and he will be forgiven; and the rest shall be the priest's, as the meal offering" [World English Bible].

It is therefore apparent that the author of the Book of Hebrews was mistaken and that the Jewish Pentateuch does teach that sin can be forgiven and atoned for without the shedding of blood. The next thing very apparent in the Book of Hebrews is the fact that the author believed and taught that the blood of Jesus did not and could not cleanse all sins indiscriminately. The author taught that only inherent sin [of Adam] and those committed in ignorance were atoned for by the bloody sacrifice of Jesus. His argument is based on the fact that Jesus died only once in order to atone for sin.

Please note the text of Hebrews 6:4-6:

"For concerning those who were once enlightened and tasted of the heavenly gift, and were made partakers of the Holy Spirit, and tasted the good word of God, and the powers of the age to come, and then fell away, it is impossible to renew them again to repentance; seeing they crucify the Son of God for themselves again, and put him to open shame" [World English Bible].

I will now demonstrate very clearly that the author of the Book of Hebrews believed that the blood of Jesus could atone only for the sins committed in ignorance just as was the case with the sin offering in the Jewish Pentateuch. This truth is seldom realized due to the fact that Christian preachers continually teach that works do not play an important role in a Christian's life but only the faith in the atoning sacrifice of Jesus. We are generally taught that virtually any sin committed after baptism and "enlightenment" can be forgiven and washed away by the "blood of Jesus." I will here demonstrate that this was not taught by those who adhered to the sacrificial cultus of the Jewish Pentateuch.

The word "enlightenment" is crucial in this text. The author said:

"it is impossible to renew them again to repentance."

The words "enlightenment" and "illuminated" are synonyms. Illumination or enlightenment was always associated with baptism. St. Crysostom of the 4th century wrote that even the heretics had baptism but not illumination or enlightenment of the soul. The word "enlightened" comes from the Greek word "photizo" which was translated as "enlightened," "illuminated" and "make to see" in the King James Bible. The word appears in Ephesians 3:9 and is translated "make to see." In 2 Timothy 1:10 the word "photizo" was translated "made manifest." The word simply means: to make one see or understand. Therefore, the author of Hebrews 6:4-6 believed and taught that no sin can be forgiven after the person was enlightened and received knowledge. That is, he taught that no sin committed with knowledge and understanding can be forgiven. In Hebrews 10:26-27 the author of Hebrews makes his point even more clear and forceful:

"For if we sin wilfully after that we have received the knowledge of the truth, there remaineth no more sacrifice for sins, But a certain fearful looking for of judgment and fiery indignation, which shall devour the adversaries" [King James Bible].

Both texts of the Book of Hebrews indisputably prove that the author believed in and actually based his argument on the principle of the Mosaic sacrifices. What most Christians do not know, but the author of Hebrews was of course aware, is the fact that the blood of animals in the Jewish Pentateuch could never atone for any sin consciously committed. That is, the sacrificial cultus of the Old Testament provided atonement only for the sins committed in ignorance. Any sin committed voluntarily could not be atoned for but the person had to be killed for his sin. There was no prescribed sacrifice which could atone for the sin committed with knowledge. I have already referred to the 4$^{th}$ and 5$^{th}$ chapters of Leviticus earlier. But I did not point out the fact that the sin offering prescribed there could only atone for the unintentional sin. Please note the following clear statements:

"And the LORD spake unto Moses, saying, Speak unto the children of Israel, saying, If a soul shall sin through ignorance against any of the commandments of the LORD concerning things which ought not to be done, and shall do against any of them" [4:1-2 King James Bible].

The rules that follow I have already covered earlier. Here is its summary. A priest who sinned without intending to had to bring a young bull as his sin offering in order to atone for his unintentional sin. The whole community which sinned unawares or unintentionally had to bring the same victim. The ruler who sinned unintentionally had to present a male goat for his atonement of sin. Any other person who sinned unintentionally had to bring a female goat or a lamb.

If they could not afford it they had to bring two doves or two young pigeons. If they could not even afford these victims then they were obligated to present an oblation in order to atone for their unintentional sin. There was simply no prescribed sacrifice for the intentional sin. Not only so, but the Jewish Pentateuch explicitly states that there can be no atonement for any intentional sin. Numbers 15 also gives a detailed account of the atonement for unintentional sins. Then in verses 29-30 we are told that whoever sins in ignorance should not be killed since the sacrifice for sin covers his sin. But whoever sins with knowledge no remedy for sin. The person must be put to death. The death penalty was applied on anyone who broke even one single command with knowledge or "presumptuously" – as King James Bible puts it. The *Zondervan Pictorial Bible Dictionary* on p. 739, sec. "sin offering" corroborates the fact that no atonement was possible for a conscious violation of the Law.

Numbers 15:32-36 lists one conscious or presumptuous sin. Even though the sin appears to be very insignificant the author states that there was no remedy or sacrificial atonement possible. The offender had to be put to death. The offender was killed for merely gathering firewood on the Sabbath. He however, according to the author, was aware that such an act was prohibited. His sin therefore was not committed in ignorance. Elsewhere we find that anyone who desecrated the Sabbath had to be put to death. There was no remedy or blood atonement possible. Realizing all these facts we are now in a better position to understand the comment of the author of Hebrews.

He clearly based his argument on the principle of the Jewish Pentateuch. We do not know for certain who actually wrote the Book of Hebrews. There is no consensus among the biblical scholars. The style differs from that of Paul and also Paul's name and personal greeting is absent. The author however had to be a close associate of Paul since he was a friend and an associate of Timothy. He obviously wrote from Italy since he extended greetings from the believers in Italy. From the writings of Paul, it appears that he also held the same view as the author of Hebrews. In 1 Timothy 1:12-13 Paul wrote to Timothy that he was forgiven for persecuting the believers only because he did it in ignorance, not knowing that he was doing wrong.

Paul here strongly implies that his sins were forgiven on the basis of Jesus' sacrifice [verse 15] only because his sins were committed in ignorance and not presumptuously. From elsewhere it appears that Paul did not believe that the sacrifice of Jesus could atone for the "great" sins of those who were believers and enlightened in baptism. But it appears that Paul thought that those people who could not claim the atonement for their sins on the basis of Jesus' blood, could somehow be forgiven and ultimately saved through the bloody sacrifice of their own.

In 1 Timothy 1:19-20 Paul states that two believing men – Hymenaeus and Alexander – fell from faith. Paul did not recommend that they repent and claim the blood of Jesus but rather he delivered them to Satan in order to learn not to blaspheme. From this text alone it is not clear what "delivering to Satan" means. But when we compare this text with that of 1 Corinthians 5 we get the clearer picture. Among the Corinthian believers there was a believer who apparently had intercourse either with his stepmother or else with one of his father's wives. As soon as Paul heard of this, he instantly condemned the man. Please note verses 3-5:

"For I most assuredly, as being absent in body but present in spirit, have already, as though I were present, judged him who has done this thing. In the name of our Lord Jesus Christ, you being gathered together, and my spirit, with the power of our Lord Jesus Christ, are to deliver such a one to Satan for the destruction of the flesh, that the spirit may be saved in the day of the Lord Jesus" [World English Bible].

Paul apparently believed that the presumptuous sin of this believer could not be atoned for by his repentance, animal blood or the blood of Jesus. He believed that the only ultimate remedy for this man would be to atone for his sin through his own blood sacrifice. Paul actually learned this practice from the Pharisees. To this day the adherents of rabbinical Judaism believe in the self-sacrifice which alone can atone for the wilful sins. In their official Prayer Book, The Complete Artscroll Siddur, compiled by Rabbi Nosson Scherman, on p. 845, we find a prayer in which it is stated that one's death may be an atonement for all errors and sins committed.

By carefully examining the Old Testament we discover that the true God and the true prophets of His did not identify with the legislator of the Jewish Pentateuch and the sacrificial system. God and the true prophets most certainly did not believe nor did they teach that a sin consciously or presumptuously committed could not be forgiven. Neither did they teach that those who sinned in this manner must be put to death or atone for their sins through their own blood sacrifice.

In Isaiah 1:11-13 we are clearly told that sacrifice and burnt offering was not prescribed by God, as we have already seen. In verses 15-18 God said that the hands of the Israelites were stained with blood and that if their sins were as scarlet, they would be as clean as snow. If they were like crimson, they would be like wool. The Israelites committed great horrors. They served the hinder gods. They worshipped molten images and many idols. They committed adulteries. They committed and continually practiced great evils and completely despised the Holy Law of God. According to the legislator of the Jewish Pentateuch these Israelites should have been put to death – since there was no sacrifice left to atone for their sins.

But God however, repeatedly testified that He was more than willing to forgive and atone for their sin on the basis of His love and mercy alone, if only they were willing to reform their ways and begin to practice righteousness. Ezekiel 18 positively proves that God did not believe in the Jewish Pentateuch nor did He prescribe all those capital punishments we find in the Jewish Torah. A person who commits all the dreadful things and sins listed in this chapter would be declared righteous, if only he would reform his ways and start obeying God's Law.

Virtually every sin mentioned in Ezekiel 18 was subject to capital punishment according to the legislator of the Jewish Pentateuch, yet God was more than glad to forgive these sins, since He did not want anyone to die. There was a king in Judah by the name of Manasseh. He was the longest reigning king in either Judah or Israel. But he was also the most wicked king – committing all sort of abominations, as shown in 2 Kings 21. He even sacrificed his son and filled the streets of Jerusalem with blood. Every sin that Manasseh committed – mentioned in this chapter – called for a capital punishment. You can verify this fact by consulting the prescriptions of the legislator of the Jewish Pentateuch.

God kept sending His prophets to warn Manasseh and the people of Judah. They urged him to return to God. He however, refused to listen. Later he was arrested by the Babylonian official and was taken captive to Babylon. In prison however, Manasseh turned to God and begged His forgiveness. God heard his prayer and forgave him all his sins [2 Chronicles 33:10-33]. God is merciful and full of forgiveness. He is our father and He loves His children. He does not need a sacrificial victim nor does He need to see the shedding of blood in order to be moved with compassion and forgive. If we as sinful fathers and mothers forgive our children simply because we really love them, how much more then will God, our heavenly Father, forgive us His children! Those who cannot see or accept this fact must indeed have a blind soul.

Jesus, the Son of God and our elder Brother, also believed that God was compassionate and loving – full of mercy and forgiveness. Jesus also rejected the legislation of the Jewish legislator concerning sin offering and the capital punishments. A woman was caught in the act of adultery and then she was brought before Jesus [John 8]. The Pharisees told Jesus that "Moses" commanded in the Law that such people should be stoned to death. They asked Jesus what was his opinion on the subject. Jesus ignored them and began to write with his finger on the ground. As they continued to annoy him, he told them that they can stone the woman to death if they were without sin and perfectly innocent from any crime. Being condemned by their conscience they simply left. Jesus told the woman that he does not condemn her. He charged her to go and sin no more – that is, reform her lifestyle. If God really commanded Moses that such people must be put to death then Jesus most certainly disobeyed and broke the Law of God. But if Jesus broke and nullified the Law of God then he most certainly was a transgressor and a sinner. But I believe that Jesus was not a sinner and I also have no doubt whatsoever that God did not command that such people should be put to death. God always gave us humans opportunity to repent and alter our sinful ways. Those who repented and reformed their evil ways were more than welcome by God – as numerous texts of the Bible and extra-canonical literature testify.

The Book of Revelation plainly reveals that those who committed even great and terrible sins could be forgiven if they would only admit their guilt and repent. Please note the following passages:

"But I have a few things against you, because you have there some who hold the teaching of Balaam, who taught Balak to throw a stumbling block before the children of Israel, to eat things sacrificed to idols, and to commit sexual immorality. So you also have some who hold to the teaching of the Nicolaitans in the same way. Repent therefore" [Revelation 2:14-15 World English Bible].

"But I have this against you, that you tolerate your woman, Jezebel, who calls herself a prophetess. She teaches and seduces my servants to commit sexual immorality, and to eat things sacrificed to idols. I gave her time to repent, but she refuses to repent of her sexual immorality. Behold, I will throw her into a bed, and those who commit adultery with her into great oppression, unless they repent of her works" [Revelation 2:20-23 World English Bible].

The keyword with Jesus was "repent." Repentance and God's love is what blots the sin away and not the blood sacrifice of an animal or Jesus. It is very plain that Jesus did not believe in the Jewish legislation concerning the sin offering and atonement as did Paul and the author of Hebrews. Jesus did not believe that only unintentional sins could be atoned for but he clearly believed and taught that even the sins of idolatry and adultery can be forgiven to them who reform their lifestyle and truly repent. Jesus addressed himself to the believers and those who were enlightened in baptism. Even though they sinned terribly, Jesus gave them opportunity to repent. The author of Hebrews was therefore gravely mistaken.

All those who acknowledge the text of Hebrews as inspired and infallible, and if they acknowledge the Jewish sacrificial cultus as inspired and infallible, are lost – because their sins which they commit after their original conversion and baptism cannot be forgiven and atoned for. They can only look forward to the terrible judgment and the punishment with fire. Therefore, my dear reader, I urge you to abandon the idea of sacrifice and bloodshed as the means of your atonement and to beg God to forgive you your sins committed presumptuously. He is loving and merciful father and He will most definitely forgive you if you truly reject the blood atonement in your heart.

Now it is essential to point out the absurdity involved in the sin offering prescribed in the Jewish Pentateuch and the Christian ludicrous teaching concerning the sacrifice of Jesus and his alleged bloody atonement. Any sacrificial victim chosen for a sacrifice had to be perfect and without any defect. This was especially true of the victim used for the sin offering. The victim was brought by the offerer to the priest and the altar of the temple. The offerer had to lay his hand on the head of the sacrificial victim and confess his sin or guilt. In this way he identified with the victim and transferred his sin and guilt on the head of the pure and innocent victim.

Although it is evil to kill an animal at least it seems logical that the victim chosen to atone for sin should be pure and blameless. It also seems logical that the sins should be transferred through the laying on of hand or hands. That the laying on of hands on the head of a victim signifies the transference of sin is very obvious from the passage of Leviticus 16:21 where Aaron was instructed to do the following:

"and Aaron shall lay both his hands on the head of the live goat, and confess over him all the iniquities of the children of Israel, and all their transgressions, even all their sins; and he shall put them on the head of the goat, and shall send him away by the hand of a man who is in readiness into the wilderness" [World English Bible].

The moment the offerer laid his hand or hands on the head of his sacrificial victim, all his unintentional sins were transferred to the head of his victim. But the sins were not atoned for until the blood of the victim was shed. Only the shed blood actually atoned for the sin. The author of Hebrews clearly shows that Jesus is the substitute of the Mosaic victim:

"then has he said, "Behold, I have come to do your will. He takes away the first, that he may establish the second, by which will we have been sanctified through the offering of the body of Jesus Christ once for all. Every priest indeed stands day by day ministering and often offering the same sacrifices, which can never take away sins, but he, when he had offered one sacrifice for sins for ever, sat down on the right hand of God; henceforth expecting until his enemies to be made the footstool of his feet. For by one offering he has perfected forever those who are sanctified" [Hebrews 10:9-14 World English Bible].

The author argues that Jesus was perfect and sinless – because he did everything God asked him to do. As a perfect sacrifice he atoned for all our past sins with his shed blood. The author was either ignorant or he deliberately ignored the real problem his teaching and that of the Mosaic Torah posed concerning the blood atonement. Before I point out this problem I first of all want to present Paul's view and teaching on the subject. Paul apparently believed and taught that Jesus was accursed. Please note Galatians 3:13:

"Christ redeemed us from the curse of the law, having become a curse for us. For it is written, Cursed is everyone who hangs on a tree" [World English Bible].

Paul obviously did not realize the absurdity and horror of his teaching. Neither did in fact the Jewish legislator of the sacrificial cultus. They believed and maintained that the sacrificial victim had to be perfect and blameless and innocent. For only an innocent and holy victim could be accepted as a substitute and could actually atone for the sins of the offerer. But at the same time, through ignorance, they have introduced a system where sin is actually atoned for through sin. Paul referred to Deuteronomy 21:22-23. Please note this text quoted from the King James Bible exactly as it is:

"And if a man have committed a sin worthy of death, and he be to be put to death, and thou hang him on a tree: His body shall not remain all night upon the tree, but thou shalt in any wise bury him that day; [for he that is hanged is accursed of God;] that thy land be not defiled, which the LORD thy God giveth thee for an inheritance."

Paul twisted the text and mutilated it in order to suit his doctrine. The text does not say that whoever is hung or crucified on a tree is accursed but only the person who deserved such a punishment. His interpretation of the text is strongly contested by certain Bible scholars and experts of philology. If the text means what Paul understood it to mean, then every single person ever crucified or hung on a tree was cursed by God. But for what purpose? If Jesus who was righteous was accursed in order to redeem mankind from the alleged curse of the Law and Adam, for what purpose was Apostle Peter accursed? The tradition tells us that Peter was crucified with his head down. John 21:18-19 says:

"Most assuredly I tell you, when you were young, you dressed yourself, and walked where you wanted to. But when you are old, you will stretch out your hands, and another will dress you, and carry you where you don't want to go" [World English Bible].

If everyone crucified is cursed by God, then how could Peter glorify God by dying on a cross? What about all believing people who were crucified by Nero and other monsters? What about all the babies and young children crucified through the ages – even as late as World War II? Were all these innocent children also cursed by God? To believe and teach so is not only incongruous but it actually borders on the line of blasphemy. Jesus said that the kingdom of God belongs to little children and that unless we become like little children, we shall never obtain salvation. Now please note what else Paul maintained in 2 Corinthians 5:21:

"For he [God] hath made him [Jesus] to be sin for us, who knew no sin; that we might be made the righteousness of God in him" [King James Bible].

Paul believed and acknowledged that Jesus lived a sinless life. But he maintained that while Jesus was hanging on the tree, God actually made Jesus a sinner by transferring all the sins of the world upon himself. Paul is saying that just as an offerer transferred his sin on the sacrificial victim by the laying on of hands, so did God transfer the sins of the whole world upon Jesus. Now Paul and the Jewish legislator were ignorant of the fact that they actually believed in and taught atonement of sin through sin. For both the animal victim of the Mosaic Torah and Jesus himself became defiled, polluted, sinful and impure by the sins transferred upon them. How then could they atone for sin in the sinful condition they were in? How could the blood of Jesus wash away sin when it was actually stained and defiled and became accursed by all the sins of the world? Please remember that the legislator in the Mosaic Torah maintained that anyone who touched anything unclean or polluted or sinful became unclean and had to wash with water and present a sin offering. The duration of their uncleanliness depended upon the decree of their defilement.

Since Paul and virtually all Christians maintain that all the sins of the world were laid on Jesus and that he actually became accursed because of this and that his own Father allegedly abandoned him because of this sinful state and condition, how then was it possible for him to atone for sin and to actually present his sinful and polluted blood in the Holy of Holies in heaven? No, Jesus was not the sacrificial victim of the Mosaic Torah. Nor did he die to atone for the sin of Adam and the world. Nor did he die in order to appease angry God and cool off His wrath.

You may ask, as many have already asked me, why did Jesus then come and why was he crucified if he wasn't a sacrifice for sin? He came to teach and reveal the true God – as Ebionites claimed all along. He was crucified because the Jewish leaders and the Jews in general could not accept his message but regarded him as a blasphemer. Had the Jews accepted him and his message then they would not have crucified him and all would have been well. Jesus was killed for the same reason that all God's true prophets were killed: the sinful world could not accept their message.

# CHAPTER 13
# Paul Had Problems With Vegetarian Believers

We have seen that the Ebionites were vegetarian and that they abstained from wine. However, if Jesus and the Twelve endorsed the flesh diet and the consumption of alcoholic beverages – moreover, if they themselves ate animal flesh and drank wine – then we would not expect believers and followers of the Twelve to insist on vegetarianism and abstention from wine and other fermented drinks. On the other hand, if Jesus and the Twelve were in fact vegetarian and if they instructed their followers to adhere to a vegetarian diet, we should expect at least some evidence in the writings of Paul that this was the case.

When we carefully sift through the epistles of Paul, we do not only discover that there were believers in the assemblies Paul established who insisted on vegetarianism and who also abstained from wine, but we also discover that they appealed to the Jerusalem Apostles in order to justify their practice. It was in fact the emissaries of James, the brother of Jesus, and the Elders from Jerusalem who actually made Paul's converts aware that vegetarianism and abstention from alcoholic beverages is a requirement which Jesus himself imposed on all his true disciples and followers. Paul of course rejected vegetarianism and sanctioned the flesh diet and consumption of fermented beverages. He claimed that food had no bearing on the relationship with God [1 Corinthians 8:8]. He instructed his followers to buy whatever meat was sold at the meat market [1 Corinthians 10:25]. He also instructed his followers to eat whatever their unbelieving friends may serve at the table. This included the sacrificial flesh, providing the host did not raise the issue.

And even if they did Paul told them to abstain not because it was wrong to eat flesh sacrificed to idols, but rather because of the unbelievers' and weak brothers' conscience [1 Corinthians 10:15,27]. Despite the fact that Paul rejected vegetarianism and was convinced that it was all right to consume animal flesh, he nevertheless instructed the meat eaters and those who drank wine not to do so in order not to cause a scandal in the congregation. Romans 14 indisputably proves that there were two types of believers in Rome. One group consumed animal flesh and wine while other group practiced vegetarianism and also abstained from wine. Please note:

"One man has faith to eat all things, but he who is weak eats only vegetables" [World English Bible].

This verse clearly proves that some believers in Rome did not eat animal flesh but were actually vegetarian. Paul of course regarded this group as "weak" while the flesh eaters as "strong." Romans 14:21 explicitly points out that the issue was flesh and wine. Please note:

"It is good to not eat meat, drink wine, nor do anything by which your brother stumbles, is offended, or is made weak" [World English Bible].

This text plainly states that eating meat and drinking wine could cause offence to other followers of Jesus. Paul used the word "scandalizo" which means "skandalize, displeasure." The word "scandalize" means: to shock the moral feelings by offensive conduct. It is evident therefore that certain followers of Jesus in Rome practiced vegetarianism and held very strong belief on the issue of meat and wine. Paul did not say that they should eat meat and drink wine as others do. Neither did he quote the alleged words of Jesus that nothing can pollute that enters the mouth. Instead, he actually instructed the "strong" to abstain from flesh and wine for the sake of those who did not eat meat and drink wine.

Paul did not regard these vegetarian believers as those who adhered to the doctrines of demons as the author of 1 Timothy 4:1-4 believed. Nor did he say that these vegetarian believers were impure and that is why they regarded meat eating impure as did the author of Titus. For the author of Titus implied that those who do not eat everything are "impure" [1:15]. To the Corinthians, Paul said that he would not eat meat all his life, since eating meat offended certain believers in that community [1 Corinthians 8:13]. Therefore, it follows that certain believers in Rome and Corinth practiced vegetarianism and they also abstained from wine. Paul did not regard them as followers of demons but rather instructed others not to eat meat and drink wine for their sake.

Practically no meat eaters today adhere to these instructions but rather they condemn the vegetarian believers. Why so many vegetarian believers in those early days if Jesus was a meat eater and if all Apostles consumed animal flesh and drank wine? Moreover, why did they criticize and condemn those who ate meat and drank wine? We should note that by 64 A.D., Paul was already dead – according to Christian tradition. Jesus died in the early 30's. If Jesus ate meat and drank wine and if the Twelve did the same, where did these believers get the idea that it was wrong to do so? Many Apostles were still alive and many believers who personally knew Jesus were still alive. So, if they all ate meat and drank wine why would these believers abstain from meat and wine? The answer is very simple. Jesus, the Twelve, and all their followers were vegetarian and they also abstained from wine. Paul knew this but he could not preach vegetarianism to the Gentiles since that would hinder his mission. If Jesus taught that all flesh is good to eat, as we are told in Mark 7, why didn't Paul quote that statement? Why didn't he tell them that Peter, James and John, and all the believers in Jerusalem consumed animal flesh and drank wine so that they had no valid reason to object to the flesh diet and stubbornly adhere to their vegetarianism?

The fact is, these vegetarian believers were influenced by the emissaries from James, the brother of Jesus. Paul had other ideas and he allowed his converts to eat meat and drink wine and to retain their slaves and eat food sacrificed to idols. When the "emissaries" from James came in contact with Paul's converts, they accepted their version of the Gospel which Paul considered "another gospel" which he did not preach. Not because he believed that it was right to do so but in order to get as many converts as he could. Some of these "emissaries" were actually important leaders. They followed Paul and disputed his views – claiming that his apostleship was illegitimate. They urged Paul's followers to conform to the doctrines taught by the Twelve and James, the brother of Jesus, who was the head of the Twelve and the seventy-two elders.

That those who swayed the believers in Rome, Corinth, Colossae, Galatia and other congregations which Paul established, were associated with James, the brother of Jesus, is evident from Galatians 2:4-5 where Paul clearly links the "Judaizers" with James the Just. Although they were James' emissaries, Paul regarded them as false bothers. Some of these emissaries of James were in fact important leaders, but Paul rejected them nevertheless. Paul accused these important leaders whom he associated with James, the brother of Jesus, of preaching "another Gospel" and "another Jesus." He urges Galatians to reject the teachings of James and his "emissaries" and return to the gospel he originally preached to them. Most Christians assume that Galatians simply accepted the admonition of Paul and rejected the teaching of James and his associates.

The evidence however, reveals that they did not and that Galatians refused to participate in the financial offering Paul organized as help for the Jerusalem Ebionites. In fact, Paul was very much afraid that the financial help he was taking to Jerusalem would not be accepted by James. The Apostles did not want to be bribed and bought with gifts and money and be obligated to accept Paul's loose version of the message of Jesus. Paul instructed the believers in Rome to pray that his financial help would be accepted by James and the Elders [Romans 15:31]. We know that towards the end of his career Paul was arrested in Jerusalem. The Jews were going to kill him for his antinomian stance. As a Roman citizen he claimed his right to defend himself in the presence of Caesar – Nero at that time. The Jerusalem Apostles refused to send a delegation to defend Paul. During his first trial before Nero, no delegation was sent either from Jerusalem or Rome. Please note:

"At my first defense, no one took my part, but all left me. May it not be held against them" [2 Timothy 4:16 World English Bible].

We know for certain that there were believers in Rome at the time Paul faced Nero. Yet none of those believers tried to help Paul in anyway whatsoever.

Not only the believers in Rome but virtually all in Asia deserted Paul and his gospel.

Please note:

"This you know, that all who are in Asia turned away from me; of whom are Phygelus and Hermogenes. May the Lord grant mercy to the house of Onesiphorus, for he often refreshed me, and was not ashamed of my chain, but when he was in Rome, he sought me diligently, and found me" [2 Timothy 1:15-18 World English Bible].

The phrase "turned away" has been translated from the Greek word "apostrepho." From this Greek word the English word "apostasy" is derived. It is number #654 in Strong's, where it is defined as "to turn away." The word simply means to turn away from allegiance; to defect. The prefix "apo" signifies separation. Believers in Asia and Rome simply abandoned Paul and separated from him. They became a part of what is now called Jewish Christianity. The final rejection and separation occurred after Paul's arrest in Jerusalem. The problem however, began much earlier. 1 Corinthians 1:12 points out that Corinthians already formed separate parties. Some recognized Paul, others Apollos, while still others Peter. In 2 Corinthians we find a dispute between Paul and the "emissaries" of the Twelve. In chapter 11:22 Paul identifies his opponents as "Christians" who were "Hebrews" of the "seed of Abraham." This immediately points out that his opponents were connected with James and other Apostles in Jerusalem.

His opponents claimed to be followers of Jesus and were accepted as such [10:7]. They claimed the authority of the Jerusalem Apostles so that Paul styles the Jerusalem Apostles as "super apostles" [11:5; 12:11] but at the same time styles them "false Apostles" and "servants of Satan" [11:13-15]. There is no doubt that Paul was actually denouncing the original Apostles of Jesus. In 11:22-23 Paul clearly states that these "super Apostles" were Hebrews, Israelites and the seed of Abraham just as he says he was. Paul acknowledged them as "ministers of Christ" but claimed that he was in fact "greater" than they because of his "greater" persecutions. In 12:11 Paul states that in no way is he inferior to these "super Apostles." Paul also plainly states that these "super Apostles" performed miracles but he also credits their miracles to Satan [11:13-15]. Paul did not deny that these "super Apostles" actually performed miracles but he claimed that their power was derived from Satan.

Biblical scholars generally recognize that in these chapters we have a strong indication of the great schism between Paul and the Apostles of Jerusalem. The emissaries of James were not the ones who preached "another Gospel" and "another Jesus" – meaning different. The Twelve preached Jesus whom they knew personally and with whom they ate and drank and they preached the Gospel that Jesus taught them. It was Paul who actually twisted the truth and who deviated from Jesus, the Twelve knew, and from the Gospel that Jesus preached. That these emissaries sent by James, the brother of Jesus, and that James and other original Apostles as well as the seventy-two elders who assisted James were actually vegetarian, is also evident from the canonical book of Acts.

The book of Acts clearly shows that there were four Nazarean-Ebionite brothers who either renewed or ended their Nazarite vow, since they had to shave their head. According to the Jewish Pentateuch, the renewal of the vow and the ending of the Nazarite vow demanded an animal sacrifice. Acts 21:26 speaks of an offering which was to be presented by the priest on the behalf of all of them. It is of great significance for you to realize that this word "offering" is translated from the Greek word "prosphora" which always implies "an oblation" and therefore "a bloodless sacrifice." The word is number #4376 in Strong's and refers to an oblation, a bloodless sacrifice. A Critical Lexicon and Concordance to the English and Greek New Testament, by the great scholar, Ethelbert Bullinger, on p. 548, points out that the word "prosphora" is antonym of the words "thusia" which means "sacrifice" and "holocautoma" which means "burnt offering." He points out that the word "prosphora" means "oblation," strictly without blood.

This text irrefutably proves that James and the Twelve repudiated the Jewish bloody sacrificial cultus – just as Jesus himself did when he interfered with the sacrifice in the temple – as we shall see in the later chapter. The Ebionites were therefore correct when they claimed that James spoke against the temple altar and the fire of the altar which consumed the animals as burnt offerings. It is also significant to note that Church Father Epiphanius testified that whenever an Ebionite was asked why he does not eat animal flesh he would reply that "Jesus revealed it to me." It is therefore fair to say that the followers of Paul who became vegetarian and who also abstained from wine, learned the practice from those who came from James, the brother of Jesus. James, the brother of Jesus, must have been a vegetarian since the Church Fathers unanimously testified the same. Hegesepius stated regarding James the Just the following:

"James the brother of the Lord surnamed the Just was made head of the Church at Jerusalem. Many indeed are called James. This one was holy from his mother's womb. He drank neither wine nor strong drink, ate no flesh, never shaved" [The Nicene and Post Nicene Fathers, Vol. 3. p. 361].

Eusebius Pamphilius stated regarding James:

"This apostle was consecrated from his mother's womb. He drank neither wine nor fermented liquors, and abstained from animal food. A razor never came upon his head" [Eusebius's Ecclesiastical History, p. 76].

St. Augustine wrote:

"St. James never ate animal food, living on seeds and vegetables, never tasting flesh or wine" [Ecclesiastical History, 2 Vols. Translated by H.J. Lawlor and J.E.L. Oulton].

James spoke against the temple and its cultus. He especially spoke against the altar of the temple, as is evident from an early manuscript used by the Jewish Christians and which is referred to as 'Ascent of James.'

James insisted that the temple was a place of prayer and not a slaughterhouse where the Sadducee priests daily immolated the innocent creatures of God. To prove his point, James went to the temple daily and prayed on his knees for a long time. The Church Fathers testified that this was James's daily practice. They wrote that his knees were like the knees of a camel from kneeling in prayer [Eusebius, Ecclesiastical History (Ἐκκλησιαστικὴ Ἱστορία), Book II, Ch. XXIII]. That prayer was emphasized rather than sacrifice, is also indirectly supported in Acts 3:1, since there we are told that at the ninth hour – three in the afternoon – at the very hour when the daily evening sacrifice was offered by the priests and when the Jewish populace adhered to the sacrificial practice, Peter and John went at that very hour to the temple to PRAY. Just as water was used in baptism for the remission of sins in opposition to blood, so the prayer was introduced in opposition to the sacrificial cult. We also know from the writings of the Church Fathers that not only James but also other apostles adhered to vegetarianism and abstained from wine. Church Father St. Chrysostom testified that Matthew was also vegetarian. Church Father Clement of Alexandria also testified that Matthew was vegetarian.

An early Christian document depicts Apostle Judas Thomas as abstaining from eating of flesh and drinking wine. We know for example that apostle Peter also preached the message in Bithynia [1 Peter 1:1]. Bithynia was actually the stronghold of "Jewish Christianity." Bithynia was the north-western province of Asia Minor. It was conquered by Romans in 75 b.c.e. During the reign of Trajan – the Roman Emperor – Plinus Secondus, the governor of Bithynia, wrote a letter to Trajan in which he stated that "Christians" in his province abstained from animal flesh. Plinus, more commonly called Pliny, was born in 53 c.e., and died in 110 c.e. Trajan reigned from 98 c.e., to 117 c.e. Some forty years before Pliny wrote to Trajan, the Roman senator Seneca wrote a letter to Lucilius in which he stated that "Christians" who were under imperial suspicion were a foreign cult who did not eat flesh of animals. This was repugnant to the Romans since they have eaten meat and since it was anathema to deny sacrificial cult in Rome in those days.

The testimonies of Pliny and Seneca must be trustworthy and significant because they would not have stated that the followers of Jesus were vegetarian if they were not. Paul sanctioned the meat diet. But not only the eating of flesh but also the food sacrificed to idols. But Jesus in Revelation criticizes those who ate the food sacrificed to idols. Paul did not only sanction the eating of flesh but he also sanctioned slavery and taught other things which Jesus and the Twelve condemned. If you would rather listen to Paul than Jesus and the Twelve – then go ahead and be a bloody butcher – slaughtering animals in order to eat their flesh.

## CHAPTER 14
# Why did Jesus Cleanse the Temple?

What we need to realize first of all is the fact that animals were not kept in the temple itself. Neither was buying and selling occurring in the temple itself. The buying and selling of animals and the exchanging of currency occurred in the Court of Gentiles – the furthest district of the temple grounds. The next thing you must realize is the fact that the priests who were of Sadducee sect [Acts 4:1; 5:17] did not turn the temple courts into a common market place where you go shopping. They kept animals allowed for sacrifice at the temple grounds so that those who came from far or those who did not have an animal for sacrifice could buy some. Since the only currency in which the sacrificial victim could have been bought was a Tyrian coin, they had money changers available to convert the common money into Tyrian coin. The money changers were also there in order to collect the temple tax prescribed in the Jewish Pentateuch. Vast majority of biblical scholars agree that activities going on in the temple courts in Jesus' day were perfectly lawful as far as the Jewish Pentateuch was concerned. In Deuteronomy 14:22-27 we find the command that those who live too far from the chosen place should take the silver with them and buy the sacrificial animals at the chosen place.

Since the Jewish Pentateuch, which is also recognized by the Christian Church, sanctions sacrificial cult and buying sacrificial animals at the chosen place – why then did Jesus take such a drastic action? Why did he charge the temple clergy of turning the temple into a den of robbers? The answer is obvious. He objected to the sacrificial cult per se. He agreed with Jeremiah that the sacrificial cult was the product of the lying pen of the scribes. It will also become apparent that Jesus regarded the killing of animals as murder. Jesus did not think that the temple should be Jewish only. Nor that it should be a place of sacrifice. He stated that the temple should be "The House of Prayer" for all nations. Jesus believed in the synagogue and not the temple. In the synagogue prayer was offered as a sacrifice. In the temple animals were butchered. In the House of Prayer all nations should participate. In the temple only those of Jewish ancestry were allowed to worship. Gentiles were allowed in the outermost court. When condemning the activities in the temple courts, Jesus referred to two Old Testament prophets: Isaiah and Jeremiah – who both opposed the sacrificial cult:

"He taught, saying to them, Isn't it written, 'My house will be called a house of prayer for all the nations?' But you have made it a den of robbers" [Mark 11:17 World English Bible].

When Jesus stated that the temple should be called the "House of Prayer for all Nations" he referred to Isaiah 56:7. Jesus emphasized that all nations have the right to participate in the House of Prayer. The second statement "den of robbers" comes from Jeremiah 7:11 – the very chapter where Jeremiah claimed that sacrificial cult did not come from God [7:21-23].

What did Jesus mean when he stated that the Sadducees [the priests] transformed the House of Prayer into a den of robbers? The answer is quite astonishing. The word "den" has been translated from the Greek word "spelaion" – number #4693 in Strong's and means: "a grotto, a cavern." "Grotto" means: "a cave." "Cavern" means: "a hollow cave." The Greek word "spelaion" has been translated "den" and "cave" by the King James translators in the New Testament. The word "den" itself means a "cave."

The word "den" in Jeremiah 7:11 comes from a Hebrew word mearah" – number #4631 which means: "dark cavern or cave." This Hebrew word has been translated "cave," "den" and "hole" in the Old Testament of the King James Bible. In the New Testament of the King James Bible, the word "den" appears three times. Each time referring to Jesus' statement a "den of robbers." The word "cave" appears only in John 11:38 in reference to the tomb of Lazarus – since his grave was a cave. In the Old Testament [according to

Jewish tradition of the Masoretic Text] we read that Abraham bought a field with a cave. This cave became the grave or burial place [Genesis 23:19-20].

Jesus charged the priests of transforming the House of Prayer into a graveyard. By perpetually cremating the holocausts on the altar – the temple became the graveyard. But what did Jesus actually want to express by the word robbers? The English word "robber" comes from the word "rob" which means: to seize and carry off the property of by unlawful violence or threat of violence. This word is distinguished from the word "thief" in that it involves violence whereas the word "thief" only implies stealing. The word "robbers" in Jeremiah 7:11 comes from the Hebrew word "periyts" – number #6530 in Strong's and means: violent ones i.e. tyrants.

This word is also translated "destroyers" and "ravenous" in the King James Bible. In the New Testament the word "robber" has been translated from the Greek word "leistes," used to render the Hebrew word. It is number #3027 in *Strong's* and means: to plunder, a brigand. The word "brigand" means: a robber in a band of outlaws. An outlaw is a violent robber who resorts to murder. When the temple guards were sent to arrest Jesus in the Garden of Gethsemane, Jesus stated:

"Have you come out, as against a robber, with swords and clubs to seize me?" [Mark 14:48 World English Bible].

Robbers were confronted with swords and clubs because they were violent ones. In John 19:40 we are told that Barabbas who was released instead of Jesus was a robber [leistes]. In Luke 23:18 we are plainly told that Barabbas was cast into prison because of rebellion and murder. Barabbas was a robber, that is, murderer. Jesus thus charged the priests with murder. He claimed that by perpetually butchering the innocent animals on the sacrificial altar they have become the violent ones. By perpetual slaughter and cremation of the victims, they have transformed the temple into a graveyard. After Jesus took control of the temple, he immediately allowed access to the blind and the lame [Matthew 21:14]. According to the Greek Septuagint Bible, King David prohibited the blind and the lame to enter the Sanctuary [2 Samuel 5:8].

The Masoretic Text uses the word "bayith" which has been rendered "house" and "temple" in the King James Bible. The Greek Septuagint however states that the blind and the lame were barred from the temple. Jesus nullified this rule and allowed the blind and the lame access to the temple. There he displayed his power by healing them. These are the last healings recorded by Matthew. Luke states that after cleansing the temple, Jesus taught there every day. The priests wanted to kill him but feared the people who were on his side:

"He was teaching daily in the temple, but the chief priests and the scribes and the leading men among the people sought to destroy him. They couldn't find what they might do, for all the people hung on to every word that he said" [Luke 19:47-48 World English Bible].

Mark tells us that after Jesus took full control of the temple, he refused to allow anyone to bring anything into the temple. In doing so he immobilized the daily activities of the priests and this proves that Jesus intervened in the temple in order to set the innocent animals free and to demonstrate his opposition to the sacrificial cult. The Greek uses the word "skeuos" which means: "vessel," and "utensil." Jesus interrupted normal activities of the temple. In doing so he interfered with the daily sacrifice. Since he drove out all sacrificial animals and prohibited anyone to bring the same into the temple, he obviously made it impossible for the priests to indulge in sacrificial rites. If Jesus identified with the Jewish Pentateuch and the prescription for the daily sacrifice, and other sacrificial offerings, then he would not have interrupted the same.

In our canonical Gospels we have an incomplete preservation of Jesus' statement regarding the temple. It is stated that he would destroy the temple and make another in three days. The testimony however does not fully harmonize. In the Gospel of Thomas however, Jesus is quoted as saying that he would destroy the temple and that no man would ever be able to rebuild it. This statement must be authentic and original. The Roman Emperor Julian the Apostate who was originally a Christian but later abandoned Christianity and reverted back to paganism, actually believed that Jesus said that the temple would never be rebuilt. In order to prove Jesus wrong, he gave a command to rebuild the temple in Jerusalem. He charged many Jews from the Roman Empire to return to Jerusalem and build the temple. He also provided materials. When the workers went on site to start building the temple, God intervened supernaturally to prevent its construction. They attempted three times to rebuild it and each time there was a supernatural intervention so that the project was abandoned. The events were recorded by the Roman historian. The facts are stated in many books that deal with supernatural and unexplained mysteries, as well as the writings of the several Church Fathers. It is now more than 1900 years since the temple in Jerusalem was destroyed. To date it was not rebuilt.

## CHAPTER 15
# Did God Allow Noah To Eat Meat?

The passage of Genesis 9:2-4 was the subject of great debate and controversy. After years of study and research and virtually leaving no stone unturned on the subject, to date I have not read a commentary on the passage which is worthy of a serious consideration. Generally, it is argued that here we have the first biblical passage where God explicitly told Noah that he may kill any animal he wanted to in order to eat its flesh.

Even vegetarians who abhor meat eating and who practice vegetarianism on ethical grounds admit that here we are faced with a biblical text which clearly sanctions the killing of animals and eating of their flesh. All they can say is that due to the fallen and corrupt nature of humanity, God gave a "concession" concerning meat diet, but that it was not His ideal as in Genesis 1:30, where God ideally prescribed a completely vegetarian diet. But nothing can be further from the truth.

The early Jewish "Christians" who were the descendants of the original disciples of Jesus argued their vegetarianism on the basis of this passage as well. The *Jewish Encyclopedia*, art. Jewish Christian Sects, points out that these early believers referred to the 4th verse of Genesis 9 in order to show that it is a sin to kill an animal and to justify their vegetarian diet. I will first of all point out how some modern versions corrupt the Hebrew text by stating that all animals, birds, reptiles and fish were given to Noah for food in addition to the plants he had always eaten. The lying pen of the scribe was not at work just in the days of Jeremiah but it is very much at work today also. At least these translations reveal very plainly that before the flood Noah was vegetarian and that he ate only grain and vegetables, even though he lived many centuries after Adam's alleged fall. Some Jewish and Christian sects actually used this passage to prove vegetarianism and the fact that killing of animals is expressly forbidden by God.

Most others however, have used and still use this passage in order to justify their butchering and mass slaughter of animals in order to eat their flesh. What a paradox! The same text is used to prove and justify two diametrically opposed ideas. So, what does the text of Genesis 9:2-4 really say? Let me first tell you what it does not say. It does not say that we can kill or slaughter animals in order to sacrifice them to God or to eat their flesh. The word "animal" does not even appear in the Hebrew text, although these translations use it in order to mislead you. The text does not say that you must not eat simply "blood" – as vast majority of Jews and Christians would want you to believe. So, what does the text actually say? God here reverses the status between all animals and humans. Just before the flood animals became corrupt and wild and killed one another and they also killed and devoured human beings. God now reversed the status to its original condition. He again subjected all living creatures to the dominion of man. This of course in no way means that this dominion of man gives him the right to kill, slaughter and butcher animals in order to gratify his lust after meat. All things were subjected under Adam and he had complete control and dominion over them but this authority most certainly did not give him permission to slaughter animals for food. Adam was told to be a fruitarian being all his life. Please note the text as it stands in the King James Bible:

"And the fear of you and the dread of you shall be upon every beast of the earth, and upon every fowl of the air, upon all that moveth upon the earth, and upon all the fishes of the sea; into your hands are they delivered. Every moving thing that liveth shall be meat for you; even as the green herb I have given you all things. But flesh with the life thereof, which is the blood thereof, shall ye not eat."

God told Noah that "all moving things which are alive" shall be his for food. This most certainly did not include his wife, sons and their wives, even though they were "living things." The Hebrew word translated in the

King James Bible "moving things" or "animals" in other versions is actually "remes" which most certainly refers to reptiles. Because Noah could not eat herbs and fruits just after the flood, since it took some months before they became available and in season, God permitted Noah to live on eggs. The Earth became dry in the second month, that is, in the spring. Vegetables had to be planted and the fruit trees would not bear fruit until months later. All animals however, were to live on grass – which was already available at the end of the flood. The Greek Septuagint Bible clearly states that God spoke only of the reptiles and not all animals. Sir. Lancelot Brenton translates the crucial parts of the text correctly since he uses the word "reptiles" and the last phrase he correctly renders as I do later.

Think for a moment. Why would God allow Noah and his family to kill any animal they desired to eat, when even carnivorous animals continued to eat herbs and grass? Even carnivorous animals had to live on grass and not on living prey as later – when the change took place. Lions could not have hunted their prey nor could have other carnivorous animals. There were only a pair of each species alive at that time. Or if you prefer the Yahwist version, then one pair of all so-called unclean animals and seven pairs of the so-called clean. If the carnivorous animals killed and ate only one of the so-called unclean animals, that specie would not have survived and God's original purpose in preserving each specie would have been destroyed. Verse 4 irrefutably proves that the passage under no circumstances could be interpreted that Noah was given permission to kill absolutely any animal that came out of the ark with him. Verse 4 explicitly states:

"But flesh with the life thereof, which is the blood thereof, shall ye not eat" [King James Bible].

This does not mean that you simply must not eat flesh or meat without blood or that meat should be koshered and blood removed from it. The biological fact is: no matter what you do you can never remove all the blood from the flesh of a slaughtered animal. The text does not say that you must not eat "blood" but it says that you must not eat "flesh with life." The Hebrew text does not speak about flesh or meat in a literal sense which is actually cut or removed from the carcass of a slaughtered animal. The expression "flesh" has been used many times throughout the Bible to mean "living creature" or "living being." In Joel 2:28 God said that in the latter days He would pour out His spirit upon *all flesh* and that they would see visions and dream dreams. Flesh in this text does not and cannot denote meat but rather living souls or animate beings. In Daniel 4:12 we read:

"The leaves of it were beautiful, and the fruit of it much, and in it was food for all: the animals of the field had shadow under it, and the birds of the sky lived in the branches of it, and all flesh was fed from it" [World English Bible].

The phrase "all flesh" clearly refers to all living souls who are alive and in whose veins the blood circulates and who possess the breath of life. In John 17:2 we read:

"even as you gave him authority over all flesh, that to all whom you have given him, he will give eternal life" [World English Bible].

"All flesh," refers to all living souls and not the meat of slaughtered animals. In Job 34:14-15 we read:

"If he set his heart on himself, If he gathered to himself his spirit and his breath; All flesh would perish together, And man would turn again to dust" [World English Bible].

Clearly the phrase "all flesh" refers to animate beings who could die and not the flesh of animals. The word "flesh" was used in chapters that deal with the flood. In every single case it refers to living souls and not the flesh of animals. In Genesis 6:12 we read:

"God saw the earth, and saw that it was corrupt, for all flesh had corrupted their way on the earth" [World English Bible].

Flesh in this statement does not and cannot mean "meat" but actually "animate beings." In verse 13 God said:

"The end of all flesh is come before me; for the earth is filled with violence through them" [World English Bible].

Again, God was not talking about meat but rather living or animate beings that corrupted their original way of life and God given ordinances. Verse 19 clearly shows that "flesh," in fact includes "all living things:"

"Of every living thing of all flesh" [World English Bible].

Verse 15 also clearly shows that "flesh" refers to animate creatures or animals as animate beings and not meat which you eat:

"And they [all animals] went in unto Noah into the ark, two and two of all flesh" [World English Bible].

Verse 21 again positively proves that "flesh" does not refer to meat but rather all living creatures:

"And all flesh died that moved upon the earth [World English Bible]."

In chapter 8:17 God says to Noah:

"Bring forth with you every living thing that is with you, of all flesh" [World English Bible].

And, finally, note Genesis 9:17:

"God said to Noah, This is the token of the covenant which I have established between me and all flesh that is on the earth" [World English Bible].

In every single case where the word "flesh" is used in chapters which deal with the flood, the word applies to all living creatures, that is, animate beings in whose nostrils was the breath of life and whose life was in the blood. Now let's take another look at the passage of Genesis 9:4 where God actually speaks and gives Noah a specific prohibition concerning his diet. In other words, here God tells Noah what he must not eat under any circumstance:

"But flesh with the life thereof, which is the blood thereof, shall ye not eat" [King James Bible].

This is the translation from the Hebrew Masoretic Text which was compiled about the sixth century after the death of Jesus. But the Greek translators of this text rendered the text into Greek as follows:

'But flesh with blood of life you shall not eat' [Author's translation].

What God actually said to Noah is this: you may eat fruit of the reptiles which contain seed just as you ate grain, herbs and fruits which contained seed, but beings or creatures or souls which are alive or animate, whose life is in the blood, you shall not eat. If we were to replace the word "flesh" in the Greek Septuagint translation with the word "souls" [designating living creatures] the reading would be as follows:

"But souls with blood of life you shall not eat."

Clearly the meaning is not to eat the living souls whose life is in the blood and not koshered meat. The text clearly prohibits the slaughter of animals for food whose life is in the blood. This is precisely how the original and earliest Jewish Christians actually understood the passage. *Jewish Encyclopedia* points out that the earliest Jewish Christian sects argued their vegetarianism on the very statement of Genesis 9:4. They argued that in this passage God expressly forbade Noah to kill animals in order to eat their flesh. Before Noah entered the ark, God told him to take with him all manner of food which is edible so that there would be food for him and the animals. This irrefutably proves that there was no carnivorous animal in the ark, since the Hebrew text plainly shows that food taken was for the herbivorous animals. The text of Genesis 9:2-4 therefore does not teach what the Church has claimed all these centuries, but it rather irrefutably proves that Noah was vegetarian and that all animals at that time reverted back to a herbivorous diet, as it was in the beginning and as it shall be in the end.

If animals could not eat meat at that time, how then could God instruct Noah to kill any animal he wanted for its meat? The allowance of meat eating could not have come at the worst time in history. But some may argue that Noah had seven or seven pairs of the so-called clean animals so that he would be able to offer sacrifices and eat meat before the fruit and vegetables were in season. This is exactly why the Yahwist source interpolated this fable and already regarded animals as clean and unclean, even though the law of such distinction did not exist as yet. He contradicts another source which clearly states that there were only a pair of each species. Also, the Yahwist source uses the name Yahweh written as LORD in King James Bible even though we are told in Exodus that the name Yahweh was not known to the patriarchs. It is hard to see how a pair of all species fitted in the ark, let alone if we add additional six pairs of all so-called clean species. That God did not speak of all animals to Noah when he told him what he may eat but rather only of the reptiles, is very simple to demonstrate.

God told Noah that "all moving things which are alive" shall be his for food. The Hebrew word translated in the King James Bible "moving things" or "animals" in some other versions is actually "remes," which most certainly refers to "reptiles." There is a definite and clear distinction in the Bible between animals, birds, and reptiles. This distinction is pointed out at the very time they were created. Genesis 1:24 shows that God created all living creatures: "cattle," "creeping things," and "beasts" of the earth. Verse 25 states:

"God made the animals of the earth after their kind, and the cattle after their kind, and everything that creeps on the ground after its kind" [World English Bible].

The beasts are those animals which we call wild beasts. The cattle refer to animals we now refer to as domesticated and herbivorous. The creeping things refer to all the reptiles. The Hebrew word used is "remes" and most definitely refers to reptiles. In Genesis 6:20 God again made the distinction between other animals and reptiles, that is, "remes," translated "creeping thing" in the King James Bible. In Genesis 7:14 we again find a clear distinction in the animal kingdom:

"they, and every animal after its kind, all the cattle after their kind, every creeping thing that creeps on the earth after its kind, and every bird after its kind, every bird of every sort" [World English Bible].

In verse 23 we find this statement:

"And every living substance was destroyed which was upon the face of the ground, both man, and cattle, and the creeping things, and the fowl of the heaven" [King James Bible].

A clear distinction between man, cattle, birds and reptiles that is, "remes," who "creep" or "move" on the ground. With this firmly fixed in our minds, let us return to Genesis 9:2-3 where we read:

"And the fear of you and the dread of you shall be upon every beast of the earth, and upon every fowl of the air, upon all that moveth upon the earth, and upon all the fishes of the sea; into your hand are they delivered. Every moving thing that liveth shall be meat for you; even as the green herb have I given you all things" [King James Bible].

The first thing we must note in this text is the fact that there is a distinction between the fishes of the sea, the birds of the air, the beasts of the earth and the one who "moveth upon the earth." The King James translators have used the word "moveth" in this case instead of "creepeth," as they have done in other passages. It means one and the same: "to glide or crawl" and is used in reference to reptiles. Cattle, sheep, goats, chickens, etc., are not reptiles and therefore they were not included in "all that moveth upon the earth," of which God spoke to Noah. Sir Lancelot Brenton translating from the Greek Septuagint Bible correctly uses the word "reptile" to translate "remes." God spoke to Noah only about "remes" that is, reptiles, who crawl or creep upon the ground and who lay eggs in order to reproduce. This law was of temporal nature and lasted only until the fruits and vegetables were in season. It is as simple as that.

# CHAPTER 16
# Did Jesus Eat Fish?

For the past twenty-four years I have abstained from all kinds of meat. I maintain that it is unethical and against the perfect will of the Sovereign God to butcher and slaughter animals in order to eat their flesh. Recently there was a debate on the subject – and, as usually, a certain Christian believer referred to Luke 5 in order to prove that Jesus helped fishermen catch fish and if this is so then he could not have opposed the eating of the same.

The person also referred to the feeding of 5000 with bread and fish. Others also quote Luke 24:41-43 to prove that Jesus ate fish and honey in Jerusalem, on Sunday evening – in presence of the Eleven – during his allegedly first appearance to them. Others point to John 21 where we are told that after his resurrection Jesus helped his disciples catch fish, cook them and serve them as breakfast. It is also pointed out that Jesus had to eat meat since he observed the Passover and hence was obligated to eat the lamb. The Passover lamb is the subject of the next chapter.

I do not refute the fact that in these passages of the Christian New Testament it is plainly shown that Jesus did indeed regard fish as acceptable for food and that he himself consumed their flesh. But I maintain that there is a satisfactory biblical explanation for these passages and when properly understood, it follows that Jesus actually was a vegetarian. Here is the first passage, that of Luke 5:1-11:

"Now it happened, while the multitude pressed on him and heard the word of God, that he was standing by the lake of Gennesaret. He saw two boats standing by the lake, but the fishermen had gone out of them, and were washing their nets. He entered into one of the boats, which was Simon's, and asked him to put out a little from the land. He sat down and taught the multitudes out of the boat. When he had finished speaking, he said to Simon, 'Put out into the deep, and let down your nets for a catch.' Simon answered him, Master, we worked all night, and took nothing; but at your word I will let down the net. When they had done this, they caught a great multitude of fish, and their net was breaking. They beckoned to their partners in the other boat, that they should come and help them. They came, and filled both boats, so that they began to sink. But Simon Peter, when he saw it, fell down at Jesus' knees, saying, 'Depart from me, for I am a sinful man, Lord.' For he was amazed, and all who were with him, at the catch of fish which they had caught; and so also were James and John, sons of Zebedee, who were partners with Simon. Jesus said to Simon, 'Don't be afraid. From now on you will catch men alive.' When they had brought their boats to land, they left everything, and followed him" [World English Bible].

It is of colossal importance to determine just at what point of Jesus' ministry this incident supposedly took place. According to Luke's version, prior to this incident Peter, Andrew, John and James were not as yet the disciples of Jesus. However, by this point of time Jesus was already known throughout Galilee and his miracles and fame spread throughout. As a matter of fact, according to Luke's version, Jesus knew Peter before this incident, for he was in his home and actually healed his mother in law who was sick [Luke 4:38-39]. At that time Peter was not as yet Jesus' disciple. If the version we find in Luke's Gospel which is a forgery – in accordance with the synoptic principle – was the only version we have concerning the choosing of Peter, Andrew, John and James, then my task to prove that Jesus was a vegetarian would be significantly more difficult. But we also have the versions of Mark and Matthew and on the basis of their versions I have no choice but discard the version given in Luke's Gospel. Please note what Mark 1:14-20 has to say about the calling of the first four disciples – the fishermen – Peter, Andrew, John and James:

"Now after John was taken into custody, Jesus came into Galilee, preaching the Good News of the Kingdom of God, and saying, "The time is fulfilled, and the Kingdom of God is at hand! Repent, and believe in the Good News." Passing along by the sea of Galilee, he saw Simon and Andrew the brother of Simon casting a net into the sea, for they were fishermen. Jesus said to them, "Come after me, and I will make you into fishers for men." Immediately they left their nets, and followed him. Going on a little further from there, he saw James the son of Zebedee, and John, his brother, who were also in the boat mending the nets.

Immediately he called them, and they left their father, Zebedee, in the boat with the hired servants, and went after him" [World English Bible].

According to Mark, Jesus chose Peter and Andrew independently of John and James and at the very beginning of his ministry. Peter and Andrew were casting their nets into the sea and not washing them as Luke's version has it. Jesus did not preach from the boat at this point of time – as Luke's version has it – but actually later. After calling Peter and Andrew he then went on and saw John and James mending their nets with their father. He called them and they became his followers. Luke's version which insinuates that Jesus helped Peter and his fishing partners catch lots of fish is a synoptic forgery. In Matthew 4:18-22 we read the following of the same incident:

"Walking by the sea of Galilee, he {TR reads "Jesus" instead of "he"} saw two brothers: Simon, who is called Peter, and Andrew, his brother, casting a net into the sea; for they were fishermen. He said to them, "Come after me, and I will make you fishers for men." They immediately left their nets and followed him. Going on from there, he saw two other brothers, James the son of Zebedee, and John his brother, in the boat with Zebedee their father, mending their nets. He called them. They immediately left the boat and their father, and followed him" [World English Bible].

The versions of Mark and Matthew nullify the version in Luke's Gospel and therefore on the basis of these testimonies I can safely conclude that Jesus did not disturb the fishes of the sea nor did he catch them for human consumption. Now we can look at the text of Luke 24:41-43 which explicitly says that Jesus asked for food and that he actually ate fish and honey which the disciples gave him:

"While they still didn't believe for joy, and wondered, he said to them, "Do you have anything here to eat?" They gave him a piece of a broiled fish and some honeycomb. He took them, and ate in front of them" [World English Bible].

This is the only passage in the entire New Testament where we are most emphatically told that Jesus in fact ate meat. Those who believe in every word of the Bible but who also practice vegetarianism [like the Reformed Adventists for example], explain that Jesus only ate of the honey but not of the fish. They argue that fish and honey should not be combined and that if Jesus ate both together, he would have been sick. The problem with this theory is that there are Greek manuscripts that omit honey. This fact is also reflected in the English translations – where most translators mention fish only and exclude honey. [See for example: The Bible for Today, The Moffat Bible, The New American Bible for Catholics, The Jerusalem Bible, The New English Bible, The Living Bible, The New American Standard Bible, New International Version, Good News Bible, Jewish New Testament, Rotherham Emphasized Bible, The Interlinear Greek English New Testament by Marshall, etc.]. All these translators omit honey since these scholars regard these manuscripts as more important. Therefore, it follows that according to most English versions of Luke, the disciples handed fish to Jesus and he ate it while they watched. If this passage is authentic and inspired then no words could justify vegetarianism – unless we reject the authority of Jesus and say that he was an impostor. I however, firmly believe that Jesus was not an impostor but rather the promised Prophet – promised by Moses who was to come. How then do I explain the passage in question where it is said that the Son of God – as a resurrected and immortal being – actually ate meat? The passage is very simple to explain. It is also a synoptic forgery.

Luke says that Jesus appeared to two disciples who were on their way to Emmaus. One of them was named Clopas. He was invited to their place late in the afternoon on the day after his resurrection. When he broke bread before meal, the two disciples realized that it was Jesus. As soon as they realized this, they immediately returned to Jerusalem which was about 10 kilometres from Emmaus. Please note:

"They rose up that very hour, returned to Jerusalem, and found the eleven gathered together, and those who were with them, saying, "The Lord is risen indeed, and has appeared to Simon!" They related the things that happened along the way, and how he was recognized by them in the breaking of the bread. As they said these things, Jesus himself stood among them, and said to them, "Peace be to you." [Luke 24:33-36 World English Bible].

Luke therefore clearly places Jesus' first appearance to his disciples on Sunday evening in Jerusalem. He says that all eleven were present – even though John, who also says that Jesus appeared to his disciples at evening on the "first day of the week" actually says that Thomas was missing. Matthew and Mark however, clearly show that Jesus was not in Jerusalem that evening and that his first appearance to his disciples was not that evening nor even in Jerusalem but rather later in Galilee. On the night of his arrest, Jesus said to his disciples that after he rises from the dead, he would go to Galilee ahead of them" [Mark 14:28].

The angel said to the women at the tomb to go and tell Peter and the disciples that he is going ahead of them to Galilee and that they would see him there" [Mark 16:7]. According to the testimony of Mark, Jesus clearly told his disciples that after he is risen from the dead he would go to Galilee and that is where the disciples were going to see him. Matthew 26:32 also quotes Jesus as telling his disciples that after he is risen from the dead, he would go ahead of them to Galilee.

Matthew states that the angel at the tomb told the women to go quickly and tell the disciples that Jesus is on his way to Galilee and that they should go there to see him [Matthew 28:7]. Jesus himself appeared to the women and told them not to be afraid but to tell his disciples to go to Galilee in order to see him alive [Matthew 28:10]. Then in Matthew 28:16 we are emphatically told that his eleven disciples went to Galilee to a place that Jesus told them to go. According to Matthew, the eleven Apostles went to

Galilee to a mountain Jesus specified. There, in Galilee, the disciples saw Jesus for the first time after his resurrection.

When they saw him some doubted. Had they seen him previously they would have no reason to doubt. Even this fact proves that this appearance was the very first to his disciples and that they did not see him on Sunday evening in Jerusalem. The account of Luke therefore cannot be reconciled with the text of Mark and especially that of Matthew. Therefore the text of Luke so often cited as proof that Jesus was a meat eater and therefore not a vegetarian – as many sources prove – is a synoptic forgery. We have already seen what the synoptic forgery did to the Gospels of Matthew and Luke. Now we can take a look at John 21.

Most critical and independent scholars believe that John's Gospel ended with chapter 20 and that this chapter is a later addition or interpolation. Be it as it may, whether interpolation or part of the original Greek version, it does not prove what is claimed here. We are told that Peter with some other disciples decided to go fishing. This was after Jesus rose from the dead and after he supposedly already appeared to them two times. They fished all night but caught nothing. At sunrise Jesus allegedly appeared to them and told them to cast a net on the right-hand side of the boat. When they did, they caught a multitude, 153 fish, to be exact. As they came to the shore, they saw a charcoal fire lighted with fish on it. He told them to bring some of the fish they caught. Then in verse 13 we are told that Jesus gave the disciples bread and fish to eat. Verse 14 states that this was the very third appearance of Jesus to his disciples since his resurrection.

This very verse proves that the passage in question is a forgery and not a historical event. According to the Gospel of John, Jesus' first appearance to his disciples was at evening on the first day of the week. John's Gospel agrees with Luke although it says that Thomas wasn't present that evening while Luke's version has all eleven present – including Thomas. John 20:19 confirms the first appearance. Then in verses 26-27 we are told that a week later Jesus again appeared to his disciples and that this time Thomas was present. This was the second appearance. The third was allegedly the time he served bread and fish to his disciples as we have seen.

# THE EBIONITES

It was already pointed out that Jesus did not appear to his disciples in the evening on Sunday in Jerusalem, but rather later in Galilee. This is an irrefutable teaching of Mark's and Matthew's Gospels. Since John's gospel is wrong about the first and second appearances, it must also be wrong about the third appearance. In Mark 16:9-19 – the additional verses – we also read of three appearances.

"Now when he had risen early on the first day of the week, he appeared first to Mary Magdalene, from whom he had cast out seven demons. She went and told those who had been with him, as they mourned and wept. When they heard that he was alive, and had been seen by her, they disbelieved. After these things he was revealed in another form to two of them, as they walked, on their way into the country. They went away and told it to the rest. They didn't believe them, either. Afterward he was revealed to the eleven themselves as they sat at the table, and he rebuked them for their unbelief and hardness of heart, because they didn't believe those who had seen him after he had risen. He said to them, "Go into all the world, and preach the Good News to the whole creation. He who believes and is baptized will be saved; but he who disbelieves will be condemned. These signs will accompany those who believe: in my name they will cast out demons; they will speak with new languages; they will take up serpents; and if they drink any deadly thing, it will in no way hurt them; they will lay hands on the sick, and they will recover." So then the Lord Jesus, after he had spoken to them, was received up into heaven, and sat down at the right hand of God" [World English Bible].

The first appearance was to Mary Magdalene. The second to two disciples on the road to Emaus. The third to the Eleven. The third appearance was the first and last appearance to the Eleven. Therefore John 21 contradicts Mark and Matthew. In John 21 Jesus supposedly appointed Peter a shepherd over other disciples. But the Book of Acts disproves this and shows that James the Just – the brother of Jesus – was in charge of the Twelve. Now we are ready to deal with the issue of feeding the multitudes with loaves and fishes. In the Gospel of the Holy Twelve which is said to have been translated by Rev. G. J. Ousely, we are told that the crowd was fed by bread and clusters of grapes. The problem is that it cannot be proven nor disproven that this gospel was not forged by Ousely. Some scholars believe that fish was not served but rather fishweeds. Church Father Irenaeus does not mention fish when he quotes the feeding of the 5000 or 4000 but only bread. The same is true when Eusebius and Arnobious refer to the feeding of the crowds. They never refer to the fish but only bread.

This could suggest that the inclusion of fish is a later interpolation. Indeed, according to the Synoptic Gospels, Jesus commanded his disciples to collect only bread in baskets and not fish. Later when he referred to the feeding of the 5000 and 4000, he always mentioned only the baskets of bread and never any baskets of fish. This, again, indicates that inclusion of fish could have been later interpolation. It is also worthy of note that the people were with Jesus two days before he fed them. It was spring – since they sat on the green grass.

The young boy had two fishes with him which he obviously took from home fried or cooked. Would the fish have been suitable to eat at least two days later? However, I have no problem at all if the story is true and if Jesus indeed multiplied the fish and if he served them to the hungry crowd. Jesus did not catch these fish nor did he kill them. They were already dead. He simply multiplied the dead fish. Having said that, I doubt very much that either grapes or fish were involved. I believe that Jesus multiplied only the loaves of bread. Be it as it may, this does not prove that Jesus condoned the butchery of animals and the eating of animal flesh.

In some parables Jesus spoke of the feasts where animals were killed and meat served. But he spoke to the people who practiced this and obviously it was logical to use the manner of speech they could relate to. I, myself, sometimes do the same, usually for convenience sake. At no time does this speech prove that I condone the practice I may use for an example. The same is true of Jesus. In the parable of the Prodigal Son the father commanded his servants to kill a fattened calf. The father represented God. Obviously, God does not butcher animals in His realm. Jesus used the speech that related to the meat eating people.

## CHAPTER 17
# Did Jesus Eat the Passover Lamb?

It is often pointed out that Jesus was not and could not have been a vegetarian since as the perfect observer of the Law he was obligated to eat the lamb during the Passover festival. It is further claimed that if Jesus did not eat the Passover lamb then he was a sinner and a breaker of God's Law. It amazes me that these same people never charge John the Baptist of breaking God's Law by not observing the Passover and by not eating the lamb during the Passover season. If Jesus was obligated to observe the Passover and to eat the lamb, then it follows that John the Baptist was also obligated to observe the Passover festival. But the Bible clearly shows that John the Baptist spent his entire life in the desert and that he never went to Jerusalem to observe the Passover. In Luke 1:80 we read of John the Baptist the following:

"The child was growing, and becoming strong in spirit, and was in the desert until the day of his public appearance to Israel" [World English Bible].

According to Luke, the Baptist spent his life in the desert and he never went to Jerusalem to observe any of the festivals. But if all the injunctions in the Jewish Pentateuch were originally given by God, then the Baptist failed to fulfil God's Law. Even after he began his ministry, the Baptist refused to observe the Passover and he refused to even eat the unleavened bread during the Passover season because he objected to the festival and considered it wrong to eat the lamb and since the unleavened bread was connected with the lamb he refused to partake of it. The Jewish historian Josephus who was contemporary of the Apostles wrote concerning John the Baptist. In the Slavonian version of the Jewish War, Josephus, among other things, states that John was an absolute vegetarian who refused to even eat the Passover bread and even to pronounce the words in memory of the exodus Passover. He also states that he never allowed wine to be brought near him and that animal flesh he absolutely refused to eat.

The Church Fathers believed and the Church in general that James, the brother of Jesus, was a vegetarian from birth. Hegesepius who lived not long after the Apostles, wrote everything he knew about them. His writings were often quoted by the later Church Fathers. This is what Hegesepius had to say concerning James the Just:

"James the brother of the Lord surnamed the Just was made head of the Church at Jerusalem. Many indeed are called James. This one was holy from his mother's womb. He drank neither wine nor strong drink, ATE NO FLESH, never shaved" [The Nicene and Post Nicene Fathers, Vol. 3. p. 361].

Eusebius Pamphilius wrote:

"This apostle was consecrated from his mother's womb. He drank neither wine nor fermented liquors, and abstained from animal food. A razor never came upon his head" [Eusebius's Ecclesiastical History, p. 76].

St. Augustine wrote:

"St. James never ate animal food, living on seeds and vegetables, never tasting flesh or wine" [Ecclesiastical History, 2 Vols. Translated by H.J. Lawlor and J.E.L. Oulton].

The *Catholic Encyclopaedia* art. St. James the Less, states:

"The universal testimony of Christian antiquity is entirely in accordance with the information derived from the canonical books as to the fact that James was Bishop of the Church of Jerusalem. Hegesepius who lived about the middle of the second century, relates (and his narrative is highly probable) that James was called the "Just," that he drank no wine nor strong drink, nor ate animal food..."

If James was a vegetarian from his mother's womb and if he never tasted flesh, then he obviously never ate the flesh of a lamb during the Passover season. If James and John the Baptist did not eat the Passover lamb and were guiltless, why then should we assume that Jesus was obligated to eat the Passover lamb and that if he didn't, that he was a sinner and a breaker of God's Law? I should also point out that there were and still are Jewish vegetarians in the rabbinical Judaism and that even some rabbis are vegetarian and that all these Jews never eat the lamb or any meat whatsoever during the Passover observance. But I will prove from the Bible itself that Jesus did not eat the lamb nor did he observe the Last Supper on the Passover night as commonly supposed.

John states that six days before the Passover, Jesus came to Bethany where Lazarus gave him a banquet [John 12:1-2]. On the next day he rode into Jerusalem [verse 12]. Then in 13:1 John states that the Last Supper took place before the Passover. He also shows that Jesus was reclining on the couch and the disciple he loved which means that the meal was not the Passover lamb for they could not eat that meal in a reclining position but in a standing position. Likewise, if that night was the Passover night then all the shops would have been closed for the shop keepers would have been in their homes, eating the lamb.

Yet the disciples thought that Judas went into the night in order to buy something they needed for the Feast [13:29]. Neither could have the trial taken place during that night for the chief priests and other priests and witnesses would have also been in their homes eating the Passover lambs. Also, in accordance with the Passover command and tradition, the Jews remained in their homes all night during the Passover night and only in the morning they burnt whatever was left of the lamb. But John clearly shows that Jesus with the disciples did not stay in the house all night but rather went across the Kidron brook [18:1]. He was arrested that very night which proves that it could not have been the Passover night. In 18:28 John makes it very plain that the night of his trial was not the Passover night since after the trial of Jesus they would not enter the Praetorium so that they would not become ritually polluted and so be unable to eat the Passover that coming night:

"They led Jesus therefore from Caiaphas into the Praetorium. It was early, and they themselves didn't enter into the Praetorium, that they might not be defiled, but might eat the Passover" [World English Bible].

Therefore, the morning of the 14th of Abib was before the Passover night and that is why they were worried lest they be defiled and thus not be able to eat the lamb that evening. Because those who were defiled or were on a journey had to observe the Passover on the 14th at evening, the following month, as prescribed in the Jewish Pentateuch. After questioning Jesus, Pilate brought him before the people about noon – still being before the Passover night:

"And it was the preparation of the Passover, and about the sixth hour" [King James Bible].

By noon, being the sixth hour of the day, the Jews removed all leaven from their homes and about three in the afternoon the priests began slaughtering and roasting the lambs on that day so that the people could eat the Passover that coming night. Because it was the preparation day and the people had to get ready for the evening meal of the Passover – the authorities wanted the bodies removed as quickly as possible, since the following day was the 15th of Abib and therefore the day following the Passover night and being the first day of Unleavened Bread Festival and therefore an annual Sabbath:

"The Jews therefore, because it was the preparation, that the bodies should not remain upon the cross on the sabbath day [for that sabbath day was a high day,] besought Pilate that their legs might be broken, and that they might be taken away" [19:31 King James Bible].

"There laid they Jesus therefore because of the Jews' preparation day; for sepulchre was nigh at hand" [19:42 King James Bible].

I have presented the evidence from the Gospel of John which irrefutably proves that the Last Supper was not the Passover night and therefore this proves that Jesus did not eat the lamb that night. However, those who embrace the Easter tradition generally believe that Jesus was arrested and put to death on Friday the 15th of Abib or Nisan. The two prominent theologians demonstrate this view. Archibald Thomas Robertson, professor of New

Testament Interpretation in the Southern Baptist Theological Seminary in his *Word Pictures in the New Testament,* Vol. I, on page 207, in regards to Matthew 26:17 states that according to the traditional view Jesus ate the Passover about 6p.m., which, according to the Jews, began the 15th of Abib and that the lambs were slain and roasted in the afternoon of the 14th.

Alfred Edersheim [born of Jewish parents but a convert to Christianity] states that early in the morning of the 15th Jesus was handed to the Romans, after he ate the Passover with his disciples. He claims that Jesus insituted the "Supper" on the very Passover night and that his crucifixion took place on the first day of Unleavened Bread Festival, the 15th [The Temple: Its Ministry and Services, pp. 200, 311].

In all honesty, this immediately creates a difficulty. The 15th of Abib was the first day of Unleavened Bread Festival. It was the Feast Day and the annual Sabbath. The chief priests decided to kill Jesus but they have uniformly agreed not to do so during the Feast Day lest the people would riot. Please note the text of Mark 14:1,2,10-11:

"After two days was the feast of the passover, and of unleavened bread: and the chief priests and the scribes sought how they might take him by craft, and put him to death. But they said, Not on a feast day, lest there be an uproar of the people..." [King James Bible].

This is also stated in Matthew 26:5. The Jewish leaders decided not to kill Jesus on the Feast Day – that is, Abib 15. This day was held in reverence because of the following injunctions in the Jewish Pentateuch:

"And this day shall be unto you for a memorial; and ye shall keep it a feast to the LORD throughout your generations; ye shall keep it a feast by an ordinance for ever. Seven days shall ye eat unleavened bread; even the first day ye shall put away leaven out of your houses: for whosoever eateth leavened bread from the first day until the seventh day that soul shall be cut off from Israel. And in the first day there shall be a holy convocation, and in the seventh day there shall be an holy convocation to you. No manner of work shall be done in them, save that which every man must eat, that only may be done" [Exodus 12:14-16 King James Bible].

"In the fourteenth day of the first month at even is the LORD'S passover. And on the fifteenth day of the same month is the Feast of Unleavened Bread unto the LORD: seven days ye must eat unleavened bread. In the first day ye shall have a holy convocation: ye shall do no servile work therein...in the seventh day is an holy convocation: ye shall do no servile work therein" [Leviticus 23:5-8 King James Bible].

"And in the fourteenth day of the first month is the passover of the LORD. And in the fifteenth day of this month is the feast: seven days shall unleavened bread be eaten. In the first day shall be a holy convocation; ye shall do no manner of servile work therein" [Numbers 28:16-19 King James Bible].

The 15$^{th}$ of Abib was the first day of the Festival and is called the Feast. The chief priests uniformly agreed not to arrest and kill Jesus on that day. Abib 15 was the Feast Day or annual Sabbath on which holy assembly was commanded and secular work expressly forbidden. On that day they were permitted to only prepare that what they would eat. When we realize this, then it becomes apparent why the Jewish leaders ruled out Abib 15 as the execution day.

When we carefully study the relevant texts of the Gospels, it becomes plain that the chief priests and the Jews in general spent the day at Golgotha. So did Jesus' family and the women from Galilee who followed him. There is no evidence to suggest that there was a holy convocation which the chief priests, elders or common people attended. The Synoptic Gospels [Matthew, Mark and Luke] refer to the day of execution as "preparation day." John calls it "preparation for the Passover." How could this be the case if the day of execution was Abib 15? How could the Jews be preparing for the Passover on Friday, 15$^{th}$ of Abib, if they have already observed the Passover the previous evening? How could they call it the preparation day when in fact the 15$^{th}$ of Abib was the Feast Day and the annual Sabbath Day? If Jesus was crucified on Friday the 15$^{th}$ of Abib, then there would have been two Sabbaths back-to-back in that week. Friday, the annual Sabbath, and Saturday Sabbath. But if that was the case it would mean that the chief priests sealed the tomb and set the guard to watch the tomb of Jesus on the weekly Sabbath, since they did so on the "next day" – the day after the crucifixion. This is unthinkable.

The Synoptic Gospels seem to contradict John by placing the Passover on the first day of Unleavened Bread Festival and therefore, if so, it would logically follow that the crucifixion took place on the 16th of Abib. Please not Mark 14:12:

"On the first day of unleavened bread, when they sacrificed the Passover, his disciples asked him, "Where do you want us to go and prepare that you may eat the Passover?" [World English Bible].

According to all biblical texts the first day of the Unleavened Bread Festival always was the 15th of Abib. Therefore, the Synoptic Gospels taken literally, according to the traditional translations, would have placed the Passover meal in the evening of the 15th of Abib and the crucifixion on the 16th of Abib. The first conjecture is that the authors of the Synoptic Gospels based themselves on the tradition recorded in Deuteronomy 16:2-8, which gives alternative injunction concerning the Passover:

"You shall sacrifice the Passover to Yahweh your God, of the flock and the herd, in the place which Yahweh shall choose, to cause his name to dwell there. You shall eat no leavened bread with it. You shall eat unleavened bread with it seven days, even the bread of affliction; for you came out of the land of Egypt in haste; that you may remember the day when you came out of the land of Egypt all the days of your life. No yeast shall be seen with you in all your borders seven days; neither shall any of the meat, which you sacrifice the first day at evening, remain all night until the morning. You may not sacrifice the Passover within any of your gates, which Yahweh your God gives you; but at the place which Yahweh your God shall choose, to cause his name to dwell in, there you shall sacrifice the Passover at evening, at the going down of the sun, at the season that you came out of Egypt. You shall roast and eat it in the place which Yahweh your God chooses. In the morning you shall return to your tents. Six days you shall eat unleavened bread. On the seventh day shall be a solemn assembly to Yahweh your God. You shall do no work" [World English Bible].

The injunction in this text deviates from other passages in the Pentateuch. First, it allows a calf to be also used for the victim and not only a lamb.

Then it commands that the victim be cooked whereas other texts prohibit cooking and commands roasting only. The Hebrew word used elsewhere is "bashal" and it states that they must not "bashal" the lamb whereas in this text they are told to "bashal" the lamb or a calf. But the most significant divergence lies in the fact that the victim should be killed as the Sun goes down on the FIRST DAY OF THE SEVEN and that it does not command holy convocation on the first day of the seven but only on the seventh. In the morning after the Passover was eaten on the FIRST of the SEVEN days, they could go home. The Unleavened Bread Festival continues for another SIX DAYS and on the final day the holy convocation is prescribed.

The Synoptic Gospels state that on the FIRST DAY the disciples came to Jesus and asked him where to prepare the Passover. Jesus told them where to and then in the evening on that first day they got together in the upper room. Later that night he was arrested and on the morrow was crucified – being the SECOND DAY of the Festival according to this reckoning. Another possibility is that the Synoptic authors followed the Jewish tradition of their time and added the Passover to the seven days – making the Festival eight days long. The first day would thus be 14th of Abib and the Passover night later in the evening of that day. The crucifixion would thus fall on the 15th of Abib. Some justification for this is found in the fact that both Mark and Luke refer to the Festival of Unleavened Bread as Passover – thus implying eight days.

Another solution is that the texts were somewhat mistranslated and that alternative reading would thus place the Last Supper at evening on the 13th of Abib and thus the crucifixion on the 14th – being the day the Jews were removing the leaven and were preparing for the Passover. John definitely places the evening meal on the 13th. I tend to think that this is the best solution to the problem. Matthew 26:17 reads:

"Now on the first day of unleavened bread, the disciples came to Jesus, saying to him, Where do you want us to prepare for you to eat the Passover?" [World English Bible].

"On the first day of unleavened bread." [Ibid].

More literally translated this should read: But before the Passover week. Therefore, the day in question is the 13th as John clearly states. But is there any justification to translate the text in this manner. The Greek word "protos" has been translated in the King James Bible also as "before" in John 1:15 and 30. James Strong under word "protos," number 4413, says that the word means: foremost – in time, place, order or importance. Then he states that it comes from the word "pro," number 4253, which means: fore, ie. in front of, prior. The word "pro" has been translated "before" in many, many places in the New Testament. The Greek word "azumos" translated "Unleavened Bread Festival" was also specifically by implication used to refer to the "Passover Week" as James Strong points out under word 106.

Mark 14:12 reads:

"On the first day of unleavened bread, when they sacrificed the Passover, his disciples asked him, Where do you want us to go and make ready that you may eat the Passover?" [World English Bible].

Here also appears the word "protos" and therefore the text correctly understood reads: And before the day of unleavened bread, when they sacrificed the passover...

The Passover was on the 14th. The day before was the 13th. Luke 22:7 reads:

"The day of unleavened bread came, on which the Passover must be sacrificed" [World English Bible].

The word "came" comes from the Greek word "erchomai" which simply means "to come." But this word was qualified by the following Greek word "de" which has not even been translated. The word opposes the previous word and qualifies it and therefore the text should read: The day of unleavened bread was coming – but did not come yet – when the passover should be sacrificed.

The Passover was killed in the evening of the 14th and the day before it was the 13th. Synoptics properly understood agree with John who places the Last Supper on the 13th of Abib. This also agrees with the Talmud statement that Yeshu was hanged on the "eve of the passover." It also agrees with the statement in the Gospel of Peter that Pilate delivered Jesus to the people "before the unleavened bread festival." It is highly unlikely that all three Synoptic authors would have placed the killing of the lambs on the first day of the Unleavened Bread Festival and thus on the 15$^{th}$, when all knew at that time that the Jews observed the passover on the 14$^{th}$. Moreover, the fact that all three Synoptic Gospels refer to the day of the crucifixion as "preparation day" and John as "preparation for the Passover" prove that it was not the 15$^{th}$ of Abib. If it was then they would have stated that the day was either the sabbath or the feast day and not the preparation day. For those who accept the New Testament as infallible, the evidence of John is sufficient to prove that Jesus did not observe the Passover night and therefore those who claim that he ate meat of the lamb are mistaken. Likewise, if Jesus was a Law breaker for not eating the Passover lamb, then also were John the Baptist and James, the brother of Jesus. It is as simple as that.

# CHAPTER 18
# Anatomy of the Human Body Proves Vegetarianism

Have you ever wondered why you eat flesh of animals and whether carnivorous diet is in accordance with God's nature? In other words, is it natural and ethically moral for a human being to be a butcher and to slash the throat of an innocent animal in order to eat its flesh? In all probability the reader has simply accepted the common trend of humanity and the diet in which he or she was raised in. I was a carnivore until the age of 38. I must admit however, that Christianity and Judaism had a great influence on me concerning my diet. I have simply taken for granted that God endorsed meat eating and the Jewish sacrificial cult.

However, when I came in contact with the Dead Sea Scrolls and when I began to seriously study the earliest form of Christianity, I realized that Jesus was not the founder of Christianity but rather a reformer of Judaism and that the earliest believers and followers of Jesus were actually vegetarian. Likewise, I have come to realize that even many Church Fathers were vegetarian and that they have condemned killing of animals for its flesh or sacrifice.

In this chapter I will argue vegetarianism simply on the principle of nature and whether humans in their natural habitat should and could be carnivorous beings. In order to find out whether the carnivorous diet for humanity is ethical and in tune with God's nature, we need to be honest, objective and open minded. We must carefully weigh the facts and examine the evidence. When we carefully observe the living beings in existence, we can see that each species is naturally equipped with everything it needs to eat its food. Carnivorous animals differ from the herbivore. Sheep and cattle, horses and giraffes for example differ from lions and hyenas. The herbivore is not equipped like the carnivore to chase and eat its prey. Their teeth are different. The mouths of the herbivore are relatively small in proportion to their heads.

Herbivorous animals could not kill their prey with their teeth nor could they rip open the bodies of other animals in order to consume their flesh. The carnivore's teeth are long and sharp so they can pierce into flesh. Herbivore's teeth are not pointed but flat edged so they could bite, crush and grind. A carnivore jaw moves up and down and they swallow their meat without chewing it. Herbivore's jaws move from side to side and back to front so that they could chew, grind and crush their food. The stomach of the carnivore forms powerful digestive enzymes with about ten times the amount of hydrochloric acid of a herbivore.

The small intestines of the carnivore are three to six times the length of its body. The flesh they eat is toxic so the intestines must be short in order to excrete the toxins fast. The small intestines of the herbivore are ten to twelve times longer than their bodies. The saliva of a carnivore does not contain digestive enzymes. A herbivore's saliva is alkaline, containing carbohydrate digestive enzymes. Carnivore animals do not sweat like the herbivore. Observe a meat-eating animal after a long run. The body is dry but the sweat drips from its tongue. The bodies of herbivore perspire through pores on the skin. Observe the carnivore when it drinks water. They lap it with their tongues. The herbivore suck water with their mouths.

Why have I pointed all this out? Put simply, in order to prove that the anatomy and behaviour of the carnivore is different from the herbivore. But in what group should we humans be classified? Everything I pointed out we have in common with the herbivore and nothing with the carnivorous animals. Does not then the anatomy of our bodies, which is like those of the herbivore, irrefutably prove that humans should be herbivorous beings? Something else should be noted. All carnivorous animals eat their flesh in its natural raw state. Therefore, if you want to eat flesh why not eat it raw and why not tear it from animals with your fingers and your teeth. Nature did not equip you with knife. Use your teeth and your fingers to rip open the buffalo, gazelle and sheep.

There is something else you need to be aware of. Carnivorous animals hunt the herbivore. Lions do not eat tigers, foxes, hyenas etc., but rather herbivore. Do you know why? Because they need all the nutrients from the herbs and plants. The flesh of a carnivore does not contain enough of these nutrients necessary for existence. If a carnivore was fed flesh only from the carnivorous animals it would not be able to live long. For the same reason humans feed on animals that are herbivore – pigs being exempted. Pigs are omnivorous animals and they also feed on flesh. Jesus said:

"Don't give that which is holy to the dogs, neither cast your pearls before the pigs, lest perhaps they trample them under their feet, and turn and tear you to pieces" [Matthew 7:6 World English Bible].

Dogs and pigs can tear you to pieces. It is not uncommon that a sow would eat her own piglets. Pigs can devour chickens and other animals. Earlier this year a man had a heart attack in a town where I was raised. He fell in a pig pen and parts of his body were eaten by pigs. Something else is of colossal importance. God did not create animals for you to kill them and eat their flesh. Animals feel pain and for that reason they run away when they sense fear. In contrast plants, herbs and fruit trees are planted and they cannot run away. This in itself proves that these are intended for food. Some would want you to believe that vegetarians are also murderers since they kill the living plants. But plants although alive do not possess brains and the nervous system. Without these it is impossible to consciously register pain. Plants cannot register pain in the same way animals and humans cannot feel and register pain when unconscious or when a total anaesthetic is administered. If God wanted us to eat meat then He would have created animals without brains and nervous systems. He could have also caused them to grow chops and sausages on their bodies so that we could harvest them the way we harvest plants and fruits.

Many try to justify their carnivorous diets on the basis that we humans are the most intelligent of all animate beings on the Earth, and therefore that gives us a license to do with other animate beings as we please. But imagine if there are aliens somewhere in space who are much more advanced than we are. Imagine if they took over our world and would do to us what we are doing to animals. Suppose they would open the dairy farms where they would breed our women for the sake of dairy industry and the babies for the slaughter houses. Could that be justified just because they are more advanced than we are? How would you like to be their home pet? They would treat you nicely, the way you treat your pets. How would you feel if they took you to their home planet and placed you in a nice and a modern Zoo together with some other animals? I think that I know the answer. Why then do we exploit and treat other animate beings with such barbarism and cruelty?

All you Christians who believe that Jesus gave you license to eat all and any flesh and who believe, like Paul, that every creature God created is good for food since it can be consecrated through prayer, go ahead then and eat cats, rats, dogs and frogs. Snakes, skunks, lizards, mice, worms and host of other crawling insects. If you truly believe that all creatures are good for food, why then do you look with contempt on the Chinese and the Koreans for eating dogs and all these similar creatures? Why are you such a hypocrite – believing one thing, yet practicing another?

# CHAPTER 19
# Cosmic Law of Preservation Proves Vegetarianism

We were all born *ignorant*. Gradually, through various methods of education we have acquired certain level of knowledge. Our perception of what is right and what wrong largely depends on our background and religious upbringing. A Jew will teach his child the ways of Judaism, a Muslim the ways of Islam, a Hindu the ways of Hinduism, just as Christians will educate their children in the ways of Christendom and Buddhists in the ways of Buddhism. What is right and permissible in one religion is wrong and illegal in another. For example, Judaism and Islam permit their followers to practice polygamy but forbid them to eat pork. In contrast, Christianity in general forbids polygamy but allows its converts to eat pork. Buddhism on the other hand encourages celibacy and prohibits the carnivorous diet altogether. Who is right? Is there a way to tell what is really right and what wrong?

Just about everything you see today exists from the very beginning. It was created during the six days as described in Genesis 1. But the Bible was not there in the beginning. In fact, people lived and died for millennia before any part of the canonical Bible was written. Just think for a moment. Adam lived and died without having the Bible to read and to show him the way to salvation. His sons Cain and Abel lived and died and yet they knew nothing about the Bible. Enoch lived and pleased God but not because he found the answers in the Bible. The Bible did not exist in the days of Enoch. But since Enoch did what is right, he must have had something to make him aware of what is right and what wrong. Noah was found righteous in his generation. But others were judged wicked. Neither Noah nor the people of his generation had the Bible to either enlighten them or confuse them. Yet there was a way to tell who was right and who wrong even in those days when the Bible was not in existence.

Abraham, Isaac, Jacob and all the other Patriarchs, including Job, the descendant of Esau, all pleased God even though they did not have the Bible to read. The Sodomites were guilty of wrong even though they did not have the Bible. Since they were found guilty, the Sodomites somehow must have known that what they were doing was wrong and against the nature and character of the loving and perfect God. The Israelites lived for more than a thousand years without having the bulk of the Old Testament books now available to us. They certainly lived and died without ever being able to read any of the Gospels or other New Testament material.

Even Jesus and all those of his time lived at the time when they did not have the New Testament. And, of course, myriads have died before the time of Jesus and after his first advent without ever hearing about the Bible. There are also millions today who have never heard of the Bible or ever read any part of it. Revelation 20:12 says that all the dead who will rise on the Last Day will be judged according to what they have done in this life. Jesus said that all those who died through the ages – yes, even millions of those who never heard about the Bible – will one day hear his voice and after hearing it will come out of their graves. Those who have done what is right will be the children of life and those who have done wrong will be the children of condemnation [John 5:28-29]. Therefore, it follows that you don't need the Bible to tell you what is right and what wrong. In fact, if you depend on the Bible to find out what is right and what wrong you may die never discovering it.

There is a Cosmic Law in existence – which always was and always shall be – which clearly shows what is right and what wrong. This Law is not recorded on the pages of books which can be destroyed and corrupted. This Law is the living Law set in motion in every living creature. It is the Law that no person could ever alter and fabricate. It is as real and as powerful as the laws which govern every facet of this universe. This Law the Essenes called *The Law of Preservation*. God created all living things to *live a life to its fullest*. From the very beginning God forbade that any living creature should kill another living creature. For that reason He implemented a fruitarian/herbivorous diet. No living soul was allowed to eat the flesh of another living soul or to bring any harm to another living creature. God made sure that every living creature would have this Cosmic Law of Preservation written in its own soul and mind. Every living being is aware of this Law but very few choose to live in accordance with it.

God made every living creature capable of feeling both pain and pleasure. An object feels neither – because it is a thing and not a living organism. These two attributes are absolutely essential for survival and the preservation of life. Imagine if you could not feel pain. You would not be able to survive. If caught on fire unaware you would burn to death because there would be no feeling of pain to warn you that your life is in danger. The feeling of pain is there to tell us that something is wrong in our system. It could be physical sickness and disease or danger or mental and psychological problem. Sometimes we resort to extreme pain in order to preserve our life. In urgent cases and in difficult circumstances people have their limbs amputated and other very painful surgeries performed even without anaesthetic – in order to save their lives.

Pain is absolutely necessary for the preservation of life. All living creatures – from the smallest and least important to the largest and most important – feel pain. But at the same time all these living creatures also feel pleasure. Pleasure is also absolutely essential for survival. Nothing gives you more pleasure than food when you are absolutely starving. The same is true of water when you are dying of thirst. Now both food and drink are absolutely required for your survival and the preservation of life. In order to insure you would eat and drink, and so preserve your life – God gave you an urge to eat when you feel hungry and drink when you feel thirsty.

At the same time, he gave you tastebuds to appreciate the pleasure of the same. Because offspring is absolutely essential for survival, God made sex pleasurable to insure the procreation of the living species. There is also great pleasure in sleep when you are tired and in everything else that is essential for your survival and perfect existence. You must realize that animals – just like you and I – are also capable of feeling both pain and pleasure. Just observe them how they react when they are hurt and how when they are full of joy. So, then, what does the Cosmic Law of life preservation has to tell us? Simply this: God intended and it is His will that every creature which has the breath of life live a life that is full of joy and pleasure. God does not want that any of His creatures that He created would be mistreated and subjected to pain. God is horrified when He beholds the slaughter of billions of animals. In America alone, so many animals are slaughtered annually for food alone, that the column of their dead bodies would stretch for a million kilometres. Imagine how God must feel about this.

He who created all life and all living beings to live and enjoy the beauty of nature never intended for man to breed animals for his own selfish needs and lusts. God created all manner of foods that we can eat. There is no need to harm and cause pain to animals by slaughtering them mercilessly. Even on New Earth God says that just as in the beginning, all living creatures will live in peace and harmony with each other and that wolf and the lamb shall dwell together. This will come about because then everyone will know God and no one will resort to harm and destruction on all His holy mountain [Isaiah 11:9]. Jesus, as vegetarian, condemned the Jewish ritual of sacrifice and the eating of animal flesh. Jesus was fully aware of this Cosmic Law and he actually summarised it in one single sentence. Jesus urged all people to observe this eternal and perfect Law by saying:

"Therefore whatever you desire for men to do to you, you shall also do to them; for this is the law and the prophets" [Matthew 7:12 World English Bible].

Jesus did not teach anything new. He taught the same thing that the true Law of Moses had taught and what the true Prophets had taught all along. Jesus was merely restoring the true teaching long lost and rejected by the hierarchy of the Jews and all other nations. Jesus urged people everywhere to restore the Edenic utopia on Earth. He taught his followers to pray that God's will be done on earth as it is done in heaven. God does not allow angels to run slaughterhouses and eat flesh. He does not allow the slaughter in war.

His will is implemented in heaven and therefore everything is in harmony. It is truly a paradise there.

But Jesus said that we should pray that God's will be implemented on earth too. How can you pray for God to implement His will on earth if your table is full of flesh from the slaughtered animals? How can you pray for His will to rule on earth if you hunt, fish, and kill in war? There is no need to argue the point any further. God created all living souls to live and it is the duty of every living soul to preserve its own life and not to do anything which would impede the safety and existence of another soul. Only when we fully comply to the demands of the Cosmic Law of Preservation will there be utopia on Earth and God's will could be administered on earth as it is administered in heaven.

Therefore, don't believe anything written in the Bible – though it be written thousand times – if it conflicts with this Cosmic Law – the Law which commands the preservation of life. For Jesus said that the true and original Law of Moses and that the true Prophets taught the things which are only in agreement with this Cosmic Law which Jesus summarized in one single sentence: "Do to others as you would want others to do unto you."

# CHAPTER 20
# The Affect Flesh Diet Has on Your Health and the Starving World

Your body is made of trillions of cells. These cells are constantly being rebuilt. To do so your body needs food – that is, building material. Your body made of cells is alive and it needs live food in order to rebuild and maintain itself in excellent condition. If you eat inorganic food – that is, dead food – your body will be sick and dying. Your body needs energy from the Sun. That energy is absorbed by the fruit trees and the green herbs and plants through the process of photosynthesis and is absorbed by the body as calories or energy. Fruits, herbs and vegetables give the first-grade energy, enzymes and vitamins. When you eat meat, you are eating second class product and lots of original and vital stuff is lost. You can see in nature that even wild carnivorous animals do not kill meat eating animals for food but rather herbivore. The carnivore meat does not contain enough nutrition to sustain the life of the carnivorous animal.

Do you know what takes place in the body of an animal when slaughtered? Are you aware of all diseases the flesh diet causes? Dr. Jethro Kloss writes in his book: Back to Eden: The Classic Guide to Herbal Medicine, Natural Foods, and Home Remedies the following:

"Meats of all kinds are unnatural food. Flesh, fowl, and sea foods are very likely to contain numbers of bacteria that infect the intestines, causing colitis and many other diseases. They always cause putrefaction. Research has shown beyond all doubt that a meat diet may produce cancer in some cases. I have treated patients who have suffered from severe headaches for many years. Every remedy had been tried without relief, but when meat was excluded from the diet they obtained most gratifying results. Excessive uric acid is caused by eating too much meat and may result in rheumatism, Bright's disease, kidney stones, gout, and gallstones. A diet of potatoes is an excellent way to rid the system of excessive uric acid. Increased uric acid excretion in the urine comes from the following two sources:

1. Uric acid taken into the body in meat, meat extracts, tea, coffee, etc. A pound of steak contains about 14 grams of uric acid. This accounts for the stimulant effect of eating a steak, since uric acid is a close chemical relative to caffeine.

2. Uric acid formed in the body from nitrogenous foods.

It is an established fact that meat protein causes putrefaction twice as quickly as vegetable protein...Meat is an expensive second hand food material and will not make healthy, pure blood or form good tissues. The nutritive value of meat broths is practically nothing. They always contain uric acid and other poisons. The argument that flesh must be eaten in order to supply the body with sufficient protein is unreasonable. Protein is found in abundance in beans, peas, lentils, nuts of all kinds, and soybeans...The meat we eat is composed mainly of part of a muscle from an animal, along with varying amounts of fat and other tissues such as nerves and blood vessels, as well as many toxic substances that we cannot see. At the time of slaughter, all the vital processes that were taking place in the animal came to an abrupt halt, and the toxins that were in the tissues at the moment of death remained there. Some of these products are urea, uric acid, creatinine, creatine, phenolic acid, adrenalin, possibly various bacteria and parasites, either alive or dead, various hormones, antibiotics, pesticides, herbicides, and other elements the animal had been exposed to or eaten while still alive...Dr. Wynder of the American Health Federation stated that it is currently estimated that some 50% of all female cancers in the Western world, and some 30% of all male cancers, are related to nutritional factors.

As the consumption of animal fat and protein increases, the incidence of breast cancer increases in females and the incidence of colon cancer increases in both sexes. Women who eat large amounts of meat have a tenfold greater chance of developing breast cancer than those who eat little animal fat. A one-pound charcoal-broiled steak, well done, contains 4 to 5 micrograms of benzopyrene, an amount equal to what a person would get from smoking about 300 cigarettes. During broiling, fat from the meat drips onto the charcoal, producing benzopyrene that distils back onto the meat. Benzopyrene is one of the main cancer-producing agents found in tobacco smoke" [Pages 597-599].

*Collier's Encyclopedia*, Vol. 21 on p. 704, states that hogs are infected with various diseases and parasites. Pigs are infested with roundworm, Trichinella spiralis. Improperly cooked meat if digested causes trichinosis. The same encyclopedia, Vol 22 on p. 468, points out that in the United States alone some twenty million people are infected. Anthropologist Marvin Harris points out that USDA does not inspect pork for trichinosis. The procedure would be far too costly and time-consuming, requiring that each cut of meat be put under a microscope for detailed examination [Sacred Cow, p. 120].

Many do not realize that when they eat meat, they also eat toxins trapped in it. When an animal realizes that it will be slaughtered it releases poisons through its entire system. Adreline pours into the blood of the animal and its muscles. We have the same reaction when angry or afraid. As soon as the animal is slaughtered the cells in the body begin to decompose. After the killing of an animal [somatic death] the activity in the body is still going on until the actual death of the cells. When the animal is alive the wastes and toxins are removed via the circulating blood. After the slaughter the remaining toxins and wastes remain trapped in the body of an animal. Thus, the dead body of an animal contains poisonous blood and venomous juices!

People generally think that we must eat meat if we want to be strong. This is the "myth" of the West. Take a look at animals in their natural habitat. The strongest creature is elephant. From where does elephant gets his strength? Not from meat! Elephant eats fruit, leaves and young branches. Take a look at the gorilla and his tremendous strength. Gorilla is fruitarian. Take a look at the beasts of burden. Horse, ox, mule, donkey, camel – all possess enormous strength. Yet they are all herbivore. They do not eat any type of flesh. Hippopotamus and rhinoceros are also powerful animals – yet purely vegetarian. You do not need meat to stay healthy and strong. In fact, meat will only make you sick and weaker.

Vegetarian and vegan athletes endure much greater strains on the body than meat eaters. This is well documented fact. Most people simply do not care just what they eat. Christians think that Jesus has given them license to eat whatsoever they wish. But they are all so wrong. Eating wrong things causes great health problems. There are those who are fully aware of all the health risks and diseases they are exposed to by consuming foods that they ought not to. But they just can't deprive themselves of these "delicacies". Just like alcoholics cannot quit their bottle, the smokers their cigarettes – even though they daily read the warnings on their packets, the tea and coffee drinkers their caffeine – so also those who crave for flesh cannot abstain from it regardless of the risks and sickness involved. I however, firmly believe that God most definitely did not make a mistake when He prescribed strictly vegetarian and fruitarian diet to Adam and his descendants.

We cannot speak of meat eating without pointing out the fact that those who eat meat are also responsible for the death of millions of people around the world. Millions of children die from malnutrition and starvation simply because we take their food in order to fatten our animals so that we can eat meat. Please carefully read the following facts:

"One concern of ecologists is that the world's food supply will not be able to keep up with the rapid increase in population, which amounts to about 208,000 persons a day. We have recently been made keenly aware of how close millions live to starvation every day, by the recent worldwide publicity given to the severe famine in Ethiopia, and other North African countries, where untold thousands have died from starvation...It has been estimated that in 1974 there was about one acre of agricultural land for every person. This is far more than enough to provide an adequate food supply for a vegetarian, who requires only about one-fourth of an acre. Those who depend on animal protein for food, however, require about 3 acres of land per person. This is a very significant difference; about twelve times more land is needed to feed a meat-eater than a vegetarian...Another way to look at it is this. If a man chooses to use his acre of land to feed cattle, he would be able to produce enough meat to supply his protein requirements for 77 days; if he used his acre to produce milk, his protein requirement could be met for 236 days; for 877 days if he grew wheat; and for 2,224 days if he used his acre to grow soybeans. This comparison is emphasized even further when you realize that 21 pounds of protein must be fed to cattle in order to get one pound of protein in return. This difference between the amount of protein fed to cattle and the amount returned comes to 48 million tons, enough to meet 90 percent of the world's protein deficiency if it were fed to them as cereal" [The Classic Guide to Herbal Medicine, Natural Foods, and Home Remedies, pp. 600-601, Dr. Jethro Kloss].

In order for an animal to produce 50 kg of protein it must consume over 790 kg of plant protein. In the United States alone 157 million metric tons of cereal, legumes, and vegetable protein suitable for human use is fed to livestock to produce 28 million metric tons of animal protein which humans consume annually. This waste of food if converted to cash would amount to about 20 billion dollars. Food economist Frances Lappe noted that this wasted food would be enough to feed all the starving people of the world.

Just think about it. In the United States alone 78 percent of all crops are fed to animals which are bred for slaughterhouses. All this food is wasted so that those who cannot control their lusts and tasty buds can eat meat. Those who waste these valuable crops do not stop for a moment to think about all those humans who have nothing to eat. They obviously do not care for all those children who die a slow and agonizing death simply because they have no food to eat. They just care for themselves and their bellies. But when Jesus returns then the wolf and the lamb shall truly dwell together and the lion shall eat straw like an ox. Jesus promised us heavenly manna and the fruits from the Tree of Life and no veal or stake which depends on butcher's knife and bloodshed.

# CHAPTER 21
# Did Jesus Die For Adam's Sin?

No doctrine is more important to the Christian Church than the doctrine of the *vicarious atonement*. All evangelical churches maintain that Adam sinned by eating of the forbidden fruit. As a result, he did not only become a sinner himself but his sin was *imputed* to all his posterity. This *imputed* sin is commonly called *original sin*. Virtually all Christians passionately believe that all humans who are ever born are consigned to eternal doom on account of this imputed and original sin of Adam. In their view the whole humanity was cut off from God and the only way back to God is through a *vicarious atonement*. For this very reason Christians urge sinners to accept Jesus as their *personal Savior* and to put their trust in his shed blood. In Christian soteriology, Jesus died to atone for sin and to reconcile the estranged world with his father.

They believe that Jesus, through his shed blood, is the *propitiation* for sin. The word "propitiate" means "to win over someone who has been offended, to appease." The word "appease" means "to pacify." When Adam allegedly ate from the Tree of the Knowledge of Good and Evil – so Christians believe – God became so angry and wrathful that He cursed the whole world on account of Adam's sin. God could not be pacified nor could He reverse His curse and sentence imposed on Adam and his whole posterity unless an innocent victim paid the penalty which Adam incurred on himself and his whole progeny.

The *International Standard Bible Encyclopedia*, Vol. 4, Art. Sin – Original Sin, on p. 519, says that original sin embraces all people without exception.

It states that through one the sin found its way into the world and because of that sin the death came and the condemnation of everything. This is the official stance not only of the Roman Catholic Church and the Eastern Orthodox Church, but actually of all evangelical churches. The New Unger's Bible Dictionary, Art. Sin – Original, on p. 1198, says that the doctrine known as Pelagianism is rejected by all evangelical churches. This doctrine denies that there is any connection between Adam's sin and his posterity. The Catholic Church and the Eastern Church also dogmatically teach that in Adam the whole posterity of Adam is accursed.

That God imputed Adam's sin and his guilt and penalty on every single individual born into this world is the most dogmatic and central doctrine of the Christian Church. If you don't believe in this fable, you are not a Christian but rather a "cultist." Did you know that this fundamental Christian doctrine does not exempt infants and little children from guilt and hellfire? The early Church Fathers introduced the infant baptism precisely because they accepted and believed in the doctrine of the "original sin" and that Adam's sin and penalty was "imputed" to all children born into the world.

Very influential Church Father Irenaeus, who lived in the 2$^{nd}$ century, regarded infants as sinful because of Adam. He spoke of infants being "born again" in baptism. African Church Father Tertulian did not only hold that Adam imputed death to all his posterity but that he also infected all his progeny with lust and sordid inclination to sin. Clement of Alexandria connected physical death and humanity's curse with Adam's original sin.

Origen, the most learned of the Church Fathers, also expressly taught that the sinful nature and the inclination to sin is inherited from the fallen nature of Adam. Origen referred to infant baptism as the purification rite from Adam's original sin. He argued that infants committed no sin of their own but only by carnal descent from Adam have they contracted the infection from ancient death. He insisted that infants were not baptized for their own sins but rather for the sin of Adam which they have genetically contracted. Cyprian also maintained that condemnation and the inclination to sin is the result of Adam's fall. St. Augustine however, was the chief exponent of the original sin doctrine and the need for a vicarious atonement.

Jesus believed that infants were holy and that the Kingdom of God belong first and foremost to them. In fact, he argued that unless we become like little infants and receive the Gospel as children – we shall never enter the Kingdom. If infants are infected with Adam's sin and if they share in his guilt and are under Adam's penalty – how then could Jesus say that the Kingdom of God was actually theirs? Jesus plainly taught that he came to save only those who were lost and sick. He said that the healthy did not need a physician and that he did not come to call the righteous but only sinners to repentance. According to the Christian doctrine – which is based solely on the teachings of Paul – all have sinned and there are none righteous. But Jesus did not agree with this idea. He insisted that there were righteous people in his time who did not need his teaching, his vicarious atonement, nor his call to repentance. Zechariah and his wife Elizabeth were just such righteous people whom Jesus did not come to call to repentance. Luke 1:6 says of them:

"They were both righteous before God, walking blamelessly in all the commandments and ordinances of the Lord" [World English Bible].

If they have blamelessly observed all the commandments and ordinances of God, then they most certainly did not need Jesus' call to repent. John the Baptist was another such man. His righteousness surpassed the righteousness of any other human being. John was filled with the Holy Spirit while he was still in his mother's womb [Luke 1:15]. No prophet was filled with the Holy Spirit while still in his mother's womb. Not even Jesus. The Holy Spirit fell on Jesus during baptism. How then can it be said that God imputed Adam's sin and guilt to John? If John was infected by Adam's sin and if God imputed Adam's sin to John, then it follows that an accursed man and a sinner actually baptized Jesus in the river Jordan. To believe so is preposterous. In the *Essene Humane Gospel*, it is abundantly clear that Jesus did not regard all people as sinners nor did he believe that he had to shed his holy blood in order to pacify his own father and thus reconcile all humanity with God. The text clearly shows that the Essenes did not need his teaching nor his vicarious atonement since they were already righteous – obeying the laws and the commandments of his father:

"But the Scribes and Pharisees murmured against Jesus' disciples, saying, why do ye eat and drink with the publicans and evil doers, know ye not better men? But Jesus hearing their complaining said unto them, they who are whole need not a physician, but only they who are ill. Thus, I come not to call the saints and righteous, those of the Holy Way, the very elect, but I come to call sinners to repentance! For I tell ye truly, if all were as the Essene brotherhood, all would be doing the will of my Father-Mother in heaven and all would be well."

Christian theologians, on the basis of the Yahwist source in Genesis, maintain that Adam was created ignorant and that he did not know the difference between good and evil. So much so, that Adam and Eve are portrayed as those who did not even know that they were naked. Only after they allegedly partook of the Tree of the Knowledge of Good and Evil did they receive the ability to distinguish right from wrong and only then did they realize that they were naked and thus felt embarrassed. Apostle Peter repudiates this idea and argues that Adam knew right from wrong from the very start and that he in fact never ate from the forbidden tree nor did he rebel against God. Peter's view is recorded and preserved in the Clementine Homilies:

"He [Adam] himself being the only true prophet, fittingly gave names to each animal, according to the merits of its nature, as having made it. For if he gave a name to any one, that was also the name of that which was made, being given by him who made it. How, then, had he still need to partake of a tree, that he might know what is good and what is evil, if he was commanded not to eat of it? But this senseless men believe" [Homily 3, ch. 21 The Ante-Nicene Fathers, Vol. VIII].

If Adam was ignorant of good and evil and could not even tell whether he was dressed or naked until the forbidden fruit allegedly opened his eyes – how, then, was he able to name all the living creatures and give them appropriate names? If Adam did not know what was good and evil how did he know that no animal that was brought before him was actually suitable to be his wife? How did he know that Eve was suitable for him and how did he know that she was "flesh of his flesh and bone of his bones" and that therefore she should be called "Ishah" – that is, woman – or man with a womb? If he was ignorant until his eyes were allegedly opened after partaking of the forbidden fruit, how did Adam know that the woman will leave her father and mother and cleave to her husband forming one family? Furthermore, how did Adam know that there were going to be parents and marriage and therefore procreation, if he was ignorant – as Christian preachers would want you to believe?

And, most importantly, if Adam was ignorant and was not able to tell good from evil until he supposedly ate from the Tree of the Knowledge of Good and Evil – how then could God hold Adam responsible and accountable for his transgression? How could just and righteous Creator then impute Adam's sin which he committed in ignorance and innocence – as a little infant does – to all his progeny? How could God subject all His creation to decay and how could He place the whole cosmos under a curse because of a single sin committed in ignorance? In the book of *Ecclesiasticus* chapter 17 – a book which was a part of the Greek Septuagint Bible – from which most of the New Testament quotes are made, we are clearly told that after God created humanity He Himself, and not the forbidden fruit, actually imparted them knowledge of good and evil and gave them a law by which to live and over each nation he appointed a governor to rule.

The author of Ecclesiasticus believed – just as Genesis 1 reveals – that the Most-High in the beginning did not only create Adam and then later his wife, as the Yahwist source says, but rather that the Most-High created humanity – males and females – in His own image and set before them His true laws and revealed to them what is right and what wrong. He also believed – as did also Moses – that the Most High created a variety of people and grouped them as "nations" and over each "nation" He appointed a "governor." I have dealt with this subject in full in my book *Yahweh Conspiracy*.

The "Jewish Christian Sects" did not believe that Adam rebelled against God by eating from the forbidden fruit. Nor did they believe that Adam was ignorant or created naked. Cardinal Jean Danilou in his book The Theology of Jewish Christianity, on p. 63, states that the Ebionites did not believe in Adam's fall but that they regarded him as the first prophet, as important as Moses. Cardinal Danilou tells us that the Ebionites regarded Adam as the true Prophet and *impeccable*. The word "impeccable" means "without sin, sinless." The *Jewish Encyclopedia* tells us that the "Jewish Christians" whose leader was James, the brother of Jesus, did not believe that Adam sinned and therefore they did not believe in his fall:

"Similarly discarded were all the passages [of the Jewish Bible] providing for kingship – an institution which they abhorred – all anthropomorphic expressions of God, and unpraiseworthy stories about the representatives of true prophecy, e.g., ADAM'S SIN, Noah's drunkenness, Abraham and Jacob's polygamy, etc." [Art. Jewish Christian Sects, p. 39].

Here we are told that the "Jewish Christians" discarded, that is, rejected as forgeries and interpolations many pericopes of the Bible. Some of these pericopes had to do with Adam's sin and the fall. The Ebionites did not believe in Adam's fall and they in fact believed and taught that Adam was a true Prophet just like Moses was for example. The Clementine Homilies preserved a saying of Apostle Peter on the subject:

"Assuredly, with good reason, I neither believe anything against God, nor against just men recorded in the law, taking for granted that they are impious imaginations. For, as I am persuaded, NEITHER WAS ADAM A TRANSGRESSOR, who was fashioned by the hands of God; nor was Noah drunken, who was found righteous above all the world; nor did Abraham live with three wives at once, who, on account of his sobriety, was thought worthy of a numerous posterity; nor did Jacob associate with four – of whom two were sisters – who was the father of the twelve tribes, and who intimated the coming of the presence of our Master; nor was Moses a murderer, nor did he learn to judge from an idolatrous priest – he who set forth the law of God to all the world, and for his right judgement has been testified to as a faithful steward" [Homily 2, ch. 52 The Ante-Nicene Fathers, Vol. VIII].

Apostle Peter flatly denies and says that he is persuaded that Adam was not a transgressor and therefore he was not responsible for the supposed curse on his progeny. Great scholar Dr. Martin Larson also confirms the fact that the Essenes and Ebionites did not believe in the fall of Adam. He points out that the fall and the great change to this world was brought about by the Watchers – the fallen angels who married women and procreated their bastard giant sons [The Essene Heritage].

The Dictionary of Historical Theology, art. Ebionites, on p. 167, points out that the Ebionites rejected Paul's teaching concerning soteriology and atonement:

"He [Jesus] was the 'true prophet' [cf. Deut. 18:15-22], a second Moses, a teacher and reformer…He was not a priest; rather, he came to abolish the sacrificial cultus and to restore the true, spiritual meaning of the Mosaic code. The Pauline construal of the death of Jesus as sacrifice was therefore wrong. The name 'Christ' was given to Jesus at his baptism, when God adopted him as his messianic prophet. The Ebionites maintained a strong eschatological hope: the Son of Man, transfigured into supra-angelic form, would return in glory. The twin foci of Ebionite Christology were thus baptism and parousia, not incarnation and atonement."

The Ebionites emphasized baptism and parousia., that is, the return of Jesus in glory – while Paul and the Orthodox Christianity emphasized incarnation [God in the flesh] and atonement [human sacrifice in order to appease God]. When we realize that the Ebionites did not believe in Adam's fall nor that God cursed the universe because of Adam's alleged sin and rebellion, then it becomes clear that either they and ultimately the Twelve [and especially James, the brother of Jesus,] were propagating the false "gospel" or else Paul and his later Catholic movement were in the wrong. The Catholic scholars candidly admit that the Old Testament prophets say nothing of Adam's fall or the need for a bloody atonement. They also frankly admit that the doctrine is traced directly to Paul and not Jesus or the Twelve [Addis & Arnold's Catholic Dictionary, pp. 609, 611].

All evangelical and conservative theologians and scholars dogmatically insist that because Adam sinned, their angry and wrathful God was furious with him and cursed the whole cosmos – subjecting every living creature to pain, suffering, misery and death. They also maintain that their God could not be appeased and reconciled with his creation unless a divine being dies and reconciles the world to their God. For this very reason they all maintain that their Jesus was a pre-existing God Being who became Man so that he could shed his blood and appease the wrath of his father. In the New International Dictionary of the Christian Church on p. 502, under *incarnation* we find the definition of the *Chalcedonian Christology,* accepted by virtually all of Christendom. In a nutshell it states that Jesus is not only divine but God Himself. Not like God, but God Himself. When he became a man, he did not cease to be God.

In a footnote of the Living Bible – Life Application Bible, in reference to verses 1 and 14 of John 1 we are told that when Jesus became man, he did not cease to be the eternal God who has always existed. The reason why the Christian Church insists that their Jesus is eternal God is so that they may claim the "full" atonement for sin. For if God Himself died for the sin of Adam, then there can be no question of forgiveness. But how absurd it is to assume that God was so angry and full of wrath that He had to put Himself to death in the form of the Second Person of the Trinity in order to appease His own anger, with His own blood! That God died in order to atone for the sin of Adam is the most-plain teaching of the Christian Church. Please note the statement of the catholic theologian by the name of Anselm. He defined the atonement for sin in such a way that the Christian Church gladly embraced it. He taught that God had to be incarnated as Jesus since satisfaction for the Fall could be acceptable only if the God-Man paid the penalty.

The *Nelson's Illustrated Encyclopedia of Bible Facts* on p. 551, explicitly states that God Himself in the person of Jesus died in order to atone for sin. This statement is the cornerstone of Christianity. It is the most fundamental doctrine. To deny this would mean to suffer eternal condemnation. Isn't it most unnatural to assume that forgiveness can only be obtained if there is punishment and killing of an innocent victim? How much more monstrous it is to believe that this victim is in fact God Himself, Who punishes Himself and puts Himself to death in order to appease His own wrath! To believe that God actually died in order to be able to forgive His own children and to be able to reconcile Himself with the world is monstrous. The great Christian theologians realized that they needed God Himself to die so that there could be no question for the victim not being suitable. But they did not realize or simply ignored the fact that it was impossible for God to become a real man and be conceived in Mary's ovum because of His pre-existence. I will argue this fact in the next chapter when we deal with the birth of Jesus and where I demonstrate very clearly that Jesus could not have had pre-existence, but was actually the natural and biological son of Joseph and Mary, just as the Ebionites insisted all along.

Christians agree that the victim was needed in order to pay the penalty which Adam allegedly incurred on himself and all his progeny. They however, do not agree as to precise reason for this. Origen and Gregory of Nyssa expressly taught that the victim was needed in order to pay the ransom to the Devil. In their view man became the property of Satan after the fall. All Adam's descendants also became his property. Thus, God had to die in order to pay the ransom and set His children free. This doctrine was rebuked and rejected by Athanasius and Gregory of Nazianzus. Anselm in his book Cur Deus Homo [1100 AD], powerfully argued that atonement was needed in order to satisfy the divine majesty. Chief opponent of Anselm was Abelard [1141 AD]. He argued that atonement was only based on the love of God. Jesus' death was the exhibition of divine love. Grotius argued that atonement had nothing to do with God's divine nature but rather with God's divine Law.

None of these three "theories"– for this is exactly what they are – do actually make any sense. Did the Devil outsmart God? Does it make sense to think that God had to die in order to pay the ransom to the "Devil"? Did God or the "Devil" have the upper hand? Would God commit suicide – for that is what voluntary death is – in order to appease and satisfy his own divine nature? The Law of God is the very character and reflection of God. How then could we think that He died in order to satisfy the norm of the Law without at the same time satisfying the nature of Himself? To think that He had to die because of the Law is to think that He was trapped by His own Law. Just who is greater – the Law or the Lawgiver? The simple fact is that God did not die. Neither did Jesus die to appease, satisfy or cool off the wrath of God. Jesus' death was in no way vicarious atonement for the sin of Adam. The father Adam did not rebel against God. He was a great prophet of God.

Ellen White – of the Adventist Church – defended the doctrine of vicarious atonement on the basis of her spurious visions. Mrs. White wrote:

"Sorrow filled heaven, as it was realized that man was lost and that world which God had created was to be filled with mortals doomed to misery, sickness, and death, and there was no way of escape for the offender. The whole family of Adam must die. I saw the lovely Jesus and beheld an expression of sympathy and sorrow upon His countenance. Soon I saw Him approach the exceeding bright light which enshrouded the Father. Said my accompanying angel, He is in close converse with His Father. The anxiety of the angels seemed to be intense while Jesus was communicating with His Father. Three times He was shut in by the glorious light about the Father, and the third time He came out from the Father, His person could be seen. His countenance was calm, free from all perplexity and doubt, and shone with benevolence and loveliness, such as words cannot express.

He then made known to the angelic host that a way of escape had been made for lost man. He told them that He had been pleading with His Father and had offered to give His life a ransom, to take the sentence of death upon Himself, that through Him man might find pardon; that through the merits of His blood, and obedience to the law of God, they could have the favor of God and be brought into the beautiful garden and eat the fruit of the tree of life. At first the angels could not rejoice, for their Commander concealed nothing from them, but opened before them the plan of salvation. Jesus told them that He would stand between the wrath of His Father and guilty man, that He would bear iniquity and scorn, and but few would receive Him as the Son of God. Nearly all would hate and reject Him. He would leave all His glory in heaven, appear upon earth as a man, humble himself as a man, become acquainted by His own experience with the various temptations with which man would be beset, that He might know how to succor those who should be tempted; and that finally, after His mission as a teacher would be accomplished, He would be delivered into the hands of men and endure almost every cruelty and suffering that Satan and his angels could inspire wicked men to inflict; that He would die the cruellest of deaths, hung up between the heavens and the earth as a guilty sinner; that He would suffer dreadful hours of agony, which even angels could not look upon, but would veil their faces from the sight. Not merely agony of body would He suffer, but mental agony, that with which bodily suffering could in no wise be compared. The weight of the sins of the world would be upon Him. He told them He would die and rise again the third day, and would ascend to His Father to intercede for wayward, guilty man. The angles prostrated themselves before Him. They offered their lives.

Jesus said to them that He would by His death save many, that the life of an angel could not pay the debt. His life alone could be accepted of His Father as a ransom for man...With a holy sadness Jesus comforted and cheered the angels and informed them that hereafter those whom He would redeem would be with Him, and that by His death He should ransom many and destroy him who had power of death. And His Father would give Him the kingdom and the greatness of the kingdom under the whole heaven, and He would possess it forever and ever. Satan and sinners would be destroyed, nevermore to disturb heaven or the purified new earth. Jesus bade the heavenly host be reconciled to the plan that His Father had accepted and rejoice that through His death fallen man could again be exalted to obtain favor with God and enjoy heaven. Then joy, inexpressible joy, filled heaven. And the heavenly host sang a song of praise and adoration.

They touched their harps and sang a note higher than they had done before, for the great mercy and condescension of God in yielding up His dearly Beloved to die for the race of rebels. Praise and adoration were poured forth for the self denial and sacrifice of Jesus; that He would consent to leave the bosom of His Father and choose a life of suffering and anguish, and die an ignominious death to give life to others. Said the angel, 'Think ye that the Father yielded up His dearly beloved Son without a struggle? No, no. It was even a struggle with the God of heaven, whether to let guilty man perish, or to give His beloved Son to die for him.' Angels were so interested for man's salvation that there could be found among them those who would yield their glory and give their life for perishing man, 'But,' said my accompanying angel, 'that would avail nothing. The transgression was so great that an angel's life would not pay the debt. Nothing but the death and intercessions of His Son would pay the debt and save lost man from hopeless sorrow" [The Story of Redemption, pp. 42-45].

Ellen White claims that all this truth was revealed to her in a vision. I, however, do not accept this vision to have been from God. It simply does not agree with the facts. If I am supposed to accept this vision on the testimony of Ellen White, then Adventists should accept the vision of Joseph Smith, the founder of "Mormonism." They should also accept the vision of Mohammed – the founder of Islam. They however, reject these visions as "spurious" or "hallucinations."

Therefore, the same can be said about the visions of Ellen White. Her teachings are based on Pauline Christianity and therefore it could not have been derived from God. When we carefully read the quotation just presented, we cannot help but notice the beautiful and lovely character she portrayed of Jesus. He is so loving and gentle that he ignored his own needs – thus he offered himself to be the sacrifice which was to stand between the wrath of God and the fallen man.

The lives of angels were rejected as insufficient to pay the great debt. Only Jesus' blood and intercessions could do the job. Where does this place God? He is portrayed as One who is full of wrath and anger – ready to crush Adam and his wife. And he would have surely done so had it not been for the proposition of Jesus. Even Paul would not agree with Mrs. White, for he taught that it was the Father Himself who predestined Jesus to be the sacrifice for sin. According to Paul, the whole plan of salvation was established before the world was even created [Ephesians 1:4-11]. If this was so, then White could not have seen a vision where God was supposedly trying to decide whether to accept the proposition of Jesus or not.

Seventh Day Adventists and other Sabbatarian groups who reject the doctrine of immortality of the soul, ridicule those who accept it. They claim that those who believe that the penalty Adam incurred through his alleged rebellion was eternal condemnation in the hellfire, are still in their sins. They insist that if the penalty for Adam's sin was eternal burning in hellfire, then that penalty was not paid by Jesus, who only died the physical death. Thus, if Adam was to be ransomed, Jesus should have been in blazing inferno forever in order to pay the debt in full. Since he only died and then rose from the dead, they claim that the immortal concept is a myth and that those who embrace it are still in their sins. But these same Sabbatarians who ridicule other Christians do not realize that their teaching on atonement faces exactly the same problem. If Adam deserved to die forever rather than burn forever, they themselves must still be in their sins, since Jesus did not and could not have paid the penalty Adam supposedly incurred on himself and his progeny. It is therefore very plain that the debt could not have been paid by Jesus since the penalty demanded either eternal suffering in the blazing inferno or an eternal sleep in the grave.

If Satan demanded the ransom he would not have been satisfied with a three days death – whether the ransom was to be eternal death or eternal punishing. On the other hand, if the ransom was demanded by God in order to appease Himself and bring Him to a state of reconciliation – would He have played a game? Would He have put Himself to death only to bring Himself back to life three days later? Just what would He achieve by doing so? Now I want you to think of something much more important than this. This fact alone proves beyond refute that Jesus did not die for the sin of Adam. Nor did he die for the sin supposedly inherited from Adam by birth. It is commonly accepted that Adam through his fall caused death to all humanity. Because of one man's sin all humanity – so it is alleged – was subjected to death penalty. This death penalty is supposedly lifted by the death and blood of Jesus – the perfect innocent victim. If this is so why then, I ask, people continue to die after Jesus shed his blood on Golgotha?

If he fully atoned for the sin of Adam and removed the inherited sin through natural generation – why then do infants still die? Why did even Adam die when Jesus supposedly offered himself as a substitute? Since death was immediately introduced upon the descendants of Adam before they were even born or done anything deserving death – why, then, was not the death also immediately removed? If all were punished because of one man's sin, then all men should be saved because of one man's righteousness. Paul actually accepts this reasoning in 1 Corinthians 15, but elsewhere rejects it.

Christians teach that Jesus did it all for us on the cross and that we only need to believe in sacrifice and his divinity. They say this because they reject God's true Law and the good works required as proof of being sanctified and righteous. Even though the penalty was paid in full, we are still lost unless we accept Jesus as a personal Savior. This, of course, is another way to say 'salvation by works.' To be saved you must believe, you must be "born again" in baptism, you must live a new life, you must not practice the old way of life. If you commit sin you must repent. Christians condemn those who teach salvation by observance of the Law – that is, by works.

But they themselves will tell you that if after your new birth you continue to murder, lie, steal, practice sodomy, homosexuality, witchcraft, or do anything else they define as sin – you will end up in the blazing inferno – burning forever! Isn't this actually saying that salvation is based on works even though Jesus supposedly paid in full the debt you owed? Even though they tell you that "JESUS DID IT ALL FOR YOU ON THE CROSS" they still have strings attached to the way of salvation. The whole atonement doctrine is a farce. It is absurd. It portrays God as a stern, wrathful and angry God who cannot forgive unless He sees the shed blood. The Christian teaching that forgiveness cannot be obtained without the shedding of blood is quoted from Hebrews. Please notice the following text:

"Therefore even the first covenant has not been dedicated without blood. For when every commandment had been spoken by Moses to all the people according to the law, he took the blood of the calves and the goats, with water and scarlet wool and hyssop, and sprinkled both the book itself and all the people, saying, 'This is the blood of the covenant which God commanded toward you.' Moreover he sprinkled the tent and all the vessels of the ministry in like manner with the blood. According to the law, nearly everything is cleansed with blood, and apart from shedding of blood there is no remission" [Hebrews 9:18-22 World English Bible].

Please compare this text with that of Exodus 24:5-8. When you do so carefully – word for word – you will realize that a number of details do not agree. Not only with the Jewish Masoretic Text but not even with the Greek Septuagint Bible or the Aramaic Peshitta of the Eastern Church. The Exodus text says nothing of the blood of "goats." It says nothing of the use of "water, scarlet wool and hyssop." It states that Moses sprinkled the blood on the altar and the people and the Book of the Covenant.

The words of Moses differ from those in Exodus. But the greatest problem the Hebrew text poses lies in the fact that it claims that Moses sprinkled the Tabernacle and all its utensils with blood in order to purify it. Whoever wrote this text was not very much acquainted with the facts. At the time Moses allegedly killed the young bulls and made the blood covenant with the Israelites, the Tabernacle and its utensils were not even in existence as yet. It was constructed some nine months later. Furthermore, even when the Tabernacle and its utensils were purified later, it was not done with blood but rather with oil [Exodus 40:9-11].

The author of Hebrews states that no forgiveness can be obtained unless the blood is shed. But this simply is not true. Even the Jewish Pentateuch in its present form plainly shows that sin could have been forgiven without the shedding of blood. Those who were excessively poor and unable to offer even "young pigeons" obtained the remission of sin by offering a "cereal" offering [Lev. 5:11-13].

Some purification could be obtained through "water" [Lev. 15:10]. Some things are purified with "fire" [Numbers 31:22-23]. On one occasion "gold" made atonement for warriors [Numbers 31:50]. On another occasion "incense" atoned [Numbers 16:46]. Of all methods – water and not blood is the real cleanser and purifier. Atonement was accomplished not through blood but through prayer and supplication – as we have already seen.

The author of Hebrews was not only wrong about the blood atonement but he did not even know when atonement was made. He claimed that the High Priest offered a sacrifice on the daily basis in order to atone for his own sin and the sin of the nation [7:27]. This was not true. The High Priest was obligated to offer sacrifice once a year only [Leviticus 16:11-19]. The author of Hebrews also made a great blunder when he claimed that the altar of incense was located in the Holy of Holies [9:3-4]. Exodus 30:6 locates it in the Holy Place. If the altar was in the Holy of Holies, how then would have the priests been able to offer daily incense? The Pentateuch clearly shows that only the High Priest had an access to the Holy of Holies and that only once a year, on the Day of Atonement.

In Hebrews we are also told that in the Ark of the Covenant was placed "golden manna jar and Aaron's budding staff" [9:4]. The Old Testament claims that only 'Ten Commandments" were deposited in the Ark. How much can you trust the doctrine of atonement taught in Hebrews, when the author was ignorant even of the basic facts recorded in the Jewish Pentateuch? Can you believe him and trust him with the complex issues when he was wrong even about the most basic principles of the Tabernacle?

Christians point to Jesus as the one who instituted the New Covenant with his own blood. They point to the cup he shared with his disciples on the night of his arrest. This cup allegedly contained wine. The Roman Catholics, the Eastern Orthodox Christians, the Anglicans and Lutherans claim that the wine was literally the blood of Jesus. They claim that even their priests literally convert bread into the flesh of Jesus and the wine into his blood. This conversion is called *transubstantiation*.

But it will be documented now that these texts in our canonical Gospels do not preserve true facts of that event. The Gospel the Ebionites used give us altogether different picture. When we realize what is claimed there and the fact that James, the brother of Jesus, was also present there and actually drank from the cup, it becomes plain that the cup could not have contained wine. St Jerome testified that he has personally saw the original Gospel of Matthew which was written in Hebrew and that he had translated this Gospel in the Latin language. In this Gospel we are told that James was present during the Last Supper and that he drank from the cup. We are also told that he had vowed that he would not eat bread until he sees Jesus alive from the tomb. After resurrection Jesus appeared to him and gave him bread to eat. This passage, often referred to by the Christian Church

Fathers, verifies the fact that James the Just was present the night Jesus was arrested. Moreover, it testifies that he drank from the cup Jesus offered to his disciples. It also reveals the tremendous confidence he must have had in the messiahship of his brother. For he vowed not to eat bread at all until he actually sees Jesus alive. In the canonical Gospel of John – James is portrayed as an unbeliever who did not accept the claims of Jesus.

Dr. Whyte in his book *Saul called Paul* degrades James. He insists that for 33 years James could not bring himself to accept the messiahship of his brother. He claims that James became a believer only after Jesus eventually appeared to him after his resurrection. Because of this act alone, so it is claimed, James actually became a follower of Jesus. This however, does not agree with the text quoted from the original Matthew. It does not even agree with the general reputation James enjoyed among the Church Fathers. They all testified that James was righteous, hence his epithet "the just." They believed that he was consecrated from his mother's womb. After his resurrection, Jesus only appeared to those who believed in him prior to his death. If James was an unbeliever then Jesus would not have appeared to him. If James became a believer only after Jesus' appearance to him, what credit is that to him? Even Pilate and Herod and Caiaphas would have believed in him, if he appeared alive to them after his crucifixion.

Once we realize the fact that James was present with other disciples the night his brother was arrested and especially that he actually drank from the cup, we must then conclude that the cup could not have contained wine. The Church Fathers testify that James the Just was a life-long Nazarite who neither tasted flesh nor wine, as we have already seen. We have already seen that the Ebionites did not use wine but rather water when they have observed the annual memorial of Jesus' death.

If John the Baptist was alive and if he would have been present that night with other disciples, he could not have drunk from the cup if it contained wine. Luke 1:15 plainly states that John could not drink wine or strong drink. We have also seen that many followers of Paul would not eat meat or drink wine and that Paul advised others not to eat meat and drink wine because of them. Since they would not drink wine, how could Paul then serve wine during the Lord's Supper? In Acts of Peter we read that Paul actually served water when he served the Eucharist [Vercelli Acts II]. We are told that this took place while Paul was in Rome. It is only logical that Paul could not have served wine to believers who did not drink it and if he instructed others not to drink wine for their sake. Jesus offered water in the cup to his disciples. His covenant was based on water and not blood. The remission of sins is based on water, not blood. The water baptism washes and purifies the sinner. John administered baptism in water for the *remission of sins* [Mark 1:4; Luke 3:3]. Peter told the Jews that only in water baptism [not blood] could they find the remission of sins [Acts 2:38]. "Remissio" means: release from penalty or guilt; pardon; cancellation, as of a debt.

The Ebionites taught that baptism, that is, water washed away the sins of the repenting candidate and not the blood of the sacrificial victim. Water is life. Without water there is no life. The blood itself depends on water. The life of the blood is actually water, the blood plasma. Not all animals have blood in their bodies. But those animals utilize water in the same way we utilize the blood. Life in the blood is water. Plasma is a complex substance and its principal component is water.

You must realize one fact. There is no life without water. Life indeed depends on blood. Life is indeed in the blood. But this life in the blood is actually water. Without water there can be no blood. Before blood was ever in existence water was there. Without water there can be no plasma and that means that no nutrients on which our body cells depend can be transported. Red and white cells cannot perform their function without plasma. No vitamins can be distributed to our body cells without plasma. Water therefore is the most important element which sustains life.

Is it any wonder then that Jesus used water in order to re-establish the covenant? Is it any wonder that water and no other liquid is used for baptism? A repentant sinner is plunged into the water. His sins are washed away by its purity and he is a new born man, free from stain. His old life is washed clean. Try to plunge yourself into the blood. Will you be washed clean or will you be stained with blood? All life depends on water but all life does not depend on blood. It is clear therefore that new life also depends on water.

The Israelites were washed in the waves of the sea as Paul himself admits. The nations of antiquity recognized the power of water. Originally water and not blood was recognized as the means of sin cleansing. The sacrificial victim itself was cleansed in the waves of the sea. Only later did pagan man rely on blood of the sacrificial victim. Even the ancient mystics realized the tremendous significance of water. They baptized their candidates in the sea and rivers and purified even the sacrificial animals in water. Even ancient Mexicans, before they came in contact with Christians, baptized their children in water. They regarded this baptism as a new life.

Pagan Mexicans knew that water baptism constituted the new birth. If you were to speak with Hindus who were never exposed to the Christian doctrine of water baptism, you would be astounded to discover that their teaching on baptism is identical to that held by the Christian Church. The Brahmans explicitly claim that they are twice born [See: Asiatic Researches, Vol. 7. p. 271]. The British Druids, the worshippers of Odin plunged their infants into the river as soon as they were born in order to wash away their sins [See: Anglo Saxon Baptism, Antiquities, Vol. 1. p. 335].

For what purpose do Hindus baptize their converts with water? Why do they regard those so baptized as "born again?" Why do they call the deity whom they recognize as the preserver by the name Vishnu? The answer to these questions may astound you. In Hindu thought Vishnu is none other than the biblical Noah. Hislop writes:

"In India, the god Vishnu, "the Preserver," who is celebrated as having miraculously preserved one righteous family at the time when the world was drowned, not only has the story of Noah wrought up with his legend, but is called by his very name. Vishnu is just the Sanscrit form of the Chaldee 'Ish-Nuh", "the man Noah", or the "Man of rest" [The Two Babylons, p. 135 non-copyrighted book published in America by Loizeaux Brothers, Inc., and in England by A & C Black, Ltd].

*Ish* even in Hebrew denotes *man*. The name *Noach* is derived from *Nuach* and means *rest*. [See: Strong's Concordance]. Wilson points out that the Hebrew-Chaldee word *ish* that is, *man* is not only preserved in **V**ishnu with the digamma but also in other words such as: **V**ishampati which means: Lord of men. [See: India Three Thousand Years Ago, p. 59].

Noah was regarded as a man who lived in two worlds: the old and the new. He was regarded as he who preserved all life. Even in Babylonish mysteries Noah was called by the name of Diphues which means: twice born. Water baptism signifies the drowning of old self which signifies sin of the Old World. New birth signifies new life in the New World. In the New Testament Noah and the flood water is used as an analogy of salvation [1 Peter 3:21].

The original world was terribly corrupted by the Watchers and their bastard sons who caused all flesh to corrupt their way of life. Thus, those who die in baptism die to the principles of the Old World of Watchers and violence as described in Genesis 6 and the Book of Enoch and Jubilees. The New World is based on justice and the principles of God's Law. The Ebionites believed and taught that this was the real fall and not the fall of Adam, erroneously believed by most of Christendom. We have seen earlier that the pagan Mexicans baptized their children in order to cleanse them from sin which originated before the creation of the world. Now Christians of course baptize their converts in order to purify them from the so-called sin of Adam and their own sins. The infants however, are specifically baptized in order to cleanse them from the inherited sin of Adam. We have seen earlier that the Ebionites explicitly rejected this idea.

They rejected the suggestion that Adam actually sinned. Neither did they believe that Adam brought death and curse in the world by eating from the forbidden fruit. Surprisingly, the Ebionites believed that sin and death was in existence before the creation of this world. It is even more surprising that this fact is plainly revealed in the Bible itself. Genesis 1:1 says that Elohim originally created the heavens and the earth. This took place in the "beginning." No one exactly knows when this was. In verse two however, we are told that the Earth "became" chaotic and empty, covered with water. Please note this verse as is translated in the King James Bible:

"And the earth was without form, and void; and darkness was upon the face of the deep, and the Spirit of God moved upon the face of the waters."

This text has been erroneously translated in the King James Bible. The correct rendering of the Hebrew text is as follows: But the Earth became desolate and empty, darkness came to be above the surface of the abyss, and the mighty wind of Elohim hovered above the waters [Author's translation].

The Hebrew word "hayah" should have been translated "became" and not *was*. King James translators did correctly render this same Hebrew word as *became* in Genesis 2:7:

"and the man became [hayah] a living soul."

In Genesis 2:10 they correctly rendered the word *hayah* as *became:*

"And a river went out of Eden to water the garden; and from thence it was parted, and became into four heads."

Genesis 1:2 states that the Earth became *tohuw* and *bohuw*. The word "tohuw" is number #8414 in *Strong's* and specifically means "a desolated wasteland."

The word "bohuw" is number #922 in Strong's and it means: indistinguishable ruin. Genesis 1:1 ays that God originally created the heavens and the Earth in perfect condition. The Earth however, became chaotic and desolate. The water covered its surface. And the darkness ruled over the waters. The word "darkness" is quite significant in this text. It comes from the Hebrew word "choshek" – number #2822 in Strong's and means: darkness; misery, destruction, death, ignorance, sorrow, wickedness. Before God actually brought order to this chaotic world He had to battle with evil forces. The great primeval Sea Monster with seven heads was the leader of the evil forces. This monster is called Rahab in the Bible. Rehab was a demonic sea monster who ruled the Abyss and was the mistress of darkness. God had to overpower her in order to create the orderly world [See: Who's Who in the Bible p. 367]. The Rahab was also identified as Leviathan with seven heads [See: The Oxford Companion to the Bible, pp. 433-434]. In Isaiah 27:1 [King James Bible] we read:

"In that day the LORD with his sore and great and strong sword shall punish Leviathan the piercing serpent, even Leviathan that crooked serpent; and he shall slay the dragon that is in the sea."

The Jerome Biblical Commentary on p. 277, says the following in regards to this text:

"The identical phrase occurs in a Canaanite myth from Ugarit where Lotham [Leviathan] is described as the "fleeing serpent" or "primeval serpent." This and other mythical monsters of ancient Near Eastern literature have become, in the OT, symbols of forces in rebellion against Yahweh."

Nelson's New Illustrated Bible Dictionary on p. 1065, under *Rahab the Dragon* says:

"a mythological sea monster or dragon representing the evil forces of chaos that God subdued by his creative power. The name Rahab as it occurs in Job 9:13 [NIV], Job 26:12 [NIV], Psalm 87:4 and 89:10, Isaiah 30:7 [NIV], and Isaiah 51:9 has no connection with the personal name of Rahab, the harlot of Jericho, in Joshua 2:1-21. The references to Rahab in the books of Job, Psalms, and Isaiah speak of an evil power overcame by God. God's smiting of Rahab is described in Job 26:12 [NIV] to signify God's power over the chaos of primeval waters at the Creation" [published in Nashville, Tennessee, by Thomas Nelson, Inc., brief quotations permitted].

In 2 Peter, the author alludes to this primeval world and chaos. Please note this text:

"For this they wilfully forget, that there were heavens from of old, and an earth formed out of water and amid water, by the word of God; by which means the world that then was, being overflowed with water, perished. But the heavens that now are, and the earth, by the same word have been stored up for fire, being reserved against the day of judgment and destruction of ungodly men" [3:5-7 World English Bible].

You must realize one fact. This text does not speak of the time of Noah. It refers to the world [Greek cosmos] being destroyed with waters in the beginning. The flood waters of the primeval times destroyed the sky and left the Earth in chaos and desolation. The waters deposited various fossils of that world. The Deluge of Noah's days did not destroy the heaven nor was the cosmos left in chaos. The Earth and Heaven of Noah's time are the same present Earth and Heaven which will be set on fire on the Judgment Day.

The previous Earth and Heaven were destroyed by waters and cosmos was left in ruin and chaos as it is to this day. After defeating the primeval evil forces, God restored our "Solar System" in six days. He set Adam in charge of this new world. Many assume that Adam was immortal and the world was perfect until he supposedly rebelled against God and brought death and decay in this world. But those who believe this are simply mistaken. There was death and decay in progress from the instant of creation. This is not hard to prove.

The leaves of the fruit trees were falling. The fruits themselves would have decomposed if left for a prolonged period. The food eaten by man and animals was digested and the waste and toxins removed. None of these could have occurred if there was no bacteria and germs in existence. For bacteria plays a vital part in this world. It causes things to decompose so that essential nutrients are supplied to the soil. If there were no bacteria then this world would become a heap of rubbish – piling to a huge mountain, thus killing and destroying life on this Earth. From the very beginning God created humankind, animals, birds...and all insects and reptiles in order to maintain balance on this Earth.

Thus, it is very wrong to assume that death and decay was introduced only after Adam supposedly sinned against God. Sin and decay existed before Adam was even created. He was put on this Earth so that he might rightly rule this world. If there was no knowledge of evil in this world at the time Adam was created, then he could have never really developed righteous character. Righteousness comes through rejection of wrong and performance of right. If there was no evil in this world then we would never know what is really right. If there was no sorrow then we could not really know what joy is. In this world there is a law of two opposites: cold and hot, right and wrong, daylight and darkness, joy and sorrow...In fact, you cannot even think of one thing without immediately becoming aware of its opposite. This is not only true of this world but also of heaven and the whole universe.

These opposites did not come into existence after Adam supposedly sinned but they were part of nature from the very start. Did you realize that God only created light on the first day of creation? He did not create darkness. Darkness was already there. But before Adam was created, darkness and light, day and night had already existed. God did not even create water on any of the six days. Water was already there covering the chaotic Earth. He did not even create the Earth on any of the six days. The Earth was already in existence but submerged under water. He merely caused the water on the surface of the Earth to be gathered into one place. By doing so He restored the dry Earth.

So, then, before Adam supposedly sinned there was already dry and wet ground. There was tiredness and sleep. Only after God completely destroys the primordial monster and all perverts on this Earth, will these opposites cease to be a part of nature. Only after He establishes His eternal kingdom, will the bad opposites disappear from existence. In the meantime, these opposites are essential so that we may built a righteous and perfect character. If we did not know what evil was, we could never know what is right. If we did not know what sorrow was, we could not know what is joy. And if we did not know the misery of death, we could not appreciate life. The Yahwist source clearly says that Adam was put to sleep [Hebrew, deep coma] while Yahweh was operating on him and removing the rib and flesh from his side and afterwards sawing the wound. If there was no pain in existence before Adam allegedly sinned and brought pain through God's curse, why then did Yahweh use the anaesthetic to prevent pain? And if Adam did not get tired before his alleged fall, why then did he sleep at all?

There is yet another way in which it can be proven that eternal life does not depend on the sacrifice of Jesus. Christians of course insist that no one can be saved without first accepting the sacrifice of Jesus. They insist that the only way to the Father and therefore to eternal life is through the blood of Jesus. The Ebionites of course did not believe this. They insisted that from the very beginning salvation and condemnation depended on the works of man. Now this claim makes sense. The generation of Noah was condemned because of their evil deeds. Sodomites were destroyed because they practiced iniquity. The Israelites were condemned because of their evil deeds. But those who obeyed God and practiced righteous works were blessed and shall live.

"I gave them my statutes, and shown them my ordinances, which if a man do, he shall live in them " [Ezekiel 20:11 World English Bible].

God also stated:

"Behold, all souls are mine; as the soul of the father, so also the soul of the son is mine: the soul that sinneth, it shall die. But if a man be just, and do that which is lawful and right, *And* hath not eaten upon the mountains, neither hath lifted up his eyes to the idols of the house of Israel, neither hath defiled his neighbour's wife, neither hath come near to a menstruous woman, And hath not oppressed any, *but* hath restored to the debtor his pledge, hath spoiled none by violence, hath given his bread to the hungry, and hath covered the naked with a garment; He *that* hath not given forth upon usury, neither hath taken any increase, *that* hath withdrawn his hand from iniquity, hath executed true judgment between man and man, Hath walked in my statutes, and hath kept my judgments, to deal truly; he *is* just, he shall surely live, saith the Lord GOD. If he beget a son *that is* a robber, a shedder of blood, and *that* doeth the like to *any* one of these *things*, And that doeth not any of those *duties*, but even hath eaten upon the mountains, and defiled his neighbour's wife, Hath oppressed the poor and needy, hath spoiled by violence, hath not restored the pledge, and hath lifted up his eyes to the idols, hath committed abomination, Hath given forth upon usury, and hath taken increase: shall he then live? he shall not live: he hath done all these abominations; he shall surely die; his blood shall be upon him.

Now, lo, *if* he beget a son, that seeth all his father's sins which he hath done, and considereth, and doeth not such like, *That* hath not eaten upon the mountains, neither hath lifted up his eyes to the idols of the house of Israel, hath not defiled his neighbour's wife, Neither hath oppressed any, hath not withholden the pledge, neither hath spoiled by violence, *but* hath given his bread to the hungry, and hath covered the naked with a garment, *That* hath taken off his hand from the poor, *that* hath not received usury nor increase, hath executed my judgments, hath walked in my statutes; he shall not die for the iniquity of his father, he shall surely live. *As for* his father, because he cruelly oppressed, spoiled his brother by violence, and did *that* which *is* not good among his people, lo, even he shall die in his iniquity. Yet say ye, Why? doth not the son bear the iniquity of the father? When the son hath done that which is lawful and right, *and* hath kept all my statutes, and hath done them, he shall surely live. The soul that sinneth, it shall die. The son shall not bear the iniquity of the father, neither shall the father bear the iniquity of the son: the righteousness of the righteous shall be upon him, and the wickedness of the wicked shall be upon him. But if the wicked will turn from all his sins that he hath committed, and keep all my statutes, and do that which is lawful and right, he shall surely live, he shall not die.

All his transgressions that he hath committed, they shall not be mentioned unto him: in his righteousness that he hath done he shall live. Have I any pleasure at all that the wicked should die? saith the Lord GOD: *and* not that he should return from his ways, and live? But when the righteous turneth away from his righteousness, and committeth iniquity, *and* doeth according to all the abominations that the wicked *man* doeth, shall he live? All his righteousness that he hath done shall not be mentioned: in his trespass that he hath trespassed, and in his sin that he hath sinned, in them shall he die. Yet ye say, The way of the Lord is not equal. Hear now, O house of Israel; Is not my way equal? are not your ways unequal? When a righteous *man* turneth away from his righteousness, and committeth iniquity, and dieth in them; for his iniquity that he hath done shall he die. Again, when the wicked *man* turneth away from his wickedness that he hath committed, and doeth that which is lawful and right, he shall save his soul alive. Because he considereth, and turneth away from all his transgressions that he hath committed, he shall surely live, he shall not die" [Ezekiel 18 King James Bible].

Did you get that? God plainly states that He shall judge each individual not on the basis of sacrificial atonement but rather on the basis of their works. Those who obey the commands of God are righteous and shall live. Those who live contrary to the laws of God are wicked and shall die. It is as simple as that. Jesus stated that all those who performed iniquity [lawlessness], shall be lost even though they performed great many miracles in his name [Matthew 7:21-23]. In Revelation we are explicitly told that the dead, small and great, shall be judged according to their works [Revelation 20:13]. On the Judgment Day, God will not ask whether you accepted Jesus as your personal Savior who allegedly died for your sins, but He will rather diligently examine your life in order to see what kind of works you have. He did the same with King Belshazzar. He placed all his works on the balance and found them wanting [Daniel 5:27].

Christianity insists that the only way to eternal life is through Jesus Christ. That is, to be saved one must believe in the deity of Jesus and his sacrificial atonement. But there were millions who lived and never heard the name Jesus. Are these people bound for hellfire just because they were born in culture where Christian teachings were unknown? Christians do not like to dwell on this subject. They do not wish to confine all these people to hellfire but at the same time they cannot see how any of them can be saved without actually believing and accepting Jesus as their personal Savior. Well, they cannot have it both ways. If salvation cannot be obtained without belief in the sacrificial atonement of Jesus Christ – then all people who never heard of Jesus will be lost forever. On the other hand, if even one person can be saved without the sacrificial atonement of Jesus, then salvation is based on works. No wonder Christians prefer to avoid this subject. The Ebionites on the other hand did not believe in the sacrificial atonement. They believed that one was saved or lost on the basis of his status with God.

Those who practiced iniquity are lost, while those who obeyed the true Law of God are saved. Now none of us perfectly observe the laws of God. At one time or another we do something that God classifies as sin. This is where repentance comes in. We confess our sins to God, pray for forgiveness and make every effort to do better. Forgiveness is not based on blood sacrifice but rather on the love and mercy of God. Salvation is therefore dependent on the faith and works of man and the love and mercy of God.

Our righteous works justify us before God while the evil works condemn us. Each confessed sin is blotted away by God because of His fatherly love.

Therefore, it is apparent that the Ebionites were right in rejecting the Christian teaching on soteriology. They were right in not connecting Adam with the so-called fall, sin and the curse. The Ebionites rejected the rite of sacrifice – whether human or animal. Christians accept both. They believe in the Old Testament sacrificial cultus.

Christians also believe and justify the human sacrifice in the Old Testament. In fact, their very salvation and vicarious atonement is based on the human sacrifice. According to their own teaching, Jesus was both fully God and fully man. Since their Jesus was also fully man who died as a sacrifice and since the only way to salvation is through his blood, it follows that Christian salvation is based on the human sacrifice which was so sternly prohibited and abhorred by the true God. One wonders how is it possible for Christian Jesus to be both fully God and fully man. Can a person be both fully man and fully woman? Or can a dog be fully dog and fully horse? But in Christian theology anything and everything is possible for those who have "faith."

# CHAPTER 22
# Did Jesus Have a Virgin Birth?

The adherents of Roman Catholicism and those of Eastern Orthodox faith sincerely believe that Mary was the "Mother of God" who remained a perpetual virgin. St. Basil stated that Jesus' friends could not tolerate anyone who says that Mary was not the Mother of God or that she ceased to be a virgin after giving birth to Jesus. Church Father Ambrose [339-397] wrote a whole treatise defending the perpetual virginity of the Blessed Mary. In 392 c.e., Pope Siricius declared that Mary was a perpetual virgin. In 431 the Council of Ephesus proclaimed Mary to be Deipara – that is, mother of God, who remained virgin for the rest of her life. The Fifth Council of Constantinople declared Mary to be "aeiparthenos" – that is, "ever virgin." The Council declared that "a virgin conceived, a virgin gave birth, a virgin remained."

Church Fathers Ambrose, Augustine and Jerome argued that the hymen of Mary was not ruptured even while giving birth to Jesus. In 1943 Pope Pius XII, in his 'Encyclical Letter,' described Mary as "she who gave miraculous birth to Christ our Lord,"

meaning that even though she gave birth to Jesus, her virginity remained intact. The Church Father Tertulian however, denied Mary's virginity post Jesus' birth. Protestants strongly embrace the doctrine of the Virgin Birth, but they do not believe in the perpetual virginity of Mary. Jehovah's Witnesses who reject the deity of Jesus nevertheless believe in his pre-existence and his virgin birth. Even Christadelphians, The House of Yahweh, and others who do not believe in the pre-existence of Jesus, acknowledge his virgin birth.

However, not many realize that original Palestinian "Christians" and their immediate and direct descendants, who became known by their derogatory name Ebionites, did not believe in the virgin birth of Jesus. They believed and taught that Joseph was the biological father of Jesus. The same view was held by the immediate relatives of Jesus – including his mother Mary.

**Matthean and Lukan Genealogies**

The word "genealogy" is derived from two Greek words: "genea" and "logia." The word "genea" means: "race, breed." The word "logia" means: "study of." The word "genealogy" therefore means: "the study of racial descent" in the same way that the word "astrology" means "the study of stars" and the word "theology," "the study of God." It is also extremely significant to point out that the English word "gene" is also derived from the Greek word "genea."

Now "gene" is one of the units located on a chromosome that determine the characteristics an organism inherits from its parent or parents. The word "genealogy" therefore also implies "the study of genetic descent." The purpose of both Matthean and Lukan genealogies is to show that Jesus is the legitimate descendant of David, Judah and Abraham. The Messiah was understood to be a descendant of David and was to be born in Bethlehem – the native town of David. Now David was a member of the tribe of Judah. Matthew 1:1 explicitly states the following:

"The book of the generation of Jesus Christ, the son of David, the son of Abraham" [World English Bible].

The text plainly states that the genealogy given in Matthew 1 is that of Jesus. Both Matthew and Luke trace Jesus' genetic descent to David, Judah and Abraham. But it is extremely important for you to realize that the ancestors of Jesus – Abraham, Judah and David are linked with Jesus through the genetic line of Joseph.

Matthew 1:17 says:

"So, all the generations from Abraham to David are fourteen generations; from David to the exile to Babylon fourteen generations; and from the carrying away to Babylon to the Christ, fourteen generations" [World English Bible].

Here is the list in its three epochs:

>ABRAHAM
>ISAAC
>JACOB
>JUDAH
>PEREZ
>HEZRON
>RAM
>AMMINADAB
>NASHON
>SALMON
>BOAZ
>OBED
>JESSE
>DAVID
>
>SOLOMON
>REHOBOAM
>ABIJAH
>ASAPH
>JEHOSHAPHAT
>JEHORAM
>UZZIAH
>JOTHAM
>AHAZ
>HEZEKIAH
>MANASSEH
>AMOS
>JOSIAH
>JEHOIACHIN

SHEALTIEL
ZERUBBABEL
ABIUD
ELIAKIM
AZOR
ZADOK
AKIM
ELIUD
ELEAZAR
MATTHAN
JACOB
JOSEPH
JESUS

You will note that the third epoch contains only thirteen and not fourteen generations. Likewise, in the second epoch three kings of Judah were omitted in order to retain the number fourteen. They were Ahaziah, Joash and Amaziah. You can verify this fact by comparing the Matthean genealogy with that given in 1 Chronicles 3:11-12. There is much I could say regarding this and other peculiarities about the genealogy given in Matthew. But this is not essential to do in this book. My sole concern here is to point out that the genealogy of Jesus is traced through Joseph. But if Joseph was not the biological father of Jesus then Jesus' descent could not be traced through his lineage, since there is no blood relation or genetic connection between Joseph and Jesus. We have already seen that the word "genealogy" means "the study of racial and genetic descent." We have also seen that Matthew 1:1 says that the names given in the list comprise the genealogical record of Jesus who is a blood descendant of David and Abraham.

Therefore, we must conclude that Joseph was the legitimate and biological father of Jesus and so through his lineage was genetically connected with David and Abraham. That Joseph was in fact biological father of Jesus by actually procreating him is explicitly stated in Matthew 1:16. But this truth is obscured in many bibles due to the fact that they are based on the Greek manuscripts which were forged by the Christian scribes. Please first of all note the verse as it now stands in the King James Bible:

"And Jacob begat Joseph the husband of Mary, of whom was born Jesus, who is called Christ."

This verse as it stands in the King James Bible and many other Greek texts, fundamentally destroys the purpose of the genealogy. Even the Catholic scholars admit the paradox of this verse. In the New Jerome Biblical Commentary, compiled by Roman Catholics we find the candid admission that it is strange indeed to present the genealogy of Joseph all the way from Abraham only to have it nullified in the end [p. 635]. If Joseph was not the natural father of Jesus then no genetic connection at all can be established between Jesus, David or the tribe of Judah. If you deny the biological fatherhood of Joseph you may as well discard the whole Matthean genealogy, because there is no way known you can prove that Jesus was a descendant of David or Judah unless Joseph actually begat Jesus.

If the translators of the King James Bible translated the 16th verse of Matthew as it stands in many Greek minuscule manuscripts, then the whole genealogy would make perfect sense, since the minuscule manuscripts plainly state that Joseph actually begat Jesus. The Greek New Testament manuscripts are divided in two categories: uncial, that is, manuscripts written in capital letters and minuscule, that is, manuscripts written with small letters. The Greek minuscule manuscripts classified as Ferrar group of Miniscules, actually give the following reading of verse 16:

"And Jacob begat Joseph and Joseph begat Iesous."

There are many other Greek manuscripts which render this verse as follows:

"Joseph, to whom was betrothed Mary the virgin, begot Jesus who is called Christ."

Greek manuscripts coded: o, f 13, I 547m, it, a, b, c, d, g, k, q, all give this reading. *Ambrosiaster* [4th century] and the *Syriac Sinaitic* version [3rd century], also support this reading. Because of this fact Von Soden comprises his text to read "Joseph begat Jesus." The Moffat Bible also follows the Von Soden rather than *Textus Receptus* or *Westcott and Hort* texts. If the Matthean genealogy is to have any credibility at all, this reading must be preferred above that of *Textus Receptus* or other Greek manuscripts. In Luke's genealogy we are told that Joseph was actually the father of Jesus. Please note the following text as it stands in the King James Bible:

"And Jesus himself began to be about thirty years of age, being [as was supposed] the son of Joseph, which was the son of Heli...the son of David... the son of Judah...*the son* of God" [Luke 3:23,31,33,38].

You will note that the words "as was supposed" are in brackets in the King James Bible. The same is the case in the Greek text. This indicates that the words are later addition. For if Jesus was only supposedly the son of Joseph then he was also only supposedly the son of God, since this implication is all through the generations. Matthean genealogy traces the lineage of Jesus through Joseph and Jacob. In other words: Joseph was the son of Jacob who was the grandfather of Jesus. Lukan genealogy on the other hand states that the father of Joseph and the grandfather of Jesus was Heli. That two distinct personages are in question is clear by the fact that Jacob traces his lineage through Solomon while Heli through Nathan. Many who believe in the Virgin Birth insist that Luke actually supplies the lineage of Mary. But we have already seen earlier that this could not be the case since Mary was from the tribe of Levi. Church Father Julius Africanus believed that both Matthean and Lukan genealogies were those of Joseph. He wrote a treatise in order to prove his view. Please note:

"But in order that what I have said may be made evident, I shall explain the interchange of the generations. If we reckon the generations from David through Solomon, Matthan is found to be the third from the end, who begat Jacob the father of Joseph. But if, with Luke, we reckon them from Nathan the son of David, in like manner the third from the end is Melchi, whose son was Heli the father of Joseph. For Joseph was the son of Heli, the son of Melchi. As Jospeh, therefore, is the object proposed to us, we have to show how it is that each is represented as his father, both Jacob as descending from Solomon, and Heli as descending from Nathan: first how these two, Jacob and Heli, were brothers; and then also how the fathers of these, Matthan and Melchi, being of different families, are shown to be the grandfathers of Joseph.

Well, then, Matthan and Melchi, having taken the same woman to wife in succession, begat children who were uterine brothers, as the law did not prevent a widow, whether such by divorce or by the death of her husband, from marrying another. By Estha, then – for such is her name according to tradition – Matthan first, the descendant of Solomon, begets Jacob; and on Matthan's death, Melchi, who traces his descent back to Nathan, being of the same tribe but of another family, having married her, as has been already said, had a son Heli. Thus, then, we shall find Jacob and Heli uterine brothers, though of different families. And of these, the one Jacob having taken the wife of his brother Heli, who died childless, begat by her the third, Joseph – his son by nature and by account" [The Ante-Nicene Fathers, Vol. 6, p. 126].

Africanus proposes interesting and possible reconciliation between Matthean and Lukan genealogies. But what he altogether avoids to say is how could Jesus be a descendant of both Solomon and Nathan if Joseph was not his biological father. Our primary concern here is not how to reconcile the two genealogies and why is Jesus said to have descended from both Solomon and Nathan, but rather how could he be a descendant of David at all if he was not the legitimate son of Joseph. Either Jesus was the biological son of Joseph or else his descent cannot be traced to David or Judah. His mother Mary was not of the tribe of Judah but rather of the tribe of Levi. Therefore, he could not be descended from David or Judah through Mary and her genealogy. Thus, Jesus could not have been a descendant of David or Judah through her genealogy. Those who think that Luke traced Mary's genealogy are gravely mistaken. The only way Jesus could have been a descendant of Judah is if Joseph – who was a descendant of Judah – was actually his biological father.

Joseph was not only a descendant of Judah but he was actually from the royal line of David [Luke 1:27]. Mary was not of the royal line of David. Therefore, Jesus could not have traced his royal blood to David through her. Apparently, the author of Hebrews whose task was to convince the "Jewish Christians" to accept the deity of Jesus and his virgin birth and to drop the observance of the Mosaic institutions, denies that Mary was in any way a descendant of Levi [Hebrews 7:13-14; 8:4]. The author of Hebrews insists that Jesus could not be a priest on earth because he is not a descendant of Levi. Since only Levites and no Judahites were ever allowed to serve as priests, the Hebrew author concludes that Jesus could not legally hold a priestly position on Earth. The author of Hebrews could not concede that Jesus was a descendant of Levi through his mother Mary. To do so would have destroyed his argument and the concept of the Virgin Birth. This is not the only place where the author of Hebrews chooses to deviate from the received tradition. He does so in other parts of his work when he feels that it is essential to prove his important point, as we have already seen previously.

**The Begettal of Jesus**

We have established that the Matthean and Lukan genealogies clearly nullify the doctrine of the Virgin Birth and actually teach that Jesus' descent from David was through the royal line of Joseph. But there is another way in which I can plainly demonstrate that Joseph was the biological father of Jesus. The Bible plainly states that Jesus was baptized by John in the Jordan river. John was baptizing with the baptism of repentance for the remission of sins [Matthew 3:11 and Mark 1:4]. Christians generally decline to comment on Jesus' baptism and when they do so they usually try to discredit its significance. However, we have already seen that the Ebionites attached a tremendous significance to his baptism. According to them it was during the act of his baptism that the Holy Spirit descended and entered Jesus and that his "begettal" as the Son of God actually occurred right there and then. This is known as adoptionist view. According to this Ebionite view, Jesus was not the Son of God before he was actually baptized. The Bible tells us that Jesus was about thirty years old when he was baptized by John in the Jordan river. During the act of baptism, the actual begetting took place. Please note the text of Matthew in connection with Jesus' baptism, as is written in the Gospel of the Twelve Apostles, the Gospel exclusively used by the Ebionites and the Nazarenes:

"When the people had been baptized, Jesus also came and was baptized by John. And as he came out from the water, the heavens were opened, and he saw the Holy Spirit in the form of a dove that descended and entered into him. And a voice [sounded] from heaven that said: Thou art my beloved

## THE EBIONITES

Son, in thee I am well pleased. And again: I have this day begotten thee. And immediately a great light shone round about the place. When John saw this, it saith, he saith unto him: Who art thou, Lord? And again, a voice from heaven [rang out] to him: This is my beloved Son in whom I am well pleased. And then, it saith, John fell down before him and said: I beseech thee, Lord baptise thou me. But he prevented him and said: Suffer it; for thus it is fitting that everything should be fulfilled" [New Testament Apocrypha, James Clarke & Co., Westminster/John Knox Press].

The most significant factor of this text is the begettal of Jesus. The text claims that God actually spoke and said to Jesus: "I HAVE THIS DAY BEGOTTEN THEE" These words do not appear in the canonical Matthew but are found in original Matthew, written in the Hebrew language. Only after his begettal at the Jordan river did the Holy Spirit actually descend and enter Jesus. This indisputably proves that Jesus could not have been born of a Virgin, nor could he have had his divine begettal some thirty years earlier. The text insists that Jesus' begettal took place at the Jordan river, during the very act of baptism. If Jesus had a virgin birth and was begotten by the Holy Spirit during Mary's alleged virginal conception, then there would not have been a need for his begettal during his baptism. Furthermore, if Jesus was the very God in the flesh – as claimed by most adherents of the Christian Church – what further need was there for the Holy Spirit to be given him during the act of his baptism?

You may discredit the words "I have this day begotten thee" because they are not found in the canonical Matthew. You may charge the Ebionites of falsely inserting the words in their text in order to bolster their anti-virginal doctrine. This however, cannot be justified on the grounds that the same statement is also found in many Greek manuscripts in the Lukan version of Jesus' baptism. Luke 3:22 preserved identical statement found in the Ebionite Gospel. This fact is obscured in many English bibles simply because the translators chose to follow certain Greek manuscripts which render the text as follows:

"And a voice came from heaven: You are My Son, whom I love; with you I am well pleased."

But many Greek manuscripts give the alternative reading which fully agrees with the original version of Matthew – used by the Ebionites:

"And a voice came from heaven: You are My Son, this day I have begotten you."

Some English versions follow these Greek manuscripts. Nestle-Alland Greek-English New Testament renders Luke 3:22 in the traditional manner. In the footnote however, we are told:

"Other ancient authorities read "today I have begotten thee."

The New American Bible for Catholics likewise acknowledges the fact that some ancient Greek manuscripts supply a variant reading and actually say that God begat Jesus on the day he was baptized. The Jerome Biblical Commentary, on page 129, states that the reading of this Western text is preferred by a large number of scholars. This reading fully harmonizes with the messianic prophecy of Psalm 2:7, where the reading is as follows:

"Thou art my Son; this day have I begotten thee" [King James Bible].

If God did not actually pronounce these words then the prophecy was never really fulfilled. I, of course, accept the Ebionite version as authentic and inspired. The epistle of Hebrews confirms the fact that God must have spoken the words to Jesus, just as claimed in the Ebionite Gospel. Please note:

"For unto which of the angels said he at any time, Thou art my Son, this day have I begotten thee?" [Hebrews 1:5 King James Bible].

"So also Christ glorified not himself to be made an high priest; but he that said unto him, Thou art my Son, to day have I begotten thee" [Hebrews 5:5 King James Bible].

Apostle Peter also quoted this statement to the people when he preached, proving that Jesus had to be begotten when John baptized him:

"God hath fulfilled the same unto us their children, in that he hath raised up Jesus again; as it is also written in the second psalm, Thou art my Son, this day have I begotten thee" [Acts 13:33 King James Bible].

Therefore, it is plain that Jesus was actually begotten as the Son of God the moment the Spirit of God entered him. If he was begotten on the day of his baptism when he actually received the tremendous power of the Spirit, how plain then that he could not have had the virgin birth. The Ebionites placed a great emphasis on Jesus' baptism and his actual begettal. From this point on he received the great power from the Holy Spirit and began his public ministry of teaching. It is most important for you to realize the fact that Christian creeds and theologians deny the fact that Jesus was ever begotten. They insist that he played the role of the Son from all eternity without ever being begotten by the Father. The view universally held by the Christian Church is that God is the father from all eternity without ever begetting Jesus as His Son. On the other hand, Jesus is the Son of God without ever actually being begotten. In other words, in the Christian sense, the Father and the Son are of the same age. Yes, the Son is as old as his Father. This fact is also explicitly stated in the Athanasian Creed:

"None is before or after the other; none is greater or less than another" [*Cyclopaedia of Biblical, Theological, and Ecclesiastical Literature*, Vol. 2, p. 561].

The *Catholic Encyclopedia*, art. "Trinity" states:

"The Trinity is the term employed to signify the central doctrine of the Christian religion...In this Trinity the Persons are co-eternal and co-equal."

If the Son was co-eternal and co-equal with God, out of necessity he could not have been begotten. If they were both co-eternal and co-equal, the Son and the Father could not be related since neither one would have been actually begotten and so genetically related. By teaching this absurd doctrine the Christian Church fundamentally rejects the Ebionite view of Jesus' begettal. They also reject the Lukan version of the baptism of Jesus, as preserved in the Western Text of the Greek manuscripts.

They also nullify and discard Psalm 2:7, which prophetically spoke of a day when God was to begat His Son. The Ebionites simply believed that Jesus was exceptionally good person whom God actually *chose* to be His Son and whom He begot in baptism. Jesus through *election* became God's Son. On the Mount of transfiguration God confirmed the fact that Jesus was His *chosen* but albeit, the text of Luke 9:35 was later corrupted and changed by the orthodox Christians in order to counter the adoptionist view of the Ebionites. Please note Luke 9:35 as it stands in the King James Bible:

"And there came a voice out of the cloud, saying, This is my beloved Son: hear him."

This is the reading of the later manuscripts. But the earlier Greek manuscripts [including $p^{45\ 75\ B\ L\ 892\ 1241}$] read as follows:

"...my Son, the one who has been chosen."

Vast majority of English bibles are based on the original reading and use the word 'chosen.' Just as Jesus chose his disciples to be his apostles, so did God choose Jesus to be his Son. Now please note how the words of John the Baptist in John 1:34 were changed. The Received Text and many others of a later date read as is rendered in the King James Bible:

"And I saw, and bare record that this is the Son of God."

But the early manuscripts coded $p^{svid}$ 77, 218 b e $ff^2$ syr$^{sc}$ give the following reading:

"...that this is the Elect of God."

The adoptionists had no problem with the term "Son of God" and this is the proof that their scribe did not alter this reading in John. For if they did then they would have altered the same term elsewhere in this Gospel. But Orthodox Christians had a problem with the adoptionist view that Jesus was God's chosen and elected and begotten Son, hence they altered the original reading. In his speech to Cornelius, Peter clearly stated that Jesus was anointed by God with the Holy Spirit and as a result he went about doing good – healing all manner of diseases [Acts 10:38]. In Acts 4:27 Peter in prayer to God refers to Jesus as a "child of God" whom God anointed [King James Bible]. If Jesus was eternal God and fully God in the flesh – as commonly believed – why then was a need for him to be anointed and to be filled with the Holy Spirit? Almighty and eternal God would be just that – almighty God – who lacks nothing. If Jesus was eternal and almighty God in the flesh, why then did he refer to his father as "my God" and why did he pray to him and worship him? Can the true God have a God above him? You must decide for yourself whether to believe and accept the Christian view or the Ebionite view – which is so clearly and simply presented in the Bible.

**The Conception of Jesus**

The adherents of Christendom do not only deny the begettal of Jesus they also deny and reject his conception. Even if I was to accept the Virgin Birth, I would still have to insist on the fact that Mary actually conceived Jesus in her ovum. Please note the following text taken from Luke 1:31:

"Behold, you will conceive in your womb, and bring forth a Son, and will call him Jesus" [World English Bible].

Although the Christian Church uses the term "conception" it does not apply it literally but rather claims that Jesus was "implanted" as an "embryo" into the uterus of Mary. The word "conceive" actually means "to start life," "to begin," "originate." Christians do not believe that Jesus' life actually started in the ovum of Mary. They insist that his pre-existent divine life was merely transferred into the uterus of Mary. Even those who reject the divinity of Jesus [such as Jehovah's Witnesses] also deny the fact that Jesus' life began at the moment of him being conceived in Mary's ovum. They claim that God transferred Jesus' run-down body to Mary's womb [Should You Believe in Trinity, p. 14].

If God merely transferred the life-force [run down body of the pre-existent Jesus] into the womb of Mary, then it follows that Jesus never began or started in the ovum. Mary, then, did not conceive but merely received the implanted, run-down spiritual being. I want you to be aware of one simple fact. The adherents of Christendom insist that their pre-existent Jesus never ceased to be what he had always been before his so-called incarnation. That the adherents of Christendom do not really believe that Jesus conceived in Mary's ovum even though they use the term "conception" is evident from the statement found in the Catholic Catechism where we are told that Jesus knew from the moment of his incarnation into the womb of Mary that he was divine. The author states that whoever supposes that Jesus only gradually became aware of his divinity denies that he was the true God [The Question and Answer Catholic Catechism, John A. Hardon, S.J., p. 62].

When the sperm fertilizes the ovum "life begins." When the nuclei of these two cells fuse, the formation of a new individual is "initiated." Now we all know that when conception occurs there is no embryo as yet. There is no awareness or consciousness in the ovum where life just started. Christians insist that their Jesus knew from the moment of his conception that he was divine. This is because he never really conceived but was rather incarnated in the uterus of Mary. Now I want you to be aware of one most significant fact. If Mary did not really and literally conceive in her ovum but Jesus was merely implanted in her uterus, then she was not really his mother nor was he actually a human being at all.

For if Mary did not actually start his life through conception then she was not his biological mother. She was merely an incubator in whom a pre-existent God Being was implanted in the form of an embryo. That means that Jesus could not have been a real human being. In our scientific laboratories fertilized ovum is implanted in the uterus of a woman unable to conceive. When the foetus develops and is eventually born, who is the biological mother of the baby, the one who carried the baby or the one who actually donated the fertilized ovum? The woman who actually donated the fertilized ovum. The woman who had carried the foetus in her womb was merely the foster mother and she passed no genes onto the foetus.

The foetus inherited the features of the father who donated the sperm and the mother whose ovum was in the first place. If Mary did not literally conceive in her ovum then Jesus was not her biological son. Likewise, if Joseph did not literally procreate Jesus then he could not have been a descendant of David or Judah since Mary, as we have already seen, was of the tribe of Levi and not Judah. This fact should help you realize that the Trinitarian concept is contrary to reason, facts, and the original belief of the Ebionites, whose chief leader was James the Just, the brother of Jesus.

**The Trinity Dogma**

I want you to be aware of another fact. The Trinity dogma was not injected into Christendom without bitter controversies and objections. Even the strongest advocates of the Incarnation concept realized the tremendous difficulties their doctrine posed. After the Nicene Council declared that God and Jesus are composed of the same substance and that both are eternal and co-equal, they had a great problem to explain how could then Jesus truly partake of the human nature and at the same time not cease to be eternal God who has always existed. Appolinarius suggested that Jesus assumed the body and soul of a man but retained his divine spirit. Nestorius affirmed his full humanity but practically split him into two distinct personages. Cyril of Alexandria and his followers maintained that as a result of the incarnation, the divine and human were fused in one nature, without successfully proving the theory. In A.D. 452 at the Council of Chalcedon, Pope Leo I, stated that Jesus was "vere Deus, vere home," that is, true God and true Man.

This doctrine which is termed the "foundation and cornerstone of the Christian faith" fundamentally denies the fact that Jesus was conceived in the ovum of Mary. It also denies the fact that God begat him through baptism. This Christian doctrine insists that Jesus was "always God" who became incarnated in the womb of Mary – becoming a person with two fused natures. This fundamental and principal Christian doctrine does not only deny the fact that Jesus was Mary's biological son but it even denies that he was God's real and begotten Son. For we have already seen earlier that Christians insist that Jesus was the Son from eternity without ever being begotten by his Father. This teaching propagated by all of Christendom and Sacred Name Assemblies, nullifies the fact that Jesus was the subject to real temptations. This teaching claims that Jesus could not sin because he was also God. In the Question and Answer Catholic Catechism by John Hardon, on p. 63, we are explicitly told that Jesus could not sin because he was God in the flesh. We are told that he had no concupiscence and unruly passion or desire because he was exempted from the original sin.

The word "concupiscence" actually means "sexual desire; lust; any immoderate desire." Thus, according to the Christian teaching Jesus was a man "immune to sin" – unable to commit sin – because of his "divine nature" which was supposedly "fused" with his human nature. This is all due to the fact that Jesus supposedly pre-existed and was incarnated in the uterus of Mary. In the Pocket Catholic Catechism, on pp. 41-42, we are told that even though true humanity in Jesus implied that he had a free human will, he could not sin. It's not that he only did not sin, but actually we are told that he could not sin, since he was God and God cannot sin.

This Christian concept makes the mockery of Jesus' temptations. It nullifies his victories over sin. It makes the mockery of his victory. It destroys the meaning of his ultimate exaltation and the reward for his obedience to God's Law and for fulfilling perfectly the Messianic role God chose him for. The Bible clearly states that Jesus was raised from the dead and was given a place of honor – at the very right hand of his Father. He inherited a name greater than any of the angels. He was given great glory and power. If Jesus pre-existed as the eternal God or some kind of a Spirit Being then all this becomes meaningless. For Jesus would then have already possessed all this. There is nothing he could have received as a reward for his obedience. Only if we accept the Ebionite view that Jesus began as an ordinary man who was born of Joseph and Mary, but who heard the call of God and perfectly fulfilled the role He gave him to play, does the exaltation and reward make real sense.

After defining at the Council of Nicaea [325 c.e.] that Jesus was pre-existent God Being, the Christian Church had a real problem of explaining just how did their pre-existent God-Savior manage to be fully human while at the same time not cease to be what he had always been – eternal God. The bishops of the Council of Nicaea have declared that their Jesus is of the same substance, Greek "homousin" with the Father. This is to say that their Jesus was composed of the same "stuff" that God is composed of. While the bishops of the Council of Nicaea had a problem of explaining the deity of their Jesus and just how he could be both God and Man, at the same time the Ebionites had no such problem. A *Lion Handbook: The History of Christianity*, on p. 113, tells us that the Trinity doctrine became a serious problem for the Church. However, it points out that the Jewish Christians, such as Ebionites, did not have a problem to explain Jesus' so-called fused nature, since they did not believe that he was truly God.

Many bishops who were present at the Council of Nicaea felt that they were pressured by Constantine to accept and agree upon a formula which they have later realized to be something that they did not really believe in. The Council of Nicaea over which Constantine, the emperor of Rome presided, gave for the first time a different meaning to the word God. It was no longer used in reference to the Father of Jesus only, but rather to the nature, substance or Godhead which God and Jesus supposedly had in common. By declaring their Jesus fully God, equal to the Father, the Church Fathers, bishops and theologians had a real problem of explaining the definition of "one substance" and just how was it possible for the pre-existent God Being to be born of a woman and be "fully man" while at the same time retain the "full Godhood."

It took seven ecumenical councils to finally settle the Christological controversy which originated with Antioch and Alexandria. I want you to be aware of one fact. All these councils were summoned by the emperors of the Western and Eastern empires. These emperors waged great wars and their only motive in summoning these councils was to preserve the unity and political stability of their empires. The bishops themselves were corrupt and bloodthirsty men. The first council took place in Nicaea [modern Nis, Serbia]. It was here where it was officially declared that Christian Jesus is fully God and fully man. The seventh council also took place in the same city. During this seventh council the veneration of icons and images were endorsed. These councils were attended by the bishops of the powerful Christian churches. They were summoned and attended by the emperors themselves.

But Jesus always spoke of his followers as a little flock. He foretold that his followers would be hated and bitterly persecuted. He insisted that only few walked on the narrow way and many followed the broad way. The Ebionites – as their name indicates – "poor ones" were despised, rejected and condemned by the Church Fathers. None of their leaders were ever invited or allowed to attend any of the Church Councils. They therefore played no part whatsoever in the Christian Creeds and abominable doctrines.

**Why Virgin Birth Impossible?**

Genesis 6 speaks of "bene ha elohim" who married the daughters of men. Their union with mortal women produced great giants, or so-called "nephilim." The same incident is recorded in the book of Jubilees and explicitly in the book of Enoch, as we have already seen. The union of the fallen Watchers [angelic beings] with the mortal women was condemned by God. Their gigantic offspring were called "bastards" because they were the result of a forbidden marriage – that of the supernatural and the mortal beings.

Now please think for a moment. Christians insist that Jesus is the offspring of Mary – that is, a mortal woman and the Holy Spirit, according to Christians a God Being – a third member of the Trinity. The offspring of this mixture is unnatural and forbidden. Why would God resort to do what He abhors? Besides, if Jesus was the result of divine and mortal "union" then he could only be a demigod and never fully God. Dionysus was a "demigod" because he was an offspring of the Greek god Zeus and a mortal woman called Semele. There is something else you need to be aware of. In Christian theology, the Holy Spirit is God and is always referred to as He. In other words, Christians treat the Holy Spirit as a masculine deity – in the same way as they treat God and Jesus. But if the Holy Spirit is a masculine being then it would follow that the Holy Spirit is the father of Jesus and not God. This must be so since in Christian theology it was the Holy Spirit that "impregnated" Mary and she became pregnant. Since the Bible insists that God is actually the begetter and the father of Jesus it follows then that it could not have been the Holy Spirit that procreated Jesus. In the Gospel of Phillip, we are told that Mary could not have conceived Jesus by the Holy Spirit since the Holy Spirit is a feminine Being and that a woman cannot conceive by a woman [The Nag Hammadi Library].

This saying may seem very strange to Christians who do not know Hebrew and are not aware of the fact that in Jewish thought the Holy Spirit is regarded as feminine. [The Holy Spirit should not be confused with the spirit of God which is only the power and energy of God which is technically also referred to as the holy spirit.] And as soon as we accept the fact that the Holy Spirit is feminine and actually our Mother, just as God is our Father, immediately we realize that the Holy Spirit could not have triggered the conception in the ovum of Mary but rather Jesus was begotten as the Son of God during the act of his baptism – in the same way as we are procreated sons of God during the act of baptism when we are imbued with the spirit of God. God's spirit is the spiritual sperm which begets. Jesus himself addressed the Holy Spirit as "Mother." In the original Matthew, written in Hebrew, we are told that Jesus acknowledged the Holy Spirit as his mother. We are also told that the Holy Spirit took hold of his hair and transported him to Mount Tabor to be tested.

Ezekiel himself was carried by the hair [Ezekiel 8:3]. Both Origen and Jerome quote the text from the Hebrew version of the Gospel of Matthew. F.F. Bruce, a Christian professor, states that it is certain that this saying is of Semitic origin for in these languages it is only logical to refer to the Holy Spirit as mother since in these languages the word 'spirit' is in feminine gender [Jesus and Christian Origins, p. 101]. Christians refer to the Holy Spirit with a masculine pronoun He. They call the Holy Spirit God. That this is wrong is evident not only from the fact that the Gospel of Philip treats the Holy Spirit as a woman, and Jesus as his mother, but also by the fact that in the Old Testament the Holy Spirit is referred to with the feminine pronoun "she." God was always addressed with the masculine pronoun "he." But the Holy Spirit was addressed with the feminine pronoun "she."

This indisputably proves that the true prophets of God did not regard the Holy Spirit as a masculine being. Therefore, if Christians wish to retain their Trinity, they should stop addressing the Holy Spirit as "God" and should rather call her "Goddess." There are two passages in the Hebrew Bible where the Holy Spirit is referred to with a feminine gender 'she' [1 Samuel 16:13 and Isaiah 11:1-2]. If the Holy Spirit was a masculine being – a third member of the Trinity – as traditional Christians adamantly maintain, then the masculine gender would have been used in the Old Testament. Not even in the New Testament do we ever find a masculine gender in reference to the Holy Spirit. In Greek, the neuter gender is always used unless the Spirit is personified as parakletos [Comforter], when the masculine gender is applied in order to correspond to the masculine form of "Comforter." Spirit in Greek is in "neuter" while in Latin in "masculine" form.

In Hebrew however, it is always in the "feminine" form. Therefore, it is an indisputable fact that the Holy Spirit is not a masculine and therefore could not have caused Mary to become pregnant. The Gospel of Philip then makes sense when it claims that those who say that Mary conceived by the Holy Spirit do not know what they are saying, since a woman does not conceive by a "woman." I want you to note the text of John 16:13-14, as is translated in the King James Bible:

"Howbeit when he, the Spirit of truth, is come, he will guide you into all the truth: for he shall not speak of himself; but whatsoever he shall hear. That shall he speak: and he will shew you things to come. He shall glorify me: for he shall receive of mine, and shall shew it unto you."

You must first of all realize that this text has been translated from the Greek. But we know that Jesus did not actually speak Greek with his disciples on the night he ate the supper with them. Neither did he speak English. He actually spoke either Hebrew or Aramaic. The next thing you must be aware of is the fact that the subject of this text is the spirit which of course in the Greek language is always referred to with the neuter gender "it." The same is true of the English grammar. The translators have therefore violated both the English and Greek grammar in order to uphold their trinitarian dogma, namely that the Holy Spirit is a third masculine member of the Trinity.

Since we know that Jesus actually spoke in either Hebrew or Aramaic, and since we know that the word "spirit" in both Hebrew and Aramaic [as well as other Semitic languages] is always referred to with the feminine gender "she," it follows then that Jesus actually referred to the Holy Spirit as "she" and not "he" as the lying and dishonest Christian theologians insinuate. Now I want you to note the same text from the Gospel of the Holy Twelve, translated by Rev. Ousely:

"Howbeit when the Spirit of Truth is come, she will guide you into all truth: and the same will shew you things to come and shall glorify me: for the same shall receive of mine, and shall shew it unto you."

Rev. Ousely correctly supplied the feminine gender "she." He was also correct in not using the word "she" elsewhere in this text because even the Greek text does not use the word "he" as the King James Bible insinuates. The Greek word "ekeinos," number #1565 in *Strong's*, actually means:

"this one, that one, the same."

Every Bible scholar knows that the Rev. Ousely was correct in applying the feminine gender "she" in reference to the Holy Spirit. But they simply do not have enough courage to do the same. They would rather resort to falsehoods and dishonesty than hurt their Christian cause. The Jewish Cabbalists clearly portray God with dual natures, masculine and feminine. God is the father of all. The Holy Spirit is the mother of all. Jesus is the Son of God. We are sons and daughters of God. Jesus is our brother. We are brothers and sisters to each other. Together all comprise 'divine family.'

The Christian theologians agree that God is the father of Jesus and all true believers who are begotten by Him. They also agree that Jesus is the Son of God and our brother. They agree that we are his brothers and sisters and the children of God. But they fail to define in what way is the Holy Spirit related to God and Jesus and all the true believers. They agree that the Holy Spirit is not the Son of God or the brother of God. They agree that the Holy Spirit is not the Father of Jesus or our father. What then is the Holy Spirit to Jesus and us? Obviously, the Mother and the spiritual bride of El Elyon, God Most-High. Many argue that the Holy Spirit is merely the spirit or power of God because they fail to distinguish between Ruah Kodesh and the spirit of God. God possesses a spirit just as we do and the animals. This is the spirit of life. The Holy Spirit [Ruah Kodesh] is not this spirit but rather our Mother. Jehovah's Witnesses in their publications insist that the Holy Spirit is merely an energy. All those who hold to Unitarian view use the same term. They compare the Holy Spirit to electrical current. Now we all know that energy is not a rational being. It can neither hear, see, smell, speak, reason, or feel. The Holy Spirit however, has all the attributes of a person. The Holy Spirit "speaks:"

"When they lead you away and deliver you up, don't be anxious beforehand, or premeditate what you will say, but say whatever will be given you in that hour. For it is not you who speak, but the Holy Spirit" [Mark 13:11 World English Bible].

The Holy Spirit "hears:"

"But when the Spirit of Truth comes, She will lead you into all the truth; for She will not speak from Herself, but what She hears She will speak; and She will reveal to you things which are to come in the future" [John 16:13 Author's translation].

This verse proves that the Holy Spirit both speaks and hears and is aware of the future, since She can reveal it to Jesus' disciples. The Holy Spirit forbids [Acts 16:6-7]. The Holy Spirit intercedes [Romans 8:26]. The Holy Spirit separates and sends out people [Acts 13:1-4]. The Holy Spirit appoints [Acts 20:28]. The Holy Spirit is a witness [Acts 5:32]. Acts 5:32 is a very important text. In verses 29-31 Peter argues that God raised Jesus from the dead and that He caused him to sit on His right hand. As proof of this Peter said:

"We are His witnesses of these things; and so also is the Holy Spirit, whom God has given to those who obey him" [5:32 World English Bible].

The Greek word "martus" means "judicial witness." It is inconceivable that the Holy Spirit would have been called as a "judicial witness" of the resurrection and ascension, if She was not a personality. To be a judicial witness one must see and hear and be a rational being. If the Holy Spirit is merely a power or energy then it could not be a rational being nor could it be used as a witness. That the Holy Spirit possesses rationalism and personality is also evident by the fact that She can be lied to [Acts 5:3], sinned against [Matthew 12:31], resisted [Acts 7:51], insulted [Hebrew 10:29]. The Holy Spirit also loves [Romans 15:30]. The impersonal force or energy cannot love. God as our Father loves us. Jesus as our brother loves us. It follows then that the Holy Spirit as our Mother loves us:

"Now I beg you, brothers, by our Lord Jesus Christ, and by the love of the Spirit, that you strive together with me in your prayers to God for me [Romans 15:30 World English Bible].

The Holy Spirit as our mother can be grieved and feel sorrow and pain.

Please note:

"Don't grieve the Holy Spirit" [Ephesians 4:30 World English Bible].

The word "grieve" comes from the Greek word "lupeo," number #3076 in Strong's, and means:

"to distress, to be sad."

The Complete Word Study Dictionary, by Dr. Zodhiates, on p. 929, defines the word "lupeo" as follows:

"sorrow; to grieve, afflict with sorrow."

The word is always used to imply personal sorrow and grief. An impersonal force or power could not be grieved or feel sorrow. That God is composed of dual natures and that He in actual fact is the father of His divine family, is very evident from the fact that the terms applied to Him indicate plurality of His Being. You must realize that in the Hebrew language there are many words which could be translated "one" in English. The words "ish" and "ishshah" [man and woman] were at times translated as "one" but never in reference to God. The word "nephesh" [soul] was also rendered "one" in the Bible but never in reference to God. The word "almoniy" rendered "one" in the Bible actually means "someone," a person referred to without a name. There are many other Hebrew words which at times are translated "one" in the Bible. But there are two Hebrew words which are crucial in our examination of the nature and composition of God.

The Hebrew word which absolutely implies "oneness" to the exclusion of all others, is yachiyd. The Brown-Driver-Briggs Hebrew and English Lexicon, on p. 402, clearly points out that the word "yachiyd" means: "only one, solitary." The word is used throughout the Bible to express this meaning. In Genesis 22:2,12,16 the word is used to designate Isaac "as the only son" of Abraham. In Psalm 25:16 it is used to imply "desolation." It is rendered "solitary" in Psalm 68:6. In Psalm 35:17 "only one." In Jeremiah 6:26 God states that Israelites will weep as they who weep for an "only" son. The same is stated in Amos 8:10 and Zechariah 12:10. The word yachiyd means absolute or solitary oneness.

This is the word used by all Unitarians to designate the absolute oneness of God. But to the dismay of all Unitarians, the word "yachiyd" was never applied to God in the Bible. This fact troubled Moses Maimonides to the point that he decided to change the Hebrew word "echad" in the Shema, with the word "yachiyd." Maimonides was the Jewish rabbinic legend. The noted Hebrew scholar David Cooper, points out this fact:

"Prior to the days of Moses Maimonides, the unity of God was expressed by echad...Maimonides, who drafted the thirteen articles of faith, in the second one sets forth, the unity of God, using the word yachiyd which in the Tenach [Hebrew Bible] is never used to express God's unity" [The Eternal God Revealing Himself, pp. 59-60].

Cooper goes on to say that the word "yachiyd" denotes "oneness" in "absolute" sense in "every" passage where it appears in the Bible. If God is one and sole indivisible Being as Unitarians insist, is it not remarkable that the word "yachiyd" was never applied to denote God's nature? Even in the great Shema of Israel the word "yachiyd" does not appear but rather the word "echad" is used. The Shema is found in Deuteronomy 6:4 where it reads in Hebrew:

"SHEMA YISRAEL YAHWEH ELOHENU YAHWEH ECHAD."

Translated into English it reads:

Hear O Israel, Yahweh our Elohim [literally masculine and feminine] Yahweh is unity.

The word "Elohim" is a plural form of "Eloah." It is used in the Bible in reference to God. It was also used in reference to goddess and goddesses. However, in here our primary concern is the Hebrew word "echad," translated "unity" or "one." Once we realize the tremendous significance of the word, then it will become apparent why the word "echad" and not "yachiyd" appears in the text. The word "echad" refers to a "compound oneness" in which a number of things together are described as one. There are many passages in the Bible which prove this fact. The following are selected to illustrate this compound meaning of oneness:

Genesis 1:5 speaks of night and day. Together they comprise one or first day. [The word "echad" appears in the text].

Genesis 2:24 states that Adam and Eve, the two, became one flesh. [The word "echad" clearly indicates compound unity]. Genesis 11:6 states that the people who were building the tower were one. [The word "echad" was thus used to at once denote many and one, clearly a compound unity].

Genesis 34:16, 22 states that Schehemites desired to become one people with the Israelites. [Clearly "echad" denotes a compound unity].

2 Chronicles 30:12 states that God gave the people one heart. [How plain that the word "echad" denotes unified heart]. In Ezra 2:64 the congregation of forty-two thousand, three hundred and sixty persons is described as one. [Again, "echad" clearly designates compound unity].

Jeremiah 32:39 states that God under the New Covenant will give His people one heart. [Again, a compound unity is implied by the Hebrew word "echad"].

Of all Hebrew words only "echad" implies "compound unity." If God was one single individual Being then the word "yachiyd" would have been used to designate His absolute oneness. If on the other hand God was comprised by more than one personage, then the only Hebrew word that could be used to imply such a compound unity is in fact the word "echad." That God is in fact comprised of two natures, male and female, is also evident not only by the fact that terms "elohim" and "adonay" both in "plural" are applied to

God, but also by the fact that God is addressed by and He refers to Himself with plural pronouns.

The Hebrew word "elohim" is a uniplural word. The word "eloah" is a feminine form and means "Goddess." The suffix "im" is a masculine plural. Therefore the word "elohim" designates God and Goddess in unity. The word "elohim" is a uniplural word like team, church, country, family. There is one team but several players in that team. One church but many members. One country but many citizens. One family but more than one member. There is one God but comprised of God and Goddess. The word/title "eloah" is of feminine gender. Webster's Dictionary gives the definition and etymology of Allah and in so doing points out that the Hebrew word "eloah" is a feminine noun:

"Allah is the Muslim name for 'the God.' Allah is derived from two words 'al,' which means 'the' and 'ilah,' which is related to the *feminine* Hebrew word for God, *"eloah."*

The words ending with "ah" generally, designate feminine gender. Consider the following Hebrew female names in the Bible and note how they end with the feminine ending "ah."

Havvah [Eve], Hannah [Ana], Iscah, Deborah, Jecholiah, Sephorah, Huldah, Haddasah [Esther], Hodiah, Hoglah, Helah, Eglah, Sarah, Rebbekah, Leah, Rizpah, Tirzah...

All are feminine names and all end with a suffix "ah" – just like the word "eloah." There is another Hebrew word used which refers to Eloah, our Mother. It is the word "shaddai" which the biblical scholars translate as "almighty." This word is a plural form of the word "shad" which means "breast." James Strong defines the word "shad" under the word number #7699 as follows:

"the breast of a woman or animal."

The plural form of this word is "shaddai" and means "breasts." Thus, when this word is applied to God it refers to our Mother. The Book of Job is one of the oldest books of the Bible, and Job himself was a descendant of Esau, who lived before Moses' time. In this book the title "eloah" is synonymous with "shaddai" our Mother – the breasted one.

Job 11:7:

Can you claim to understand the depth of Eloah? Can you grasp the limit of Shaddai? [Author's translation].

Job 22:26:

Then you will delight in Shaddai, and your face you will lift to Eloah [Author's translation].

Job 27:10:

Can he be pleased with Shaddai? Can he always call on Eloah [Author's translation].

Job 32:1:

Now what portion does Eloah give from on high? What destiny does Shaddai apportion from heaven?" [Author's translation].

In other passages El [God] is distinct from Eloah [Goddess] and Shaddai [breasted one].

Job 5:8:

I would look for El, and unto Eloah I would entrust my case [Author's translation].

Job 8:3,5:

Does El judge wrongly? Does Shaddai pervert justice? If you seek El and plead for mercy from Shaddai [Author's translation].

Job 20:29:

This is the lot from El for the wicked man, and the heritage allotted him by Eloah [Author's translation].

Job 27:2:

I swear by El, the living, who deprives me of justice and by Shaddai who has filled me with bitterness [Author's translation].

Psalm 7:11:

The righteous is judged by El, and every day Eloah is annoyed by the wicked [Author's translation].

Two feminine words are used to depict our Mother, the Holy Spirit. The word "hochmah" and "shekinah." The word "hochmah" means "wisdom" and "shekinah" means "divine presence." Both words possess a feminine gender in Hebrew and end with a suffix "ah." Therefore, the Holy Spirit – Ruah Koddesh – is our Mother and the spiritual spouse of El, our Father. The Church herself teaches that Jesus will marry the Church – his bride – so why then do they find the spiritual marriage between God and Goddess who are "echad" that is, "one," blasphemous?

# CHAPTER 23
# Is Jesus God?

To answer this, we first of all must clarify and define the word 'God.' In English language the word is capitalized thus 'God' when applied to the true God and written with a small letter thus 'god' when applied to someone other than the true God. But this is not the case in either Greek or Hebrew languages. The title 'theos' is written in the same way whether it referred to the eternal and self-existent God or some other subordinate deity. The same is true of the Hebrew title 'elohim.'

*Inconsistency in Translation*

As a matter of fact, the Hebrew title is even more problematic than the Greek and hence different renderings of the same title by different translators. The Hebrew word 'elohim' has been translated as God, god, gods, mighty, spirit, spirits, spectre, ghost, judges, and even goddess in 1 Kings 11:5 and 33. There are cases when the translators are puzzled and do not know whether to translate the word 'elohim' in singular or plural. In Genesis 3:5 some use the term "you shall be as gods, knowing good and evil," while others "you shall be like God, knowing good and evil." In Judges 9:13 some use the term "wine which cheers the hearts of gods," but others "of God." In 1 Samuel 28:13 the Medium of Endor told King Saul that she saw "elohim" come out of the earth. Some translate the word 'elohim' as gods, others as spirit, spectre, ghost, divine being... In Psalm 82:1 we read:

"God standeth in the congregation of the mighty; he judgeth among the gods" [King James Bible].

There are so many conflicting translations of this passage. Why such a disagreement among the biblical translators of the simple Hebrew text? Because of the delusion and the reluctance of the biblical scholars to acknowledge the truth. Namely, that the biblical authors identify beings other than the Creator as elohim. But before I demonstrate the fact that there are gods or Gods other than the true and eternal God who created the universe, I will first of all point out the correct translation of Psalm 82:1. The first crucial Hebrew word is 'elohim' – being a plural form. The second is 'el' – a singular form but also used as a name of the Divine Being who was also recognized as the God Most High [El Elyon] in the Bible. The third word is also 'elohim.' So, the correct way to render the text is thus:

Gods stand accompanied by El who judges in the midst of the gods.

**Gods other than the Creator**

The first command prohibited the Israelites to have other gods beside their own God Yahweh. If other gods did not exist then there would be no such a prohibition. This command does not deal with idol-gods, for the second command deals with idols and graven images. The Israelites were prohibited to have other gods, as well as idol-gods who are not living gods. Jephtah, regarded as hero of faith in Hebrews 11, most definitely recognized that Chemosh was an existing god and actually a legitimate God of the Ammonites. Israel annexed a territory which belonged to the Ammonites. In his letter, Jephtah explained to the king of the Ammonites why the Israelites would not return the territory. Jephtah argued that it was Yahweh who personally conquered this portion of land and then gave it to the Israelites. In this letter Jephtah acknowledged Chemosh as the great war lord and the legitimate God of the Ammonites:

"So now Yahweh, the God of Israel, has dispossessed the Amorites from before his people Israel, and should you possess them? Won't you possess that which Chemosh your God gives you to possess? So, whoever Yahweh our God has dispossessed from before us, them will we possess" [Judges 11:23-25 World English Bible].

Please note how Jephtah spoke of Yahweh as "our god" and the "god of Israel," but of Chemosh he spoke as "your god." Jephtah acknowledged that the Ammonites had the right to hold onto any territory that Chemosh gives them just as they had the right to keep onto the territory that their god Yahweh conquered for them. Numbers 21:29 says that the Moabites were "the people of Chemosh" and that they were actually "sons and daughters" of Chemosh. The text also says that Chemosh abandoned his people and allowed them to be taken captive. Obviously because of their disobedience to him. The inscription on a Moabite Stone – the oldest Semitic writing discovered – says that Chemosh was angry with his people and allowed other nations to conquer them.

Jephtah, and most of other Israelites of his day believed that each nation was governed by its own national god. They believed that originally the Most High divided the nations and over each nation He appointed one of His sons to rule and take care of that nation and administer His government [Deuteronomy 32:7-9]. The Israelites boasted about their national god and believed that he was superior to all other gods appointed over the nations. It seems that this was the case since he apparently inflicted the punishment over the gods of Egypt. Exodus 12:12 says:

"Against all the gods of Egypt I will execute judgments" [World English Bible].

The word 'judgement' comes from the Hebrew word 'shephet,' which actually means "infliction, punish." The word 'infliction' means "pain, punishment." The word 'punish' means "to subject to pain." A mere idol of gold or stone or any other material could not be punished nor can pain be inflicted on an idol. Only the real and living gods could be punished. In Numbers 33:4 we are also told that Yahweh punished the gods of Egypt. The Jewish chronicler apparently believed that the gods of Damascus were real and powerful. He believed that these gods actually defeated King Ahaz in battle. In 2 Chronicles 28:23 we read:

"For he sacrificed to the gods of Damascus, which struck him; and he said, Because the gods of the kings of Syria helped them, [therefore] will I sacrifice to them, that they may help me. But they were the ruin of him, and of all Israel" [World English Bible].

Obviously, King Ahaz believed that Yahweh was not the only god but this is neither here nor there. What is imperative to grasp is the fact that the author of Chronicles believed that the gods of Damascus were real since the author made a statement that these gods struck him, that is, defeated King Ahaz. For them to defeat him they had to be real and for the author to make such a statement he had to believe that they were real and not just idols of gold or stone or simply an imagination of a deluded mind. The Bible clearly shows that the authors of the Bible prior to the Jewish exile to Babylonia believed that other gods existed but they only thought that their god Yahweh was more powerful. Please note the following passages:

"Who is like you, Yahweh, among the gods?" [Exodus 15:11 World English Bible].

"Now I know that Yahweh is greater than all gods" [Exodus 18:11 World English Bible].

"For Yahweh your God, he is God of gods, and Lord of lords" [Deuteronomy 10:17 World English Bible].

"For you, Yahweh, are most high above all the earth. You are exalted far above all gods" [Psalm 97:9 World English Bible].

"For Yahweh is a great God, A great King above all gods" [Psalm 95:3 World English Bible].

If other gods did not exist then Yahweh would not prohibit the Israelites to have other gods besides him and to serve and worship them. If other gods did not exist then Yahweh could not say that he is a jealous god. The authors of the above passages believed that other gods existed, but at the same time that their national god was more powerful than any god of other nations. We are not talking about idols of stone or gold. It would be absurd to say that Yahweh is above all idols of stone who do not even have breath. The comparison is only valid and meaningful if other gods were living deities but not a match for Yahweh. That these gods were living gods and not a mere idols or imagination of the deceived worshippers, is evident in the Bible. In Psalm 138:1 the writer says that he will sing praises to Yahweh in the presence of all the gods:

"I will give you thanks with my whole heart. Before the gods, I will sing praises to you" [World English Bible].

The word 'before' comes from the Hebrew word "neged." Gesenius' Hebrew-Chaldee Lexicon to The Old Testament, on p. 530, states that this word primarily means "in the presence off; in the sight off." The understanding of the early Israelites was that Yahweh was the local and national god of Israel. He was worshipped in Israel – the land of his own inheritance. In other nations other gods ruled. [This is fully documented in my book 'Yahweh Conspiracy' available from amazon.com and other retailers.

In Psalm 97:7 we read:

"Let all them be put to shame who serve engraved images, Who boast in their idols. Worship him, all you gods!" [World English Bible].

These graven images and idols were representative figurines of the heathen deities. That it is so is apparent from the final remark where the author states that all the gods should worship the true God. Graven images and idols of stone and wood or gold and silver could not worship anyone or anything since they are objects and have no personality. But the gods represented by idols and graven images could, and as far as the author was concerned, should worship the true God. There are other passages which prove that ancient Hebrew authors of the Bible believed that the gods of other nations were actual deities and living beings who could be punished and upon whom judgement can be executed. In Jeremiah 46:25 Yahweh said the following:

"Behold, I will punish Amon of No, and Pharaoh, and Egypt, with her gods, and her kings; even Pharaoh, and those who trust in him" [World English Bible].

Amon was a tutelary deity in the city of No [Thebes]. Amon of No [Thebes] is also mentioned in Nahum 3:8. It would be impossible to punish and inflict punishment and pain on Amon if he was a nonexistent being and merely an idol of stone and an imagination of a corrupt human mind.

## *Many gods and lords*

Paul in 1 Corinthians 8 states that there are many gods and lords but that we identify only with one God, the father of Jesus and with one Lord, even Jesus. In 1 Corinthians 4:4 Paul identifies Satan [Adversary] as "god of this world." If Satan is god then how much more can it be said that Jesus is god or God! Jesus is the begotten Son of God and therefore he is and must be divine since dog begets a dog, man begets a man and God begets a god. All those who are begotten of God are divine and gods and members of God's divine Family. This is an irrefutable fact.

Jesus is our elder brother, the firstborn in God's divine Family. The Bible reveals that even certain angels were called Gods. The being who appeared to Moses was identified as God, yet Stephen clarifies that this being was in fact an angel [Acts 7:30]. Jacob wrestled with God and saw him face to face [Genesis 32:30]. Yet Hosea identifies this God as an angel [Hosea 12:4]. The true God is elohim above all other elohim. Did you know that the word 'demon' which is derived from the Greek word 'daimon' – actually means 'deity'? If certain angels, Satan and even demons are deities and are called GODS in the Bible, why do Christians make such a big deal when Jesus is occasionally referred to as GOD?

## *Jesus not the Sovereign God*

Even though Jesus is God, he is not the Most-High God [El Elyon] who alone is the self-existent and from all eternity. Let's face it. The true and eternal God who is the source of everything cannot have someone else who is His God and anything that is above Him. But Jesus himself identified his Father as "the only true God" [John 17:3]. Jesus plainly stated on several occasions that this only true God was not only our God but also his God. After his resurrection, he told Mary:

"'I am ascending to my Father and your Father, and my God and your God." [John 20:17 World English Bible].

Jesus, as a resurrected being told Mary that God was not only her God but also his own God. The authors of the New Testament unanimously identify Jesus as 'kurios' [Lord/Sir] while his father as "God." In 1 Corinthians 8:6 Paul identifies the Father as the only God from whom all things come while Jesus he identifies as 'kurios.' Whenever Paul introduced his salutation to the believers, he always offered praise only to the Father and he always identified the Father as the God of Jesus. Please note the following passages:

"Grace and peace to you from God our father and the Lord Jesus Christ. Praise be to the God and father of our Lord Jesus Christ" [2 Corinthians 1:2-3 World English Bible].

"Praise be to God and father of our Lord Jesus Christ…I keep asking that the God of our Lord Jesus Christ, the glorious Father, may give you the Spirit of wisdom and revelation, so that you may know him better" [Ephesians 1:3,17 World English Bible].

In these passages Paul clearly identifies God not only as the father of Jesus but also as his God. In 1 Corinthians 11:3 Paul explicitly says that as Jesus is the head of every man so is God the head of Jesus. This clearly shows that Jesus is not the Sovereign God but rather a subordinate God. In Ephesians 4:4-6 Paul clearly distinguishes between the Father and Son and makes it plain that the Father alone is God:

"There is one body, and one Spirit, even as you also were called in one hope of your calling; one Lord, one faith, one baptism, one God and Father of all, who is over all, and through all, and in us all" [World English Bible].

As there is one body, one Spirit and one baptism, so there is only one Lord [Jesus] who is clearly distinguished from the one God who is over and above all and who is also the head of Jesus. In Romans 16:27 Paul gives glory to the only God through Jesus Christ – proving that Jesus is not and cannot be part of that only God to whom Paul was giving glory. In 1 Timothy 6:13-16 the Father is identified as the

"only Ruler, the King of kings, and Lord of lords; who alone has immortality, dwelling in unapproachable light; whom no man has seen, nor can see: to whom be honor and eternal power. Amen" [World English Bible].

Jesus is not the life of all since he conceded that his own immortality was actually the *gift of his Father*:

"For as the Father has life in himself, even so he gave to the Son also to have life in himself" [John 5:26 [World English Bible].

Eternal and self-existent immortality was not Jesus' own but it was rather granted or given to him by his father and God. He is not the *most sovereign* since he conceded that his father is greater than he [John 14:28]. He could not grant the left and right seats to James and John in the kingdom. Only his God and father had that right [Matthew 20:23]. He did not know all things. He conceded that no one knew the day of his return, not even he, but only his God and father [Matthew 24:36]. Even as the resurrected and glorified being he stated that this secret was still within the power of his God and father [Acts 1:7].

God existed and can exist without Jesus or any other being in this universe. But Jesus and any other being in the universe cannot exist apart from God and if He did not will it so. This is the most fundamental teaching of the Bible. That is why God the Father alone is the Most-High and the Supreme God of the universe who never had and never will have an equal partner. Other authors of the Bible, besides Paul, also believed that the Father is not only Jesus' father but *also his God*. In Revelation 1:6 we are told that Jesus made us to be kings and priests of his God and father. In Revelation 3:12 Jesus stated:

"Him that overcometh will I make a pillar in the temple of my God, and he shall go no more out: and I will write upon him the name of my God, and the name of the city of my God, which is new Jerusalem, which cometh down out of heaven from my God: and I will write upon him my new name" [King James Bible].

Four times the resurrected and glorified Jesus refers to his father as "my God." In 1 Peter 1:3 the author writes:

"Blessed be the God and Father of our Lord Jesus Christ" [World English Bible].

The author gives praise to the Father alone and claims that the Father is in fact Jesus' God. When Jesus asked his disciples who they thought he was, none of them replied that they thought that he was eternal God who in the beginning created the universe. Peter said that Jesus was the Anointed and the Son of the living God [Matthew 16:16-17]. Jesus did not correct him nor did he tell him that his conception of him was wrong. At no time did Jesus tell his disciples that he is God or anything more than the Son of God. After Peter made his profession, Jesus pronounced a blessing upon him saying that this truth was not revealed to him by the flesh and blood but rather by his father who is in heaven. Peter therefore acknowledged Jesus as Christ [anointed] and the Son of God by the revelation and the inspiration of God.

If Peter's perception was limited or if Peter had a misconception of who Jesus really was, then the Father would have revealed it to him or at least Jesus would have corrected him. Since neither did so, we can be absolutely certain that Jesus is not the Sovereign God as the Trinitarians would want you to believe. Even the demons never acknowledged Jesus as God but on every single occasion they identified his father as the Most-High God and Jesus only as the Son of God and the Holy One of God. Please note:

"When he saw Jesus from afar, he ran and bowed down to him, and crying out with a loud voice, he said, "What have I to do with you, Jesus, you Son of the Most High God? I adjure you by God, don't torment me" [Mark 5:6-7 World English Bible].

Luke reports the same incident but has the demons say:

"When he saw Jesus, he cried out, and fell down before him, and with a loud voice said, "What do I have to do with you, Jesus, you Son of the Most-High God?" [Luke 8:28 World English Bible].

In Luke 4:33-34,41 we read the demons identified Jesus as the "holy one of God" and the "son of God" but never as God or the Most-High God as they identified the Father. The demons well knew who Jesus was. They also knew who was the Sovereign God. They never identified Jesus as God Almighty but only as the Son of God and the Holy One of God. His father however, they identified as the Most-High God. The demons know who is the true and real God but the Christian theologians and preachers don't.

**Jesus a Human in All Things as We Are**

In Hebrews 1:1-9 we read:

"God, having in the past spoken to the fathers through the prophets at many times and in various ways, has at the end of these days spoken to us by his Son, whom he appointed heir of all things, through whom also he made the worlds. His Son is the radiance of his glory, the very image of his substance, and upholding all things by the word of his power, when he had by himself made purification for our sins, sat down on the right hand of the Majesty on high; having become so much better than the angels, as he has inherited a more excellent name than they have. For to which of the angels did he say at any time, "You are my Son, Today have I become your father?" and again, "I will be to him a Father, And he will be to me a Son?" When he again brings in the firstborn into the world he says, "Let all the angels of God worship him." Of the angels he says, "Who makes his angels winds, And his servants a flame of fire." but of the Son he says, "Your throne, God, is forever and ever; The scepter of uprightness is the scepter of your kingdom. You have loved righteousness, and hated iniquity; Therefore God, your God, has anointed you With the oil of gladness above your fellows" [World English Bible].

The passage is pregnant with significance. The author could have never written this text as he did if he was a Trinitarian – believing that Jesus was eternal God who is of one substance with the Father. He first nullifies the notion that the God of the Old Testament was actually Jesus – as many Trinitarians seem to believe. He does so by saying that the true God of the Old Testament who spoke through the prophets did later speak through His Son. This irrefutably proves that the Son was not the God who spoke through the prophets but that this God was in fact the father of Jesus. The author then goes on to say that this God who spoke to us through His Son did in fact appoint Jesus an heir to all things.

An heir is the person who inherits things from another. This proves that the Son is not and cannot be an eternal and supreme God since he is an heir – appointed to inherit the things his own father and God possesses. The author also points out that Jesus is the *reflection* of God's glory. Jesus in all his glory and exalted state is only a shadow of the eternal, almighty, self-existent supreme God. After all, his exalted state is due to the fact that his own God and father promoted him and gave him the glory and self-immortality.

By comparing the rank of Jesus with the angels it is apparent that the author believed that Jesus could not be the supreme and eternal God, since his superiority is due only to the fact that his God and father preferred him above all others and gave him a name that is superior than theirs. Let's face it. Supreme and Most High God could not be exalted above the angels nor could he inherit a greater name. Who in the universe for example could promote God the Father and appoint him an heir? Who can bestow upon him more glory and the nobler name? Even though in verse 9 Jesus is addressed by the title God, at the same time it is pointed out that he is not the true and supreme God since his own God anointed him to be king. We have already seen that other beings are referred to as Gods even though they are not what the true and eternal God the Father really and truly is. When the title God is applied to Jesus and other beings it is done so only in the extended manner as an honorific title. It is never meant that Jesus or any other being who ever bore the title God is the God who originally was the cause of all and who alone is unbegotten and uncreated.

If the author meant that Jesus was the Most-High God and the supreme Ruler of the universe, then he could not say that he himself has a God above him who is actually his own father and begetter. This is irrefutable fact if you are unbiased and if you really believe what the text in Hebrews actually says. In the writings of John, we learn that whoever does not accept the fact that Jesus came in the flesh is an antichrist:

"Every spirit that confesseth that Jesus Christ is come in the flesh is of God: and every spirit that confesseth not that Jesus Christ is come in the flesh is not of God: and this is that spirit of antichrist, whereof ye have heard that it should come; and even now already is in the world" [1 John 4:2-3 King James Bible].

"For many deceivers are entered into the world, who confess not that Jesus Christ is come in the flesh. This is a deceiver and an antichrist" [2 John 7 King James Bible].

Only one way, Jesus could have come in the flesh: by being conceived by Joseph's sperm in the ovum of Mary. And only in that way he could have been a real and true human being in every way as we are. The word 'come' is translated from the Greek word "erchomai." Liddel and Scott in their Greek-English Lexicon on page 694 say that this word also means "to start." The word "start" means "to begin, to commence." Thayer's Greek-English Lexicon on page 250 points out that this word "erchomai" does not only mean "to come" but also "equivalent to come into being." Every human being comes into the world. In John 1:9 we read that the true light illuminates every man that "cometh [erchomai] into the world." In order for a man to come into the world he needs to be conceived in the ovum of his mother and then born in the flesh. He begins and starts in the flesh by coming into being in the ovum of his mother. Jesus was conceived in his mother's womb. The word means "to start life." God was Jesus' God from his "mother's womb" and not from all eternity – as we are plainly told in the 22$^{nd}$ Psalm verses 9 and 10. This is a prophetic psalm and refers to Jesus. That Jesus literally came into being and began in the flesh is evident from Hebrews 2:14-17:

"Since then the children have shared in flesh and blood, he also himself in like manner partook of the same, that through death he might bring to nothing him who had the power of death, that is, the devil, and might deliver all of them who through fear of death were all their lifetime subject to bondage. For most assuredly, not to angels does he give help, but he gives help to the seed of Abraham. Therefore he was obligated *in all things* to be made like his brothers..." [World English Bible].

Since all humans are real flesh and blood, that is, since they are all born of a human fathers and mothers, so was Jesus also born of Joseph and Mary. He was obligated to be in ALL THINGS as we are. Do you know why the Church teaches that Jesus was born of a virgin? So that he could be exempted from the fallen sinful nature of Adam. According to their teaching, Adam sinned and his sin was imputed to all humanity and thus all children born inherit the sinful nature and are subject to sin. For this very reason the Church Fathers introduced the infant baptism. Not because of the children's own personal sins but rather because of the inherited sin from Adam. They argue that original sin is imputed to a child through the father and not mother. The Bible nowhere states so. On the contrary, Luke's genealogy proves that Jesus was the son of Adam and if so then as his son he would have inherited a sinful nature. Jesus did not believe that children are sinful and the children of wrath because of Adam. On the contrary, he stated that the kingdom of God belongs to the little children and if we do not become like little children we would never enter the kingdom.

If Jesus' nature was different from ours then he was not made "in all things as we are" and anyone who would be born as God in the flesh would never sin. If Jesus' nature was immune to sin, as the Church dogmatically teaches, and if he was either Almighty God in the flesh or the Son of God from birth, what praise and reward could he be given? Even demons would be sinless if they would be born with divine nature. In the days of John many taught that Jesus was not truly human because they believed in his pre-existence as the divine being and so they could not see how could divine and eternal being actually truly possess a human body. They regarded flesh and matter as evil and so they taught that Jesus only seemed to be human. As a matter of fact, all those today who teach that when Jesus was born, he never ceased to be what he had always been, deny the fact that he was really and truly human in all things as we.

They only in words teach that he was fully man while also being fully God, knowing that this is actually impossible. To teach that Jesus had a special nature and divinity from birth is to teach the doctrine of antichrist. For this doctrine nullifies everything Jesus accomplished while in the flesh. Furthermore, what reward could he expect and how can he be our example if he was God in the flesh? We are not Gods in the flesh from birth. If we were then we would have been perfect and sinless. But if Jesus was God in the flesh, why did he receive the Holy Spirit when he was baptized and why was he then begotten by God as His Son? From Christian perspective Jesus was perfect from birth only because of his divine nature. Had he inherited an absolutely human nature as we do, then, they say, he would have been subject to sin. Therefore, from their perspective, Jesus had to be incarnated as God in the womb of Mary in order to be immune to sin. They say that he knew all things and that he was God from the moment of incarnation.

But Luke states that he gradually grew in power and spirit [Luke 2:52]. They downplay the significance of his baptism. But the fact is, if he was not baptized, he would not have received the Holy Spirit and thus he would not have been begotten by God as His Son. The baptism and begettal proves that Jesus' nature was identical to all humans. Only through the begettal of God he was able to accomplish everything God set before him. Without the power of the Holy Spirit he would have failed. Even we are begotten through baptism and the Holy Spirit and only through the power of the Holy Spirit we could defeat sin and the world. We could be perfected also if we gave our all as Jesus did. But we don't and that is why we fail at times. Jesus was tempted [tested] in all things as we are. In Hebrews 2:18 we are told:

"For in that he himself hath suffered being tempted, he is able to succour them that are tempted" [King James Bible].

During these temptations he suffered and cried. If he was God in the flesh and if he was immune to sin, as we are told, then these temptations would have had no meaning and he would not have suffered while being tempted. In Hebrews 4:15 we read:

"For we don't have a high priest who can't be touched with the feeling of our infirmities, but one who has been in all points tempted like we are, yet without sin" [World English Bible].

In Hebrews 5:7-9 we read:

"Who in the days of his flesh, having offered up prayers and petitions with strong crying and tears to him who was able to save him from death, and having been heard for his godly fear, though he was a Son, yet learned obedience by the things which he suffered; and having been made perfect, he became to all of those who obey him the author of eternal salvation" [World English Bible].

Eternal and Almighty God in the flesh would not need to depend on another God for help. Nor would he need to learn anything or to be made perfect through reverence and constant obedience and suffering. If Jesus was God in the flesh, then he would have been perfect from the moment of incarnation. But the author of Hebrews clearly tells us that Jesus gradually was perfected, that is, made perfect [Hebrews 5:9 and 2:10].

We are taught that Jesus' will was always in tune and harmony with God's because he was God in the flesh and perfectly one and equal with God. But if so, why did he then pray to bypass crucifixion? An Almighty God who is equal to the Father would be exempted from human fear and fleshly weakness. But because he was a real and true man, it could only be expected to fear death and torture. By praying to bypass the death – if at all possible – only proves two things: that he was a man like we are but who put his destiny in God's hands, and that he was not all knowing since he said to the Father "if it be possible." There is another point I want to make. That he felt, as we feel, when we are suffering, is evident also from his cry:

"My God, My God, why hast thou forsaken me?" [King James Bible].

God did not forsake him, but he in all human weakness felt so. The cry proves that his father was also his God and that he had a human nature in every way as we do. When he was about to die, he said to his God:

"Father, into thy hands I commit my spirit" [Luke 23:46 King James Bible].

This statement is of colossal importance. The Bible clearly states that it was God who raised Jesus from the dead. If God did not raise Jesus from the dead, he would be dead even today. This is an irrefutable fact. But if Jesus was eternal God who never ceased to be so while in this world, as we are told, then he could neither die nor would he need to entrust his spirit in his God's hand. Also, the Bible states that after God raised Jesus from the dead, He exalted him and caused him to sit on His right-hand side and gave him a name that is above all others.

Where was Jesus before he was born of Mary? In heaven, according to Trinitarians. Was he then Almighty God equal with the Father? Yes, according to them. Was his name higher and above of angels? Indeed. Did he sit on his father's right-hand side already then? Obviously. What did Jesus then receive more than he had? The exaltation after the resurrection and the reward has meaning only if Jesus was a human being who was called and chosen by God and who was begotten by God as His Son and who was perfected by what he learnt while suffering, as the Ebionites claimed all along. The text of 1 Corinthians 15:24-28 explicitly and in no ambiguous terms states that it was very father and God of Jesus who made everything subordinate to Jesus, except Himself. When God eventually conquers all Jesus' enemies then Jesus himself will bow before God Who is all in all:

"Then the end comes, when he will deliver up the kingdom to God, even the Father; when he will have abolished all rule and all authority and power. For he must reign until he has put all his enemies under his feet. The last enemy that will be abolished is death. For, "He put all things in subjection under his feet." But when he says, "All things are put in subjection," it is evident that he is excepted who subjected all things to him. When all things have been subjected to him, then the Son will also himself be subjected to him who subjected all things to him, that God may be all in all" [World English Bible].

How plain! There is only One infinite and unique God – the source of all life. Jesus is His Son who was begotten as His Son when baptized by John. Jesus has inherited great glory and majesty but is not Almighty God and never was and never shall be. He prays to God and he worships God and he acknowledges his father as his God. He is the Mediator between God and the world. He prays for our sins and the sins of the world. As a Mediator he has to be a neutral party between God and the world. And he is. He was a real and true man who has earned his privilege and position as the Mediator – who is now neither Almighty God nor a mortal man as we are.

### *Corrupted texts in order to prove Jesus' Divinity*

There are myriads of conflicting readings but in here we are primarily interested how the orthodox Christian scribes forged many original readings in order to bolster the anti adoptionist view of the Ebionites and to substantiate the orthodox view of Jesus' pre-existence and his divinity. We can begin with the fact how these lying scribes tried to hide the fact that Joseph was actually the biological father of Jesus. There were manuscripts which emphatically show that Joseph was Jesus' biological father. The Syriac or Aramaic manuscript discovered in St. Catherine's Monastery on Mount Sinai gives the following version of Matthew 1:16:

"Jacob begot Joseph; Joseph, to whom was betrothed the virgin Mary, begot Jesus, who is called the Christ."

Then in verse 25 we are told the following:

"and he [Joseph] had no relations with her [Mary] until she bore to him a son."

Compare this with the King James Bible, based on the Textus Receptus:

"And knew her not till she had brought forth her firstborn son."

Various manuscripts show how the Orthodox scribes have corrupted the original renderings whenever we are told that Joseph was the father of Jesus or where the phrase "the parents" of Jesus occur in the earlier manuscripts. In Luke 2:33 some manuscripts read:

"father and mother began to marvel."

But majority of the manuscripts read:

"Joseph and his mother."

In Luke 2:48 one important but fragmentary Greek manuscript $C^{vid}$ and two Old Latin manuscripts β and e read:

"Your relatives and I have been grieved."

Other manuscripts [a b ff$^2$ g$^1$ l r$^1$ and syr$^c$ read:

"We have been grieved."

The earlier reading was:

"Your father and I have been grieved."

This is the reading even in the Textus Receptus and the King James Bible. Why such variations if not because someone wanted to remove the idea of the Ebionite adoptionist teaching concerning Jesus? When Jesus stayed behind in the temple, his parents did not know it. They assumed that he went to Galilee with their relatives and friends. The original reading was:

"his parents knew it not,"

but this was changed in other manuscripts to

"Joseph and his mother knew it not."

The Textus Receptus and the King James Bible are based on this version of Luke. In the speech of Peter [Acts 2] he stated that Jesus was to come "from the loins of David – clearly implying that through Joseph [the royal line] he would be David's biological descendant. But this was changed to "from the heart of David" in Codex Bezae it$^d$.

In John 1:13 we read:

"But as many as received him, to them he gave the right to become God's children, to those who believe in his name: who were born not of blood, nor of the will of the flesh, nor of the will of man, but of God" [World English Bible].

Please note the plural "who were born," implying that all those who are born of God are God's children. But this was later changed in Old Latin manuscript to singular "who was born." This change had to take place before the end of the second century for the Church Father Irenaeus was aware of this and argued that the text referred to Jesus. Tertulian later also argued in favour of the singular rendering in order to counter the Ebionite adoptionist view. In John 1:14 the earlier reading was: "the word became flesh," but this was later changed to "God became flesh." In John 1:18 the earlier reading was "the only begotten son," but this was later changed to read variously as "the unique God," "the only begotten God" and "God the only son."

In John 19:40 we are told that Nicodemus and Joseph wrapped the "body of Jesus." This was later changed to the "body of God" [Codex Alexandrinus]. In Luke 2:26 we are told that the Holy Spirit told Simeon that he will not die until he sees the "Lord's Christ." Old Latin MS ff² changes this to "Christ, namely God." In Luke 9:20 Peter acknowledged Jesus as "Christ of God," but this was later changed to "Christ, God" in the Coptic manuscripts. In Mark 3:11 the demon referred to Jesus as "Son of God," but this was later changed to "God, the Son of God" [MS 69].

In Luke 7 we are told how a Roman centurion went to Jesus in order to ask him to heal his sick servant. In verse 9 we read: "when Jesus heard." This was changed to "When God heard" [miniscule MS 124]. In Luke 8:28 the demon referred to Jesus as "Jesus, Son of God Most High." This was changed to "Jesus, the Highest God" [MS 2766].

In Luke 20:42 Jesus quotes the words of David: "The LORD said to my Lord." This was changed to "God said to my God" [Persian Diatesseron]. In Jude verse 5 we are told that "the Lord" saved the people from Egypt. This was changed to "Jesus" in MSS A B 3381 1241 1739 and 1881. In the following MSS C² 623 and VG^ms the reading is "God." In one manuscript P⁷² the reading is "the God Christ."

In Galatians 2:20 the earliest reading is:

"...I live by the faith of the Son of God, who loved me, and gave himself for me" [King James Bible].

This was changed in MSS P⁴⁶ B D F and G to read:

"by the faith of God even Christ."

Miniscule MSS 330 reads:

"by the faith of God."

MS 1985 reads:

"by the faith of God the Son."

In Titus the original reading "through Jesus Christ our Savior" was changed to "through Jesus Christ our God." In Hebrews 13:20 "our Lord Jesus" was changed to "our God Jesus" [MS d]. In Ephesians 3:9 the words "by Jesus Christ" are added later in some manuscripts. Majority of English bibles omit these words as do also Greek manuscripts coded A B C D F G, Syriac, Arabic of Erpen, Coptic, Ethiopic, Vulgate, and Itala. These words were added so that the reader would think that Jesus was present with God when the creation took place and that everything was made by Jesus. The most significant and evil text added to the New Testament is found in 1 John 5:7 – a text bolstering the Trinity dogma. This verse was not in any of the Greek manuscripts prior to the fifteenth century. The *Emphatic Diaglott*, p. 803, omitted this text and explains why:

"The received text reads, For there are three that bear witness in heaven, the Father, the Word, and the Holy Ghost, and these three are one. And there are three that bear witness in earth. This text concerning the heavenly witnesses is not contained in any Greek manuscript which was written earlier than the 15th century. It is not cited by any of the Greek ecclesiastical writers; nor by any of the early Latin fathers, even when the subjects upon which they treat would naturally have led them to appeal to its authority. It is therefore evidently spurious."

Do you realize what this means? People who lived prior to the fifteenth century simply knew nothing about 1 John 5:7. They never referred to it because they could not refer to something that was not in existence. St. Gregory urged the Roman hierarchy to delete this text since "God does not need our lies" – he said. However, his church most certainly does and consequently on January 13, 1897 Pope Leo XIII forbade anyone to question the authenticity of this text. Despite the fact that this text is a wicked forgery, many Christians still use it in order to prove their erroneous teaching on Trinity. Moreover, they sternly condemn those who reject this text as scribal interpolation. Even some Bible scholars retain this verse in their translations even though they frankly admit it to be a forgery. J.P. Green retains this verse in his Interlinear Bible, yet in the preface he plainly states that he does not regard this text as true Scripture.